STRAVINSKY'S BALLETS

YALE MUSIC MASTERWORKS SERIES

GEORGE B. STAUFFER, GENERAL EDITOR

CHARLES M. JOSEPH

STRAVINSKY'S BALLETS

YALE UNIVERSITY PRESS
NEW HAVEN AND LONDON

For information about this and other Yale University Press publications, please contact:
U.S. Office: sales.press@yale.edu   www.yalebooks.com
Europe Office: sales@yaleup.co.uk   www.yalebooks.co.uk

Set in Arno Pro by IDSUK (DataConnection) Ltd
Printed in Great Britain by TJ International Ltd, Padstow, Cornwall

Library of Congress Cataloging-in-Publication Data

Joseph, Charles M.
    Stravinsky's ballets / Charles M. Joseph.
      p. cm.
    ISBN 978–0–300–11872–8 (cl : alk. paper)
    1. Stravinsky, Igor, 1882–1971. Ballets. 2.   Ballets--20th century—History and
criticism.   I. Title.
    ML410.S932J675 2011
    781.5'56092—dc22
                                                                            2011011116

A catalogue record for this book is available from the British Library.

10 9 8 7 6 5 4 3 2 1

For William, Julia, and Susan

CONTENTS

ILLUSTRATIONS

(Music) Examples

FOREWORD

IGOR STRAVINSKY has long been associated with ballet music, in particular with *The Firebird*, *Petrouchka*, and *The Rite of Spring*, the trio of works that propelled both dance and music into the modern age. In the present volume Charles M. Joseph shows the remarkable degree to which these pieces were but a prelude to Stravinsky's lifelong exploration of dance and dance idioms. As Joseph demonstrates, dance music was *the* artistic constant in Stravinsky's career, drawing him to composition again and again and spurring him to new realms of inventiveness. No other modern composer has been linked so closely and completely with dance: fully one-third of his music was written for the ballet or ballet-related productions, and another 60 percent has been choreographed at one time or another. Joseph makes the case that the evolution of Stravinsky's musical style is viewed best through the prism of dance.

For Stravinsky, ballet proved to be a receptive forum for new music and new ideas. The ethnic exoticism of Serge Pavlovich Diaghilev's Ballets Russes set the stage for the primitivism of *The Rite of Spring*, just as the tradition-bucking asceticism of City Ballet created a welcome environment for the neoclassicism of *Orpheus* and the serialism of *Agon*. Writing for ballet gave Stravinsky the opportunity to explore a wide array of extra-musical sources for composition—Nicolas Boileau's *L'Art poétique* for *Apollo*, Hans Christian Andersen's story "The Ice Maiden" for *Le Baiser de la fée*, or T. S. Eliot's poetry for *Agon*. And working in the professional world of ballet allowed Stravinsky to rub elbows with producers, choreographers, dancers, set and costume designers, and other impassioned artists, including Michel Fokine, Vaslav Nijinsky, Bronislava Nijinska, Anna Pavlova, Pablo Picasso, Jean Cocteau, and René Auberjonois. The 1966 Lincoln Center production of *L'Histoire du soldat* alone featured Aaron Copland as Narrator, Elliot Carter as the Soldier, and John Cage as the

Devil. While many composers labored in isolation, Stravinsky worked arm in arm with energizing colleagues who prodded, probed, and pushed one another to try unorthodox things.

Joseph constantly reminds us that Stravinsky was not writing abstract scores for orchestra but rather music in which every dimension was determined by the requirements of dance production. Pointing to compositional sketches, he shows how the precise timing of sections, notated by Stravinsky in minutes and seconds in early drafts, commonly determined the shape of musical material, or that the inclusion of Russian folk songs in the early ballets had less to do with patriotism than with the fact that it helped to win over Parisian audiences, who had come to expect exotic enchantment from the Ballets Russes. In the case of *Apollo* the sketches show that Stravinsky often composed discrete blocks of musical material that he then maneuvered into place only as the score and choreography took shape. Stravinsky can also be observed writing pivotally important passages first, and then composing up to the climactic moment. In the early materials of *Agon* choreographic gestures appear directly in the score, conceived simultaneously with the notes. With *Jeu de cartes* an eager Stravinsky practically took over the production, drafting the story, establishing timings, determining the size of the orchestra, making suggestions for stage design—in short, deciding all the important details. Writing for dance became an obsession for Stravinsky. In rehearsals of *L'Histoire du soldat* he pounded out the music at the piano "in a frenzy of enthusiasm," becoming so involved with the production that at one point he proposed dancing the figure of the Devil himself.

Joseph surveys Stravinsky's development as a ballet composer by taking us on a guided tour through the dance productions that defined his career. After an opening discussion of Stravinsky's youthful years in Russia, individual chapters are devoted to *The Firebird, Petrouchka,* and *The Rite of Spring*—the early triptych that put Stravinsky on the international map. Chapter 5 turns to *Apollo*, touching on its roots in *Le Chant du rossignol* before showing how Stravinsky successfully moved beyond his Russian heritage by creating a score free from ethnicity—white music for a *ballet blanc*, as he put it. Stravinsky's life after Diaghilev is examined in chapter 6: the new partnership with Balanchine, the move to America, and the steps that led little by little from *Le Baiser de la fée* to *Jeu de cartes* and finally, in 1942, to *Orpheus*, in which the concept of architectural choreography emerged in full form.

Chapter 7 analyzes the final component of Stravinsky's second triptych, *Agon*, demonstrating how the composer achieved the work's supreme synthesis of musical styles (seventeenth-century dance and twentieth-century serialism) and modern ballet (Balanchine's illuminating choreography). Chapter 8 looks at Stravinsky's genre-crossing hybrid pieces—*Renard, L'Histoire du soldat, Pulcinella, Les Noces, Perséphone,* and *The Flood.* While achieving varying degrees of professional success, these six works reveal Stravinsky at his creative best, seeking to break down the traditional definitions of ballet to produce innovative, mixed-media theatrical forms. Finally, chapter 9 traces the promotion of Stravinsky's ballet scores after his death—by Balanchine, in particular, but by others as well. This closing discussion brings us full circle from Stravinsky's early days, when music was an aural accompaniment to dance, to the years following Stravinsky's death, when in the hands of Balanchine dance became a visual accompaniment to music. Stravinsky's works stood at the center of this transformation.

Joseph offers us far more than a majestic survey of Stravinsky's ballet music, however. He takes us behind the scenes for a firsthand look at the composer's negotiating tactics, working methods, dealings with colleagues, behavior at rehearsals, and responses to fame and to failure. He paints a vivid picture of an artist bored with convention and obsessed with breaking new ground—a creative genius determined to succeed in a rapidly changing political and cultural environment. After reading his account one sees and hears Stravinsky's ballets with new eyes and ears and senses how each work forms a logical step in the composer's journey to artistic greatness. In reviewing an early performance of *L'Histoire du soldat,* Boris Asaf'yev declared, "Dance is the primary agent of form and movement in Stravinsky's art." *Stravinsky's Ballets* demonstrates just how true this is, and why.

George B. Stauffer
General Editor

INTRODUCTION

Igor Stravinsky (1882–1971) left an indelible stamp on both his own generation and those that have followed. In a survey of the major mileposts of western music history over the last millennium, Stravinsky's one-hundred-plus compositions stand alongside the redoubtable masterworks of that historically celebrated trinity Bach, Beethoven, and Brahms. In many ways, he is their twentieth-century counterpart, so great is his historical significance. Moreover, the achievements of his prolific career, as well as his extraordinary notoriety as a classical composer, elevated his status beyond the pages of music history. His was a public legacy. Among the emboldened artists who shaped the age of modernism, Stravinsky served as music's most iconic flag bearer. His influence quickly earned him a place in the broader cultural history of an era written by such artistically diverse protagonists as Louis Armstrong, Charlie Chaplin, T. S. Eliot, Martha Graham, Pablo Picasso, Virginia Woolf, and Frank Lloyd Wright. He shared with such movers and shakers a wonderful compulsion to interrogate existing conventions. And as it served his expressive purpose, he frequently restructured the internal dynamics of established musical paradigms.

When one thinks of Stravinsky's contribution to twentieth-century music, *The Rite of Spring* most often comes first to mind. Pierre Boulez's anointing of the 1913 ballet as the "birth certificate" of modernism still rings true. Its cataclysm served as a lightening rod, an artistic proclamation that would transmogrify both music and dance. Even more, its audacity spurred the reconsideration of the boundaries of creativity and forced us to think anew about the dialectics of art. *The Rite*, justifiably, acquired the gravitas of a manifesto. History, however, must guard against the enormous eclipse cast by its preternatural force. For within Stravinsky's catalogue, *The Rite of Spring*, while monumentally emancipating in its epochal spirit, constitutes but one testament to the composer's lifelong affinity for ballet. Stravinsky's predilection for classical dance still often strikes some historians as odd, inasmuch as ballet seldom afforded a fertile channel for the great composers of any age. Why then would Stravinsky devote an inordinate amount of his creative energy over the breadth of his long career to such a historically bereft genre? How do we account for the fact that dance provided a remarkably successful platform for some of his most memorable music?

Throughout Stravinsky's early years in Russia, then later in Switzerland, France, and America, a steady stream of ballets serve as markers that track the pathway of the composer's constantly evolving interests. *Apollo* (1928) and *Agon* (1957), for example, while less well known to the general public, are every bit as illuminating as *The Rite* in plotting Stravinsky's compositional trajectory. For over fifty years, the composer's ballets continued to flow. Each of them posed different questions. Each accepted the challenges presented by any collaborative venture. And each represented a different side of the composer's interests and genius. When one includes music originally written for ballet, imaginative hybrid forms that incorporated dance, and concert works ultimately brought to the stage through choreography, dance music accounts for nearly a full third of Stravinsky's works—by far the highest proportion of any major composer's total output. His devotion to dance was evident. His understanding of the art was profound. Consequently, Stravinsky would become the pre-eminent ballet composer in the annals of music history.

As such, his ballets warrant a comprehensive study—but comprehensiveness within the framework of dance is a particularly challenging proposition. By its very nature, ballet involves an interwoven fabric of music, dance, theater, drama, and the plastic arts. As with opera, it is a layered art form that begs the unpacking of its contributing and often convoluted parts. Competing and at times conflicting ingredients are brought into play. For centuries, however, these elements occupied subsidiary roles at best. Dance masters often blithely dismissed the music as mere choreographic accompaniment. A score's highest aspiration was most often nothing more than a desired unobtrusiveness. Still, from his earliest collaborations with Diaghilev and Michel Fokine, Stravinsky sensed and eventually insisted that an equilibrium—however delicate—had to be struck in achieving coherence and integrity. And while the entrepreneurial composer was never faint-hearted in promoting his ballet scores as legitimate concert pieces in themselves, he was also quite aware of the complexly subtle counterpoint of a ballet's interlocking elements. In bringing a work to the stage, there had to be a genuine synthesis. This was particularly true in his collaborations with George Balanchine, in whom he found his most sympathetic partner. Together they reconceived ballet in the twentieth century as a coordinately structured, thoughtfully balanced, and fully blended mix of all the partnering arts. In this sense alone, the Stravinsky–Balanchine repertoire especially signaled a sea change in conceiving ballet as a unified art form.

In addressing some of these issues, the book's nine chapters proceed simply enough. Each of the composer's ballets is examined chronologically in chapters 2 through 8, although no single template is employed. At times I focus on musical elements of a particular ballet rather than dance; while in taking up other less often performed works, I forego a score's compositional details, focusing instead on the choreography or the storyline. Throughout these seven chapters, I have occasionally felt it necessary to provide brief excursions into ballet history and its politics, as well as other broadly mitigating circumstances useful in constructing relevant contexts. As a means of tracking the evolution of the composer's ideas, as he formulated and answered specific compositional questions, several musical examples invoke a comparison of Stravinsky's sketch materials with the final version of a particular passage.

Also, given the centrality of Balanchine's role in Stravinsky's ballets from the mid 1920s forward, their collaborations are frequently emphasized. Inasmuch as my interest in the journey of their partnership was addressed in an earlier study, I do borrow freely from some of my previous work in detailing their most important ballets. Chapter 1 serves as a broad introduction to dance within the context of the Russian musical traditions and cultural history Stravinsky inherited. Chapter 9 addresses the continuing devotion to the composer's ballets after his death, initially by George Balanchine and the New York City Ballet, but eventually by many others. That interest continues to expand, even globally as dance historian Stephanie Jordan has demonstrated, providing a testament to the longevity of the composer's dance works and their historical significance.

My initial knowledge of Stravinsky came through listening to *The Firebird*. The colorfully orchestrated score won me over immediately. At that moment, however, I knew nothing of Diaghilev or Fokine, let alone the artistic upheaval triggered by the Ballets Russes. Years later I encountered the serenely captivating music of *Apollo*, yet I had no sense of how Balanchine had managed to envision Stravinsky's music with the perfect choreographic complement. Only later was I able to appreciate these wonderful scores within the context of ballet. Over the ensuing years I have come to see that Stravinsky's ballets, collectively, constitute one of the genuine landmarks of the twentieth century, as well as one of the pinnacles of western music history. It is my hope that this monograph may in some small way help lead the reader toward a similar conclusion.

*   *   *

Finally, a few technical matters. Readers interested in following some of the compositional details of various ballets will find the easily available scores of Stravinsky's ballets and concert suites useful. Although Stravinsky himself often refers to specific rehearsal numbers, I have, in most instances, chosen to discuss particular passages using measure numbers, enumerated from the beginning of each individual scene or *pas*. Most often I rely upon the piano reductions prepared by Stravinsky, although orchestral scores are employed as appropriate. At times I detail some of the choreography created by Fokine, Nijinsky, Balanchine, and others. Obviously, therefore, access to DVDs or videotapes (most of which are again readily available) would be helpful. The spelling of names (such as *Petrushka* or *Petrouchka*) may occasionally vary, depending upon which source is quoted. But for the most part, I have tried to be consistent.

The ever-increasing abundance of Stravinsky sources has by now proven not only invaluable, but daunting. Among the many authors upon whom I have relied, the writings of Richard Taruskin, Stephen Walsh, and Robert Craft emerge often. Among dance historians who have taken a special interest in ballet's relationship with music, Lynn Garafola, Nancy Reynolds, and Stephanie Jordan must be mentioned. Richard Parks was helpful in clarifying Debussy's important relationship with Stravinsky. Maureen Carr's recent compositional studies of several Stravinsky dance works provide a treasure trove of sketches useful in tracking the composer's working process.

Several repositories and curators were helpful in facilitating my study of Stravinsky's primary source materials. Fredric Woodbridge Wilson, former curator of the Harvard Theatre Collection, was, as always, extraordinarily helpful in guiding me through the collection's important papers and images. For the better part of twenty years, Ulrich Mosch and his colleagues at the Paul Sacher Stiftung in Basel, Switzerland, have proven continually cooperative in making available so many of Stravinsky's archival materials. The Morgan Library and Museum in New York was also helpful in allowing me to work with materials from the Robert Owen Lehman Collection and the Mary Flagler Cary Music Collection. Closer to home, funding from Skidmore College has enabled me to pursue research and present papers at various venues over the last few years. Let me also express my special appreciation to Chrisana McGill, who patiently listened to my ideas as they grew, all the while making valuable suggestions. Finally, thanks to Candida Brazil of Yale University Press for her expertise in editing the final manuscript of my work. Her assistance was invaluable. I would also particularly like to express gratitude to the general editor of the Music Masterworks series, George B. Stauffer, who was a wonderful partner in helping to bring this study to fruition.

C. M. J.
Saratoga Springs, New York

CHAPTER ONE

FROM ST. PETERSBURG TO PARIS
The Road to Recognition

IGOR STRAVINSKY was barely twenty-eight years old when the Ballets Russes premiered *The Firebird* on June 25, 1910, at the Théâtre National de l'Opéra. Almost overnight the composer vaulted into the Parisian limelight. Until that fateful juncture, he had been relatively unknown beyond a rather obscure circle of young St. Petersburg composers, and not particularly distinguished even among these. Now, suddenly, the young Russian became the darling of *haute société*, as well as an instant sensation within Diaghilev's troupe. A century later, many acknowledge *The Firebird* as the composer's first masterpiece, so beautiful is his orchestration of Fokine's beguiling fairytale ballet. But how did Stravinsky's short journey from obscurity to pre-eminence unfold? What is the history of the road traveled from his home in St. Petersburg to his initial triumphs in Paris? For not only was it a journey that dramatically changed the composer's life; it would also significantly alter the annals of both music and ballet.

Classical dance initially held little compositional appeal for the young composer. The bright glare of Parisian celebrity would change all that. Certainly Stravinsky was quite familiar with ballet and opera from his early days spent at the Maryinsky Theater in St. Petersburg. He admits the colorful spectacle of theater bedazzled him, just as anything ritualistic deeply impressed him. As a boy summering in Ustilug and elsewhere, he also delighted in observing village peasant dances and contests. Moreover, he demonstrated an affinity for physical movement and acting, frequently performing in amateur plays. Yet as memorable as these experiences surely were, nothing suggests that Stravinsky possessed any innate desire to rush headlong into writing ballet at any point before the success of *The Firebird*. Why would he? By the end of the nineteenth century, "grand ballet" was all but moribund. With the notable exceptions of

Tchaikovsky's and to some extent Alexander Glazunov's ballets, the genre itself was widely spurned as the deadest of dead ends. Would-be composers of the St. Petersburg vanguard had no wish to churn out humdrum accompaniments for the prima ballerinas and *danseurs* who swept across the Maryinsky stage. This was perfunctory work better left to hired hands such as Ludwig Minkus, who worked at the Maryinsky from 1872 to 1886 manufacturing one pastiche after another; or the slightly earlier Cesare Pugni, who, amazingly, bundled together well over three hundred ballet arrangements between 1823 and 1868. Ballet composers acquiesced to subordination in the cause of choreographic ostentation. It was often hard to spot the thinnest glaze of a story—harder still any thread of musical coherence. Consequently, ballet writing was adjudged jejune in the eyes of most budding composers unwilling to risk stigmatization.

The truth is that Stravinsky came to write ballet music by happenstance, seizing a fortuitous opportunity when he saw it. His acceptance of Diaghilev's providential invitation to work for the Ballets Russes would prove the right choice for all the parties involved. It could not have been a difficult decision for the ambitious young composer to make; nor should it be misconstrued as any particular attraction to dance as a medium. His interest arose from an eagerness to make an early and very public statement of his abilities. Chronicling the important path leading to the inception of *The Firebird*, however, is not so simple. This famous ballet—the first truly Russian ballet, as Diaghilev proclaimed it—finds its birthright in a whorl of intermingling and convoluted histories stretching back two centuries. Exploring this labyrinth, even summarily, throws light on the composer's life during his formative years, especially as it relates to dance. These influences not only pertain to *The Firebird*; they also figure prominently in viewing all his ballets, collectively, as a distinctive repertoire. Indeed, if ever there were a composer whose heritage shaped virtually every note written and every proclamation made, it was Stravinsky. Tracing the underlying impact of that heritage, and specifically the multiple forces that constitute its complexity, is instructive in understanding the journey that led to the composer's initial recognition as the most acclaimed ballet composer of the twentieth century.

*   *   *

A brief glance at dance history from 1700 to 1900 offers a point of departure. The roots of that history begin with the modernist vision of Peter the Great's autocracy in the early eighteenth century. Ballet's immediate precursors are traceable to fourteenth-century Europe. In Italy, and later in France, social dancing (masquerades, divertissements, banquets, and marriages) was common. For Russia, ballet came by way of importation, a trophy of the Enlightenment designed to position the empire on the European map—the only map that counted for some. Traveling abroad in 1697–98, a very young Peter toured Europe. It would be an odyssey of incalculable consequence. He returned with the grandest of blueprints rooted in his unbridled enthusiasm for the achievements of the West, including everything from maritime strategies to the technologies of industrialization and the beauties of the arts. These tangible advances stimulated Peter's imagination and set in motion a sweeping reformist government whose ripples would spread over the next two centuries. Moreover, the aristocratic urbanities of Europe also captivated Peter, especially the gracefulness of classical dance. Not to be outdone by the monarchy of his counterpart, Louis XIV, who danced in court as the "Sun King" in the 1653 *Le Ballet de la nuit*, Peter likewise actively participated in masquerades with notable aplomb. More germane, he introduced western stylized dances to his own court.

Westernization emerged as the desired goal of Peter's reign, at times with a highly corrosive impact upon a country whose national identity would remain mired in what seemed an insuperable perplexity. Peter intended his paternalistic vision as a corrective. For him, westernization provided, as Geoffrey Hosking observes, "a vivid sense of what was missing in Russia, together with the desire to begin making up the deficit."[1] It is easy to imagine the cultural turbulence that such a not so subtle disparagement of one's own country would incite. Unsurprisingly these violent winds, driven by deeply rooted emotions, continually sculpted the diverse visions and expressions of Russian artists. Frequently, such ideologically powerful statements proved hugely divisive.

Nearly two centuries after his rule ended, the aftermath of Peter's egoistic vision would still haunt the country's psyche. Stravinsky would not be exempt. The composer spent his childhood and early adult years in a world of a chronic political tumult that grew ever fiercer during the pre-revolutionary days of his St. Petersburg youth. His memoirs at times seem almost penitential, reflecting an anxious wavering in alternately engaging with or distancing himself from the disturbances all around him. Indeed, the vacillation persisted long after his departure for Switzerland, which came on the brink of the first World War—a war whose virulence decimated much of his country, wounded him psychologically, and deeply influenced his composition. His ambivalence left an inescapable wake.

Stravinsky's pent-up emotions came pouring out on his return to Russia in 1962. On October 1, at an evening reception in his honor, the composer spoke wistfully of his Russian birth as a lifelong influence. He expressed sorrow, perhaps even guilt, that he had not created his compositions in his homeland; and that he had been forced to flee his beloved country so many years earlier. It was an odd reversal. Shortly before departing California for this historic trip, the composer remarked, "Nostalgia has no part in my proposed visit to Russia . . . No artist's name has been more abused in the Soviet Union than mine, but one cannot achieve the future we must achieve with the Russians by nursing a grudge."[2] Yet there is no hypocrisy here, for these seemingly conflicting sides of the composer are wholly compatible. They speak to his life-long, ambivalent relationship with his ancestral past. It was a past the composer sometimes openly celebrated and at other times covertly buried beneath the surface of his words and music. He would continually struggle with personal and artistic choices throughout his life. And as will become apparent, from *The Firebird* to *Agon*, his ballets reflect the choices he made.

The roots of those ballets are traceable to the French court of the late 1500s, whose blanketing influence shaped Russian classical ballet throughout the nineteenth century. Thoinot Arbeau's 1588 *Orchésographie* is an early "how to dance" manual detailing the period's courtly dances. The seventeenth century brought Louis XIV's 1653 Apollonian "Sun King" portrayal in *Le Ballet de la nuit,* and in 1661 Louis established the Académie Royale de Danse, a school that would eventually lead to the Paris Opera Ballet. Ménestrier's important dance history, *Ballet Ancient and Modern,* appeared in 1682, exactly two hundred years before Stravinsky's birth. Pierre Beauchamps codified classical ballet's five basic positions at the dawn of the eighteenth century.

Peter the Great's shift of political power in 1713 from Moscow to the newly built cosmopolis christened St. Petersburg—a westernized city that would provide a "window on Europe," as Pushkin wrote—was transformative. The construction of St. Petersburg took the better part of a decade to complete, and was achieved at great human and material cost. Shortly thereafter Russian ballets began appearing regularly in the architecturally sumptuous capital. In 1731, during the brief reign of Tsarina Anna Ivanova, courtiers danced one of the most memorable tales of Russian folklore, that of Baba Yaga. St. Petersburg saw the founding of the Imperial Theatrical Academy (to which the Maryinsky's lineage is traceable) seven years later. In 1783, now only one hundred years before Stravinsky's birth, Catherine the Great, whose sovereign rule embraced far more than her western expansionist policies, reigned as a strong patron of the arts. Her royal largess supported music, theater, and especially ballet, as witnessed in her establishment of the Imperial Opera and Ballet Theater (more commonly referred to as the Bolshoi). Mikhail Glinka's operas

A Life for the Tsar and *Ruslan and Lyudmila* premiered there. Tamara Karsavina remembers that *A Life for the Tsar*, considered the most patriotic of operas, opened each season at the Maryinsky. Stravinsky recalled hearing both of Glinka's operas at the Maryinsky when he was young, and catching a "glimpse" of Tchaikovsky at the gala fiftieth anniversary performance of *Ruslan*. Another key figure in understanding Stravinsky's early ballets, the ballet master Marius Petipa offered many of his ballets at the Maryinsky over a very long and distinguished career.

Of the innumerable historical landmarks in nineteenth-century Russian ballet, as well as a constant stream of political upheavals and national reformations acutely affecting the empire, a few are particularly noteworthy. Charles-Louis Didelot, the "father of Russian ballet," accepted the directorship of the Imperial Russian Ballet School in 1801, having first worked in Paris and London. He overhauled ballet teaching, instituting measures that led to the development of the St. Petersburg ballet style, which Stravinsky regularly witnessed in performances at the Maryinsky Theater toward the other end of the century. Ballet was then very much in vogue, but its popularity, let alone its prestige, waxed and waned. As Peter Lieven commented in his *Birth of the Ballets-Russes,*

> During the nineteenth century the Russian Imperial Ballet had experienced several vicissitudes of fortune. During the thirties, it was still in full bloom, and the great national poet Pushkin was writing immortal verse in praise of the classical dancing of the ballerina Istomina as she daringly raised *en pointe*. After the death of the famous choreographer Didelot ballet began gradually to decay, though it never became completely extinct. It always retained a small but loyal public. Although the balletomanes were rather mocked at and ridiculed, they still persisted in their loyalty to the art.[3]

All the while, disputations between European modernization and Russian nationalism continued to roil. Tensions escalated following the 1812 invasion of Russia and Tsar Alexander's untrammeled pursuit of an on-the-run Napoleon through central Europe and back to Paris itself. Russian troops returned from France with newly acquired tastes for all things western, thus widening the chasm. The Decembrist revolutionaries of 1825, fueled by a liberalism military officers came to embrace while in the West, vowed not to pledge allegiance to the new Tsar, Nicholas I. Meanwhile the restiveness of those who took the westernization of Russia as pure coercion continued unabated. In 1828, Nikolai

Gogol arrived in St. Petersburg and, like so many other writers, wrestled with the overarching question of tsarist rule as fervently contested by Slavophiles, whose insurgency turned particularly seditious around 1830. It was the year Alexander Pushkin would complete *Eugene Onegin*. Nearly fifty years later, Tchaikovsky premiered an opera of the same name.

Pushkin's message proved a bellwether. The novel's polemic, best captured by Hosking as the "depiction of the spiritual consequences of living in a society which regulates itself by foreign models, models which have been deeply absorbed by educated people without penetrating to the people," would raise profound questions.[4] Largely consisting of liberals and intellectuals, the Slavophiles constituted a formidable agency in stridently denouncing the decadence of the West. Advocacy from all sides intensified, and the internecine politics among differing groups escalated. Unsurprisingly, the many polarized viewpoints contested within this crucible found reflection in the great works of literature and painting that poignantly recorded an emerging national pathos.

Nor were dance and music immune. Tours of internationally popular ballerinas featured such stars as Marie Taglioni, who, dancing *en pointe*, delighted Russia's nobility in the late 1830s and early 1840s. In 1847, Petipa arrived in St. Petersburg from Marseilles as a dancer. Twenty-two years thence, he would become ballet master in chief to the Imperial Tsar Alexander II. Petipa methodically elevated dancing to an unprecedented level of respectability. His accomplishments culminated in an especially productive partnership with Tchaikovsky during the 1890s. Under the Tsar's sponsorship, the Maryinsky Theater opened in 1860 as one of the most resplendent performance houses imaginable. Two years later Anton Rubinstein founded the Germanized St. Petersburg Conservatory—a state-sanctioned institution that, while reviled by some, would finally recognize its graduates, including Tchaikovsky in 1865, as members of a profession. The composer was now a "free artist"—a notable step forward in defining one's social status according to the still rigidly applied Table of Ranks established by Peter in 1722.[5]

Nor can one ignore the subsequent effect of the most consequential edict in modern Russian history: the 1861 emancipation of the serfs. The Russian climate would change radically in cities such as St. Petersburg, where the liberated serfs as well as the peasantry demanded increased rights. For too long, in a state of immense frustration, they had served the nobility under considerable restraint. Now there was hope for change. Industry mushroomed and the middle class grew exponentially. A proliferating population brought with it the problems of any city unprepared to deal with issues of health, overcrowding, dissension, and crime. Nonetheless, societal hopes swelled, and young artists everywhere increasingly grappled with the important questions of their time. It was the age of Lermontov's *A Hero of Our Times*, Gogol's *Dead Souls*, Turgenev's nihilistic *Fathers and Sons*, Dostoyevsky's *Crime and Punishment*, Tolstoy's *War and Peace*—all released within a thirty-year span around the century's midpoint. Collectively such literary voices stoked the political fires of the day through their psychological and moralistic ruminations. The impassioned authors of these texts were the radical provocateurs of Stravinsky's youth, and their inflammatory words surely stirred him. Optimism commingled with despondency. The antipodes of Russian politics as reflected in contemporary literature impelled courageous writers to speak out. The arts flourished in new directions—directions Stravinsky's generation would inherit, ingest, and ultimately modify.

Twenty-five years after the abolition of serfdom, the Maryinsky Theater—an enduring achievement in itself—became not only the new home of the Imperial Ballet, but also "a second home" to Stravinsky, as he once described it, where his father regularly performed, and where the young musician eagerly breathed in so many formative lessons. Shortly after the Maryinsky opened, Enrico Cecchetti, a legendary teacher who would rise to become a mainstay of Diaghilev's company, first appeared in St. Petersburg, in 1887, eventually becoming one of the prominent figures in the Ballets Russes from whom Stravinsky would learn the art of dance. Moreover, as ballet master for Diaghilev's troupe, Cecchetti was instrumental in fostering the careers of so many of the prominent dancers now enshrined by history.[6]

The three Tchaikovsky ballets performed at the Maryinsky during Stravinsky's youth furnish the closest bridge to his earliest meaningful contact with classical dance. Only by dint of Tchaikovsky's patience and fortitude was he able to deliver the scores for *The Sleeping Beauty*, *The Nutcracker*, and *Swan Lake*. Given the mostly feckless musical scores consigned to the ballet master over most of his career, Petipa's full capabilities went unrealized until then. In the end, however, these three masterpieces of the 1890s represent a pinnacle in the repertoire of what many characterize as the golden age of the Imperial Ballet. Thereafter the Ballet's fortunes steadily declined. If anything, as the new century approached the state of ballet worsened, the pre-revolutionary years bringing a tightening of tsarist rule. Moreover, an understanding of the Petipa– Tchaikovsky partnership helps to shed light on Stravinsky's often prickly relationships with many of the eventual choreographers of his ballets.

The original version of *Swan Lake*, first performed at the Bolshoi Theater in Moscow in 1877, proved problematic on many levels. The music was simply too good (a criticism that would attach itself to some of Stravinsky's own ballets). It ran the risk of suffocating the stage action, or at least confusing the audience as to what was most important. The original choreographer, Julius Reisinger, did not quite know what to make of this first truly symphonic ballet score, choosing to cut large portions of it. The first definitive version of the full-length ballet was premiered at the Maryinsky nearly two decades later, in 1895, two years after Tchaikovsky's death. By then the music had again been altered by Petipa and conductor Riccardo Drigo, resulting in a revised score that incorporated additional music not originally intended for the ballet by Tchaikovsky. From the outset, Tchaikovsky had been quite reluctant to undertake the commission. The genre initially struck him, as it did most Russian composers, as petrified. "They tell me that during the production of a new ballet, ballet masters treat the music very unceremoniously and demand many changes and alterations. To write under such conditions is impossible," the composer commented.[7] Boundaries were drawn and strictures applied in an effort to curb what choreographers bemoaned as a composer's overactive imagination. Formal contracts explicitly spelled out very tight constraints. For *The Sleeping Beauty*, a work that Stravinsky is likely to have seen in 1890, and one that touched him perhaps more than any other, Petipa had instructed Tchaikovsky as follows: "No. 1. At the rise of a curtain, a salon march for the entrance of the lords and ladies. No. 2. For Catalabutte's little recitative, the march becomes somewhat more serious. No. 3. Fanfares—broad grandiose music."[8]

According to Lieven, Nikolai Rimsky-Korsakov complained that his *Mlada* "was rehearsed without an orchestra, without even a piano, the only accompaniment being provided by two violins. Neither ballet master and dancers, nor the musicians themselves, could understand the first thing about the orchestration. When the orchestra was supposed to play a *tutti* with trombones *fortissimo*, Petipa rehearsed light aerial movements, and when the score demanded the soft tone of strings mass ensembles were staged." Moreover, directives to composers often came in such simple terms as the number of measures that were needed—and this was often determined upon nothing other than "the limit of a dancer's endurance," according to Tamara Karsavina. The music was filled with wooden, run-of-the-mill formulaic patterns built upon inelastic symmetrical groupings of four, eight, and sixteen bars.[9]

The impermanency of a work's choreography allowed for the interpolating and excising of musical passages at will. This often occurred without a composer's knowledge, let alone his permission. Choreographers frequently sanctioned the insertion of music by an entirely different composer at any point in a ballet. Coherence was not an issue: the only justification needed was that such alterations served the dance. Naturally, this irritated the perfectionistic

Tchaikovsky. He had no choice but to watch a finished score subjected to the whims of a particular all-powerful dancer or choreographer. Stravinsky, too, would constantly bristle at such license, especially when played as a trump card by the ironhanded Diaghilev, who considered managing musical scores to be part of his jurisdiction. Eventually Diaghilev's control would emerge as a major point of contention, since Stravinsky balked at any such artistic intrusion.

The aristocracy doted on ballet, sparing no expense in mounting lavish productions that were often attended by the Tsar's family. Ballet rivaled opera in its theatrical allure. Nevertheless, it knew its place. During the reign of Nicholas I, dancers and ballet masters occupied the lowest rung on the ladder of society's artists and artisans. Likened to indentured government employees, they took whatever tenuous security they could. Ballet was an adornment, and certainly not meaty enough to mirror the serious questions swirling in the broader culture. These concerns were better left for the more revered and appropriately contemplative sphere of literature and painting to tackle. By the time Tsar Alexander placed Petipa in charge of the Imperial Ballet in 1869, whatever interest there had been in earlier, romantically styled ballet was beginning to vanish as well.

In 1881, a year before Stravinsky's birth, Alexander II was assassinated. His demise continued a series of acts of violence against state officials at the height of nihilism's unremitting stonewalling of tsarist authority. During the brief reign of Alexander III—a staunch advocate of the restoration of native Russian traditions—there were a number of governmental attempts to foster a sense of pride and ownership within individual ethnic communities, and more widely throughout the empire. Through the Tsar's broadly based but alas often persecutory policy of Russification, a window opened. In 1882, Alexander decreed the closing of the Imperial Theaters and with it productions of Italian opera. Held in high regard for so long, the popular works of Donizetti, Bellini, Verdi, and others now faced growing competition from operas by Russia's own composers. Some of ballet's luster returned during the early 1890s with the works of Petipa and Tchaikovsky. Nonetheless, given the growing antagonism between Slavophilism and a less relevant "Europeanized" music, as Tchaikovsky's detractors branded his compositions, reactions varied. From a musician's viewpoint, at least, Russia's golden age of ballet was at best fleeting.

While some important ballets continued to appear between the 1895 *Swan Lake* and the 1910 *Firebird*, thanks mostly to Michel Fokine's prolific talents, compositional quality was markedly uneven. There was not much new music. Fokine choreographed pre-existing, familiar scores by Albéniz, Arensky, Bizet, Borodin, Brahms, Chopin, Glinka, Victor Herbert, Andrei-Karl Kadletz,

Mendelssohn, Johann Strauss, and others—over thirty works in all before 1910. Fokine first danced at the Maryinsky in 1898. Thereafter, his emergence as an imaginative and musically sensitive artist becomes hugely important in the years leading to *The Firebird*.

Fokine's story similarly unfolds within the politically unstable environment that continued to beset St. Petersburg. As Lynn Garafola points out, his rise "coincided with the Revolution of 1905 and reflected the social and artistic discontents that contributed to the turmoil within the Maryinsky."[10] It was also at this time that the dancers and choreographers of the Maryinsky whom Stravinsky would either observe or collaborate with began to make their presence felt. Anna Pavlova made her debut in 1899; Vaslav Nijinsky began his studies in St. Petersburg in 1900; Tamara Karsavina, first seen at the Maryinsky in 1902, would dance the principal role in *The Firebird* eight years later; Fokine produced the first of his ballets in 1905, including the immensely popular *Dying Swan* to the music of Saint-Saëns; George Balanchine was born in 1904 and later attended Cecchetti's classes at the Ballets Russes. With the exception of the young Balanchine, in fact, Enrico Cecchetti trained all of these artists in the years immediately preceding Diaghilev's establishment of the Ballets Russes in 1909.

Stravinsky's entry into the world of classical ballet dates from the time of Diaghilev's era-defining presence. Many artistic forces at work in literature, theater, and painting, both in combination and individually, contributed to the bold venture undertaken by Diaghilev. In painting, for example, the earlier Peredvizhniki (the Wanderers) broke free from the Academy of Arts in 1863. They focused their attention on realist works, landscapes, and portraits depicting the everyday struggles of the peasantry and serfs, who, although emancipated by decree, were in reality still enslaved. The movement found a parallel in Konstantin Stanislavsky's desire to introduce theater to the merchant class by familiarizing this burgeoning community with Russian drama. The evolution of Russian music during the second half of the nineteenth century warrants special attention given dance's relationship to music, its closest partner.

The Firebird, in common with virtually all of Stravinsky's other ballets, is directly traceable to several historical models that evolved during this period. Even more than dance, Russian history frames the musical world into which Stravinsky would soon be born, while also echoing quite pointedly the political and philosophical beliefs of a country still very much in ferment. As much as any contemporary art form, music took two very different paths in the second half of the nineteenth century. As Robert Ridenour observed, music became increasingly prominent after the Crimean War, which "provoked an artistic renaissance full of new energies. The musical rivalries of the 1860s illustrate the vigor with which at least a portion of educated Russian society responded to the reforming spirit and apparent opportunities for personal advancement thrown open by the accession to the throne of Alexander II."[11]

These rivalries inevitably invoked the opposition between westernization and Slavophilism. Glinka completed his *Life for the Tsar* in 1836, twenty years before the end of the Crimean War. The opera stands as an early historical benchmark in Russian music's quest to establish a national identity by relying heavily upon aboriginal folk song. In so doing, it represented a derogation of western academicism for some. It was quickly enlisted as a battle cry by vocal Slavophiles such as Vladimir Stasov, whose blustery and imperious advocacy of a homegrown, nationalistic Russian music (as well as artistic endeavors generally) stretched well into the years of Stravinsky's earliest pre-Ballets Russes works. Even earlier, a taste for change had been ripening. There were calls to unearth the buried musical treasures of Russian folklore as symbols of nationalistic strength and pride. The poignancy of Russian literary authors, the awakening of a cultural awareness hastened by renewed optimism following the Crimean War, the emancipation of the serfs, a tidal wave of population growth in St. Petersburg, the rise of the peasantry as a voice to be heard—all of these proved catalytic in galvanizing interest in Russia's cherished and too long neglected riches.

In contrast, the purveyors of an idolized West, particularly as manifested in a solemnly venerated German Romanticism, had considerable cachet in Russia during the first half of the century. The alternately thundering and poetic Romantic musical repertoire was heard ubiquitously throughout the country, thanks to well-supported and highly successful tours undertaken by such luminaries as Robert and Clara Schumann, Hector Berlioz, and Franz Liszt. Italian opera—whose influence on Stravinsky would be more important than one might assume—took firm root in Russia in the early eighteenth century. Thereafter, it remained wildly in vogue, culminating years later in the commissioning of Giuseppe Verdi's 1862 opera *La forza del destino*, first performed at the Bolshoi Theater.

Indeed, Italian opera would not relinquish its clutch throughout most of the century, even as Russian opera itself emerged as a competitor.[12] Celebrated singers at the Maryinsky, including Stravinsky's father Fyodor, performed both the Italian and the Russian repertoires with equal ease and affection. Additionally, Fyodor's repertoire included some of Wagner's operas, which Igor would also hear and study. Moreover, in one overarching way, at least,

Italian opera was not so different from classical ballet. Peter Lieven, who attended both often, offered a simple but instructive comparison: "The production of Italian opera concentrated on the voice and the art of the singer, and the orchestra provided scarcely more than an accompaniment, its dramatic function being kept in the background; in the same way the classical dance was the central part of the classical ballet and the music was merely an aid to the dancer."[13]

Russian folk music, evangelized by Stasov, and European art music, prized by the aristocracy, arose as opposing forces. Moreover, these powerful polarities reflected the divergence that had been steadily unfolding ever since Peter the Great had stood at the Baltic Sea's edge envisaging a modernistic new land. As Tolstoy asserted, the dichotomy pointed to the unaffectedness and sincerity of an agrarian people in contrast to the hubris of an alien culture that was externally imposed and thus unlikely to be assimilated. Perhaps the history of a submissive Russia's inferred inferiority as a nation had left too many scars. Enculturation of any kind had to be resisted. Inevitably, these two competing musical movements, each nearly choking on the vitriol of its own rhetoric, would converge in a public campaign promulgating two sets of compositional approaches. Ultimately, these highly charged contrarieties would prove not so contrary after all. Still, the two allegedly distinctive worlds would lead directly to Stravinsky's door. Their musical reconciliation would eventually fall into his capable hands. How oddly appropriate that the early triumph of *The Firebird*, the first truly public statement of the composer's deeply ingrained Russianness, would take place at the Paris Opera, one of the West's most sacred musical citadels.

Musically, St. Petersburg staked out its own occidental ground—hallowed ground paying full homage to Bach, Beethoven, and their disciples. Anton Rubinstein, given his ultra-westernized views, was immediately vilified as an interloper in establishing the Russian Music Society (RMS) in 1859. The organization quickly gained status as a public concert venue featuring mostly but not exclusively a narrow range of works from the classical Germanic tradition. Critics were predisposed to disparage Rubinstein's efforts. In responding to their attacks, Rubinstein offered as an appeasement the inclusion of Russian composers in programs. The St. Petersburg Conservatory, also under Rubinstein's direction, followed in 1862. It set the standard for conservatory education in Europe and America. Its faculty, again steeped in Germanic training, offered a rigorous curriculum in counterpoint, harmony, composition, performance, and conducting, all based upon the traditionalist conventions of the common-practice period. The RMS and the Conservatory stood as unassailable sanctuaries of classical programming and training. Their common stance, made more explicit by Rubinstein's own very public and imprudent disparagement of Glinka's music as clumsy and philistine, could not have been more incriminating. The scene was set for yet another conflagration.

The response—or rather antidote as some perceived it—came in the form of a loosely knit Russian *Gesellschaft* of musically untrained, avocational composers. They banded together in the mid 1850s, championing a more folkloristic, distinctly un-westernized approach. Under the leadership of Miliy Alexeyevich Balakirev (the only full-time musician among them) and with the encouragement of Stasov, the group coalesced in 1862 as the "Moguchaya kuchka," commonly known as "the Mighty Five" (Balakirev, Alexander Borodin, César Cui, Modest Mussorgsky, and Rimsky-Korsakov). The collective strength of their union—raw, impudent, and dauntless in its mission—would touch a nerve. They took dead aim at the unconcealed conservatism and self-styled pieties of Rubinstein's institutionalized initiatives. The time had come to set the record straight. Modernism would not spring from the transplanted pedantries proffered by the apostles of classical conservatism such as Rubinstein. Outlanders could know nothing of Russia's heritage. Truly new music, therefore, must find its source in a different wellspring: one that had been right under their noses all along. Relying upon indigenous source materials for inspiration, and unabashedly embracing their own ignorance of classical conventions, they would teach themselves how to compose. Help was neither sought nor needed.

Balakirev, however, did need a very public venue for his compatriots and himself, one that would provide an alternative to the biddings of the RMS and Conservatory. The Free Music School, which he helped to organize, was thus established in 1862 with the aim of teaching the masses, especially singing, the only musical training worth its salt in the eyes of such realists as Pushkin, Dostoyevsky, and Chekhov. Deserving students registered gratis, in keeping with the institutional mission to educate the merchant class then flourishing in St. Petersburg. The school set out to raise the musical consciousness of the public. Of course, entrusting the education of pliable minds to the proselytizing studios and classes of these young nationalist composers and their advocates was part of the bargain. Nor did Balakirev's rabidly combative faculty miss an opportunity to besmirch what "Stupinstein," as their calumny would have it, was teaching on the other side of the street, particularly given the superior level of performance and imperial concert subvention offered by the RMS. While the Free Music School attained some early success with choral performances, Balakirev soon fielded instrumental ensembles, providing him and his colleagues with at least some platform for the performance, even if by much less proficient personnel, of their own orchestral works.

The lines were drawn. The breach between Rubinstein, the despicable westerner, and "The Five," reactionary Slavophiles in the extreme, seemed irreparable. Characterizing them as warring parties, however, invokes a falsehood mainly attributable to Stasov's promotion of his own agenda. In the end, he overreached. Pitting one camp against the other in the most vituperative terms, Stasov's obloquy backfired, and the seams of his fervency began to fray. Following Rubinstein's 1867 resignation from the directorships of both the RMS and the Conservatory, a softening of positions occurred. Tchaikovsky, once thought almost traitorous in his adoption of Rubinstein's principles, and Balakirev, the uncompromisingly bellicose leader of the kuchkists, gradually negotiated a mutually beneficial truce, even achieving a measure of reciprocal respect. In another unpredictable twist following Rubinstein's departure, Balakirev, demonized by the conservatives as an antichrist, accepted an invitation to conduct several RMS concerts in 1867 and beyond. For the nationalists, it was a coup, as well as a way for Balakirev to infiltrate the opposing camp.

The squabbles apparent throughout this history directly affected Stravinsky's own musical education in the years preceding The Firebird. A pivotal moment occurred with the arrival of Nikolai Rimsky-Korsakov, the youngest, most complex, and most successful of Balakirev's New Russian School. Somewhat surprisingly, Rimsky accepted an appointment to the faculty of the St. Petersburg Conservatory in 1871—the very institution that had once stood in steadfast resistance to the effete musical beliefs of the circle of the Mighty Five. Thirty-two years later he would become Stravinsky's mentor. Rimsky was only seventeen when he joined Balakirev's crusade in 1861. Remarkably, by the time Stravinsky began his relationship with Rimsky in 1903, the tables had turned. The descendants of the New Russian School now constituted the majority of the St. Petersburg Conservatory faculty. Nevertheless, Stravinsky would never study there. Rather, he would work with Rimsky privately, and closely.

Ironically, Rimsky's acceptance of the Conservatory appointment was hardly the anomaly it might have seemed. It corroborated his own interest in acquiring the fundamental compositional techniques his more parochial colleagues spurned. By his own admission, teaching fundamental techniques forced him to learn them from the inside out—techniques of which he knew virtually nothing. "I could not decently harmonize a chorale; not only had I not written a single counterpoint in my life, but I had hardly any notion of the structure of a fugue." Perhaps it also hinted at a desire for a rapprochement. He even consulted Tchaikovsky (for whom he would later profess dislike). He learned the art of fugue, and worked tirelessly. Most importantly, Rimsky's appointment to the faculty represented a turning point not only for him personally but also for Russian music. Consequently, it would make all the difference for his future student. Through Rimsky's eyes, Stravinsky surely saw the provincialism of placing westernized compositional techniques on one side of an arbitrary line and the synthesis of folk song as richly compatible source material on the other. He was perceptive enough to sense the potential of blended musical styles as evident in Rimsky's thinking; and he would soon put the lesson to good use.[14]

While Stravinsky recounted memories of Rimsky in the conversation books he produced with Robert Craft, more revealing are the unedited comments he made to television producer David Oppenheim as part of the 1966 CBS documentary *Portrait of Stravinsky*. Cut from the film, on account of the time limitations of the forty-two-minute documentary, they portray Rimsky as disagreeable and jealous of Tchaikovsky's music. Stravinsky recalls that he and Rimsky often discussed Wagner's music, with special emphasis on Wagner's penchant for employing an orchestra quite dynamically. Likewise, Beethoven's orchestrations arose as a discussion topic. Stravinsky also remembers that Rimsky expressed his admiration for the "academics," an admiration Stravinsky attributes to Rimsky's envy of their well-honed compositional techniques. But at other times, this jealousy, Stravinsky contended, would erupt in anti-intellectual homilies.[15]

The young Stravinsky was well aware of Rimsky's undisguised critical view of ballet in the early years of the twentieth century. It was a view shared, for the most part, by members of the New Russian School, and for that matter by many of St. Petersburg's intelligentsia, whose nihilistic leanings continued to find an uncomfortably saccharine excess even in such celebrated works as *The Sleeping Beauty*. In his autobiography, *My Musical Life*, Rimsky wrote that he would "never write such music," presenting his reasons in the most caustic terms. He considered ballet a "degenerate art," adding that it was "boring, since the language of dance and the whole vocabulary of movement are extremely skimpy." There was simply no need "for good music in ballet" and such work was not suitable for a "highly talented composer." In his own autobiographical account, Stravinsky remembered that Rimsky begrudgingly tolerated national dances as inserted into operas such as Glinka's *Ruslan*. Certainly any interest in classical ballet among Rimsky's students would have been discouraged, despite the successes of Tchaikovsky, or perhaps because of them. How could such a pointed impeachment not have rubbed off on the impressionable Stravinsky, especially given his obeisance to Rimsky?[16]

Still, Stravinsky's familiarity with ballet began long before he commenced his formal tuition with Rimsky. Dance was part of the Russian culture for those of Stravinsky's social class, and he would have been acquainted with dance's classical vocabulary when he was quite young. As he recorded in *Memories and Commentaries*, he knew the stories of the great Tchaikovsky ballets. He recalled seeing Petipa, and remembered watching Anna Pavlova dance. Tamara Karsavina lived in the flat just above the Stravinsky apartment; and he attributed his knowledge of dance technique to Cecchetti. How many of these memories had grown tattered by the time Stravinsky and Craft discussed them one cannot say. But unquestionably ballet was an integral part of the young composer's life. What we do know is that as a boy Stravinsky regularly walked to the neighboring Maryinsky to see performances.

As Lieven writes, "The Imperial Ballet was never given as an adjunct or *divertissement* to other arts. Wednesdays and Saturdays were set aside for performances of nothing but ballet, and the half-empty auditorium contained a special public—a mixture of children accompanied by mothers or governesses, and old men with binoculars." It is unlikely, however, that Stravinsky would have heard anything of particular value, especially since ballet was still very much part of a social milieu that placed a premium on conservatism in the service of courtly amusement. Rather, it would simply have been one of many experiences imbibed during his young artistic development. Indeed, by the time Stravinsky was twenty-one and began studying regularly with Rimsky, his youthful experiences had brought him into contact with many of the arts. Moreover, he accumulated this growing body of knowledge during the political turmoil of a particularly volatile period wherein disillusionment ran high.[17]

Stravinsky was born on June 17, 1882, in Oranienbaum, a small town on the Gulf of Finland where for several years Catherine the Great held court. His earliest years were musically unremarkable. His memoirs claim a precocity as demonstrated by his ability to repeat songs he heard sung at an early age. Yet there are no portents of the firebrand composer of *The Rite*. He remembered starting to read music at age nine, studying piano with indifference, although enjoying improvising and discovering ideas on his own. Certainly his mother, Anna, was a constant presence in the home, and probably more so than her husband, who attended to his career. Consigned to a subsidiary role in Stravinsky's musical upbringing, Anna exercised a quiet but important early influence. Her pianistic skills seem to have been limited. Nonetheless she knew the easier Romantic piano works of Chopin, Schumann, and Schubert, and also studied the works of Bach, Mozart, and Beethoven. Put most simply, music was always in the air. Moreover, Stravinsky claimed that his mother was a fluent sightreader, and that his taste for using the piano as a tool to learn the repertoire had been inherited from her.

Even though distinguished composers and performers frequented the household from the time of his birth, music was certainly not Igor's only childhood interest. Summers in the country, beginning in his very first years, were among his fondest memories. They also provided an artistic stimulus. Letters indicate that painting and drawing occupied much of his time, and there is evidence that he continued to paint during these vacations as late as 1903. Taking part in amateur theatrical productions was another attraction, presaging his lifelong devotion to the stage. Such productions were more than a recreational way of passing time. They sprang from the seriousness of Russian theater that was so prevalent in the last decades of the nineteenth century. He literally learned the "ropes" of mounting a production by performing, building the stage, procuring props, and acquiring a sense of the behind-the-scenes aspect of theater.

Moreover, Stravinsky often attended plays, especially those of Chekhov as first produced during the late 1890s and early 1900s in St. Petersburg. He and his friend Stepan Mitusov partook of other theater performances as well—plays by Molière, Shakespeare, and Racine, standard fare ever since the Russian Cadet Corps had opened in 1732 and encouraged its pupils to learn such European classics. Stravinsky seems to have had little contact with the world of Stanislavsky or Meyerhold at the very moment that the Moscow Arts Theater was making international waves destined to change the way the twentieth century conceptualized the art of theater. Indeed, it was the innovative approach of Stanislavsky and others that drove much of what would be attempted by Diaghilev's Ballets Russes. Stravinsky's education here, as in most aspects of his youth, was blandly conservative. Nor was there any desire on his part to challenge the wisdom of his elders.

Letters home further indicate that Stravinsky read "omnivorously," to use his own term, and at a very early age, especially during his country excursions. Back in St. Petersburg, his father's library, recognized as one of the finest in the city, would furnish a safe haven for inspiration and reflection, and no doubt nurtured the future composer's own bibliophile instincts. Although not always verifiable, other memories as well as several letters to his parents suggest the breadth of his reading. Gogol and Pushkin, Dostoyevsky and Turgenev (the latter two said to be friends of his parents), Tolstoy, foreign writers such as Dickens and Twain, all were consumed. So too the standard texts from the Greeks to Shakespeare, Dante, and Molière, and even a hefty work on aesthetics by the nineteenth-century French philosopher Jean-Marie Guyau, *The Problems of Contemporary Aesthetics*.[18]

Beyond these summer experiences, St. Petersburg left an indelible imprint upon the young composer, both politically and culturally. The colorful reminiscences of Stravinsky's later conversations with Craft as recorded throughout *Expositions and Developments* make for wonderfully etched prose. Whether or not the city's open piazzas were the original inspiration for *Petrouchka*, or if he truly remembered seeing Tsar Nicholas parade by, or how many of these vividly recounted memories are accurate, it is clear that the city's splendors enchanted him. His tellingly confessional comment is illuminative: "St. Petersburg is so much a part of my life that I am almost afraid to look further into myself, lest I discover how much of me is still joined to it." Stravinsky's memories of the Maryinsky are assuredly true, at least with regard to its lasting influence. It was indeed his second home. Vitalized by his attendance at rehearsals, as well as "five or six nights a week at the opera" courtesy of his father's position, it is little wonder his interest in music surged.

Moreover, his growing keyboard proficiency enabled him to read and study operatic scores from his father's library at the piano at a relatively early age. He would continue similarly once he began his studies with Rimsky, when teacher and student read symphonic and operatic scores together at the keyboard and frequently attended performances. Nor should one dismiss the importance of this tactile learning. Surely, this personal, empirical examination of each score significantly deepened the knowledge he acquired at each Maryinsky rehearsal and performance. Whether the words are precisely recalled or not, the sentiment he remembered fifty years later resonates with his lifelong desire to experience ideas directly and personally: "Sitting in the dark of the Maryinsky Theatre, I judged, saw, and heard everything first hand, and my impressions were immediate and indelible. And, after all, the world of St. Petersburg in the two decades before *The Firebird* was a very exciting place to be."[19]

Exciting indeed, and given their family birthright, the Stravinskys enjoyed the cultural trappings of nobility. While certainly not rising to the status of true aristocrats, they were in many ways privileged. The family's political thinking was cautiously liberal, and mostly expressed out of sight in private letters. Even so, there is no doubt that they, like their son Igor, were acutely aware of the unsettled world outside their door. Accordingly, they subscribed to long-held traditions of rank. It is therefore unsurprising that neither parent supported their son's developing musical aspirations. The goal of Igor's eventual university studies in jurisprudence was to assure him a place within the proper social rank. But his interest in formal studies was halfhearted at best, and his transcript undistinguished. Stravinsky admits that most of his classes at St. Petersburg University went unattended, although he did receive his certificate in the spring of 1905. Increasingly, music preoccupied his mind.

His real education came by way of his private tutoring with Rimsky, beginning in 1903, and even then took the form of observation rather than regular lessons, which commenced a bit later. Rimsky's home, which Stravinsky happily recalls visiting almost daily from 1903 to 1905, opened a new world of dialectics, of protagonist thinking. Polemicists of all stripes—scientists, painters, scholars, as Stravinsky remembers—gathered to argue their progressive views amidst Russia's increasingly combustible environment. It was at about this time too that Stravinsky became aware of Serge Diaghilev, whose stimulating and some would suggest incendiary ideas were arousing commotion within the St. Petersburg artistic community.

Rimsky himself was no stranger to political activism. The most intellectually inclined of the Mighty Five, he surely encouraged the heated discussions that took place in his parlor. His dismissal as director of the St. Petersburg Conservatory came soon after Bloody Sunday and the ensuing imperial sanctions, the result of what his superiors considered the impolitic support of student protestors. His blunt statements and actions helped to temporarily shut down the institution in 1905. So suspect were his freely expressed opinions that for a while the Tsar also banned all of the composer's works from performance in the city. For many artists, insurrection was in the air, and Stravinsky, being in his early twenties, found such zealotry seductive. The dancers of the Imperial Ballet raised a series of grievances against the government, and a strike at the Maryinsky Theater included several artists with whom Stravinsky would collaborate five years later, including Tamara Karsavina and Michel Fokine. As Garafola suggests, "The strike kindled a feeling of common artistic identity not unlike the bonds uniting artists grouped around Diaghilev's journal *Mir Iskusstva*." Indeed the journal would lay the cornerstone of the modernist movement to which Stravinsky would contribute so significantly.[20]

Although Stravinsky projected an apolitical public posture throughout his life, he nevertheless confessed that he was cognizant "of the political world into which I was born." His private letters often refer to his concern for others, but also for his own welfare and for the advancement of his own work. The gathering storm clouds of 1905 did not escape his attention during his time either at the university, where demonstrations were frequent, or at Rimsky's home, where ideas found free exchange. In *Memories and Commentaries*, he recounted an incident as a university student during which he was inadvertently arrested together with other protesting students in the politically tense months following the Russo-Japanese War. "I was detained seven hours, but seventy years will not erase the memory of my fears."[21] He recalls the hardship of travel following his marriage in 1905, of finding "a safe train back to St. Petersburg" where "soldiers stood guard everywhere" in the aftermath of the *Potemkin* mutiny, one of many confrontational lines drawn in the sand by military personnel. The country was on the precipice of a national revolt. In a letter written a year later, the composer acknowledged "the tremendous revolution that is inevitably coming," even submitting that the grievances of those less fortunate than he were understandable and their expression long overdue.[22]

Even so, the young composer eagerly took advantage of the benefits bestowed by his family's status, especially the entrée to St. Petersburg's musical life that was provided by his renowned father. Fyodor's friends and colleagues, very much members of the local *culturati*, occupied positions of prominence in the city's artistic circles. Igor remembered that his father treasured an inscribed photograph of Tchaikovsky, as well as the accolades the composer heaped upon Fyodor's performance in his opera *The Sorceress*. How close Tchaikovsky's relationship to Fyodor was is difficult to determine, but the younger Stravinsky also recalls that his father served as a pallbearer at Tchaikovsky's funeral in 1893. As a singer and actor, Fyodor constituted almost a personal performance wing of the Mighty Five, presenting much of their music in lavishly staged productions while enjoying the friendship of Borodin, Cui, Mussorgsky, and Rimsky. While Igor would have been too young to engage in meaningful interaction with these visitors to his home, he was old enough to appreciate his father's celebrity.

A graduate of the St. Petersburg Conservatory, Fyodor Stravinsky began singing in Kiev but soon made his professional operatic debut in St. Petersburg in 1876. From that moment on, he won the praise of audiences and critics alike as one of the leading bass singers in the Imperial Opera. His achievements also received an imperial imprimatur. In 1899, Tsar Nicholas presented him with a gold watch in recognition of his contributions to the cultural life of St. Petersburg. Seven years earlier Fyodor had contributed to a celebrity autograph album to benefit victims of the 1891–92 Volga famine and cholera epidemic that followed. Thus, Igor was keenly aware of his father's status, though the son's memoirs disclose mixed feelings about him as a cold, unsupportive paterfamilias. By the time of adulthood, these feelings turned to bitterness (also in relation to his mother's less than supportive attitude), leading to his tellingly dismissive comments regarding the question of parental influence. Even so, when the composer returned to St. Petersburg in 1962, he delighted in returning to the Maryinsky, the theater in which his father had performed so often, and where so many of his own youthful artistic impressions had been formed.

Fyodor's widely ranging repertoire included many of the established and contemporary Russian operas of the day—everything from Glinka's *Ruslan and Lyudmila* to Mussorgsky's *Boris Godunov*. Tchaikovsky, Borodin, and of course Rimsky were among the composers he sang, but he also appeared in several operas by Wagner, including *Tannhäuser*. Igor's later disparagement of Wagner belies the fact that these operas captured his attention as a young musician, so much so that he studied the scores closely at the keyboard. As the archives reveal, Stravinsky was a lifelong annotator. The colorful marginalia of his books and scores, which mostly flag something he wished to remember or pursue, include annotations to the pages of *Parsifal* and *Tristan und Isolde*.[23] A decade later, Rimsky's own admiration for Wagner would come through in his lessons and conversations with the young, acquisitive Stravinsky.

If the Maryinsky was a second home to Stravinsky, then Rimsky was, by Stravinsky's own admission, "a second father to me." Rimsky was in a position to influence Stravinsky even more than his father might. Fyodor's connection to Rimsky by virtue of the singer's stellar performances of such operas as the 1882 *Snow Maiden*, in which Fyodor premiered the role of Grandfather Frost, certainly curried some favor, as did Igor's friendship with Rimsky's two sons, both classmates from university days. This was fortunate, for there was little of compositional promise in the young Stravinsky's portfolio when he first shared his nascent attempts with the elder composer during the summer of 1902. In meeting with Rimsky, Stravinsky took with him a letter of reference from Fyodor, and one can only imagine that Rimsky factored in his respect for Fyodor in suggesting, cautiously it seems, that the young Stravinsky continue to compose. Perhaps Rimsky's own admitted naiveté and ignorance of fundamental compositional techniques, as acknowledged at the time of his appointment to the Conservatory, spawned some measure of compassion. Maybe he also saw in Stravinsky's rough first efforts some flicker of aptitude that might develop once the young composer had the opportunity to acquire the basics— basics that two of Rimsky's own students would have to inculcate before he would take Stravinsky on as his pupil a few years later.

Even so, Rimsky must have strained to catch any glimmer of potential. Stravinsky's earliest pieces are more revealing in terms of what they lack than in terms of what they foreshadow. There are no Mozartian moments here. Nor is there even a whiff of the precociousness of Prokofiev, who at half the age of the twenty-year-old Stravinsky was already far more advanced. Another wunderkind, Alexander Glazunov (1865–1936) was much the rage at the time. Touted as one of Rimsky's protégés, he would soon become a nemesis for Stravinsky. Beginning in the 1880s, Mitrofan Belyayev, an amateur chamber musician—and more to the point, a wealthy one—promoted the teenaged Glazunov's climb to notoriety by publishing his early symphony, begun at age sixteen in 1881. Not only did Belyayev found a publishing house for Russian composers in 1885, he also established a series of public concerts the same year, further advancing the visibility of Glazunov himself and of both other younger and also more established Russian composers. Rimsky served as Belyayev's advisor and seems to have aggressively pushed Glazunov's music to the fore.

Known as the Belyayev Circle, a group of composers fiercely loyal to Rimsky's academic views, this new generation became the heir to the Mighty Five. However, just as Rimsky had changed, so too this newer neonationalist coalition was not so interested in wearing its folkloristic, social consciousness on its sleeve. Stravinsky regularly heard the music of the "Belyayevtsï" composers, including Glazunov, Nikolai Cherepnin, and Anatoliy Lyadov. Understandably, he patterned his music after these academically rooted proponents at Rimsky's urging. Eager to join this fraternity, whose music won regular performances (if only at Rimsky's discretion), what incentive had he to do otherwise? While Glazunov possessed the fundamental tools of composition early on, Stravinsky had to work assiduously to acquire even the rudiments of music theory and composition. His jealousy of Rimsky's fondness for Glazunov erupted at various points throughout his life, perhaps because Stravinsky realized early on that Glazunov's post-Romantic idiom was stolidly formulaic and heading nowhere. Still, during the drought of talented ballet composers that followed Tchaikovsky's death, Glazunov wrote three ballets, including the successful and still popular *Raymonda* (1898), one of Petipa's last important works, and later staged by several choreographers including George Balanchine and Rudolf Nureyev.[24]

In acquiring and honing the tools of composition, the distance the twenty-year-old Stravinsky traveled between 1902, the date of his earliest-known complete piece, and 1909, when he began writing *The Firebird*, is nothing short of extraordinary. It constitutes a remarkable spurt of compositional growth that is too often underestimated in defining Stravinsky as the overachiever he was. His rapid maturation from a compositionally unsophisticated teenager to the toast of Paris is perhaps the most revealing story of his youth. In looking for his earliest compositional attempt, we find a negligible, musically inchoate fragment of a *Tarantella* for piano dating from 1898. The year 1902 brought several other student pieces probably written while the young composer was completing elementary assignments with Rimsky's pupils, who, like their own teacher, were now more inclined to formal academicism and far less kuchkist in their outlook. A few of Stravinsky's juvenilia have survived. A Scherzo for piano, while disappointing to those unrealistically hoping for some augury of the more sophisticated works of ten years later, is predictably derivative. Still, it demonstrates that some development had occurred over the intervening four years, as well as Stravinsky's idiosyncratic approach to the keyboard—an approach that would have compositional consequences in the years to come. As one of his earliest extant efforts, it is more important than often credited. A short song setting a poem by Pushkin, entitled "The Storm Cloud," argued by some to show potential, is likewise not particularly distinguished. There is nothing compositionally objectionable here, but neither can it be considered a diamond in the rough.

Increasingly substantial works began to appear once Stravinsky embarked on his more formal relationship with Rimsky in 1903, although even then the elder composer was not prepared to act as his official tutor. Rather, Stravinsky spent time in the Rimsky home, listening to music, acquainting himself with the party line taken by Rimsky's advanced students, and broadening his artistic horizons. There is a large, or perhaps better stated, bloated Sonata in F-sharp Minor for piano completed in 1904, heavily reliant upon Glazunov and other contemporary Russian composers whose music Stravinsky clearly wished to emulate. Still, its advance over the artistically and technically scant works of a few years earlier is notable. There is also another short song, "How the Mushrooms Went To War," memorable for its oblique commentary on conscription and the quickly disintegrating state of affairs brought about by the disastrous Russo-Japanese War. Such a musical setting would have reverberated with the tone of political conversations at Rimsky's home. This little piece too, however, marched along in the style of the composers by whom Stravinsky was surrounded, breaking no new ground. Other small to modestly proportioned works emanate from the five years preceding *The Firebird*: the *Faun and Shepherdess* (1906), clearly indebted to Glazunov and Wagner; the *Pastorale* (1907); the Four Studies for piano, op. 7 (1908), the first of his published works and legitimate concert etudes that deserve performance; the *Chant funèbre* (1908), written in tribute to Rimsky who had died in June; and a few other smaller unpublished works. Most ambitious was the Symphony in E-flat, probably begun before his lessons with Rimsky but completed under his guidance in 1907. Stravinsky and his teacher worked through its composition slowly over an extended period. In essence, it was the young composer's "coming out" work, performed before a private audience in 1908, although reviewed rather tepidly.[25]

Perhaps even more relevant than the symphony is the fact that Rimsky began assigning orchestration projects to the young composer in 1904 as part of his curriculum. These undoubtedly included works by Beethoven and Schubert, which was quite customary for Rimsky's students. He also gave Stravinsky some of his own compositions to orchestrate, including an unpublished opera. The orchestral brilliance of Stravinsky's ballet scores from *The Firebird* onward is surely indebted to the lessons learned under Rimsky's tutelage. As we shall see, it was Stravinsky's powers as an orchestrator that originally caused heads to turn and opportunities to arise. Stravinsky spoke of Rimsky's instructional method in his autobiographical remembrances: "He would give me some pages of the piano score of a new opera he had just finished (*Pan Voïvoda*), which I was to orchestrate. When I had orchestrated a section, he would show me his own instrumentation of the same passage. I had to compare them, and then he would ask me to explain why he had done it differently. Whenever I was unable to do so, it was he who explained."[26]

The two pre-*Firebird* works of greatest significance are the *Scherzo fantastique*, begun in 1907, and *Fireworks*, completed in 1909, both pertinent to Stravinsky's initial foray into the world of ballet. The *Scherzo fantastique* is a large symphonic work (at twelve minutes' duration ambitious indeed) displaying the composer's already well-developed orchestral palette. Rimsky lived to see only a completed draft, but was himself impressed. As with the earlier and more ponderous symphony, Stravinsky employed a large orchestra (originally including three harps and a celesta), but here the orchestral writing is notably less turgid. The composer evocatively painted the shades of color needed to emphasize the chromatic character of the music. By this date, it is not surprising that the score is drenched in the octatonicism he was constantly hearing, and dutifully amalgamating, in the music of Rimsky and others. Richard Taruskin, for example, addresses Stravinsky's "composing out" of the many symmetrically structured harmonies so often found in Rimsky's works, citing the passage beginning at Rehearsal 56 of the *Scherzo fantastique* as a particularly rich example. Although the composer doubtlessly had such whole-tone and diminished-seventh-chord pitch collections in mind from the start, he was apparently not so sure about the most effective way to orchestrate the music. The autograph manuscript suggests that the sixteen measures between Rehearsal 56 and Rehearsal 60 were initially sketched quite differently from those of the final published version. Stravinsky literally rewrote the passage on new manuscript paper and pasted the revision over the earlier version, as recorded in the autograph.

As other emendations in the autograph full score reveal, Stravinsky worked assiduously on the piece, even given its continued dependence upon the models of Rimsky and others.[27] Moreover, it would later become the first piece of his concert music to be employed for ballet. Ten years after its composition, the *Scherzo fantastique* premiered under the title *Les Abeilles* at the Paris Opera in early 1917, with choreography by Leo Staats. In its balletic incarnation, the music accommodated a scenario based upon a portion of Maeterlinck's *La Vie des abeilles* (The Life of the Bees). That Stravinsky had been aware of Maeterlinck's book is now certain, to judge from a letter to Rimsky. His imitation of the sound of buzzing bees in this score is as programmatically clear as clear can be. Most importantly, the *Scherzo* is an unmistakable harbinger of the striking orchestral devices employed in *The Firebird*. It is the most definitive signpost on the road to that ballet. Coming only five years after Stravinsky's first completed work, the juvenile Scherzo for piano of 1902, the accomplishment of the larger orchestral *Scherzo fantastique* speaks directly to the amount of ground covered in such a brief period.

Fireworks represented another step forward. The first performance took place the following winter in St. Petersburg. It is a brief composition, so orchestrally radiant and rhythmically vibrant that it begs for dance. As with the *Scherzo*, *Fireworks* has all the elements of a programmatic piece, but without the need for any constraining story. There is an unmistakable indebtedness to works such as Paul Dukas's *The Sorcerer's Apprentice*, written a decade earlier. If nothing else, Stravinsky's score continues to demonstrate a transition beyond the music of St. Petersburg models, as he begins to stake out what will evolve into an independent style. He was not quite there, even with the more mature *Fireworks*, but the integration of his harmonic and rhythmic vocabulary within a continually expanding sense of the orchestra's capabilities grew ever more apparent. The use of the celesta and the string writing in particular unequivocally foreshadow the "Infernal Dance of All Kashchei's Subjects" in *The Firebird*. Both the *Scherzo fantastique* and *Fireworks* appeared on concert programs in the winter of 1909, conducted by the influential Alexander Siloti. Their inclusion in this prestigious series constituted further confirmation of Stravinsky's growing reputation. The *Scherzo* premiered at a public concert in January. *Fireworks* followed a few weeks later. As Stravinsky recalled, that winter marked "a date of importance for the whole future of my musical career."[28]

The composer now appeared more frequently in public venues. He served as the pianist that winter in a performance of his 1907 *Pastorale*, playing in an "Evenings of Contemporary Music" program in St. Petersburg. Of course, there were in-house auditions of some of his works at Rimsky's home as well. Increasingly accomplished players began to perform his music. Gradually, Stravinsky began to shed the role of an apprentice. Still and all, it was his father's name that typically came to mind when most St. Petersburgers heard the name Stravinsky. As Lieven wrote, even "in 1909 the Russian public had to mention the father in order to make clear who this unknown young man was."[29]

That was all about to change.

CHAPTER TWO

THE FIREBIRD

Diaghilev, Fokine, and Stravinsky

For Stravinsky 1909 was nothing short of an *annus mirabilis*. Whatever his hopes, he could not have imagined how pivotal the performance of his *Scherzo fantastique* in Siloti's program of January 24, 1909, would be. Serge Pavlovich Diaghilev (1872–1929), for many the gatekeeper to twentieth-century modernism, was in the audience. Even as he listened that winter night, his mind must have been preoccupied with preparations for his soon-to-be unveiled Ballets Russes in Paris. He would launch its inaugural season less than four months later. The new venture would be a gamble, and Diaghilev needed all the visibility he could get. The *Scherzo*'s coruscating orchestral sound caught his ear that evening. He immediately discerned Stravinsky's potential usefulness. The short composition had just the pungency needed to complement the exotica he envisioned for the Parisian stage. At that moment, Stravinsky could not have realized that his compositional fortunes would soon fall into Diaghilev's hands. Indeed, the destiny of these two artistic giants would intertwine for the next twenty years as their turbulent, on-again-off-again partnership evolved, constantly teetering on the edge of collapse.

It is likely that they met immediately after the Siloti concert. Not long after the *Scherzo*'s public premiere, Stravinsky performed the piano reduction of *Fireworks* at an informal Conservatory concert. Apparently Diaghilev was again present, although the formal orchestral premiere did not occur until almost a year later. Diaghilev invited Stravinsky to meet with him. The composer arrived on time but was made to wait outside the impresario's office. Growing impatient, Stravinsky had one hand on the door to the street, ready to leave, when Diaghilev suddenly emerged from his quarters and asked him in. "I've often wondered," Stravinsky later recalled, "if I'd opened that door, whether I would have written *Le Sacre du printemps*."[1]

Born in Perm, Diaghilev attended the St. Petersburg Conservatory where opera quickly became a passion. Graduating in 1892, it became evident that his talents would be better channeled in an administrative direction. With broad interests and experiences—dance, painting, literature, publishing, opera, and theater—Diaghilev became an accomplished critic and collector. And with a bigger-than-life personality, as well as a quixotic and flamboyantly irrepressible temperament, the indomitable entrepreneur instinctively knew how to make things happen. Even while juggling a dozen competing business interests, he acted as a puppeteer, cajoling friends and associates to see matters his way. Moreover, he knew who he was. Writing to his stepmother, Elena Panaeva, he pronounced himself "a great charlatan, albeit *con brio*," a person with charm, cheek, logic, "no genuine talent," but a vocation "to lead the life of a patron of the arts."[2] He was an aesthete, whose tastes ranged widely, encompassing both classical traditions and the avant-garde. Personally ambitious and fiercely devoted to extolling Russian culture, Diaghilev exported the country's artistic heritage to all points west, from Paris to New York; and he did so with unrivaled ingenuity.

As one of the founding architects of the free-spirited, frequently irreverent 1898 art journal *Mir iskusstva* (World of Art), Diaghilev's impact upon the consciousness of St. Petersburg and Moscow over the publication's six-year run was considerable. Its contributors preached an unbending insistence on core aesthetic values that skipped back over the recent tsarist reigns of Alexander II and Alexander III to the more patrician rule of the earlier Nicholas I. The "miriskusniki" offered perorations on the ennobling rewards of beauty for beauty's sake. Diaghilev and his elitist circle embraced a strange *noblesse oblige* mix of condescension and egalitarianism, declaring it was high time for Russian artists to concede the existence of hierarchical layers of art—some layers more meaningful than others. The run-of-the-mill trials and tribulations of the bourgeoisie, for instance, as darkly lamented by popular painters and writers, were of little interest to the journal's editors. They felt morally obliged to denounce the superficialities of social realism as nothing more than a barefaced sentimentality belying the shallowest meaning.

Diaghilev made his manifesto plain from the start, authoring a series of four allocutions under the rubric "Complicated Questions."[3] Boundaries were to be pushed, mediocrity excoriated, and ideas meant to clash. Only twenty-six years old when he assumed the role of editor-in-chief of *Mir iskusstva*, the supercilious young provocateur was contemptuous of anything commonplace. Unsurprisingly, his didactic approach met with resistance from conservative academics, who had no use for such empty erudition. Alexandre Benois and Léon Bakst, whose innovative thinking in theater helped revolutionize set designs and costuming, were mainstays among contributing writers. They provided essays on contemporary issues and reviewed exhibitions, concerts, and theatrical performances. Long after the journal's demise, such likeminded thinkers would collaborate closely with Diaghilev's Ballets Russes, notably in its first successful venture, *The Firebird*. Soon Diaghilev's troupe exhibited an increasingly iconoclastic sense of experimentation traceable to *Mir iskusstva*'s ideologically confrontational esprit.

Diaghilev's acumen transcended the voluble intellectualizing of which he was often accused. He was also a practical man. Eager to learn all that he could, he accumulated a wealth of experience through directing the daily business of the Imperial Theaters. Toward the end of the century he also produced several operas. But despite his successes, personal indiscretions soon led to his dismissal. In 1905, shortly after Bloody Sunday, he mounted an astonishing exhibit of Russian portraiture in St. Petersburg, subsidized by Nicholas II. Its encyclopedic breadth encompassed over four thousand paintings, spanning a period reaching back to Peter the Great in laying out the expanse of Russian history. It was a leviathan achievement, matched only by his own sweepingly prophetic "At the Hour of Reckoning," delivered shortly after the exhibit's opening. "Do you not feel that the long gallery of portraits of people great and small . . . is but a grand and convincing reckoning of a brilliant, but, alas, mortified, period of our history? . . . We are the witnesses of a great historical moment of reckoning and ending in the name of a new unknown culture."[4]

So comprehensively towering was its scope that Paris—ever eager to place itself at the cutting edge—had to host the exhibition too. It marked the beginning of Diaghilev's close ties to the West. He would return to the capital annually, concocting some artistic allurement that was sure to woo the French. High-profile artists such as the hugely popular singer-actor Fyodor Chaliapin (in operatic circles, Fyodor Stravinsky's heir) and Sergei Rachmaninov would dazzle the public with their artistic genius; but for many jaded Parisian sophisticates, they were little more than dancing bears. As Tamara Karsavina reported, "The whole of our vast country to the average occidental mind still remained a land of barbarians."[5] Welcoming such artistically talented but intellectually coarse Russian vulgarians into a culturally urbane Paris was thought to be oh-so-voguishly continental, so *très chic*.

By 1907, Diaghilev was regularly presenting concerts of Russian music to the Parisian glitterati, whose appetite for the risqué "orientalism" of these curiously exotic Russian composers and performers seemed unquenchable. Diaghilev's 1908 *Boris Godunov*, grandly staged at the Paris Opera with Chaliapin in the title role, proved so marketable that Diaghilev returned the next season not only with more operas, but with Russian story-ballets as well. Even so, he was anything but a devoted balletomane. On the contrary, it fell to Benois and others to convince him of ballet's potential as a collaborative enterprise. The efficacy of its silence, unfettered by words, provided a more pristine content and physical expression. Its power would derive from the vocabularies of music, painting, dancing, and theater working symbiotically, rather than relying upon literary denotation. This made it all the more incumbent upon musicians and dancers to design clear, coherent statements through sound, sight, and movement. And pragmatically, it was a lot less costly than opera to produce.

Had opera been self-sustaining, Diaghilev may not have been so willing to stage dance; but by the time the Ballet Russes arrived, Paris had become Europe's amusement park. It was ripe for a resurgence of ballet. As Peter Lieven observed, "In Paris the ballet had sunk to nothing more than a display of pretty women in tempting costumes."[6] It took but a minute for the often doctrinaire Diaghilev to determine that while there was nothing inherently oriental about Russian music, if the Parisians chose to associate "tempting costumes," exotica, and indeed eastern eroticism with "du vrai Russe," then so be it. And if it improved ticket sales, so much the better. Borodin's Polovtsian Dances from Prince Igor, offered in 1909, and Rimsky's Scheherazade, produced in 1910 only three weeks before the premiere of The Firebird, would create the titillation that modish French society desired.[7] The Ballets Russes became the hottest ticket in town, and audiences flocked to see what delectable indulgence Diaghilev's eccentric menagerie of artists would offer up next. Further, in aggressively marketing productions under the banner of Russian neonationalism, the machinating Diaghilev had no compunction in drawing on or mixing whatever sources and styles served his purpose. Benois was particularly outspoken in declaring a proprietary ownership of all that Russian history included. Whether it was native folklore or the Europeanized artistic tastes cultivated over the preceding two hundred years in the wake of Peter the Great's audacious westernization policy, all was fair game. "That is why we focus equal attention on what was created both before and after Peter," Benois exclaimed with a rationalization that quickly disposed of any presumed limits as to what subject, content, or style the Ballets Russes might next pursue.[8]

For the next twenty years, the Ballets Russes functioned as a tastemaker, not only transforming ballet but shaping other arts as well. Often flouting convention, it embraced everything from theater to fashion. Diaghilev's company provided a very well lit stage for the ideas Mir iskusstva had championed over the preceding decade, including a synthesis of the arts in mounting coherently structured artistic statements. Whatever "ism" emerged during the century's first quarter, it found sponsorship under Diaghilev's aegis. Music was no exception. A constellation of contemporary composers including Prokofiev, Ravel, Debussy, Richard Strauss, Satie, Falla, and Nicolas Nabokov participated in an unprecedented grand experiment. With his first ballet, Stravinsky's star shone the brightest. His stunning success instantly furnished Diaghilev with a marquee composer whose music piqued audience interest. Following *The Firebird*, Stravinsky's name appeared more and more prominently in promotions and programs—remarkably so, given that the focus of ballet had always been squarely on the dancers. And while Diaghilev, Benois, and Fokine served as the principal architects in sculpting the 1910 story-ballet, Stravinsky's music won the day. Enthralling Parisian society, it soon captured the wider world as well.

Seventeen months before *The Firebird*'s June premiere, in January 1909, Diaghilev had been immediately charmed by Stravinsky's *Scherzo*, especially its instrumental flair. Perhaps he had Stravinsky in mind for his new 1909 ballet season, although he was still not particularly interested in the composer's own music. Caution prevailed. There was a lot at stake during Diaghilev's inaugural ballet season. He invited the composer to reorchestrate two works by Chopin for a revised version of the ballet *Chopiniana*—audition pieces, really—scheduled for production in Paris under a new title, *Les Sylphides*, in June of that year.[9] Stravinsky prepared Chopin's Nocturne in A-flat Major, op. 32, no. 2, and the popular Grande Valse Brillante in E-flat Major, op. 18. While the commission required only transcriptional work, Stravinsky knew a passport when he saw one. Associating with the Ballets Russes and the other composers who contributed to the revised ballet (which included orchestral arrangements by Cherepnin, Lyadov, and Alexander Taneyev) was incentive enough. To have his music danced by a galaxy of the most iridescent classical ballet luminaries—Anna Pavlova, Tamara Karsavina, and Vaslav Nijinsky, costumed by Alexandre Benois—was surely immensely gratifying, or as he later recalled in his memoirs, "intoxicating." Moreover, he understood the moment's importance, even though his own role was relatively subsidiary. *Les Sylphides* opened a door for the young Stravinsky, if only a back door to the *beau monde* sparkle of Paris. He was now an international composer, and letters to friends who attended the premiere reveal that he anxiously sought word from Paris as to how the ballet fared.

Siloti, among others, solicited additional orchestration projects immediately before *The Firebird*. Stravinsky's setting of a Mussorgsky song was so successful that Chaliapin recorded it. Diaghilev requested that Stravinsky orchestrate a short piano piece by Edvard Grieg, one of the *Lyric Pieces*, op. 71, no. 3, of 1901, entitled "Kobold." What choice did the indebted composer have but to accept this eleventh-hour commission intended by Diaghilev as a gift for Nijinsky, to be danced during a benefit performance in St. Petersburg in the winter of 1909–10? Doubtlessly, Diaghilev wished to showcase the young Nijinsky, his newest rising star. Stravinsky's ability to produce the short piece quickly, as well as his eagerness to become part of Diaghilev's retinue, would serve him well at such a critical moment. "Kobold" premiered at the Maryinsky on February 20. It subsequently became part of Les Orientales, a loosely structured olio of dances to the music of Arensky, Borodin, and Glazunov. Clearly, Stravinsky was now keeping good company. The divertissement premiered on the same program of June 25, 1910, that included The Firebird.[10]

By the time Diaghilev approached Stravinsky about orchestrating the Grieg piano piece, the composer was already deeply involved in sketching The Firebird, for by that point Diaghilev had officially invited him to prepare the ballet score. The composer later recalled, "It was highly flattering to be chosen from among the musicians of my generation, and to be allowed to collaborate in so important an enterprise side by side with personages who were generally recognized as masters in their own spheres."[11] Flattering, yes, but in truth Stravinsky had hardly been Diaghilev's first choice.

Despite Stravinsky's potential, why would Diaghilev hazard everything on an inexperienced, virtually nameless composer, with so much riding on his company's Parisian debut? Initially he had turned to others with more experience: Cherepnin and Lyadov for sure, Glazunov and perhaps one or two other composers as well. The choice of Cherepnin made eminent sense, as he had already produced the successful Le Pavillon d'Armide with Benois and Fokine. He had actually begun composing the music for The Firebird, but according to Benois was losing interest in ballet generally about this time and withdrew.[12] On September 4, 1909, while vacationing with Nijinsky on the Lido, Diaghilev next wrote to Lyadov, hoping to inveigle him: "I want a ballet and a Russian one; there has never been such a ballet before. . . . We all consider you now as our leading composer with the freshest and most interesting talent." Leading composer or not, the notably dilatory Lyadov also failed to come through, leaving Diaghilev in a quandary.[13]

Time was running short. That same autumn, and following a few more declinations, Diaghilev looked to Stravinsky out of need and perhaps even a touch of desperation. He wagered that the ambitious young composer would fully devote himself to completing the score at short notice, whatever the time constraints (in fact, Stravinsky put aside his new opera, Le Rossignol, and began composing the ballet score even before Diaghilev had officially offered him the commission in December 1909). Whatever the reasoning, there was simply no alternative; and although Grigoriev reports that an "ominous silence" fell over the artistic committee when Diaghilev announced his choice, it was clear that nothing would deter him.[14] Besides, Stravinsky would be a benign choice. His score most likely would be comfortably derivative. It would be orchestrally appealing; unfailingly Russian; exotic, but not offensively so. Moreover, Diaghilev knew that if he did not like what he heard, Stravinsky would have no leverage with which to bargain. The composer would be compelled to revise the music in accordance with the wishes of Fokine and others. To a considerable degree it becomes evident that the composer of *The Firebird* was, for one fleeting moment, little more than an heir to Pugni—something that would quickly change after the June 10 performance.

Stravinsky dedicated the score to Andrei Rimsky-Korsakov, with whom he had spent considerable time at the Rimsky-Korsakov family dacha in November 1909 during the early stages of the ballet's composition. The French organist and opera composer Gabriel Pierné was to conduct the premiere. Karsavina danced the Firebird, Fokine himself portrayed Ivan Tsarevich, and Alexis Bulgakov (who had danced in several earlier Fokine ballets, including *Chopiniana*) portrayed the essentially mimed character role of the wizardly Kashchei, a role later assumed by Cecchetti and Balanchine. By the time Stravinsky officially joined the Ballets Russes enterprise, the overall outline of the ballet's two tableaux was in place. How the authors of the scenario went about assembling the story remains somewhat unclear, but assembled it was by Diaghilev's artistic committee. Many Ballets Russes principals had a hand in stitching together bits and pieces of this most enchanting Russian fairy tale—a fairy tale that would need to be reconstituted so as to engage the interest of adults, naturally.

Although legend of the Firebird had grown out of Russian folklore, the story of this bewitching bird, whose feathers would illuminate the night and whose powers were magical, was universally familiar.[15] Diaghilev and Benois oversaw the production, Alexander Golovin created the costumes and designs with the exception of the costume of the Firebird, which was fashioned by Leon Bakst, and Fokine prepared the choreography.[16] In addition, Fokine purportedly authored the libretto, even though Stravinsky later commented that Diaghilev considered Bakst his principal advisor, Bakst thus having more to do with the story than he is credited with. Karsavina, too, remembered that Bakst was a quiet, sturdy presence in guiding the evolution of the scenario. Diaghilev and his cohorts chose this particular Slavic story in the hope that its fantastical elements would intrigue the French audience. They did. After all, fantasy, overflowing with goblins and sorcerers, was precisely what the Parisian press demanded of the newly formed Russian troupe. The storyline was thoroughly neonationalistic, perhaps even to excess. Upon arriving in Paris in early June, Stravinsky immediately perceived a distasteful tone in Diaghilev's marketing. Whatever the over-embroidered ethnic pitch, Diaghilev had wisely calculated the ballet's fascination. It was exactly what Paris wanted.

The plot of the *ballet d'action* was programmatically simple. The story flowed from the diametric contrasts that are common to most children's fairy tales: good versus evil, dark versus light, mortal versus supernatural, loss versus redemption, and ultimately, just as one would hope, the triumph of love. What could be more readily digestible for Diaghilev's eager-to-be-charmed audience? Of course a villain was *de rigueur*, and so Kashchei the Immortal, complete with his menacing green talons (particularly threatening to young women, so the legend goes) found his way into the ballet courtesy of a different Russian myth. The Kashchei lore held the ogre to be deathless since his soul lived in an encased and virtually impenetrable egg. The transliterations of Kashchei's name are many, including Koschei, Kashchey, and Kastchei. Kashchei was the embodiment of evil. His soul was virtually immortal. Great powers would be bestowed upon the person who could vanquish him. The importation of Kashchei from another fairy tale into *The Firebird* was not difficult to achieve, especially given that Russian fairy tales abound with such egg stories. Without hesitation, Diaghilev and his collaborators were prepared to annex whatever parts of whatever myths worked in designing a scenario that would be easy to follow, and thus congenial to an audience wanting nothing more than to be entertained.

In the first tableau, Prince Ivan comes upon the Firebird in Kashchei's garden, where she is about to eat a golden apple (a recurring theme in most versions of the myth). Ivan captures the beautiful bird, but doing her no harm, he signals his benevolence, or better still, his morality. Kashchei eventually succumbs to Ivan because Ivan himself, according to Stravinsky, "yielded to pity, a wholly Christian notion that dominates the imagination and the ideas of Russian people. Through pity [Ivan] acquired power to free the world from the wickedness of Kashchei."[17] The composer's moralizing notwithstanding, in order to win her release the Firebird offers the Prince one of her feathers—an extraordinary gesture in that her plumage was never to be plucked. Fokine describes the scene thus: "The Bird trembles frantically and quivers in his arms, begging to be released. The Tsarevich does not let go. But the Firebird pleads and cries so pitifully that the kind and compassionate Ivan releases her. In gratitude, she gives him a fiery feather. 'It will be of use to you,' the Firebird tells him, flying away."[18] Ivan soon comes upon thirteen maidens and falls in love with Tsarevna (danced by Fokina, the choreographer's wife, although the role was originally to have been Karsavina's), who is imprisoned by Kashchei's evil spell. The Prince uses the magic feather to call upon the Firebird, who reveals that the monster's immortality lives within an egg, which Ivan crushes. Kashchei dies, immediately lifting the curse. The brief second tableau follows in which Ivan and Tsarevna, as well as the entire ensemble, engage in a stately, sustained processional to the kingdom's royal throne. Prince and Princess pledge their eternal love to one another, while the grandest Stravinskyan music, reminiscent of a Mussorgskyan coronation, provides, literally, the fairytale ending. (Just so, Diaghilev employed the scenery from his earlier *Boris Godunov* production, originally prepared by Golovin.)

While Fokine surely exaggerated his claims of authorship, it was he who assembled the threads of the various stories consulted in constructing the libretto.

In my original story, the Firebird presented Tsarevich Ivan with a magic gusli, which, when he played it, forced the inhabitants of the evil kingdom to dance. I abandoned the idea at the suggestion of Benois, and because it was planned to present in Paris, during the same season, Rimsky-Korsakov's opera *Sadko*, in which the gusli also figures importantly. Later, yielding to the wish of Igor Stravinsky, I agreed to substitute a coronation for the gay processional dances with which I had wanted to end the ballet.

In that concluding tableau, Fokine recounted, Kashchei's wicked kingdom disappeared, to be replaced by a "Christian city" in the form of a cathedral. The once petrified knights are revived, each finding his princess. Ivan Tsarevich "also finds his beloved Princess Unearthly Beauty. He pronounces her his wife, and queen of the liberated kingdom."[19]

As the original Firebird, Karsavina confirms that Diaghilev regularly convened his collaborators to thrash out ideas. They discussed everything from strategies to budgeting. She witnessed debates over the music in one corner of the room and discussion of the scenario in another, the participants all the while "hatching daring ideas." She especially remembers Benois, whose "inspiration was coupled with clear thought, wisdom with practical adaptability. He over-flowed with benignity, and his erudition was unique. His mastery of blending fantastic with real was the more wonderful because he effected his magic by the simplest means." Of particular concern to the committee were the originally planned symbolic horsemen of Day and Night. "Impossible, horses stamp all over the stage, pull the scenery to pieces," some complained, but Benois insisted. Karsavina also wrote of Bakst, whom she found "exotic, fantastic—reaching from one pole to another. The spice and somberness of the East, the serene aloofness of classical antiquity was his." She writes of Stravinsky and Fokine huddled in another corner, discussing each section of the score and appealing "to Diaghilev in every collision over the tempi." He brought a "quick, unhesitating decision to every doubt. . . . Engrossed as he was in his part he kept a vigilant eye on his collaborators: 'Gentlemen, you are wandering off your point,' came now and then from his corner."[20]

Stravinsky attended all of the ballet's preliminary rehearsals that spring in St. Petersburg. Often, according to Serge Grigoriev, *régisseur* of the Ballets Russes (who claims to have created the libretto with Fokine), the principals would meet in Diaghilev's flat where Stravinsky would take an active role, interjecting ideas. Frequently he would play passages as they were composed. It is likely that he also improvised ideas as Fokine requested certain actions, emotions, or moods.[21] The composer would often join the regular rehearsal pianist at the keyboard to demonstrate a particular passage. Karsavina's recollections regarding Stravinsky's work ethic and demeanor are also illuminating. The music was not easy to absorb, the dancer reported:

> It was not learning without tears. . . . I found it difficult to follow the pattern of a musical theme through its rich orchestral ramifications. . . . He was kind and patient with my shortcomings. Often he came early to the theatre before a rehearsal began in order to play for me, over and over again, some especially difficult passage. I felt grateful, not only for the help he gave me, but for the manner in which he gave it. . . . It was interesting to watch him at the piano. His body seemed to vibrate with his own rhythm; punctuating staccatos with his head, he made the pattern of his music forcibly clear to me, more so than the counting of bars would have done.[22]

Grigoriev confirms that the music's novelty baffled some of the dancers and musicians. Stravinsky would demonstrate passages and some of the rhythmic complexities at the keyboard, where he would "demolish the piano" according to some. He paid particular attention to the rhythms, "hammering them out with considerable violence, humming loudly and scarcely caring whether he struck the right notes," Grigoriev remembered. He also recalls that Fokine began with the choreography for the "Infernal Dance," in view of its difficulties.[23]

Fifty years later, Stravinsky recalled that he had acted brashly, often criticizing his elder and more established collaborators. Karsavina's comments, and those of others, tell quite a different story, portraying the young man as a most amenable and genteel contributor. Karsavina's own anxiety had several sources, including the fact that she, like Stravinsky and Golovin, had not been

Diaghilev's first choice. Pavlova had turned down the role, contending that the music was too complex and was not written so as to best serve the dance.[24] Benois, who was particularly fond of Stravinsky, recalls that as musicians go the composer was uncharacteristically conversant with other arts, and insatiably curious about theater. Benois characterized the young composer as "a very willing and charming pupil. . . . Discussion with him was very valuable to us, for he *reacted* to everything for which we lived."[25] Stravinsky's zeal was evident to all. At Diaghilev's invitation, the French critic Robert Brussel (who had reviewed Diaghilev's earlier Russian concerts in Paris) observed Stravinsky at one St. Petersburg rehearsal. "The composer, young, slim, and uncommunicative, with vague meditative eyes, and lips set firm in an energetic-looking face, was at the piano. But the moment he began to play, the modest and dimly lit dwelling glowed with a dazzling radiance. By the end of the first scene, I was conquered: by the last, I was lost in admiration. The manuscript on the music-rest, scored over with fine pencillings, revealed a masterpiece."[26]

The production, lavishly appointed to create what looked like an ornate tapestry, called for an orchestra of nearly one hundred musicians. An especially large percussion battery included tambourine, triangle, cymbals, bass drum, timpani, tam-tam, glockenspiel, xylophone, celesta, piano, and three harps. Moreover, a stage band called for three trumpets, two tenor tubas, and two bass tubas. In addition to the Firebird, Tsarevna, Prince Ivan, and Kashchei the Immortal, there were Twelve Other Enchanted Princesses, Petrified Knights, Adolescents, Kashchei's Wives, Indian Women, Kashchei's Retinue, Goblins and Demons, Two-headed Monsters, and other attendants populating the final tableau.[27] The stage was bursting with the huge *corps*, as pockets of activity from various constituencies often unfolded simultaneously, notably in the "Infernal Dance." Among the thirteen princesses was Bronislava Nijinska, who would later collaborate with the composer on *Les Noces*. Of all the eyewitness accounts, hers is particularly useful in describing the ballet's preparation and first performance.

The orchestral writing should not have seemed all that foreign to the musicians, especially since the music of Borodin, Rimsky, and others was at least somewhat familiar to them. But it did prove challenging. Nijinska and the other dancers initially found the "rhythms and movements" disconcertingly awkward. She remembered that rendering "the new rhythms correctly" was difficult, even though the steps themselves were not complicated. To which rhythms is she referring? Perhaps the music at m. 1 of the "Appearance of the Thirteen Enchanted Princesses," and a bit later at the opening of "The Princesses' Game with the Golden Apples"? The first passage is cast in simple duple and the second in simple triple meter. What could be easier? The internal rhythms of these sections, however, proved problematic, on account of the music's florid recitative- and cadenza-like writing at places such as m. 31, where the solo flute's avian warbling ambles almost randomly through quickly changing duple and triple meters.

The "Intercession of the Princesses" (marked *Andantino dolente*), in which the thirteen princesses danced over a plethora of figurations built upon metrically undefined string tremolos, also constituted a challenge. Woodwind and harp glissandi constantly obscured the prevailing beat. The idea was to create a free-flowing, improvisational dialogue. Understandably, Nijinska and others had to be alert. In each of these instances, Fokine's choreography furnished a counterpoint to Stravinsky's melismatic writing, which seemed more operatically inspired than danceable. In the context of ballet, therefore, Stravinsky's score turned out to be quite venturesome. The dancers were unaccustomed to the often unarticulated and disguised meters of his music. Consequently, Nijinska and members of the *corps de ballet* initially struggled.

Nijinska also remembers that Diaghilev and Golovin frequently attended rehearsals, both being admirers of Fokine's choreography. The number of rehearsals was another issue. Nijinska's recollections of the ballet's frenzied final preparations and premiere are worth remembering:

> We did not have many rehearsals onstage, and the dress rehearsal for *L'Oiseau de feu* and *Les Orientales* did not take place until the afternoon of the premiere. I recall the turmoil and the nervous atmosphere, how confused we dancers were by the music. We had rehearsed for *L'Oiseau de feu* to the accompaniment of a piano, and now we heard Igor Stravinsky's music played for the first time by the orchestra; many dancers missed their entrances. So did the musicians, apparently, given that the music was new to them as well. To the confusion created by the music were added other problems for the dancers because of the quick changes of sets and the many lighting effects during the action of the ballet. Backstage it was crowded—Diaghilev, himself, was directing the lighting—with stage-hands trying to learn the quick changes and large numbers of *figurants* in their masks standing in the wings blocking the entrances. . . . Sergei Grigoriev, our *régisseur*, was giving orders to the *figurants*, who were even more confused by the music than the dancers, for they too had rehearsed only with a piano. . . . Fokine was furious not to have more rehearsals on stage with the orchestra before the premiere. . . . Things were made worse by the presence backstage of two horses [which] were used only for the first two performances and then were discontinued. . . . Diaghilev

remained backstage during the performance that night to direct the lighting, and so did not watch this last premiere from his usual seat in the audience. . . . I did not expect that this fairy tale would interest the audiences, but . . . the ballet was a great success."[28]

While the ballet was a feast for the eyes, the orchestra, was employed splendidly in enriching the ballet's storybook themes. As in the *Scherzo fantastique* and *Fireworks*, the gifted orchestrator employed the instrumentation imaginatively and strategically, seldom tapping the power of his complete forces. Instead, he frequently wrote for smaller combinations. The full grandeur of such a large orchestra was reserved for the dramatic highpoints of the ballet's action, as in the "Dance of the Firebird" and the justly celebrated "Infernal Dance of All Kashchei's Subjects." The latter, Stravinsky remembered, stunned the audience. Its ferocity became synonymous with his "barbaric" style. Like so many other passages, the "Infernal Dance" evoked the ghosts of many other Russian composers. Moreover, the prodigious force of the music with its incessant percussiveness and throbbing rhythms was inexorable. For the audience, it was unprecedented in its willfulness. Finally, the slow, magnificent accretion of sound that steadily builds throughout the second tableau, entitled "Disappearance of Kashchei's Palace and Magical Creations, Return to Life of the Petrified Knights, General Rejoicing," was majestic, and quite literally the showstopper.

Fokine espoused definite ideas about music supporting the dance. Perhaps more than any previous ballet master, he perceived that music's emotive power could serve choreography by rising above the level of an ancillary embellishment. He constantly questioned the "canons of tradition" in dance. His suggested reforms, sent to the director of the Imperial Theater, Vladimir Teliakovsky, provoked a rethinking of ballet performance. In 1904 he spoke boldly, even impudently in the view of some, contending that ballet should not merely consist of a string of trifling dances constantly subjected to the interrupting applause of spectators. Acknowledging artists during a performance only compromised the scenic illusion. Furthermore, "The music should not consist of waltzes, polkas, and final galops—indispensable in the old ballet—but must express the story of the ballet, and, primarily, its emotional content."[29] Such aberrant notions were greeted with derision, Karsavina recalls. Fokine further insisted that "music is not the mere accompaniment of a rhythmic step, but an organic part of a dance," and that "the quality of choreographic inspiration is determined by the quality of music."[30] It is ironic that Stravinsky later railed against Fokine's consignment of music to a much lower status, claiming that the choreographer had pronounced the music of *The Firebird* to be Stravinsky's "musical accompaniment," as opposed to Fokine's own "choreographic poem."[31]

As a young man, Fokine had displayed an affinity for native Russian instruments such as the gusla, dombra, mandola, and balalaika, all of which he played. He performed in amateur orchestras fond of presenting national songs on such instruments, and he could see how such performances touched the emotions of the proletariat. Fokine also studied orchestrations carefully, transcribing parts for some amateur performances. Whatever his training, Fokine had at least some applied experience in making music—experience that, while serving his choreography, also annoyed Stravinsky, since the self-assured choreographer felt entitled to interfere with the composer's work (as did Diaghilev). He also made a specific point of stating how closely he worked with Stravinsky. Rather than waiting for finished music, Fokine would ask to see the composer's "basic ideas", which he then choreographed fully, using the music only as a guide. For his part, the composer spoke caustically of Fokine's "wearying homiletics . . . on the role of music as *accompaniment* to dance."[32] He also recounted how much he had disliked Fokine's choreography. "The female dancers in The *Firebird*, the Princesses, were insipidly sweet, while the male dancers were the *ne plus ultra* of brute masculinity; in the Kastchei scene, they sat on the floor kicking their legs in an incredibly stupid manner."[33]

Fokine's unoriginal ideas compromised the dancers' ability to match the music, the composer further carped. The convoluted choreography was suffocating in its overbearing "plastic detail." Whatever the production's defects, however, in the view of many an otherwise rather lackluster ballet was rescued by Stravinsky's incandescent score. Disappointed in the ballet's failure to demonstrate a genuine collaborative synthesis, Benois believed that the music itself "achieved complete perfection" in eclipsing Fokine's stolid choreography. "Music more poetic, music more expressive of every moment and shading, music more beautiful-sounding and phantasmagoric could not be imagined." Peter Lieven also recalled that the music alone attained distinction. He thought even the "Dance of the Firebird" to be weak in its staging, redeemed only by the composer's brilliant orchestration, which was so imaginative that "people seemed to want to rise and peer into the orchestra pit, inquiring, 'Who made those strange noises?' "[34]

In truth, the noises were not so strange, or at least not unprecedented. Most of the orchestral effects employed by Stravinsky were rooted in earlier Russian models. It is the temporal pacing of Stravinsky's release of information in enhancing the drama, and the imaginative coloring of that information by the orchestra, that is of greatest significance. For example, in the "Introduction" preceding the opening curtain, Stravinsky incrementally builds tension so as to heighten the audience's anticipation. The ballet begins with muted lower strings in unison outlining the Firebird's fundamental motivic material. That material continues with violas joining the unison texture in m. 3, followed by the addition of trombones at m. 5. The orchestral buildup moves forward in a steady sequence: bassoons, horns, harp glissandi, bass drum, clarinets, flutes in m. 11, and finally the appearance of the first violins in m. 13, with a series of muted glissando natural harmonics overlapping with *divisi* violins and cellos in their highest registers. The strings literally chirp and squeal. If ever there was "bird music," here it is. That Stravinsky withheld the use of the first violins until this moment is significant. The illusory effect surely surprised the audience, although it was not truly new.[35] More informatively, the effect was fleeting. Stravinsky knew exactly when to introduce the colorful device—only a few measures before the curtain's rise and the Firebird's initial appearance. It hinted at things to come, building a sense of suspense. It is this pacing, in particular, that reveals the sense of theater commented on by Benois and others. Simply stated, dramatic as the device is in itself, its strategic placement at precisely the right moment within the context of a staged work tells us more.

Throughout the ballet, Stravinsky employs the orchestra as a handmaiden to the dance—exactly what Fokine and Diaghilev had asked of him. In the "Dance of the Firebird," for example, there is a constant dovetailing of piccolo, flute, oboe, clarinet, and bassoon, this woodwind choir providing an orchestral counterpoint to the full complement of strings, oftentimes muted.[36] Marked *Allegro rapace*, the music unfolds ethereally, with brass (also often muted), celesta, and harps used sparingly to punctuate the gossamer fragility of the Firebird. It is a choreographic tour de force. Here Stravinsky's writing is accompanimental in the best sense. Fokine recalls that he staged the dance "on toe and with jumps which predominated in the choreography. The dance was highly technical but without *entrechats, battements, ronds de jambes.* . . . The arms would now open up like wings; now hug the torso, and head, in complete contradiction of all ballet arm-positions. In the ornamental arms of the bird . . . there was an Oriental element."[37] His description echoes what he had passionately advocated six years earlier in challenging classical ballet's traditions. "Why must the arms be always rounded," he wrote in 1904, "the elbows always held sideways parallel to the audience, the back straight, and the feet always turned out with the heels to the front?"[38]

Just so, Stravinsky's music for the Firebird's dance is anything but rounded; for the music often gives the impression of sputtering, or perhaps better said, of flitting. It is all in keeping with the Firebird's often erratic, exaggerated gestures.

As for the interwoven rhythm of dance and music, here too there is an alternation between metrically clear passages and passages that defy definable beats. No wonder Karsavina struggled with the sometimes complex music written specifically for the Firebird's signature dance. Karsavina's shining moment was spectacular, making a lasting impression on Diaghilev's committee, even in rehearsal, Grigoriev recalled.[39] It was undoubtedly the ballet's choreographic highpoint. Still, it could not overpower the score's enveloping richness. The genius here is Stravinsky's writing to script in enhancing Fokine's innovative concept. The orchestral layering evident in the dance's two minutes of music is as ingeniously written as anything Stravinsky had previously accomplished.

The "Infernal Dance of All Kashchei's Subjects" startled the audience at the premiere, its opening chord, played by full orchestra and sharply accentuated, taking them by surprise. The score's intensity evoked the exoticism of Rimsky's works. Music and dance were laden with eastern stereotypes: abundant pentatonic scales; an unceasing percussiveness evident from the timpani's opening ostinato; an unremitting brass section pounding out the "relentless syncopation" (as the composer once described it) of the driving rhythms; special effects such as tuba glissandi and trumpet tremolos; and a stream of cascading perfect fourths and fifths at strategic moments. So unlike the wispy music of the Firebird's dance, the full-throttle sound of the orchestra greatly overshadowed Fokine's choreography.

Rimsky's pitch vocabulary, predictably, still pervades *The Firebird*. Stravinsky organizes his pitch structure, both thematically and harmonically, according to the laws of "the Rimsky-Korsakov scale," as it was once dubbed. Tritones, ladders of juxtaposed major and minor thirds, diminished and augmented triads, and symmetrical tetrachords all arise from a progenitor source that has become a near obsessive object of analytic attention.[40] These colorfully chromatic structures are intended to portray the evil, supernatural forces of Kashchei's kingdom, in contrast to the purer diatonicism associated with the human vulnerabilities of Ivan, Tsarevna, and the other princesses—contrasts again traceable to Rimsky, especially his politically controversial 1907 opera *Le Coq d'or*. Diatonicism is apparent in the few memorable folk melodies that Stravinsky uses in the ballet, such as in the "Khorovod (Round Dance) of the Princesses" or the "Lullaby." Would we have expected otherwise? Such pitch structures (also pervasive in Debussy's music) were precisely the sound that Diaghilev and Fokine desired in evoking the "East." In that sense, Rimsky's permeating octatonic pitch vocabulary was still quite apropos in delivering the imagery desired.

Both the Firebird and Kashchei often stood at the periphery of the stage, framing the individual constituencies of the *corps de ballet*, which took center stage. Maidens, demons, knights, princesses, as many as fifty at any given moment, each took part in small and large combinations as the action pulsated over four minutes of deftly written music. Fokine choreographed a medley of stiffly folkloristic gestures, some acrobatic, some mimed, and all very much removed from classical ballet. Men clicked their heels, women locked arms or covered their faces submissively, and the entire troupe frequently stood in place hopping from one foot to the other as they metronomically marked time. It was a gratuitous affectation of choreographic and nationalistic clichés evoking stilted images from Taras Bulba to Scheherazade. But for Diaghilev's public, it worked.

In a sense the "Infernal Dance" may be said to have succeeded by sheer force, inexorably hammering home the ballet's ostentatiously ethnic flavor. In the end, however, it resulted in no more than a conglomeration of short, self-contained dances, each section platitudinously emulating a well-known Russian gesture in very circumscribed terms. The pacing of the music, consequently, had no choice but to be segmented rather squarely. In complementing the fast-moving pageant of images that Fokine wished to elicit, Stravinsky composed short passages of no more than fifteen to thirty seconds in duration. Whatever coherence emerged from this hodgepodge came by way of the composer's ability to weave these disparate parts together. Stravinsky accomplished this by utilizing recurring thematic motives associated with the principal characters (the Firebird's motive at m. 98, or the leitmotiv of the thirteen princesses also at m. 98 and again at m. 208). Nonetheless, the dancing still appeared disjointed. The cost was a mismatch between score and choreography—a disparity that surely accounts for some of the criticism leveled at the production as a whole.

Although far from innovative, the music's adeptly applied compositional techniques reveal a remarkable culmination of the young composer's much-accelerated apprenticeship. Stravinsky had attained a first plateau, an "assertion of active sovereignty over lesson and precept," as Asaf'yev put it.[41] As an example, we might consider the passage of the "Infernal Dance" beginning at m. 142, marking a recapitulation of the opening material although orchestrated quite differently. Timpani and bass drum now provide the contrapuntal ostinato while pizzicato strings offer a version of material initially given to the lower woodwinds. Kashchei's leitmotiv (consisting of diminished intervals and the tritone) is again assigned to the brass, first trombones and tuba, then horns and trumpet. The result is a variation, familiar enough to be recognized but new enough to re-engage one's attention as dance and music set off in new directions. The refurbishing continues between m. 156 and m. 172, except that whereas originally at m. 39 the Firebird's leitmotiv had appeared, here Stravinsky further develops Kashchei's thematic material.

Measures 173–76 continue the harmonically open fourths and fifths, with an occasional tritone. At m. 177, these yield to an arpeggiation of these same fifths, assigned to the harps and lower strings in the orchestral score, over which Stravinsky now syncopates Kashchei's major- and minor-third motive in two-measure pairings. Measure 181 continues the motive, now doubled in thirds, all the while intensifying. At m. 185, the syncopation is transformed into duple groupings of four beats, for upper woodwinds and strings, superimposed over the continuing triple-meter arpeggiations in the bass clef. This duple/triple metric conflict, certainly traceable to Stravinsky's models, continues at m. 189 with three more four-beat groupings, rising in pitch as the lower voice now descends chromatically. This wedged voice-leading creates further drama as the texture splits, leading to the sudden return of the triple meter at m. 193, although with the *Più mosso* change it gives the impression of one beat per measure—in effect a violent acceleration. As for pitch, Stravinsky continues to pit major and minor thirds against one another, pointedly so from m. 193, where their starkness is most dramatic. Thereafter an implied acceleration continues wherein quarter-four-eighth-note figures give way to all eighths. The passage culminates at m. 209, where Stravinsky reinstates the princesses' theme heard in mm. 99 through 143, where the recapitulation just discussed begins.

All of this said, we must remind ourselves that Diaghilev hired Stravinsky to write music for the dance. And indeed it is possible that Fokine, and perhaps the entire artistic committee, may well have inserted themselves into decisions about the score. The piano autograph, completed on March 21, a month or so before Stravinsky undertook the ballet's orchestration in earnest, was undoubtedly the manuscript from which Fokine and Stravinsky worked as the ballet went into rehearsal that spring. It is a revealing document. It shows, for example, that Stravinsky originally composed sixteen additional measures of music just before the structurally important first beat of m. 192, but that at some point he crossed these measures out in the piano score, wrote a shorter version of them (eight measures—that is, without the original repetition) on a separate sheet of manuscript paper, and then taped that version into the piano score at m. 30 of the ballet's earlier "Magic Carillon, Appearance of Kashchei's Monster Guardians, and Capture of Prince Ivan."

The interpolated music ultimately employed at that juncture makes perfect compositional sense, in that it is seen to grow out of a shorter motive adumbrated eleven measures earlier, at m. 18. That leitmotiv, Kashchei's in fact, appears more fully developed in mm. 27–29, immediately before the passage that Stravinsky added. This added material displays now familiar pitch resources, thoroughly chromatic in portraying the evil Kashchei and his subjects. The canon that

Stravinsky composes between the two lower clefs (orchestrated for strings) and the augmentation of the highest of the three lines (assigned to the brass) is clear.

Why did Stravinsky initially place this passage in the "Infernal Dance," where it would only have impeded the acceleration leading to m. 193? And why did he extract it at that point, and insert it in the earlier dance? The answer could be as practical as a need on Fokine's part for more music earlier and less music later; thus Stravinsky simply transferred fifteen seconds of music to the earlier juncture, where it made compositional sense. Indeed, further examination of the piano rehearsal score reveals several excisions. Stravinsky frequently cut short passages for no apparent compositional reason, suggesting that such decisions were in response to choreographic needs.

As a final example, consider that the piano score originally included an additional six measures of music at the conclusion of the "Enchanted Garden of Kashchei," just before the beginning of the "Appearance of the Firebird, Pursued by Prince Ivan," which Stravinsky at some point deleted. He had already employed the same motive at m. 4 of the "Enchanted Garden," and compositionally it made sense to use it at the end of the dance as a transition to the next section. Perhaps Fokine did not need the music at that juncture. In fact, the excised passage does indeed appear later in the ballet, at m. 75, as the transition from "The Firebird's Supplications" to the "Appearances of the Thirteen Enchanted Princesses," and yet again at m. 15 of the "Arrival of Kashchei the Immortal, Dialogue of Kashchei and Prince Ivan, and Intercession of the Princesses," a passage "where the music is as literal as an opera," the composer declared.[42] Stravinsky's manuscripts frequently reveal that he would salvage deleted passages by repositioning them—a testament both to his frugality and to the seamless nature of certain compositions.[43]

The well-known "Lullaby" (or "Berceuse") follows the "Infernal Dance." Based upon one of the score's three documented folk sources, it provides a final opportunity for the Firebird to command the stage. As her dance ends, she directs Ivan to the chest containing the egg. The Prince hoists the casket above his head for all to see. He threatens to drop it as Kashchei quakes. The corps follows every taunting gesture, as the Prince, juggling the egg precariously, moves from one side of the stage to the other. Here Stravinsky's music, severely hampered by the demands of the libretto, is almost embarrassingly histrionic in its imaging, even though dramatically it leads to the climactic moment of Kashchei's death. Fokine must surely have stipulated such insipidly programmatic music. The score's characteristic major and minor thirds tumble downwardly as Ivan destroys Kashchei's soul. Moreover, the tritonal separation of a C-major chord over the F#–A# tremolo dyad serving as a pedal for mm. 33–44 of "Kashchei's Death" anticipates one of the cornerstone harmonies of Stravinsky's next ballet, *Petrouchka*. The passage initiates an upward ascent as chromaticism melds into diatonicism in preparation for the final tableau.[44]

The music elides into B major (the key of the much earlier folk song setting of the "Khorovod") as this string music converges texturally in framing the beginning of the second tableau—or as Stravinsky originally conceived it, an "Apothéose" (in effect, a finale).[45] As Stravinsky admitted, the euphonious melody beginning at m. 17 is traceable to a pre-existing folk song, another *khorovod* from a Rimsky anthology. The material has a familial relationship with the ballet's earlier "Khorovod (Round Dance) of the Princesses"—unsurprisingly, since the theme of this, too, was based upon Rimsky's anthology. The magic kingdom, now glistening in bright sunlight for the first time in the ballet, reunites the formerly ossified slaves of Kashchei, as well as the princesses and other captives. Ivan and Tsarevna stand center stage. Their investiture, complete with ceremonial vestments, scepter, and the resplendent trappings of sovereign rule, signals their royal benevolence. Although some immediately criticized the saccharine taste of this fairytale ending, the public got what it wanted. And once again, despite the predictability of the story's end, the music itself continues to stand as the true achievement here.

As with most of the ballet, the music of this closing tableau is derivative; but to underestimate its power by simply citing its Rimskyan model would be an injustice. The slowly building crescendo of its beauty grows as each of the theme's twelve appearances mounts grandly. Each iteration reveals a slight modification, rhythmically, orchestrally, or harmonically. It is an aggregating process that reaches its peak at m. 47, where a metric shift to 7/4 occurs—new for Stravinsky's music, but hardly unprecedented in Rimsky and others. The variations continue through the final measures, where the Firebird's leitmotiv, first heard at the ballet's opening, presents itself once again at m. 63.[46]

The March 21 piano score again provides insight regarding Stravinsky's attention to detail. Probably as a result of changes made during rehearsals, the composer was especially attentive to performance issues, tempo indications, and dynamic markings as to shades of *forte* and *piano*. Moreover, he makes several insertions concerning the exact duration of passages, even articulating the values of fermatas, and calling attention to how the metric shifts should be handled. He notated several of these directions on an index card taped into the score. Some of the differences between the manuscript piano score and the printed orchestral score are quite dramatic. For example, in the piano score Stravinsky pencils in "*accelerando* to Tempo I" at m. 61; yet by the time the piano and orchestral scores were engraved that direction had been reversed to "*poco a poco allargando*"—quite a reconception, indeed. One can only imagine that such changes were occasioned by the dancers' needs as dictated by the choreographer, in what would have been considered the best interests of the visual.[47]

Despite the frenzy surrounding the preparations for the premiere, Stravinsky remembers *The Firebird* being "warmly applauded," and that he returned to the stage several times. In his memoirs he praises Pierné's conducting specifically and the production generally. His comments regarding Fokine, however, remained captious. Moreover, the composer reported that Debussy's comments on the premiere were quite complimentary.[48] Some reviewers immediately signaled the collaborative nature of the production as the beginning of a new artistic pathway. Writing for the *Nouvelle Revue française*, Henri Ghéon lauded *The Firebird* as "the most exquisite miracle imaginable of the harmony of sound and form and movement. . . . Stravinsky, Fokine, Golovin, in my eyes, are but one name."[49] While most of the production's principals were ecstatic, Benois alone remained unhappy with the less than fully integrated spirit of the ballet. Generally, however, members of the old *Mir iskusstva* coalition deemed the work an affirmation of all they had advocated a decade earlier.

Eager to dictate what was *au courant*, the French adoringly crowned Stravinsky their newest discovery. Parisian reviews lionized the young composer while hailing the ballet as an unqualified success. Russian critics would not hear its music until Siloti gave its first public performance in Russia in the autumn. By then, Stravinsky had quickly assembled a suite that drastically pruned what he saw as the wastefully discursive recitative demanded by Fokine.[50] But this is not to say that the Russian press was uninterested in the ballet's premiere, or more broadly, in the impressions made by the internationally acclaimed Ballets Russes. Several dancers, including Karsavina, maintained a relationship with the Imperial Theaters, and were eager to know how their performances were viewed back home. There were also concerns about the image of the Russian homeland that was being crafted by Diaghilev's company in Paris, especially "issues such as nationalism, the role of art in creating an appropriate image of the Empire, or questions of what was meant by modernity and modernism."[51] All of these bubbled up in Russian criticisms of Stravinsky's instantly popular ballet. The St. Petersburg reviews were tepid at best, meretriciously recognizing the composer's orchestral mastery, but complaining that the music was either too unpalatably modernistic or too mired in the style of outworn models.

Understandably, the young composer, just then riding the crest of celebrity's first wave, was both perplexed and disappointed by the rebuking response of his St. Petersburg colleagues, including that of his oldest friends. Especially hurtful was the obvious jealousy of Andrei Rimsky-Korsakov, who surely knew that Stravinsky's future would soon supplant all that had come before, including his father's own accomplishments. Following the premiere, the composer wrote to Andrei's mother, lamenting their absence at the premiere. He spoke of *The Firebird*'s reception as the highlight of the Ballets Russes season, entreatingly seeking their approbation. Andrei did travel to Paris in time to see the final performance of Diaghilev's production in early July (several additional performances had been scheduled following the work's favorable reception), but the accolades Stravinsky sought were not forthcoming. Perhaps the suddenly famous composer had come too far too quickly in the view of those once considered his closest friends—friends who now harbored envy. His frustration erupted in a letter to Andrei of November 20, which makes clear the pettiness to which he ascribed the deafening silence of his Russian colleagues. "No one writes anything, from which I conclude that my *Firebird* made either a very small impression or a negative one on all of you, as well as on the public."[52]

Despite his friends' apathy, the composer knew he had rounded a corner. With the success of *The Firebird* Stravinsky entered an exciting new world. In the process, as several letters to the Rimsky family attest, he began burning bridges. His creative energy was illimitable, and as would be the case throughout his career, Stravinsky was prepared to move on. It was a courageous moment. Success often carries the burden of replication, and Stravinsky could easily have fallen victim to his own celebrity in rewriting *The Firebird* several times over. But whatever the vicissitudes of his career, complacency was never in his blood.[53] Scholars nowadays seem somewhat dismissive in pointing to the *démodé* sound of the ballet, not to mention its obsolete theater, as if it were merely a charmingly quaint antique. It is more than that. Despite its obvious indebtedness to past models, one detects the seeds of a very different future.

The roar of *The Firebird*'s plaudits had fueled an explosion of self-confidence. Even as Stravinsky had rushed to complete the score in March 1910, a "fleeting vision," as he termed it, of what would become *The Rite of Spring* flashed across his imagination. He was eager to turn his attention in that direction. Still, business was business, and Diaghilev was in a hurry to capitalize immediately upon Stravinsky's now marketable reputation. The grand pagan ritual Stravinsky envisioned would have to wait. Diaghilev wanted another ballet, and he wanted it for his next season. Sensing the promising road that now stretched before him, Stravinsky would depart Russia shortly after *The Firebird*'s triumph. He now realized that St. Petersburg would no longer be able to provide the opportunities he needed in order to grow. Paris, however, could.

CHAPTER THREE

PETROUCHKA
The Piano and the Puppet

DIAGHILEV HAD struck gold. With the triumph of *The Firebird* the enterprising impresario had achieved all that he hoped, including placing his youthful troupe on a firm footing. If he had harbored any uncertainty concerning the untested Stravinsky's talents, they vanished with the composer's radiant score. Success breeds success. Diaghilev realized that Stravinsky was now indispensable. The path was clear. The composer must provide another score for the next season, one that would dazzle Parisian sophisticates every bit as much as his first. "Do you remember what Napoleon said?" he cautioned Grigoriev on the eve of the premiere of *Petrouchka*, "It is not enough to take the Tuileries. The problem is to stay there. . . . This is our third season in Paris, and the most critical."[1] Ballet now embraced the spirit of artistic collaboration that had long ago been endorsed by Savva Mamontov's operatic productions and *Mir iskusstva*. If the Ballets Russes was to prosper in Paris, it would invest its energy primarily in the production of ballets.[2]

The artistic feat accomplished by Diaghilev's Ballets Russes had not escaped Stravinsky's attention. He was now a marketable commodity, and he knew it. *The Firebird* taught Stravinsky to trust his own instincts. It was indeed those instincts, especially his ear rather than any lockstep adoption of particular compositional techniques, that had unfailingly served as both the primary guide and the final arbiter in making choices. The achievement of his first ballet came as a liberating epiphany, bestowing on him the strength of his convictions. The aplomb of the twenty-eight-year-old composer's correspondence, his interactions with others, the decisions he made, and the new compositional course he undertook all betoken a growing confidence. No longer would he kowtow to the likes of Fokine, whose choreographic strictures had handcuffed the young composer's own imagination. No longer would Diaghilev's obtrusions and bombastic manner bully him into compliance. After only one ballet, Stravinsky would flatly refuse to serve as a Pugni-like formulaic composer, ready to fabricate mechanical scores on demand. If Lincoln Kirstein overstated the matter in declaring that Stravinsky "made music, not to serve dance, but to control it," he did so only slightly.[3] The composer intuitively understood the intricate and subtle interplay of sound and movement in a way no previous ballet composer had. In achieving a genuine artistic equipoise, he elevated the importance of the ballet score to a plane others could not have imagined. Casting off its subsidiary role, music emerged as a principal partner.

Stravinsky and his wife Katya (together with their three-year-old son Theodore and two-year-old daughter Lyudmila) left Russia shortly after *The Firebird*'s Paris premiere. Following a brief relocation in Brittany, they moved to Lausanne, where Katya gave birth to their second son, Soulima (a second daughter, Milena, followed in 1914). The move was prompted by an ongoing search for a more salubrious climate that might relieve his wife's pulmonary ailment. By then he had begun what would eventually become his second ballet, although he had not originally intended the work for dance. The Stravinskys would move again, this time to the seaside resort of Beaulieu-sur-Mer, only a few miles from Nice. There he continued work on his new composition. His ideas quickly taking form, he returned to St. Petersburg in December 1910 to see his mother and to meet with Benois and Diaghilev. The trip proved both arduous and disencumbering. After living in the sunny climes of the Riviera, St. Petersburg struck the composer as bleak and worn-out. *The Firebird* had not only changed the fortunes of Diaghilev's company, it had changed the composer as well, and profoundly. He felt the dreary academicism of the St. Petersburg Conservatory, whose injunctions continued to strangle the ideas of young Russian composers. Since his departure only seven months earlier, he had become aware of the Conservatory's lifelessly prescriptive provincialism. If any fading fealty for its antiquated canons still stirred in him, it was rapidly being dispelled by Diaghilev and his colleagues. France became a desideratum, as the voracious Stravinsky eagerly absorbed once unfathomable ideas. He consorted with freethinking young writers, composers, and artists. He felt afire, unshackled, and emboldened to test his talents in works that went beyond the boundaries imposed by his first ballet.

It had been only a few months since *The Firebird*'s premiere when in October 1910 Diaghilev and Nijinsky went knocking on Stravinsky's door in Clarens. The agenda was clear: Diaghilev would prod the composer about a follow-up ballet for the company. Stravinsky had already completed two large chunks of a new composition in the months immediately following *The Firebird*. And while his visitors surely expected to hear something new, they had no inkling that the composer was in the midst of writing a work for piano and orchestra—a concert piece, so he dubbed it. The hubbub of fame that followed his first ballet had taken its toll. He needed to step back for a moment, to process what had happened. Toward revitalizing his spirits, Stravinsky turned to the keyboard, a source of comfort throughout his career. In reviewing all his early orchestral works one detects the unmistakable signs of a pianist everywhere.[4] The composer outlined a general scenario for his *Konzertstuck*, a program in which a puppet springs to life. "Petrushka," the popular, folkloristic puppet, "the immortal and unhappy hero of every fair in all countries," would play the protagonist in the manner of a puffed-up Romantic virtuoso pianist, foiling the orchestra with, as Stravinsky put it "diabolical cascades of arpeggios." And further, "The orchestra in turn retaliates with menacing trumpet blasts. The outcome is a terrific noise that reaches its climax and ends in the sorrowful and querulous collapse of the poor puppet."[5]

Scholars often tend to marginalize the pianistic roots of the composer's ideas, seeing them only as initial stimuli. They underestimate their role as a primary shaping force. Certainly in this instance the piano represents Petrouchka's very essence. More than that, however, the actual layout of the keyboard plays a significant part in the molding of lines, in the actual spacing of chords, and in sculpting the basic figurations of the pianistically born and often counterintuitive orchestral writing. The composer consistently declared his reliance upon instinct in identifying the raw material that would jumpstart his compositions. He spoke of discovering the "auditive shape" of ideas. Only after deciding upon those shapes would he move on to composition as "a later expansion and organization of material."[6]

If ever there were an "auditive shape" that sprang from the very black-and-whiteness of the keyboard it is surely the arpeggiated "Petrouchka Chord." It first appears in the second tableau, "In Petrouchka's Room," in m. 9 (Example 1). One

Example 1 *Petrouchka*, second tableau, mm. 9–13.

of the very first ideas Stravinsky drafted, its built-in edginess sharpens the fundamental conflict of the composer's original programmatic conception. This celebrated moment, in which the composer juxtaposes two major triads at a tritone's
distance, marks one of several insignia sonorities in the Stravinsky repertoire.
Whether one chooses to see the chord as an example of bitonality or a hexachordal subset of an octatonic scale, its sound has everything to do with the division inherent in the keyboard's layout.[7] Stravinsky writes with the physical
structure of the keyboard in mind, whereby the black keys and white keys retain
their own autonomy in sharpening the clash he desired. This black and white
sonority, literally, is an entity in itself, owing none of its identity to the larger pitch
collection to which it might be traced. The sweeping pianistic cadenzas that mark
the writing at m. 26, for example, are those of a virtuosic performer giving free rein
to the extemporaneous figuration characterizing the puppet's frenzy. There is a
sense of flight here, of capriciously abandoning any boundaries in highlighting the
drama of the moment. Even the tightly organized octatonic pitch structure of this
often-cited section should not blind us to the more improvisatory platform from
which Stravinsky launches Petrouchka's tortured fantasy.[8]

In urging the composer to convert his already well-developed piano
work into a ballet, Diaghilev suggested Benois as the ideal collaborator, aware
that he and Stravinsky had developed a mutual respect during the evolution of
The Firebird. Perpetually afraid of artists colluding against him, Diaghilev was
surely chary. Benois was just then at odds with him, having taken umbrage at
Diaghilev's crediting of Bakst, rather than him, for the libretto of *Scheherazade*.
Yet Stravinsky's writing of a non-commissioned, independent *Konzertstuck*
might lessen a sense of ongoing dependency upon the Ballets Russes, and
Diaghilev knew he had to keep the composer within his circle. And in the end,
whatever their muffled qualms about Diaghilev, neither Benois nor Stravinsky
could resist working with one another.

Benois was eager to bring Petrouchka to the stage. "I immediately had the
feeling that 'it was a duty I owed to my old friend' [Petrouchka] to immortalize
him on the real stage. I was still more tempted by the idea of depicting the
Butter Week Fair on the stage, the dear *balagani*, which were the great delight
of my childhood, and had been the delight of my father before me."[9] Others,
too, fondly remembered the vividly colorful Russian fairs of the nineteenth
century. Bronislava Nijinska and her brother Vaslav experienced the panoply of
colors of the Great Annual Fair in Nijni Novgorod in 1895:

We felt excitement in the air as we were surrounded by a multitude of
people of many races, all wearing their own colorful costumes. I was

overwhelmed by the noise, the sounds of the accordions, the whooping of the coachmen, the ringing of bells, the drunken songs, and I marveled at everything there was to see. . . . We saw magicians, jugglers, weight lifters, strongmen, midgets, man-lions . . . but our special joy and delight was the puppet show—"Petrouchka" . . . Each time we visited the Fair we made sure not to miss seeing our beloved, unhappy Petrouchka, encouraging him in his fight with the puppet-soldier. We laughed and we cried.

Indeed, Nijinska and her brother often staged their own performance of their favorite puppet show, using the back of their parlor sofa as a stage. "Vaslav and Stassik [their brother] let their bodies hang over it from the waist with their arms dangling and swinging."[10]

Whatever Benois's exact models, his own vision was clear: "The dolls should come to life at the command of a magician . . . and should be somehow accompanied by suffering. The greater the contrast between the real, live people and the automatons who had just been given life, the sharper the interest of the action would be." Such a clearly delineated contrast would complement the music Stravinsky had already composed. "It would be necessary to allot a considerable part of the stage to the mass of real people—the 'public' at the fair—while there would only be two dolls, the hero of the play, Petrouchka, and his lady."[11]

Stravinsky and Benois maintained a revealing correspondence between October 1910 and March 1911, their letters chronicling an affable, give-and-take collaboration. Initially both men genteelly abnegated their claim to the libretto's inspiration—a *combat de générosité*, as Benois joked. In later years, however, each tried to claim credit as the principal author, mostly in view of the distribution of royalties and production rights. Whatever the appropriate division of credit, the surviving letters track the ballet's evolution. For example, it appears that Diaghilev virtually absented himself from the development of the story and the score—a notable reversal from his issuing one directive after another in completing *The Firebird*. The correspondence further reveals the extent to which both story and score had jelled in Stravinsky's mind before Benois became involved. In a letter from Clarens dated November 3, 1910, Stravinsky expresses a

definite desire that "Petrushka" end with the magician on the stage. After the Moor kills Petrushka, the Magician should come on stage and, having gathered up all three, that is Petrushka, the Moor, and the Ballerina, he should exit with an elegant and affected bow, the same way he exited the first time. I have already composed the Shrovetide in the first tableau before the magic trick, and the Russian Dance after it. I still haven't begun the magic trick itself: I am waiting to get it from you—and right away, otherwise it will hold up the composition of the ballet.[12]

Other letters detail Benois's skepticism over the ballet's ending, which proved difficult to resolve. In early December he outlines a scenario in which Petrouchka and the Ballerina lock themselves away from the crowd's ballyhoo. The Magician appears, "lifts up a *puppet*-Moor from whom, with a smile, he extracts a cardboard knife." There is no mention of Petrouchka's murder (as occurs in the final version), but rather "general relief and endless happiness" and a "torchlight bacchanale" in which the merrymakers dance and continue their cavorting as the curtain falls. Curiously, in a subsequent letter Benois cavalierly states that while he sees Petrouchka as "freeing himself from the Magician's depraved spells" it was not so crucial, and that directing the Moor to murder Petrouchka would provide just as suitable a conclusion.[13] Apparently Benois was more concerned with the elision of the four scenes, "the sorest spot," he informs Stravinsky. The composer's letters often include brief musical examples of folk or popular tunes he planned to use. In early January 1911, he informs Benois that most of the fourth tableau is complete. Stravinsky itemizes orchestral choices, frequently explaining his preference for the accordion or tuba here rather than there. Throughout their cordial dialogue, a confident Stravinsky tenaciously refuses to concede ground to the more experienced Benois. As for the ballet's ending, which had caused such consternation, Stravinsky credited himself with "the resurrection of Petrouchka's ghost."[14] The idea was a long time coming. Amazingly, he did not write the music for the sobering ending until he arrived in Rome in May 1911, only shortly before rehearsals began.

Diaghilev had previously scheduled several ballet performances in Italy, as a consequence of which *Petrouchka* had to be rehearsed in the basement restaurant of the Teatro Costanzi. "On a dirty red spotted carpet in these shabby, stuffy premises, and in an atmosphere of terrible heat, Fokine staged the dances, while Stravinsky played the music without sparing himself," Pieter Lieven recalled.[15] Fokine grumbled that the score "affected him disagreeably."

With the Paris season just around the corner, the score remained unfinished. Diaghilev pushed forward as tempers grew short amidst the company's rush to mount the production. Benois complained of the theater staff's incompetence and the management's hostility. Local dancers were recruited to fill out the *corps de ballet*, but they were amateurish. Conditions were deplorable, the dilapidated state of a stage floor threatening physical injuries. A vocal and ill-disposed audience greeted each performance contemptuously. Sabotage was evident, and

Diaghilev warned his dancers of an anti-Russian demonstration. Nijinska remembers that "tacks and small nails were again found strewn on the floor" just before a performance of Le Pavillon d'Armide. And outside the performances of such familiar ballets, the anxious troupe continued to labor in its rehearsals of Stravinsky's new score. The music simply bewildered many of the dancers. Karsavina recalled the rehearsals: "It felt not unlike the toil of galley-slaves. . . . Fokine, ruffling his hair, enervated, hysterical; reprimands and tears and general tension electrifying the atmosphere. Stravinsky alone, performing the menial duty of a pianist, remained unperturbed." By the time the company departed Rome for Paris in early June, the ballet had still not been fully rehearsed. With the premiere's curtain at hand, Nijinska recalled, "there were still many roles to be filled and lots of work for those who had just arrived in Paris."[16]

The final rehearsals, directed by Pierre Monteux, were marked by derision and outright antagonism, since the French musicians were as baffled by the music as the dancers. The score was altogether new to them, especially in its quirky rhythmic demands and textural complexities. Monteux, whose patience was tested, split the orchestra into groups to facilitate teaching the music to one section at a time. Once the orchestra and large cast of dancers assembled for a full rehearsal, Fokine and Stravinsky openly contested the music's tempi, complicating matters further. The composer adamantly stated that he knew precisely what he wanted, while Fokine insisted that the dancers could not perform the choreography at the breakneck speed Stravinsky required.[17] In the end, however, the first performance of Petrouchka was given without incident at the Théâtre du Châtelet on the evening of June 13, 1911.

The ballet's principal characters are, unsurprisingly, traceable to several Russian precedents. Lincoln Kirstein provided a conspectus for the history of the ballet's dramatis personae:

> The characters are old friends: Ballerina [danced by Karsavina] is cousin to Columbine and Coppélia; Moor [premiered by the character dancer Alexandre Orlov], a medieval wild man, an instinctive, savage bully, is descendant of the cruel or generous Turk; Showman [Enrico Cecchetti] derives from the charlatan doctor familiar from Italian comedy; Petrouchka [Nijinsky] is at once Little Ivan the serf, Pierrot, and Pedrolino. A fifth character is collective—the bustling crowd, here more particular and contemporary than in Perrot's Esmeralda (1844).[18]

The published synopsis of the scenario, as included in a souvenir program booklet of the Ballets Russes, is worth reprinting:

Petrouchka is another fantasy of the amazing Stravinsky. It is a Russian pendant to "Pagliacci." The tragedy is enacted in the large square of Petrograd. Crowds are coming and going, and an old necromancer, manager of a puppet show, displays his grand, life size marionettes—a pretty dancing girl, her two admirers, the ugly but romantic Petrouchka, and a wicked but fascinating Moor. Their creator has endowed these images with human emotions, and the hero bitterly resents his uncomeliness, as contrasted with the Moor's gorgeous appearance, which enslaves the dancing girl. The poor, grotesque Petrouchka is mad with jealousy and when the Shrovetide festivity in the square is at its height, he is suddenly killed by his black rival. Consternation seizes the crowd, but the old showman assures them that Petrouchka was only a thing of sawdust and plaster—a creature of his own magic power. When the people disperse, however, he is horrified to see the tragic ghost of his marionette menacing him from the quiet shadows of the booth.[19]

The score of *The Firebird* had opened lugubriously, the orchestra setting a fantastical scene by exploring the lowest region of its range. The tempo was dirge-like and the mood tenebrous, and even before the celesta signaled the rising curtain an ominous sense of some chimerical kingdom was lurking. The set revealed itself in the darkness of a dimly lit forest wherein the magical Firebird suddenly appeared. The audience would be transported into a land of good and evil. The opening of *Petrouchka*, conversely, could not have been sunnier. Even before the curtain rises at m. 33, the music is joyfully buoyant as the orchestra explodes with the mimicking of full-throated street cries of vendors huckstering their wares. And although we cannot yet see for ourselves that we are about to be engulfed by the bustling clamor of the first tableau's Shrovetide Fair, we hear a tumultuous outburst of sound as Stravinsky enlists the entire orchestra in building our anticipation of the curtain. Both Stravinsky and Benois had seen Petrouchka puppet theater as children. Thus the composer was thoroughly acquainted with the enrapturing potpourri of these colorful fairs. Such deeply implanted experiences carried for both Stravinsky and Benois the weight of hierology.

Few youthful reminiscences triggered the composer's delight more than the sensorial memories of this cultural heritage. Stravinsky constantly referred to the smells, sights, colors, and other visceral experiences of his ethnic past. Such indelible remembrances affected him to the bone. In attempting to recreate the world of the Shrovetide Fair on stage, the composer uses the piano, harps, and celesta to provide a sturdy tide of sound that binds the music together, against which he weaves other instruments in and out of focus. Moreover, the well-known

Russian folk songs that he incorporated, such as the "Song of the Volochebniki" (from an 1877 Rimsky folk song collection), while largely unfamiliar to Parisian audiences were still memorable enough to engage the listeners' attention. It was not so much the litany of folk quotations themselves, however, as the manner in which Stravinsky so imaginatively deployed them throughout a richly variegated web of rapidly changing textures that made an indelible impression upon the audience. It was immediately drenched in a flood of sound, while the folk songs shone through. The composer often helps the listener along by scoring the folk songs at both ends of the orchestral spectrum (for example, in the flutes in the very first measure and in the lower strings at m. 14). From the outset the audience hears the stratified layers of sound that are employed throughout the tableau to replicate the bustle of the fair. The exhilaration of a Mardi Gras atmosphere, hinted at in the opening pages of the score, becomes visually concrete the moment the curtain rises.[20]

Brightness floods the stage. Balloons float about, amid street vendors costumed in primary colors and an animated crowd—all aimed toward recreating an 1830 Shrovetide Fair in a huge public square in St. Petersburg.[21] The theatrical action adds to the blizzard of musical color established in the whirring opening measures. Pockets of flurry prevail in every corner and at every level of the stage. A windmill turns to one side while a merry-go-round revolves at the other. Higher up is a box, from which people wave to the crowd below, tall spires decorating large buildings in the background. A large cast of dancers provides the central action—so large that it included virtually every dancer in Diaghilev's company. With such a large troupe, however, came problems. How would Fokine manage the traffic constantly in motion on stage?

The choreographer seized the challenge as an opportunity to redress a long-held peeve. The crowd would serve him, as Garafola comments, as "an antidote to ballet's visual and social hierarchies."[22] He would use the assembled revelers to emphasize the range of attitudes such a diverse body represented, as well as their collective emotionalism as a separate, empowered force. Fokine captures this wonderfully in the first and fourth tableaux. It is, in fact, this power to act conjointly that Kirstein was referring to when he characterized the crowd as the ballet's important fifth character. It enters and exits the stage in rapid succession, sometimes performing short solos, sometimes grouped in threes and fours, all contributing to the rising buzz of activity that ensues. The fragments of folk song material that Stravinsky introduces at m. 14, where they appear then quickly evaporate, now coalesce at m. 42, where the orchestra in unison heralds a Rimsky folk song, the scenario directing, "A small group of tipsy merrymakers, prancing, passes by."

Smaller ensembles of male and female dancers offer an array of choreographic gestures ranging from classical pirouettes to familiar folk dance movements. A jumble of styles intrude upon one another, just as Stravinsky's musical layers constantly mingle with and interrupt each other in creating a dizzying mélange of sound. The musical styles are as different, and as recognizable, as the choreographic figures that appear (note the fluffy waltz accompanied by a triangle at m. 116). The unrelenting pace of the music is accompanied by an equally constant rush of acrobats, soldiers, buskers, gypsies, merchants, tricksters, coachmen, nursemaids—sometimes performing independently, but frequently interacting with one another. It is an unbroken chain of comings and goings reminiscent of what one might see while sauntering down a festival's thoroughfare. The accumulative bustle seems improvisational, but in fact Fokine carefully delineated the movements of each participant, often relying upon national dances from within Russia's ethnically distinct provinces. He aimed for and achieved a sense of spontaneity and improvisation.

Stravinsky's score introduced musical episodes consecutively and very distinctly, each focusing on a specific choreographic event. Fokine had to avert a sense of statis in dealing with the multitude of dancers and actors not directly involved in a particular episode but still on stage. His own summary is worth quoting: "For example, when the drunks enter on stage, no characters, other than they, are interpreted in the music—without regard to the mass of other people I have on the stage at that moment . . . I made an effort to have everyone on stage interpret a separate, individual character."[23] Fokine later complained that Diaghilev provided insufficient time to rehearse these intricately woven crowd scenes. Virtually excluded from the ballet's inner circle (he was rapidly falling from grace as Nijinsky ascended in Diaghilev's professional and personal life), an embittered Fokine criticized Stravinsky, Benois, and the work's other architects. Meanwhile, Diaghilev, eager to prevent the collaboration between Benois and Stravinsky from flourishing too vigorously, devoted considerable energy to monitoring their interaction, to the further exclusion of Fokine.[24]

Whatever the politics, *Petrouchka*'s complex score represented a new challenge for Fokine. He complained of the asymmetrical rhythms, as well as the abundance and rapidity of musical ideas unfolding at Stravinsky's accelerated pace. For instance, how would he handle the swiftly shifting rhythms beginning at m. 74, perhaps the most jolting figure Stravinsky had thus far written (Example 2)? Such unorthodox metrical schemes baffled the dancers. When did the customary laws governing the flow of an underlying rhythmic current cease to exist, the choreographer surely wondered. The "unnatural" rhythms

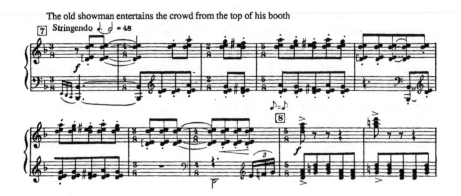

Example 2 *Petrouchka*, first tableau, mm. 74–83.

forged by Stravinsky violently dislocated any expectation of patterns, creating a
sense of musical vertigo. In its use of such genuinely innovative, asymmetrical
rhythmic strata, *Petrouchka* broke definitively with the *kuchkist* tradition. The
music's power drew its energy from elasticity rather than predictability, creating
a new paradigm. Even the many conventional three- and four-beat groupings
that remain take on a new starch within the overall accretion of rhythmic and
metric ambiguity conjured by Stravinsky. Layers of rhythmic propulsion are
piled one above another. Not knowing what is likely to pop up next, the listener
remains uneasy. As Boris Asaf'yev wrote, "The bar-line has lost its tyrannical
hold and has reverted to its original purpose: a coordinator of moments in time
that does not in any way predetermine the bounds of lines."[25]

The score directs the action every few measures: "An old showman enter-
tains the crowd from the height of his booth" (m. 74); "In the crowd an organ-
grinder appears with a street dancer" (m. 90); "The street dancer dances,
beating time on the triangle";[26] "At the other end of the stage a music box plays"
(m. 134). All the while, the crowd revels in the gaiety of the moment. The
action intensifies, culminating in a recapitulation of the opening measures'
musical material at m. 250. The crowd disperses, moving to the sides of the
stage to reveal a small puppet theater. Drummers beckon the crowd's attention,
as directed by the score at m. 258. At m. 271, marked "The Magic Trick," the
Magician appears, peeking from behind the theater's bright blue curtain,
turning his head mistrustfully from side to side, and peering at the audience as
the first of several drum rolls accentuates the moment's dramatic importance.
He sneers at the crowd rather disdainfully, immediately inviting suspicion of
his legerdemain. Lieven characterized the Magician as a misanthrope who

conjured "the dolls in mocking travesty of mankind, making them half-human beings who remain under his domination."[27]

Following the drum roll, seven measures of music aimed at arousing apprehension are heard as the merriment of the fair dissipates. The arpeggiated figures of the celesta and harp, as well as the sliding scales of the violins, descend over a pedal F#, creating an air of foreboding. At m. 278 the Magician begins to play his flute in an improvisational, rhythmically free cadenza, as the audience listens spellbound and then applauds (Figure 1). His serpentine solo suggests his charlatanic character, with its melismatic twists and turns. He exerts his control as the imperious puppeteer.

The crowd presses closer to the little theater as the curtain opens to reveal the three puppets. The score directs, "The magician animates them by touching

Figure 1 Enrico Cecchetti as the Magician in *Petrouchka*, 1916.

each with his flute"—in effect a magic wand—in the measures immediately before the beginning of the famous "Russian Dance." After a pregnant silence, the puppets begin to dance, startling the audience. The melody is based upon the folk song "A Linden Tree Stands in the Field," a *khorovod* Stravinsky must have borrowed from an 1877 Rimsky anthology.[28] Their shoulders are suspended on pegs (just as puppets always were in the *balagani*), with the Ballerina in the middle, flanked by Petrouchka to her left and the Moor to her right. Their choreographic movements unfold to some of the most popular ballet music Stravinsky ever composed.[29] They cast their heads down as they dance. The composer divides the folk tune into four separate two-measure segments, each antecedent phrase beginning with the same motive but followed by a slightly different consequent phrase. The dancers help to articulate the ending of each rhythmically subtle variation by raising their heads on the last beat of each phrase, mesmerizing the crowd. Their torsos remain perfectly still—stilted, really—thus exaggerating the raggedy movement of their dangling legs alone. The piano assumes a prominent, concertante role throughout—hardly surprising given the music's origins as a keyboard work.

Suddenly the puppets spring to life as they miraculously break free from the constraints of their inanimate existence. It is a wondrous moment as they jump down to the level of the crowd in the street below (during mm. 29–37 of the "Russian Dance"). They burst forth from the confines of the little theater's stage as well as from those of reality. Whether the Ballerina then came to life seems to have depended upon the dancer. Karsavina danced the opening tableau as if she were a doll but the two interior scenes as if she were human. Nijinska, who played the same role in subsequent productions, saw things quite differently. She understood that the Ballerina "lives in the body of a doll, and not for a moment does she leave that state, not even when she dances and acts in Petrouchka's or the Moor's room.[30] The principal tune returns as all three puppets, now anthropomorphically transformed, continue to dance woodenly among the dumbfounded listeners. Fokine sculpted each puppet very precisely, as Kirstein remembered: "For the Ballerina, he accented pizzicato points. The Moor was turned out (*en dehors*); Petrouchka turned in (*en dedans*). By limiting movement and gesture to a flat and rigid single plane, he proposed mechanical, semi-automatic regularity, in contrast to the semi-accidental haphazard naturalism in his conglomerate vignetted *corps*."[31]

A few measures before m. 96 the music slows as the clarinet and English horn each play a fragment of the folk tune introduced in the opening measure. It is a pivotal moment, for as the Ballerina raises her arms defensively toward Petrouchka the Magician calls him to his side, the Ballerina then moving toward the Moor and coquettishly perching herself upon his knee. She has made her choice. The piano then restores the original tempo with its invocation of the principal folk melody of the "Russian Dance". The three dancers spring back into action, the two males now literally falling over one another in their quest to win the Ballerina's affection. As the scene concludes, all three join hands, leaping in a straightforward rhythm as a backdrop to Stravinsky's eighteen syncopated chords beginning at m. 120 and extending to the end of the scene. The music itself is jarring in its asymmetrical groupings, disrupting the duple meter with fitful starts and stops, including a one-beat measure that magically breaks the flow of the dance.[32] These intermittent explosions toy with our expectations, heightening our anticipation of what is to come. It is a Stravinskyan technique that would function as a hallmark of his music for the rest of his life. As the music ends, the Magician appears imposingly at center stage, hovering over the transformed puppets.

A sustained drum roll introduces the second tableau, "Petrouchka's Room." This historically memorable dance (actually the first music Stravinsky composed) placed Nijinsky center stage in every way. Just as *The Firebird* had provided Stravinsky with a portal to his future, so Nijinsky's nonpareil portrayal of Petrouchka marks a turning point. The formidable dancer's accomplishments had been quite evident in earlier Diaghilev productions, but here Nijinsky becomes the very embodiment of Petrouchka (Figure 2). Of the various encomia that were inspired by Nijinsky's performance, those of two eyewitnesses are worth citing. First, his sister Nijinska:

When Petrouchka dances, his body remains the body of a doll; only the tragic eyes reflect his emotions, burning with passion or dimming with pain. The heavy head, carved out of a wooden block, hangs forward, rolling from side to side, propped on the shoulder. The hands and feet are also made of wood, and Vaslav holds his fingers stiffly together inside the black mittens like wooden paddles. . . . Petrouchka dances as if he is using only the heavy wooden parts of his body. Only the swinging, mechanical, soul-less motions jerk the sawdust-filled arms or legs upwards in extravagant movements to indicate transports of joy or despair. Despite these limitations imposed on his body, these restricted movements of a doll-like character, Vaslav is astonishing in the unusual technique of his dance, and in the expressiveness of his body. In *Petrouchka*, Vaslav jumps as high as ever and executes as many *pirouettes* and *tours en l'air* as he usually does, even though his petrouchkian wooden feet do not have the flexibility of a dancer's feet.[33]

Figure 2 Vaslav Nijinsky as Petrouchka, 1916.

The second eyewitness account comes from Benois, who recalled Nijinsky struggling somewhat in rehearsals, failing to grasp what it was he and Stravinsky were attempting to portray.

> He even asked me to explain his role to him, which was very unusual for Nijinsky . . . I was surprised at the courage Vaslav showed, after all his *jeune premier* successes, in appearing as a horrible half-doll, half-human grotesque. . . . [He] is not given a single *pas* or a *fioriture* to enable him to be attractive to the public, and one must remember that Nijinsky was then quite a young man and the temptation to "be attractive to the public" must have appealed to him far more strongly than to an older artist.[34]

The tableau unfolds without folk song quotation. The piano dominates the entire scene. Its cascading arpeggio and cadenza-like figures quickly become synonymous with Petrouchka's frantic, flustering efforts to escape the imprisoning room into which the Magician has thrust him. The beginning of the scene also highlights the bitonal C major–F# major tritone, the intervallic span that defines the music's diabolical sentiment throughout Petrouchka's solo dancing. From the very opening, a timorous Petrouchka covers his head, trembling, as he lies prostrate. He rises to his knees extending his arms outwardly to the audience in what has become the signature gesture of the Petrouchka character (one of the few elements of Fokine's choreographic conception that Stravinsky approved of). He is in pain, clutching his side and his heart as a clear signal of his distress. As the white-and-black-key arpeggios quicken in scampering through the keyboard's screeching higher register, Petrouchka rises to his feet (m. 26). The brittleness of the sound matches the shrillness of his misery. Fruitlessly, even hysterically, he searches for an escape from his captivity as he dances, jouncing around the room's perimeter.[35]

As the piano cadenza flies out of control, the C–F# bitonality returns, blasted, literally, by the orchestra's cornets and trumpets at m. 33. At the same moment, a portrait of the Magician shines on the wall (marked "Petrouchka's curses" in the score), incensing the saturnine Petrouchka even more. The image itself emits an air of terror and evil, as if the baleful charlatan were monitoring Petrouchka's every move. It is an important moment in the ballet. Little wonder that Benois was eager to have his original painting employed, although Diaghilev conspired against its retention.[36] Nijinsky's movements grow increasingly convulsive as the *Adagietto* theme, much like a music box, begins at m. 44. Petrouchka's supplicatory gestures are now more marionette-like, as he once again grasps his heart, extending his hands as if to tell us that it aches for the Ballerina.

The Ballerina enters at m. 68 to the innocent, child-like unaccompanied music of the piano, its naiveté matching the empty-headed persona she herself projects. Pushed into the room by the Magician, she moves perfunctorily, retaining her doll-like image. In terms of the drama, however, she is much more than that. Puppet or person, the ostensibly harebrained Ballerina wields the real power here, over both the hapless Petrouchka and the braggart Moor. Her rubicund face is blank, and she reacts to everything without a trace of emotion. Yet her vacuity only adds to her allure, playing upon the stereotype of the nineteenth-century ballerina for which Fokine felt such disdain. As Garafola comments, "The Ballerina . . . stood for everything he despised; technical trickery (her coy *échappés* and tiny hops on pointe, *passés, relevés* and whipping *fouetté* turns were variation staples) and empty display, as well as a number of lesser sins: drawn-out preparations, the extremes of turnout, arms *en couronne*, segmented phrasing—all of which he refused to countenance in his 'straight' choreography."[37] The Ballerina is no more than a device for the guileful Magician's depraved amusement, a sexual prop in stoking the feud between the two hopelessly infatuated males.

Whatever the Ballerina's on-stage machinations, Petrouchka rejoices at the sight of his beloved. In a letter to Stravinsky of December 1910 Benois outlines his thoughts on this episode. It constituted an especially important dramatic moment that must complement closely the music Stravinsky had already completed. Benois suggests a "duet full of perfidy; pitiful Petrushka tries to seduce the flighty beauty with his dancing and writing . . . At any rate you must express the fact that P. does not get anything from C. [Columbine, i.e., the Ballerina] and that he is left high and dry. The scene ends . . . with the knock of the Magician and with C's flitting away."[38] In the final version, the two begin dancing together, although never touching or interacting in any way. No sooner has this duet begun than it ends. After the briefest of moments (only thirteen measures of music), the Ballerina exits. It is clear that despite his efforts to win her favor, she does not wish to be there, nor indeed to be with the piteous Petrouchka. It is equally evident that the Magician, in his despicableness, intended her fleeting presence to taunt the already disconsolate Petrouchka. The clarinet engages in another extended cadenza marked *fortissimo* at the moment where the puppet realizes all is lost. He is left clawing at the door, pounding his head against it, and holding his heart. The piano returns with another cadenza beginning at m. 88, becoming increasingly agitated as Petrouchka continues to seek a way out of his cell. His real despair (as marked by the score) mounts at m. 101, as his disposition and entire physical demeanor become more and more tormented. He curses the Magician's painting on the wall. It is futile, and he recognizes his fate. As the scene ends, he flings himself to the floor again.

"In the Moor's Room" follows, with music marked *feroce* capturing the drama of this third tableau. Stravinsky sets the mood with rhythmic figures that recall the Petrouchka theme, including stentorian trumpet solos. The curtain rises at m. 18 to quieter music, rhythmic accompaniment being provided by a percussion section that includes gong, timpani, cymbals, and bass drum. Once again, the bright colors of red and blue provide the scenery for the Moor's room. We find the festooned Moor looking quite pleased with himself.[39] He is supine, casually reclining on a bed, tossing a coconut up in the air and catching it. Grigoriev recalls this scene taxing Fokine more than others. He simply did not know what to do with the Moor, and Stravinsky's music seemed both confusing and undanceable. "He lost his temper, throwing the music on the floor and leaving the rehearsal," Grigoriev recalled. "Next day, however, he appeared looking happier, and said he had thought of some 'business' for the accursed Moor: he would give him a coconut to play with—which would carry him at least through the first part of the scene."[40] Edwin Evans remarked that the coconut was symbolic of a sacred power, a cocoon both irresistible and impregnable. "He then decides it must be stronger than himself, and bows down and worships it."[41] He juggles it nonchalantly, as if without a care in the world. The music itself, on the contrary, is scored rather starkly for bass clarinets, bassoons, and the lower strings. The resplendent Moor continues to play with the coconut until he falls off the bed at m. 36, whereupon the English horn signals a new theme. The Moor now sits cross-legged at the center of the stage and continues to make the coconut the object of his attention.

The adjacency of the second and third tableaux emphasizes the difference between the males and all that they symbolize. Fokine recalled the contrast for which he was aiming, while also offering an analysis of the two characters' obvious body language:

> The Moor is all *en dehors* ("turned out"); Petrouchka all *en dedans* ("turned in"). I have never seen a better example of choreography which discloses so eloquently the personality of two such different characters. This self-satisfied Moor, an extrovert, completely turns himself out; while the pathetic, frightened Petrouchka, an introvert, withdraws into himself. Has this been borrowed from life? Most certainly. It has been borrowed from life to be introduced into the most unlifelike puppet pantomime— puppet movements built on a psychological foundation. We often see a self-assured man who sits in a chair with widely spread legs, feet turned out, hands resting on his knees or hips, holding his head high and his chest out. There is another type: he will be sitting on the very edge of the chair, knees together, feet turned in, with his back hunched, head hanging down, and arms like dropping branches. We can immediately conclude that this one has had little success in life.[42]

Stravinsky adopts a fragmented approach wherein different orchestral layers interlock in a textural mosaic that presages his next ballet. The *sul ponticello* figures of the lower strings interspersed with the woodwinds in alternating *stringendo* and *a tempo* shifts are remarkable. So too are the metric shifts every few measures: 4/4, 2/4, 6/8, 5/8, 4/8, 3/8, 3/4, all compounding the passage's asymmetry. The similarity to *The Rite of Spring*, especially its "Ritual Action of the Ancestors," is conspicuous, and further indicates just how far Stravinsky had traveled in less than a year. Fokine may not have fully appreciated the compositional direction Stravinsky was now pursuing. Nonetheless, he grasped the dramatic thrust of the composer's purpose: "No matter how sudden the frequent variations of the tempi in the score . . . I believe them to be an indispensable element. For they are introduced to express and illustrate the rapidity and abruptness of the ever-changing emotions."[43]

The Moor mimes rather than dances his way through this intricately woven section. He grabs a scimitar in an effort to split the coconut and release its secrets. He is absorbed in his own frippery, oblivious to his internment. The Ballerina enters as the "Dance of the Ballerina with Cornet" begins with the martial cornet solo accompanied by the snare drum. She is *en pointe*, tramping in strict step with the rhythm while marking every note. Holding the coronet, she prances (more than dances) around the stage, circling the Moor who remains recumbent at the center. The equally well known "Waltz (The Ballerina and the Moor)" commences with a cornet and flute duet, now accompanied by a bassoon ostinato. The Ballerina again dances jerkily, as if her strings are being pulled. The Moor dances too, but independently. Waggishly, he teases her, offering his own mockingly performed pirouettes. The overt lampooning of a classical pas de deux is immediately evident. The Moor supports her at the waist as she turns, stomping his feet roughly in heightening the buffoonery. Both the tempo and the key change suddenly at m. 20, marking a second music box waltz played slightly faster, and even more clownishly.

The Ballerina continues to dance mechanistically, while the Moor now moves from her side and sits down, observing her every movement. He claps scoffingly as if she is not to be taken seriously. She remains no more than a bauble. Stravinsky's imaginative music unfolds at two distinct levels, rhythmically and texturally. While the waltz prevails from the start, with the harp accompanying the flute, the contrabassoon and English horn intrude a few measures later, clearly marked in 2/4 and thus defying the waltz's thoroughly consistent triple meter. The bass drums and cymbals provide an underlying accompanimental layer that alternates between 3/4 and 2/4, producing a wonderful muddle. The two layers of sound clearly replicate the two gallivanting characters on stage, each going his or her own way.[44]

Eventually the Ballerina falls into his lap. The Moor now nibbles lustfully on her side, without any reaction from the doltish object of his amorous attention. All the while, the same waltzes, together with fragments of other thematic materials, continue to underlie the action. At m. 60 the Moor's advances grow too lascivious, the Ballerina raising her hands as if to resist. It is merely a momentary prudence, however, and their romantic dalliance resumes. At m. 82, marked "The Moor and the Ballerina listen," they raise their hands to their ears, cupping them as they hear the trumpet announcing Petrouchka's theme. The sound distracts them from their flirtation. Petrouchka enters the room at m. 86 as the trumpets again herald his theme. The Magician thrusts Petrouchka into the room as he once again clasps his heart and reaches out entreatingly for the Ballerina, who, as he can plainly see, has fallen for his nemesis. The Moor chases him around the room as the Ballerina watches. He hoists Petrouchka into the air like a rag doll and drags him around the room, exhibiting his command. The nadir of Petrouchka's abuse comes at another musically pertinent moment (m. 115), wherein Stravinsky incessantly articulates a repeated chord in rapidly changing meter, again portending a repetitive figure he will use in *The Rite*. The Moor hurls his fists on the beleaguered Petrouchka, literally booting him from the room. He thumps his chest pompously with all the implications associated with such a virile gesture. With notable indifference to what has just occurred, he resumes his licentious wooing of the Ballerina as the scene ends.

The fourth tableau returns us to the Shrovetide Fair and the "Grand Carnival." It is evening and the festivities are peaking. Stravinsky's kaleidoscopic orchestra emits waves of sound reminiscent of a hurdy-gurdy or accordion rhythmically breathing in and out. The tableau's opening material returns at m. 32 as the curtain rises. The stage is awash with activity. The revelers are merrymaking, squabbling, laughing, and engaging in slapstick comedy, with constant motion onto and off the stage. It is a recapitulation of the spirit of the first tableau, but now the spectacle unfolds in a whirlwind of separate scenes. We begin with the "Dance of the Nursemaids" to thirds played by the bassoons. An oboe intones a folk song that would have been familiar to Stravinsky and many other Russians, entitled "Down the Petersburg Road." Appropriately employed by the composer, it is a lighthearted dance song about a party and the bibulous indulgences often associated with Shrovetide bacchanals. "I drank with delight, vodka so divine, pony not for mine, nor a glass for wine," and "Hold me straight in line, tipsy as I am, tipsy as I am, stupid drunken lamb," so a few lines go.[45]

The Russian folk dancing employed by Fokine is unmistakably reminiscent of choreographic gestures evident in *The Firebird*, although here they are highly extended.[46] One of the revelers encircles a nursemaid until she begins her own dance as the folk song returns, now played by the French horn. (If one listens closely one hears the very first tune of the ballet in the flutes and piccolos at m. 15, helping to unify both the musical material and the dramatic action.) A popular Russian folk tune is taken up by the oboes at m. 33.[47] The entire ensemble continues to dance as Fokine evokes even more familiar Russian folk dancing. The frivolities are interrupted abruptly at m. 64 ("A muzhik with a bear enters. Everyone scatters"). Stravinsky inserts an unanticipated 6/4 measure marked by blatting brass and descending chromatic figures in the strings. The crowd reacts to the intrusion and disperses to the sides of the stage.

A peasant enters with a bear—the ultimate Russian stereotype sure to amuse the Parisians—as a trembling crowd scatters and a nursemaid faints. The trainer plays his instrument (here the clarinets play a chromatic figure shrilly and at one point in counterpoint with the tuba) while coaxing the animal through an array of tricks, such as rolling over, and standing up on its hind legs. The musical transition around m. 76 (*Tempo del principio*) from this scene to the return of the earlier hurdy-gurdy effect is seamless. A merchant enters with two gypsies at m. 89, tossing bank notes to the crowd (marked by Stravinsky "Le marchand et les bohémiennes" in the 1911 manuscript, although the title did not survive in the published score). Violins sound yet another popular Russian tune from an 1866 Afanas'yev collection of folk songs. "The gypsy girls dance. The merchant plays the accordion," so the direction is given at m. 98. There is a great deal of ensemble dancing, although here females dance in smaller groups of duos and trios as fragments of several of the earlier folk tunes reappear and vanish one after another. The music begins to fade as the merchant and his dancers leave in preparation for what will be the ballet's grandest ensemble dance, the "Dance of the Coachmen and Grooms."

The men stand center stage on their heels, performing splits, and warming themselves by wrapping their hands around their bodies.[48] The quarter-note chords are grouped in fours to a syncopated accompaniment, providing a steady background rhythm—this in anticipation of the folk song "The Snow Thaws" (taken from a Tchaikovsky anthology), which Stravinsky quotes in its entirety. He divides sections of the tune between instruments—trumpets, violins, trombones, horns—creating a textural sequence. The previously heard folk song "Down the Petersburg Road" reappears at m. 57 ("The nursemaids dance with the coachmen and grooms"), as the intensity of the dancing swells into a huge crowd scene. The merry-go-round revolves; people are looking down at the carnival from above; balloons add to the color; spectacle permeates every inch of the stage. It begins to snow as the lighting dims and the illusion of night overtakes the scene. Fantasy figures appear as "The Mummers" begins, with animals and women cowering as a character dressed as a devil enters, portrayed orchestrally by huge leaps of a ninth in the lower brass around m. 10. The scene continues to unfold as the crowd joins the dancing mummers. The music becomes increasingly homophonic, thinning to single notes as "Cries begin to emerge from the little theater."[49]

The Petrouchka theme reappears as those gathered in the square drop to their knees in front of the puppet theater. A palpable gravity replaces what was all lightheartedness as the crowd sees a ruffling movement from behind the curtain. All three principals emerge, the Moor, scimitar in hand, scurrying after Petrouchka and soon slaying him. The now silenced revelers encircle the fallen figure. The programmatic music underscores the dying puppet as he extends his hand out from his heart, still ardently pledging his love for the Ballerina, even as he expires. The Moor and Ballerina exit the stage as Petrouchka lifts his head spasmodically. A police officer summons the absconding Magician, who implies with his gestures that the deranged Petrouchka's death was not of his doing. The crowd suspects his prevarication, exhibiting its anger. The Magician cradles the corpse, shaking the body to confirm that the puppet is dead. The stunned revelers disperse under a darkened sky as the Magician drags the body off stage, all of this to the now soft, mournful hurdy-gurdy bellowing of the scene's opening. Suddenly, fourteen measures before the ballet's end, muted trumpets sound the Petrouchka theme, as the Magician incredulously glimpses the puppet's ghost hovering above the theater, gesturing derisively. The petrified charlatan drops the body and flees. As the ballet ends, Petrouchka flops down limply over the top of the theater. The respiring of the accordion-like figure slows (played by the horns), and the music ends with a slow pizzicato tritone ominously intoned a final time.[50]

Stravinsky later commented that he was "more proud of these last pages than of anything else in the score."[51] The work's diatonicism, mostly obvious in the quotation of folk songs but evident almost everywhere, would come together in the ballet's final moments with the chromaticism associated with the tormented Petrouchka. The conjunction itself was shocking, and quite unlike the sumptuously melodious and uplifting finale of The Firebird. One can only wonder what the Parisians made of Petrouchka's disjunctive, perplexing ending. The final curtain brought with it questions rather than answers, inviting the audience to contemplate the hazy line separating fantasy from reality. Diaghilev had every right to be concerned. Benois remembers the impresario's initial reaction: "When everything was ready, Petrouchka was played to Diaghilev and me from beginning to end. Diaghilev was no less delighted with it than I; the only thing he argued about was the 'note of interrogation' upon which the ballet score ended. For a long time he would not agree to it, but demanded a more traditional solution—a curious proof of how strongly influenced Diaghilev was by 'academic prejudice' even in 1911!"[52] Yet when the work proved a success, Diaghilev seems to have denied ever questioning the ending. Such a bold, intentionally mystifying conclusion represented a moment of quiet audacity on Stravinsky's part, one that would set the tone for the even riskier ideas to be explored in his next ballet.

The premiere "took Paris by storm," reported Nijinska, with Stravinsky, Benois, and the dancers garnering "thunderous applause," and "the enraptured public [pouring] behind the wings, into the dressing rooms of the artists, onto the stage." Yaakov Tugenhold, reporting for the influential journal *Apollon*, carped a bit over the "excessive psychologism of the last moment (the resurrection of the slain Petrushka, a hint at the existence of a Doppelgänger)," but admitted that the production exhibited an "amazing wholeness," an "infinitely near-and-dear profoundly Russian *harmony*." His acclamation was particularly generous, referring to Stravinsky as "the collective soul of the Russian people." *Comoedia* carried a review by Louis Vuillemin, who praised Stravinsky's courage and the work's orchestral color.[53]

The coterie of progressive French composers who had recently embraced Stravinsky was equally impressed. Satie had attended the dress rehearsal, where several critics (present at Diaghilev's behest) glowed with enthusiasm. Ravel, Delage, and others also expressed their approbation. Most tellingly, and doubtlessly most meaningful to Stravinsky, Debussy described the young Russian composer as possessing "an instinctive genius for color and rhythm," exclaiming, "What a mind he has! His music is full of feeling for the orchestra, conceived directly for the orchestral canvas and concerned only with conveying an emotional intensity. He is afraid of nothing, nor is he pretentious." In a letter to Stravinsky himself, Debussy singles out *Petrouchka* as a masterpiece: "I do not know many things of greater value than the passage you call 'Le tour de passe-passe.' There is in it a kind of sonorous magic, a mysterious transformation of mechanical souls, which become human by a spell, a spell of which you so far seem to be the unique inventor."[54]

High praise indeed. Russian reviews, however, were mixed. Writing for *Muzika* in January 1912, Nikolai Miaskovsky submitted that Stravinsky's "exceptional, radiant talent" would have pleased Rimsky-Korsakov—for many still the yardstick of musical excellence in Russia. Stravinsky was "flesh of his flesh and blood of his blood," Miaskovsky exclaimed. The young and brashly assured Sergei Prokofiev, however, remarked that Stravinsky represented moments in the ballet brilliantly, but that such *remplissage*, or 'filler,' should not be confused with writing genuine music. "If he can't compose music for the most crucial moments, [but] only stuffs them with whatever's at hand, then he's musically bankrupt."[55] Andrei Rimsky-Korsakov's invective seemed the most gratuitous and personally hurtful. It would be the final blow to his friendship with Stravinsky. Even as the writing of the ballet progressed in late 1910, Stravinsky had written to Andrei requesting that he send some folk song material, since he could not quite remember the tunes accurately. In the end, however, Rimsky's son impugned the use of these ethnographic and vernacular sources as nothing more than debris—"trash," as Stravinsky later recalled.[56] Such diatribes, however, could not conceal the denial of what was obvious to those beyond the Conservatory's clannishly hidebound circle. The young Stravinsky had managed to free himself from the circumscription that continued to choke St. Petersburg. Even more difficult to swallow, he did it with true innovation, surpassing the brilliance of the very conservatively written, derivative, and thus easily digestible *Firebird*.

Stravinsky pressed for some acknowledgement of his ballet's value. In a letter of July 21, 1911, barely a month after the ballet's premiere, he wrote to Vladimir Rimsky-Korsakov, emotively repelling recent attacks on the viability of ballet as a compositional genre—an old grumble that his St. Petersburg colleagues continued to voice. Stravinsky vehemently affirms his rejection of ballet's all too familiar stigma as the "lowest sort" of art, adding that he feels the opposite:

> I love ballet and am more interested in it than anything else. And this is not just an idle enthusiasm, but a serious and profound enjoyment of scenic spectacle—of the art of animated form. . . . And I am simply bewildered that you . . . consider ballet to be a lower form than opera. If a Michelangelo were alive today . . . the only thing his genius would recognize and accept would be the choreography that is being reborn today. Everything else that takes place on the stage he would doubtless call a miserable farce. For the only form of scenic art that sets itself, as its cornerstone, the *tasks of beauty*, and *nothing else*, is ballet. And the only goal Michelangelo pursued was visible beauty. . . . I think that if you would attend the ballet regularly . . . you would see that this "lower form" brings you incomparably more artistic joy than any operatic performance.[57]

Stravinsky's exasperation leaps from the page as he fervidly argues his case. He defends the "clairvoyance" of Benois's position on the purity of dance—a position Benois further articulated in praising *Petrouchka* "as an artistic achievement all the more remarkable in that it proves that by balletic means one can convey dramatic situations and sensations that are absolutely impossible in drama or opera."[58]

Asaf'yev offered a particularly insightful appraisal of the distance Stravinsky had traveled in creating his new ballet. "The score of *Petrushka* is entirely different from that of *Firebird*. With *Petrushka* Stravinsky finally reaches a fulfillment, [and] with it he steps out in front of his generation. All those who did not wish to be counted among the 'living dead' realized that a great event had taken place, that Russian music had really made a new and unprecedented conquest."[59] In truth, the conquest was larger still. *Petrouchka* deserves landmark status. With it, the charter members of *Mir iskusstva* finally realized their dreams. Realism and fantasy achieved the blend that had for so long seemed unattainable. *Petrouchka* had managed to bring a consummate sense of coherence to all of the theatrical arts integral to ballet. By the time of the Ballets Russes' 1916 tour of sixteen American cities, the company's identity, as well as the notable prominence of Stravinsky, was publicly declared. Indeed the role of music seems to have been elevated to a status equal to that of dance, as hinted in the tour's program booklet:

> Artistic unity and harmonious cooperation are the keynotes of the Russian Ballet. It is important to remember that the supreme technical excellence of individual dancers is the least remarkable element contributing to the sensational success of M. Diaghileff's organization. The art of his famous *maître de ballet* would lose half its significance in a commonplace setting, or accompanied by banal music. On the other hand, to appreciate properly the genius of a Stravinsky, we must be assisted by the interpretations of the mimes and dancers.[60]

With *Petrouchka*, Stravinsky attained an eminence that had been unthinkable only two years earlier. Moreover, "the artistic unity and harmonious cooperation" of ballet itself led to a more serious, more legitimated role as an expressive art form. Perhaps the ossified criticism of ballet as mere trumpery could now be silenced. The composer looked back on the nineteenth century and bid it adieu. The piano work about a naive, star-crossed harlequin that had begun its life in a seaside resort would alter the new century's thinking about contemporary composition. *Petrouchka* provided a gateway to a higher plateau. The composer now shifted his focus from an 1830 Shrovetide carnival to a pagan mythology steeped in the power of ritual, as remote from the subject matter of his second ballet as that work's had been from that of *The Firebird*. He had moved swiftly from a first ballet exhibiting a skillful orchestral handling of derivative materials to a second ballet marked by ingenuity in both dramatic and compositional approach. Increasingly confident within the orbit of Diaghilev's own ambitious vision, he now renewed his thinking about what would become his third ballet, "The Great Sacrifice." And with this resumption, Stravinsky stood poised to exert a shaping, even defining force on the emerging world of modernism.

CHAPTER FOUR

THE RITE OF SPRING
Gateway to Modernism

STRAVINSKY'S FIRST two ballets premiered in a European capital that exuded optimism. *Fin de siècle* Paris gave way to a robust artistic colony's fresh thinking aimed at nothing less that forging a bold new future. Everywhere artists questioned conformity in charting the future; and none more so than the Ballets Russes. In surveying the shifting terrain of modernism's early years, the year 1912 emerges as a turning point. It was a year of extraordinary global transitions, failures, and triumphs. In April, the RMS *Titanic*, publicly heralded as a testament to the achievements of modern technology and declared unsinkable, sank. Aviation continued to grip the world's fancy as the first non-stop flight from Paris to London was successfully completed. Thomas Edison began producing disc phonographs. Jean Metzinger and Albert Gleizes published the first major treatise on one of several "isms," in this case cubism. Picasso, moving through rapidly evolving stylistic periods, created *Violon, verre, pipe et encrier*, while Chagall and De Chirico exhibited early proto-surrealist paintings in Paris. Advances in understanding the nascent power of X-ray diffraction continued. A more refined probing into the concatenate riddle of atomic structure yielded increasing clarity. Freud's controversial theories of psychoanalysis further provoked questions about the inner sanctum of our most private thoughts. Albert Einstein turned physics upside down with his first published writings on a general theory of relativity, released in 1913, the year in which Stravinsky's third ballet, *The Rite of Spring*, stunned the artistic world.

All the while, the distance between St. Petersburg and Paris grew ever greater. Russia's rigidly autocratic government continued to disintegrate. During the summer in which *Petrouchka* premiered, the assassination of the Tsar's prime minister, Pieter Stolypin, whose suppression of the growing revolution was fated to fail, amplified a widening fissure between the monarchy and the proletarian classes. The Lena execution, in which tsarist troops massacred hundreds of mistreated workers in northern Siberia, followed in April 1912. A month later, the ideology of an underground communism acquired a powerful pulpit in the form of *Pravda*, whose appearance in May 1912 instantly captured a far-reaching sympathy. Everywhere tensions grew as oratory supplanted whispered testimony and public demonstrations and strikes replaced caution. All signs pointed to a mounting dissidence that would soon precipitate a decimating national revolution.

Still, emboldened by the artistic triumphs of his first two ballets, Stravinsky rose above the blanketing political despair, embracing an integral role in contributing to the new century's momentum. He realized that he no longer need suffer the prosaic strictures of tsarist Russia, nor allow its catechism to manacle him creatively. The composer was fully cognizant of his own remarkable growth. "It seems that twenty years, not two, have passed since *The Firebird*," he wrote to Rimsky-Korsakov's son Andrei.[1] Indeed, as an artist he had matured more swiftly than Diaghilev, Benois, Bakst, and others could have guessed. Perhaps more than any disciple of the Ballet Russes, and unquestionably more than any musician, Stravinsky understood how ballet must transform itself if it was to become a revitalized, coherent art form in the new century. The composer knew he was on to something new; and others knew it too. Buoyed by the artistic vigor of Paris, his beliefs resonated with the passionate convictions of other young modernists seeking to refashion the thinking of a new generation. All around him, questions were raised about the impregnable truths of inherited wisdom. The world found itself drawn into an intellectual vortex that contested the canonical assumptions that lay at the base of accepted knowledge. It was a time for doubting, for reassessing, for establishing a new order.

For many, the unparalleled violence of Stravinsky's next ballet overstepped the limits of propriety in ballet music. Yet it was hardly the music alone that met with wide condemnation. Immediately decried as a maleficence foisted upon artistic sensibilities, its violation of tradition was seen by many as sacrilegious— a "crime against grace," to use the epithet associated with Nijinsky's profane choreography. Enrico Cecchetti, Nijinsky's own teacher and one of Diaghilev's own ballet masters, found fault enough to pass around: "I think the whole thing has been done by four idiots. First, M. Stravinsky who wrote the music. Second M. Roerich who designed the scenery and costumes. Third M. Nijinsky who composed the dances. Fourth M. Diaghilev who wasted money on it."[2] Others consecrated the new Stravinsky ballet as the shibboleth of modernism, supporters eagerly hoisting its impudence upon the shoulders of a much broader insurgency. The volatility of the times warranted its volcanic rage. Borders were crossed, boundaries redrawn. Stravinsky's ballet indignantly begged the question of what constituted meaningful artistic expression, as repellent as such expression might need to be in honestly addressing the human condition.

In Russia, especially, *The Rite of Spring* was seen as a symbolic capitulation to the hopelessly caustic forces that were eroding the world's vanishing sanity. A year after its premiere, by which time Stravinsky had long departed his homeland to find asylum in the countryside of Switzerland, St. Petersburg became Petrograd en route to its rechristening as Leningrad. The future was agonizingly clear. The Bolshevik Revolution of 1917 seemed for many a predictable apocalypse. The First World War would trigger multiple consequences, many of which would play out in hostile social actions and responses. A frenzy of artistic schisms and "isms" would ensue. Whether Stravinsky liked it or not—and to some extent he probably relished the turbulence unleashed—he found himself portrayed as an anarchist, creating a chaos that touched artists deeply. Lincoln Kirstein saw *The Rite* not only as a watershed in balletic and musical terms, but as an augury of the gathering political storm clouds. "Five years before the October Revolution," he remarked, "Diaghilev glorified popular rather than imperial aspects of Russian power, daemonic, undeniable, in a collaboration that would never have been permitted in any tsarist opera house, which would be heard in Russia only some thirty years after 1919."[3]

Historian Modris Eksteins, whose social theories revolve around the devastating human price of the war, offered a similar viewpoint. Eksteins went so far as to describe Stravinsky's third ballet as the single most powerful artistic manifesto to exemplify the boiling temper of the modernistic epoch:

> *The Rite of Spring* . . . is, with its rebellious energy and its celebration of life through sacrificial death, perhaps the emblematic *oeuvre* of a twentieth-century world that, in the pursuit of life, has killed off millions of its best human beings. To demonstrate the significance of the Great War, one must of course deal with the interests and emotions involved in it. . . . Cultural history must at least try to capture the spirit of an age. That spirit is to be located in a society's sense of priorities. Ballet, film, and literature . . . can provide important evidence of these priorities, but the latter will be found most amply in the social response to these symbols.[4]

In recounting the perniciousness of the First World War—this purging war to end all wars, as it was thought—Eksteins asserts that history too often marginalizes the plight of the common soldier in favor of focusing on the strategies and merciless generals of warfare. Metaphorically, he suggests that the unknown, unsung soldier is the ballet's victim. "The theme of *Le Sacre* was birth and death, Eros and Thanatos, primitive and violent, the fundamental experiences of all existence, beyond cultural context."[5] As such, *The Rite* stands as a universal statement that not only prefigures the consequences of one impending war, but also speaks to the reassuring power of regeneration. We are genetically bound to replenish ourselves, the pre-literate story of *The Rite* poses, and to do so by whatever Darwinian means are necessary. More broadly, *The Rite* celebrates the pristine beauty of primitivism in its unembellished power; for "primitivism," writes Francis Maes, "went a long way toward satisfying the dream of a restored unity of man with the elementary forces of nature." It did so naturally—that is, it came from the depths of the most fundamental and sincere expressions of a Slavic past, rather than through the transplanted cultural veneer of inherited European traditions.[6]

For Pieter Lieven, the score's unprecedented dissonance drew its primary strength from the unmitigated "power of 'barbarism,' of true primitivism."[7] While Russian artists had long been preoccupied with their own people's history of ancient rituals, a resurgence of this interest in the early twentieth century would have drawn the composer's attention. Alexander Blok's essay "The Poetry of Magic and Spells" appeared only two years before Stravinsky began thinking about *The Rite*: "What for primeval man was a living necessity, men today must reconstitute by the roundabout means of imagery. The ancient soul, in a manner we cannot fathom, experienced as something united and whole all that seems to us not only discrete but also mutually antagonistic. In contemporary consciousness, such concepts as life, knowledge, religion, mystery, and poetry are all distinct. For our ancestors it was all one."[8]

The Rite's inexorability, even its repellency, spoke loudly to those willing to shed their preconceptions about the illusory prettiness of music and dance. Moreover, historians realized that it was Nijinsky's choreography, particularly its obtrusively angular and overtly unballetic gestures, that especially abraded the audience. Stravinsky's score was more than an accompaniment: it was the perfect accomplice. Brawny, aggressive, and repellant, the music was "seriously ugly," Lincoln Kirstein wrote, "a manifesto against tyrannical symmetry or timid dislocation that had governed ballet since its beginning."[9] Musicians and dancers were forced to face the reality that bar lines, those hitherto dependable but subjugating forces, could no longer be counted upon as temporal pillars. Stravinsky had hinted as much in some break-free moments of *Petrouchka*, but these were merely momentary blips by comparison with what lay ahead. *The Rite* offered no litany of recognizable folk songs or shopworn choreographic gestures; rather, it sought to undermine, to "subvert," as some critics saw it, the fossilized assumptions of simplicity—or more to the point, simplemindedness—that were associated by westerners with ethnicity. Moreover, the ballet elected not to go anywhere. One was coerced into accepting its individually pounded-out ideas for what they were. It stood on its own, a *res ipsa loquitur*, rejecting the need to explain itself. One had to accept its unorthodoxy as an unvarnished, unrefined "being," one that pretended no compulsion to develop into something else.

Indeed, unorthodoxy of every stripe was pored over in the bustling milieu of the Parisian café where Stravinsky often met with a widening circle of like-minded colleagues, some of whom would eventually become his collaborators. *Les Apaches*, a group of French musicians, authors, artists, and critics who followed the changing tides of the times, fostered Stravinsky's growing curiosity and cosmopolitism. These Apaches, or "hooligans" (to translate roughly their moniker), included Debussy, Ravel, Maurice Delage, the painter Paul Sordes, and the influential critics M. D. Calvocoressi and Émile Vuillermoz. They had sensed the budding qualities of genius in *Petrouchka*. They knew that Stravinsky had something to say as an artist, and that artists collectively had something to say about the unsettled world in which they lived. Offering the counsel the composer needed, they were among the first to hear the embryo of a master-piece as it began to take shape. As Florent Schmitt recalled in November 1912, Stravinsky played a large part of *The Rite* for his friends: "This work has, all by itself, more importance than all other music that can be played at this moment anywhere in the world. It contains liberty, newness and life."[10] (Only a month earlier, ironically, the composer had visited St. Petersburg where he performed a few excerpts from *The Rite* for a former friend and fellow composer who was left "bewildered and unhappy.")[11] Schmitt's "newness and life" might have come at a cost to Stravinsky and Diaghilev. It would have been infinitely easier to continue manufacturing the formulaic Russian ballets that were then so popular. But Diaghilev knew what he was doing. He brilliantly brewed a potion that had proven immensely marketable for the Ballets Russes. Still, he needed to strike a delicate balance between ruffling and chafing. Where was such an elusive line to be drawn? *The Rite* was meant to jolt, even incense. Thus it constituted a considerable gamble.

Long before *The Firebird* was completed, Diaghilev had realized he had a problem on his hands. Even as Stravinsky dutifully followed Fokine's directives, his imaginative mind had stretched beyond the clamps imposed upon his first ballet score by Diaghilev and others. Following the 1910 production, Stravinsky left Russia, but not before dreaming, literally, of a new work. He grew eager to begin, and did so the following summer. "The Great Sacrifice" would serve as a working title (although his preferred title was "The Holy Spring"). He envisaged a ritualistic, prehistoric pagan ballet, a sacred ceremony steeped in Russian pre-literate history. Diaghilev sensed something was afoot, although Stravinsky was guarded about the details. Diaghilev grew increasingly uneasy about such an unappetizing scenario, perhaps fearing it would meet with contempt in Paris. Was a story culminating in the sacrifice of a young virgin something the urbane Parisians would embrace? After all, while audiences were enchanted by the exoticism and even soft eroticism of Diaghilev's productions, ballet was still largely a white tutu affair. Ultimately, it came down to ascertaining the reaction of the public in terms of box office appeal, while placating the young star composer who was now hell-bent on expanding his creative compass rather than merely repeating himself. Diaghilev could not hazard losing his latest discovery, for Stravinsky had become a marketable commodity to rival the troupe's most brilliant dancers. Indeed, with *The Rite* the composer exercised considerable authority in making decisions. He approached a directorial leverage that was unequaled by any other composer in Diaghilev's circle.

Stravinsky fancied himself a visionary and staunch advocate for change. His personality, his instincts, and now his newly embraced notoriety nudged him toward assuming the role of an apologist for new music. He wanted to be noticed. Increasingly he delighted in confronting the inviolability of existing paradigms—a trait that would characterize the remainder of his long career. But his was not vacuous grandstanding calculated to be different for difference's sake. As he approached thirty, Stravinsky was brimming with self-assurance, even hubris. Moreover, he knew exactly what he was provoking, and he relished the apostasy of which others accused him. The composer's voice was that of a young artist, even an angry artist, staking out his own poetic claim. *The Rite* was every bit as exhibitionistic as the nude photographs he had made of himself around this time and sent to friends. Diaghilev grew convinced that the new ballet's shattering of all that had come before was worth the risk. "In retrospect the preparations for *Le Sacre* have an almost conspiratorial air," suggests Eksteins. "By 1913 Stravinsky was caught up in his own importance, and with *Le Sacre* he had every intention of setting the musical and ballet world on its ear." Many came away suggesting that Diaghilev was obsessed with the idea of the mayhem the work would incite. Lieven (quite aware of earlier incidents the entrepreneur had shrewdly instigated) conjectures with good reason that "Diaghilev had a faculty for creating scandals. . . . In an atmosphere of uproar he knew better than anyone how to emerge with credit."[12]

Stravinsky remembered dreaming of a new ballet during the spring of 1910, just as he was completing *The Firebird*:

One day, when I was finishing the last pages of *L'Oiseau de feu* in St. Petersburg, I had a fleeting vision which came to me as a complete surprise, my mind at the moment being full of other things. I saw in imagination a solemn pagan rite: sage elders, seated in a circle, watched a young girl dance herself to death. They were sacrificing her to propitiate the god of spring. Such was the theme of the *Sacre du Printemps*.[13]

Whether or not Stravinsky's musings were actually so comprehensive, the emphasis on the critical element of dance rings true. The story would center upon a sacrifice to the Slavic deity Yarilo, known in many mythologies both pagan and Christian. He was associated with the fertility of the earth arising each spring, from seed, to vegetation, to harvest, and the sacrifice itself was intended to propitiate him. Homage to Yarilo was thus a fertility rite, a bestowal intended as a ritualistic *quid pro quo* wherein the sacrifice of a virgin, the ultimate oblation, would appease the gods, thus winning their favor and providing for the earth's own fruitfulness.[14] Folk festivals held in the pagan god's honor were staged annually in Russia. How much Stravinsky truly dwelled on his "fleeting vision" over the next two years is unknown. But surely this "solemn pagan rite" simmered in his mind even as he worked on his first two ballets.

Stravinsky confided to André Schaeffner that it was the vision of the dance itself rather than any thoughts about the accompanying music that was clearest in his mind—a confession worth noting in ascertaining how theatrically Stravinsky first envisaged the work as a "choreodrama," to use his own term. And in a letter to Nikolai Findeizen of December 1912, by which time rehearsals were underway, Stravinsky remarked, "The whole thing must be staged in dance from beginning to end. I give not one single bar for pantomime. Nijinsky directs it with passionate zeal and with complete self-effacement."[15] Moreover, as hazy as it may have been, the composer's vision revolved around a dance of terror as the ballet's climactic scene. It would take shape as the "Sacrificial Dance," wherein the young maiden, the "Chosen One" as she was seen, literally dances herself to death. The notion of portraying a communal murder on stage would strike many as heinous and vulgar, especially in a choreography that reveals a helpless, quivering young girl forced to submit to this pre-ordained ordeal. It was an unspeakable act, and within the unlikely context of ballet, simultaneously magnetic and abhorrent.[16]

After the 1911 Paris season, Diaghilev moved his troupe to London, as usual; but he would not stage either of Stravinsky's recently acclaimed ballets there, given the conservatism of English tastes. Consequently, Stravinsky soon returned to Russia, where he was reunited with his young family. He ensconced himself in Ustilug during the summer months, with the purpose of pursuing at long last the ritualistic ballet that had appeared in his dream. Other projects intervened, however, as did an increasing involvement in family life. In July he wrote a few short songs setting the poetry of the Russian symbolist Konstantin Balmont. A slightly more ambitious cantata for male choir and orchestra followed, entitled *Zvezdoliki* (The King of the Stars), also to a Balmont text and dedicated to Debussy, whose influence on Stravinsky was already evident. It was time well spent; these little-known vocal works may have paid dividends in fleshing out a suitable scenario for the new ballet.[17]

Stravinsky needed a knowledgeable, sympathetic collaborator. He was committed to staging an accurate replication of prehistoric rituals upon which he could build music, dance, costumes, and scenery. Soon after dreaming of his pagan ballet in 1910 he contacted Nicholas Roerich. Given the ambitious scope of *The Rite*, Roerich's role in the work's evolution would be crucial. From the outset the composer understood that he must rely upon the scholar's expertise in archeology and Slavic mythology. "Who else could help?" Stravinsky wrote to Nikolai Findeizen. "Who else knows the secret of our ancestors' close feeling to the earth?"[18] Roerich's Slavophile devotion to ethnography and in particular his knowledge of anthropology and archeology proved critical in anchoring *The Rite*'s ritualistic content. As a child, Roerich had come to know Glinka's operas, which he had often seen at the Maryinsky. Even more relevantly, he had become thoroughly familiar with and devoted to Slavic history, especially as a result of his own expeditions and digs. "He was absorbed in the rituals of Neolithic Russia, which he idealized as a pantheistic realm of spiritual beauty where life and art were one, and man and nature lived in harmony," writes Figes.[19]

Roerich's scholarship complemented his literacy, as well as his education as a painter. It was a resource that served him well when he came to work on a series of paintings addressing an array of Russian subjects. Many were stunning in their starkness and detachment, winning the admiration of the *Mir iskusstva* circle. His painting *The Idols* (1901), for example, clearly presages the bleakness of the scenery he would envision for Stravinsky's *Rite* over a decade later. Indeed, the Scythian look of his costumes for Stravinsky's ballet, together with Nijinsky's choreography, was in no small part responsible for the commotion the ballet caused.

Diaghilev initially scoffed at Roerich's involvement (as he often scoffed at collaborators suggested by Stravinsky). He had commissioned Roerich to prepare the designs for some of the Polovtsian Dances from Borodin's *Prince Igor* during the Ballets Russes' Paris season of 1909, designs which had in fact met with great success. Evidently Stravinsky was not the only person thinking

of a ritual ballet. In early 1909—thereby predating the composer's dream—
Roerich had shared his thoughts of "a scene of Stone Age Life" as a possible
scenario. He wrote of the celebration "of a springtime sun," of "whole trimmed
furs [and] floral garlands," of "hides . . . drying on kilns: bear, wolf, lynx, vixen,"
and of "beautifully decorated footwear and of skins."[20] In an interview in the
St. Petersburg Gazette of August 28, 1910, Roerich fully described the story for
a ballet he entitled "Supreme Sacrifice": "The new ballet will depict several
scenes of a sacred night of the ancient Slavs. At the start of the ballet it is a
summer night, and it ends with the sunrise, with the first rays of the sun. Strictly
speaking, the choreographic part comprises the ritual dances. This will be the
first attempt to reproduce antiquity without any explicit story."[21]

The composer first wrote to Roerich on June 19, 1910, conceding that for
better or worse they would need to enfold Diaghilev in their discussions. A
huffish Stravinsky already raises the question of a choreographer, grumbling that
while Diaghilev wished to engage Fokine, both he and Roerich should have been
consulted before Fokine was approached.[22] Stravinsky moved forward with
preliminary sketches, such that by August he was inquiring about Roerich's own
progress. Even though *Petrouchka* would soon absorb his energies, thoughts for
The Rite continued to percolate. What is clear, therefore, is that Stravinsky made
considerable headway in at least conceiving the scenario together with Roerich,
as well as roughing out preliminary compositional ideas, long before Diaghilev
approached him about *Petrouchka* in the fall of 1910.

Upon returning to Ustilug in the summer of 1911, Stravinsky made plans to
visit Roerich in July, intending to settle the entire scenario for the new ballet.
Writing on July 15, he cautioned Roerich, "It is imperative that we see each
other and decide about every detail—especially every question of staging—
concerning our 'child.' " The composer traveled to Talashkino where Roerich
was completing a project for his patron princess Tenisheva, an early supporter
of Diaghilev's *Mir iskusstva* initiatives. On the Talashkino estate, where she
housed an impressive archive of peasant handicrafts and folk art, designers were
encouraged to explore new directions. In essence, her home was a cultural
hothouse, and Roerich and Stravinsky surely breathed in the rarefied air. They
made decisions that would help guide their work over the next two years in
identifying suitable dances, designs, and the outlines of a rough libretto. Over
late summer and fall, Stravinsky and Diaghilev agreed the specifics of the
commission, and the composer finally began writing the music for the ballet in
earnest. Six months later, in March 1912, Stravinsky reported to Roerich that
he had not only composed and orchestrated the first part of the new ballet, but
was already working on the second tableau. Later that same month, Stravinsky

informed Benois that *The Rite* could not be produced that spring; rather, it would have to wait until the following year.

Although the composer had made significant strides, the postponement was fortuitous, allowing additional time to complete the massive project. More importantly, the delay permitted the Ballets Russes to come to grips with its most ambitious undertaking to date. Meanwhile, Stravinsky willingly previewed the score for those wishing to listen. By April 1912 he was eager to share his progress with Diaghilev and Monteux. They met in a rehearsal room in Monte Carlo, where Stravinsky was attending rehearsals of his first two ballets. Monteux's description captures the "ruthless impetuosity" with which Stravinsky rendered the score at the keyboard as he performed the first part of the ballet:

> Stravinsky sat down to play a piano reduction. . . . Before he got very far I was convinced he was raving mad. Heard this way, without the color of the orchestra, which is one of its greatest distinctions, the crudity of the rhythm was emphasized, its stark primitiveness underlined. The very walls resounded as Stravinsky pounded away, occasionally stamping his feet and jumping up and down to accentuate the force of the music. Not that it needed much emphasis. I was more astounded by Stravinsky's perform-ance than shocked by the score itself. My only comment at the end was that such music would surely cause a scandal.[23]

A few months later, in June, the composer read the four-hand piano score with Debussy at the country house of Debussy's friend the critic and scholar Louis Laloy. In a subsequent letter to Stravinsky, Debussy commented, "I still think of our performance of your *Le Sacre du printemps* at Laloy's house . . . It haunts me like a beautiful nightmare [*un beau cauchemar*] and I try, in vain, to recall the terrifying impression it made. That is why I wait for the performance like a greedy child who's been promised some jam."[24]

In August the composer played the score again for Diaghilev, Benois, and Nijinsky in Lugano. In his *Reminiscences*, Benois describes the famous encounter, wherein the composer previewed excerpts from the evolving ballet: "It was *Sacre du printemps*, a 'primitive' ballet, with no romantic subject, but devoted to the evocation on the stage of certain rituals of the pagan Slavs." Tellingly, Benois adds,

> The original idea was probably Roerich's; if, in fact, it came first to Stravinsky it must have been due to the influence of his painter friend. Roerich was utterly absorbed in dreams of prehistoric, patriarchal and religious life—of

the days when the vast, limitless plains of Russia and the shores of her lakes and rivers were peopled with the forefathers of the present inhabitants. Roerich's mystic, spiritual experiences made him strangely susceptible to the charm of this ancient world. He felt in it something primordial and weird, something that was intimately linked with nature.

Benois further suggests that since there were no precedents, Stravinsky was free to create a completely new aural imagery, giving him "free scope in search for unusual rhythms and sounds." The sheer rawness of the ballet, its guttural shrieks, intrigued Diaghilev. It fully satisfied the entrepreneur's own "barbarian instincts," Benois observed, in preparing a ballet that would present "a magnificent opportunity for 'shattering' the Parisian audience."[25]

In December Stravinsky corresponded with Roerich, who had sent sketches of his costumes for Stravinsky's approval. The composer readily endorsed the designer's conceptions. Writing to Findeizen on December 15, the composer outlined the scenario that had by now been adopted by the designer as well.[26] Years later, in his conversations with Robert Craft, the composer provided his own rather detailed chronology with regard to how the composition unfolded. He completed most of the work in Switzerland in "a *pension* in Clarens." He began with the famous chord of the "Augurs of spring," first played for Diaghilev in Venice, and finished the first part of the ballet from that point forward, later returning to compose the "Prelude." He composed the second part strictly in order. The scenario outlined in late 1912 underwent a process of evolution over the next sixteen months. A few weeks before the premiere, Stravinsky summarized the essence of the scenario in *Le Figaro*: "*The Rite of Spring* is a musical choreographic work. It represents pagan Russia and is unified by a single idea: the mystery and great surge of the creative power of spring. The piece has no plot." There followed a synopsis of the action:

First Part: The Kiss of the Earth. The spring celebration . . . The piper's pipe and young men tell fortunes. The old woman enters. She knows the mystery of nature and how to predict the future. Young girls with painted faces come in from the river in single file. They dance the spring dance. Games start . . . The people divide into two groups, opposing each other. The holy procession of the wise old men. The oldest and wisest interrupts the spring games, which come to a stop. The people pause trembling . . . The old men bless the spring earth . . . The people dance passionately on the earth, sanctifying it and becoming one with it.

Second Part: The Great Sacrifice. All night the virgins hold mysterious games, walking in circles. One of the virgins is consecrated as the victim and is twice pointed to by fate, being caught twice in the perpetual dance. The virgins honor her, the chosen one, with a marital dance. They invoke the ancestors and entrust the chosen one to the old wise men. She sacrifices herself in the presence of the old men to the great holy dance, the great sacrifice.[27]

Stravinsky later stressed the almost trance-like state in which he claimed the score had been created. He actively promoted the fiction that his breakthrough composition was neither based on any compositional methodology, nor influenced by any historical model. *The Rite* was a gift, divinely bestowed upon him. He depicted himself as a willing medium, faithfully transcribing what was channeled to him by a greater mystical power. "I was guided by no system whatever," he remarked, adding with purpose aforethought that *The Rite* was nothing like the intellectually plotted "theoretical" music of Berg, Webern, and Schoenberg. "Very little immediate tradition lies behind *Le Sacre du printemps*," he proclaimed. "I had only my ear to help me. I heard and I wrote what I heard. I am the vessel through which *Le Sacre* passed."[28] Beguiling as this is, a trail of extant primary sources tells quite a different story.

As his numerous sketchbooks and drafts reveal, the composer worked consciously and carefully in matching the sound he heard with the vision he saw. Nor should the two be separated. Too often exegetic theories—some informative, others self-indulgent—purporting to find the elusive Rosetta stone that unlocks the work's deeply embedded coherence have come at the expense of *The Rite*'s fundamental theater, as well as its physicality. The ballet's surviving sketches furnish a valuable record of the work's evolution; but it is only a partial record.[29] What of the innumerable pre-notational experiments improvised at the keyboard? Doubtlessly the composer experimented with any number of rough ideas, then quickly amended several in rapid succession as his ear weighed what might or might not provide fertile materials for the compositional process to follow. After all, why would Stravinsky—ever the disciple of frugality—take the time to notate ideas that lacked potential utility?

In his early commentaries, and indeed in his later conversations with Robert Craft, the composer spoke about nothing as often and as definitively as he did about this trial-and-error process. Tactility, more than abstraction, served as the catalyst in determining the vocabulary he would employ. "I think it is a thousand times better to compose in direct contact with the physical medium of sound than to work in the abstract medium produced by one's imagination," he wrote in his chronicle. In the case of *The Rite*, at least, that physical medium was the keyboard, "the fulcrum of all my musical discoveries." Moreover, he continued, "Each note that I write is tried on it, and every relationship of notes is taken apart and heard on it again and again."[30] It was through these unrecorded empirical tryouts that his ear discovered ideas as translated through his fingers. Make no mistake: this was the metaphorical "vessel" through which *The Rite* passed. There is an uninhibited earthiness to the score that was literally beaten out of the piano. Several eyewitness descriptions of the unbridled passion with which Stravinsky literally banged away at the piano ring true. Moreover, as one examines the available sketches, one easily discerns the feverish pace at which Stravinsky sometimes sketched out ideas, as quickly as his hand would allow, no doubt rapidly moving from hitting upon something at the keyboard to getting it down on paper. His calligraphy occasionally rivals the scrawls of a Beethoven sketch, although more often the sketches suggest a slower-paced method of work.

The profusion of keyboard figurations evident in *Petrouchka* was to be expected, given the ballet's pianistic genesis. But many of the fundamental constructions of *The Rite* similarly derive, literally, from the shape of Stravinsky's hand. One immediately thinks of the similarities between the black/white juxtaposition of chords in the second tableau of *Petrouchka*, perhaps the work's most identifiable sonority, and the equally famous "Augurs" insignia chord initiating the "Dance of the Young Girls," where a major chord is assigned to the left hand and an inverted dominant-seventh chord is assigned to the right. Both passages, as so many analysts have remarked, are traceable to an octatonic wellspring; yet viscerally octatonicism has little to do with the powerful emotional impact produced by the juxtaposition of two stable sonorities brought into conflict.[31]

As the composer's sketchbook reveals, it was the deployment of such chords, the textural setting of his ideas, that occupied Stravinsky far more than the determination of pitch. In both *Petrouchka* and *The Rite*, the built-in clash of these progenitor chords (noting that *The Rite*'s pre-curtain "Introduction" was written at the end rather than the beginning of the compositional process) was built upon the most simple, consonant triadic configurations. It was their conflation at the most dissonant intervals of a tritone in *Petrouchka* and a semitone in *The Rite* that intensified the drama of the moment. Indeed the dissonance of so many Stravinskyan moments is most often the dynamic consequence of these "vertical coagulations," as Boulez describes them, which bring stabilities into direct, purposely crude conflict.[32] But it is more than that: *The Rite*'s landscape is marked by constant textural shifts, as opposed to the more continuous, more organically structured *Petrouchka*. Quite intentionally, Nijinsky's choreography would physically stress the difference. As Kirstein summarizes, "It was more in the separate uses of all musical elements—rhythm, harmony, melody—in their disjunction—that lay the novelty of *Sacre*. Nijinsky chose deliberately to accentuate the rhythmic pattern in its disparateness above any other interpretive idea."[33]

The composition's pianistic roots—as awkwardly laid out as they often are—are apparent in the four-hand version read by Debussy and Stravinsky. The very first page of the sketchbook, for example, presents the material for the "Augurs of Spring." Perhaps most revealing is Stravinsky's notation of the celebrated sonority itself, notated only once and followed by eight measures in which the composer notates only eighth-note stems with accents—a clear indication of his intent to emphasize a texturally and harmonically distinctive idea complete in itself, rather than to develop it into something else (Figure 3). If any one moment in the entire ballet captures the essence of its incisiveness, its hypnotic nature wherein a Scythian stasis simultaneously generates a relentless animation, it is the pulverizing power of this single, cornerstone chord.[34]

Stravinsky seldom committed an idea to manuscript without eventually employing it at some point in the score. Throughout his compositional archives, in fact, it is clear that the composer never squandered ideas. It was simply a matter of determining the best location for their use.[35] For instance, the principal idea for the "Ritual Action of the Ancestors" is initially notated among the sketches for the much earlier "Mystic Circles of the Young Girls." And just so, the basic ideas for that section find precedent among the sketches for the still earlier "Dance of the Earth"—sketches that begin with an inscription by Stravinsky proclaiming that "music exists when there is rhythm, as life exists when there is a pulse" (as appropriate a description as one will find of the work's elemental power in depicting the seasonal process of growth and decay, of life and death).

The music of these three sections could not be more different, and the composer's transformation of the material to fit his needs at a moment of the dramatic action for which it was not originally envisioned is remarkable.

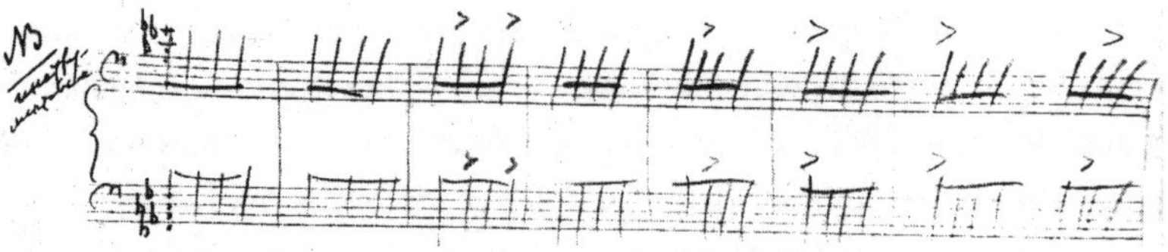

Figure 3 *The Rite of Spring*, sketch for the "Augurs" chord.

Moreover, between the composition of the "Mystic Circles" and that of the "Ritual Action" Stravinsky changed his mind about the orchestration. The haunting English horn melody that begins in m. 3 of the "Ritual Action" was first sketched for bassoon—one of numerous coloristic alterations made by the composer. Indeed, despite Stravinsky's claims that the particular color of a sonority came to him fully formed, compositional sketches throughout the archives constantly reveal his rethinking of orchestral assignments. Other sketch materials suggest that Stravinsky initially chose to conclude the ballet at the end of the "Ritual Action," with its descending bass clarinet solo that gradually deflates all of the energy accumulated up to that point. The composer clearly marks this "The End." But could this really have been his intent? Or did he rethink the dramatic let-down this would entail, ultimately opting for the maniacally asymmetrical rhythms of the "Sacrificial Dance?"[36]

The composer frequently reordered small chunks of material, even single measures—independent rhythmic entities, really—in creating longer, more electrically charged sequences (Figure 4). In the "Sacrificial Dance" much of the music beginning at m. 202 is based upon his shifting of six such units labeled in the sketches with the letters A through F (Figure 5). At one point, the rotation of these measures is marked abstractly without re-notating the music (why take the time to write it out again?) by simply specifying: "A B C D F A B D E." Here and elsewhere the sketches were doubtlessly notated in the heat of the moment, as the composer attempted to get his thoughts on paper before they escaped him. Moreover, red and blue pencil markings, arrows, "Nota Bene" cautions,

Figure 4 *The Rite of Spring,* "Sacrificial Dance," sketch showing discrete compositional blocks.

Figure 5 *The Rite of Spring,* "Sacrificial Dance," sketch showing the ordering of compositional blocks by letter.

directions as to where something should be inserted, transposed, or relocated down or up an octave—all of these stipulations provide a running commentary throughout the sketches. Once more, such markings are hardly uncommon in the composer's drafts, especially in many of the ballets, including *Apollo, Jeu de cartes,* and *Orpheus,* where similar directives provide a revealing road-map of the composer's thinking.

Finally, the sketchbook, like various other primary sources, puts to rest the fiction that *The Rite* is virtually free from pre-existing folk songs, with the exception of the opening bassoon solo, which is drawn from a Lithuanian anthology. If there are moments in the score that remind listeners of "aboriginal folk music," Stravinsky suggested, it was probably because his "powers of fabrication were able to tap some unconscious 'folk' memory."[37] As for *The Rite* specifically, given both his and Roerich's determination to create a work that would be as ethnographically authentic as possible, we might have guessed that the composer would have turned to such models as a starting point. Yet historians had to wait until after Stravinsky's death for Lawrence Morton to produce hard evidence that the composer had indeed begun the ballet with several folk tunes cribbed from the same Lithuanian anthology, to which Stravinsky had given only a passing nod. With the door now opened, Richard Taruskin pursued Morton's discovery in earnest, demonstrating just how thoroughgoing the composer's reliance upon both this collection and others had been.[38] While these melodies may serve as the work's substratum, however, Stravinsky's invocation of these simple folk tunes surpasses mere quotation or superficial alteration (as in *The Firebird* and *Petrouchka* respectively), often entailing a transmogrification beyond the point of recognition.

Whatever the fabrications about *The Rite*'s musical origins, the composition's dance element must be factored into any equation calculating the work's original artistic genesis as well as its historical impact. Stravinsky's on-again-off-again dismissal of the work as a ballet in favor of its performance as a symphonic work was characteristically self-serving.[39] The twenty-five-year-old Nijinsky was blamed for the ballet's failure. Yet during the arduous rehearsals (one hundred of them in all) Stravinsky generously praised the choreographer, as attested by his aforementioned letter to Findeizen of December 1912. Only a few days after the infamous premiere, Stravinsky rebuffed Nijinsky's critics, asserting that he and the choreographer had "never failed to be in absolute communion of thought" in producing a *Rite* that was absolutely "fruitful." A month after the first performance Stravinsky wrote to Rimsky's relative Maximilien Steinberg, "Nijinsky's choreography is incomparable and, with a few exceptions, everything was as I wanted."[40] Even four years later, by which time the choreography had long been abandoned, Stravinsky still volunteered, "The dance that had been evolved was the most perfectly beautiful."[41] But by 1936 Stravinsky's chronicle was complaining of the choreographer's ineptitude in setting the "Sacrificial Dance," claiming that "Nijinsky was incapable of giving intelligible form to its essence, and complicated it either by clumsiness or by lack of understanding," adding that he had "never known any [choreographer] who erred in that respect to the same degree as Nijinsky."[42]

At the heart of the composer's criticism was Nijinsky's lack of musical training. By the time Stravinsky answered Craft's questions about the choreographer in the late 1950s, his position had hardened. The composer asserted that Nijinsky understood neither meter nor tempo—a deadly ignorance in dealing with the ballet's "last dance where poor Mlle Piltz, the sacrificial maiden, was not even aware of the changing bars." Further, according to Stravinsky, Nijinsky misapprehended the ideas for the "Dance of the Young Girls," where the composer had "imagined a row of almost motionless dancers. Nijinsky made of this piece a big jumping match."[43] From the very start, Stravinsky vehemently opposed Nijinsky's inclination to visualize the score's many ostinato patterns and asymmetrical accents too mechanically. The counterpoint of sound and physical motion that Stravinsky sought went unrealized. As an observant Jean Cocteau remarked, "The defect was in the parallelism of the music and the movement, in their lack of *play*, of counterpoint. We were given proof that the same chord often repeated is less tiring to the ear than is the frequent repetition of a single gesture to the eye. The laughter came more from a monotony of automata than from the violation of posture, and more from the violation of posture than from polyphony."[44]

Vaslav Nijinsky's prodigious gifts as Diaghilev's star dancer (or "show pony," as some detractors quipped) represented the most public aspect of his role in the Ballets Russes. But long before he danced his signature role of Petrouchka, he was, according to his sister's memoirs, quite familiar with and supportive of *Mir iskusstva*'s mission, often attending meetings of the artists who constituted Diaghilev's inner circle. As his reputation as a dancer grew, so too did his desire to choreograph. By the spring of 1912, even as Stravinsky was completing the meat of his work on *The Rite* in Switzerland, Nijinsky's first important ballet, Debussy's *L'Après-midi d'un faune*, was being rehearsed in Monte Carlo. *L'Après-midi* would prove to be a crossroads in ballet history, the first genuine break with classical tradition in four hundred years, writes Kirstein.[45] Fokine's tenure with the Ballets Russes went unchallenged from 1909 to 1912, as he produced an astonishing series of successful ballets; but in 1912, Diaghilev unceremoniously pushed him away, as he sought more innovative statements consonant with the developing precepts of modernism. Diaghilev's choice of Nijinsky for *L'Après-midi* would be the last straw. Stravinsky had understood from the start that Fokine, naturally, would choreograph *The Rite*. As early as the spring of 1910, the composer had met with both Fokine and Roerich to discuss the scenario. Two years later, with Fokine still on board, Stravinsky expressed his continuing reservations in a letter to his mother, referring to the choreographer as an "exhausted artist . . . who writes himself out with each new work . . . New forms must be created, and the evil, the gifted, the greedy Fokine has not even dreamed of them . . . There is no salvation in *habileté*. Genius is needed, not *habileté*."[46] Nonetheless, as late as May 1912 Fokine was still prepared to undertake the choreography. All of that was soon to change.

Nijinsky attended the meetings of Diaghilev's inner sanctum as "The Great Sacrifice" took shape. One can appreciate his attraction to the subject, especially given his instinctive taste for its raw, primitive nature. (Referring to *The Rite* in a letter to the *Daily Mail* in 1913 the choreographer remarked, "I like to eat my meat without sauce Béarnaise.") Although eager to promote Nijinsky as a choreographer, Diaghilev knew that *The Rite* would present the most complex musical problems imaginable. The inexperienced Nijinsky would need help. As the 1913 premiere approached, both Diaghilev's and Stravinsky's misgivings grew. Because the troupe was constantly on the move, Nijinsky was forced to piece together the new choreography whenever and wherever he could: Vienna, Budapest, London, Monte Carlo, and finally Paris. In November 1912, the troupe visited the studios of Émile Jaques-Dalcroze in Hellerau near Dresden. Diaghilev knew of Dalcroze's new techniques as promoted in St. Petersburg a year earlier. Dalcroze, the "inventor" of eurhythmics, might provide Nijinsky with a concrete method by which to instruct his dancers in Stravinsky's asymmetrical rhythmic groupings.

Diaghilev contracted one of Dalcroze's finest instructors, Marie Rambert (quickly nicknamed "Rhythmitchka"). Joining the Ballets Russes, she first worked on the Debussy–Nijinsky *Jeux* (which was not without its own rhythmic hurdles), while also assisting Nijinsky with *The Rite*.[47] Loathing the work immediately, the dancers were slow to respond. "They wanted to show off their beauty and the grace of their arms and legs," Rambert recalled. Of course such elegance countered the overt coarseness Stravinsky desired. Nijinsky had unnecessarily complicated the music by methodically assigning specific movements to virtually every articulated beat. Given the ever-shifting meters and rhythmic complexity of the score, the task of dancing each individual event was overwhelming. Lydia Sokolova (who would dance the role of the Chosen One in the 1920 Massine production) remembers that in the Nijinsky original, "some of the girls used to be running around with little bits of paper in their hands, in a panic, quarrelling with each other about whose count was right and wrong." Nor was the sheer physicality of the very un-balletic, flat-on-one's-feet stomping with repetitive jumps easy to absorb. "Jumps were no longer completed on toes with slightly flexed knees, but flat-footed and straight-legged in a fashion to preclude the possibility of lightness, and to convey an impression of antediluvian festivity that nearly killed us. With every leap we landed heavily enough to jar every organ in us," wrote Anatole Bourman of the rehearsals. "Our heads throbbed with pain, leaving us continually with nerves jangled and bodies that ached."[48] Nijinsky left no room for anything remotely approaching interpretation. He proceeded with the precision of a general, first mapping out virtually every beat of the music, and then instructing his *corps de ballet* troops to execute his directions exactly.

Moreover, Rambert was forced to transfer to the female body a physiology of dance designed for a male. What might have been natural for Nijinsky, especially given his gifts of elasticity and powerful springs, became awkward for other males, let alone females. But no matter; the choreographer was determined to contest long-held assumptions, including how dance for both men and women should be conceived. Just as Stravinsky's music confronted the fundamental concepts of rhythmic symmetry and motivic development, so too Nijinsky defied the sacrosanct principles of classical dance. Movements were downwardly oriented rather than upwardly—as more traditionally found in ballet's customary efforts to escape the force of gravity. Gestures were compressed rather than stretched. Knees and feet turned in upon themselves. Virtually the entire body closed in rather than opened up. With *The Rite*, Nijinsky tore apart the venerated principles of nineteenth-century dance vocabulary, leaving any sense of its traditional balletic elegance in tatters.

Given the immense difficulty of the score, as well as the notably slow pace at which Nijinsky choreographed the individual sections of the ballet, Diaghilev pushed Stravinsky to assist with the preparations. A telegram from Munich in November 1912: "Have you finished *Sacre*? Can you come to Berlin again November 20?" Another from Berlin on December 18: "Rehearsals have not yet begun. We do not have the designs. No need for pianola arrangement." Then a third cable dated January 2, 1913, from Budapest: "If you do not come here immediately for fifteen days *Sacre* will not be given."[49] By then, Rambert had joined the company as an instructor. Moreover, she also joined the *corps de ballet*, mainly, she recalls, to maintain order by keeping count for the other dancers. Perhaps as importantly, Rambert is remembered by many of the dancers as a calming force at the eye of the storm, mediating heated arguments between composer and choreographer. Stravinsky frequently attended rehearsals; and he expressed his views adamantly, having envisioned the dancing with such precision. His four-hand piano arrangement (lost for many years and rediscovered in 1967), records the specificity of the composer's intent. "Every mark in the score is in my own hand," Stravinsky comments in notes appended to the score, "and this account of the choreography supersedes all others." An example may be found toward the end of the "Sacrificial Dance," where Stravinsky writes in the score, "For the next two measures the Chosen One does not dance, according to the blue pencil score. When she resumes [in m. 55] her beat pattern is not the same as the music, nor are her phrase patterns, two measures of 7/8 and one of 6/8, three times repeated."[50]

In the staging of the ballet's complex closing section (which was, in fact, Roerich's first idea in assembling the scenario) Nijinsky's sister was originally cast as the Chosen One. When she became pregnant she was replaced by Maria Piltz, who had worked with Nijinsky in earlier ballets. Nijinska remembers her brother's preparation of the concluding movement: "Vaslav listened attentively to 'Danse Sacrale' repeated several times, then told the pianist to play the whole piece again, indicating that this time he wanted to hear each musical phrase separately. Vaslav would stop the pianist in the middle of a phrase and ask him to play a few measures over and over again, until he had thoroughly comprehended the rhythm."[51] How much Nijinsky could have understood the subtleties of Stravinsky's rhythmic asymmetries is dubious.

Nonetheless, while much of his grumbling about Nijinsky's inadequacies was surely exaggerated, the composer's complaints about the choreographer's inability to understand "the very rudiments of music: values—semibreve, minim, crochet, quaver, etc.—bars, rhythm, tempo, and so on" seem fair enough.[52] "Vaslav and the pianist worked on the music . . . until Vaslav was satisfied that he had assimilated it," Nijinska observed. Perhaps, but not to Stravinsky's satisfaction; for while Stravinsky openly admitted of the whirling conclusion to the ballet, "I could play but I did not at first know how to write [it]" (and attempted to notate its rhythms more clearly throughout much of his life), he knew the sound he wanted. In her colorful interview for Tony Palmer's 1982 film documentary *Once at a Border*, Rambert vividly recalls Stravinsky "jumping up like a mad man." He would brusquely push aside the rehearsal pianist, Maurice Steinman (who had also served as the rehearsal pianist for Debussy and Nijinsky's *L'Après-midi*), demonstrating the tempo he desired as he literally beat the music out of the piano. And in a scene reminiscent of Fokine's complaints about *Petrouchka*, Nijinsky criticized *The Rite*, insisting that the music was impossible to dance at such a feverish pace, while Stravinsky demanded that it had to be danced as he envisioned it. The composer played the closing dance with "frantic speed," banging the rhythms out on the top of the piano, with exasperation, to make his point, Rambert observed.[53]

This was the climatic ritual of abduction by which the maiden was forced to succumb to the tribal will. It was imperative the music be perceived as frenetic. It had to be both played and danced at the brink of madness and despair, as Stravinsky prescribed. Trembling helplessly and terrifyingly, the Chosen One collapses with the music's final measure in a choreographic and musical gasp. This was a dance of death, constituting the ultimate sacrifice. Sally Banes colorfully captures the essence of the historically important "Sacrificial Dance":

As the ancestors close in . . . the Chosen One emerges from her trance and tries to escape. She runs from one side of the circle to another, but there is no way out. She gallops, crouches, trembles, and moves her outstretched arms like a prehistoric bird's powerful wings, ambiguously suggesting both her desire to escape and her aspiration to meet her mate in the heavens. . . . If the earth is female and the heavens male, this suggests a primal struggle between the sexes that mirrors the ritual abduction.[54]

Tensions grew as the performance neared. The extraordinary number of rehearsals demanded of the dancers led to both frustration and physical exhaustion. Most of the rehearsals were held without the orchestra, Steinman—often in tandem with the composer (who had arrived in mid April to direct the rehearsals)—continually making corrections at the keyboard. Moreover, given the density of the orchestration and the idiosyncratic way in which many of the instruments were treated, the dancers faced yet another nearly impossible challenge upon hearing the unusually massive orchestra.[55] Monteux remained undaunted in plowing through a morass of ensemble problems as the orchestra itself struggled. Stravinsky attended the final seventeen orchestra rehearsals, "pointing out little phrases he wanted heard," Monteux remembered. The composer endured the players' initial sarcasm regarding the awkwardness of the parts they were to perform.

The dancers joined the orchestra for only five full rehearsals on the stage of Gabriel Astruc's opulently appointed Théâtre des Champs-Élysées. Opening only a month before the premiere, the architecturally stunning building was an attraction in itself, and controversially so, given its Germanic design. In the two weeks leading up to the premiere of *The Rite*, Diaghilev offered not only the first performance of *Jeux* on the program of the May 15 opening night, but also popular productions that were fast becoming chestnuts: *The Firebird*, *Le Spectre de la rose*, the dances from *Prince Igor*, and *Scheherezade*. The official rehearsal of *The Rite*, the *répétition générale*, was given on the evening of May 28. Intended mainly as a private preview for other artists and for the invited aesthetes of the Parisian beau monde, it was attended by several critics. Their reports appeared in the daily papers the next morning. The highly anticipated premiere, they wrote, promised to be a landmark. *Le Figaro*, for example, published the kind of purple press release one had come to expect. As in so many of Diaghilev's titillating productions, the mostly decorous audience would be treated to the uncultivated ravings of a foreign people. The new ballet would illustrate "the strongly stylized characteristic attitudes of the Slavic race with an awareness of the beauty of the prehistoric period. The prodigious Russian dancers were the only ones capable of expressing these stammerings of a semi-savage humanity, of composing these frenetic human clusters wrenched incessantly by the most astonishing polyrhythm ever to come from the mind of a musician." This final run-through had, by all accounts, gone smoothly enough. Both Stravinsky and Nijinsky seemed pleased and relieved. Although the reception at the May 29 premiere was to some degree unanticipated, Diaghilev seems to have sensed something of the magnitude of the gathering storm. As Grigoriev recalled, the impresario "had misgivings about the reception of Stravinsky's music and warned us that there might be a demonstration against it. He entreated the company of forty-six dancers to keep calm and carry on, and asked Monteux on no account to let the orchestra cease playing. 'Whatever happens,' he said, 'the ballet must be performed to the end.' "[56]

May 29, 1913. Was there ever a more epochal moment in the annals of music history?—or so we have been led to believe. The sum of hyperbolical tabloid reports anecdotally detailing the "riot" that broke out during the premiere may indeed exceed the number of studies devoted to the ballet itself. To say the least, our understanding of what really occurred is blurred. How could it not be? The audience was a prisoner of the moment, and caught in the worst possible position to assimilate what it had witnessed. The program began at 8:45 P.M. with Fokine's *Les Sylphides*—no doubt Diaghilev's attempt to smooth the way for *The Rite*; but in fact programming the works back-to-back seemed to backfire. The comfortable medley of Chopin waltzes, preludes, mazurkas, and nocturnes that underscored Karsavina and Nijinsky's classical dancing of this gossamer *ballet blanc* served less as an emollient than as a reinforcement of the audience's conventional musico-balletic expectations. For those who remained after *The Rite*, the second piece in the program, order was restored following the intermission by *Le Spectre de la rose* and the Polovtsian Dances from *Prince Igor*—crowd-pleasers both, but hardly enough to wash away the bitter taste of Stravinsky and Nijinsky's unruly brainchild. *The Rite* was literally trapped in the middle.

Even before the curtain went up on Roerich's barren, "prehistoric" scenery only a few minutes into the score, the fidgeting began at the sound of Stravinsky's craggy, layered introductory music. The composer had attempted to portray the awakening of spring through accruing levels of sound, one line atop another. This superimposition, creating the illusion of motion, is notably similar in intent to Marcel Duchamp's painting *Nude Descending a Staircase No.2* of 1912. And like Duchamp's controversial portrait, the composer's music met with "derisive laughter," as he later recalled in his chronicle. "I wanted to express . . . nature's terrible fear for the beauty which is rising, a scared terror in the noonday sun, a sort of cry of Pan," Stravinsky is said to have commented in an article published the day of the premiere. "The musical material itself inflates, grows, spreads. Each instrument is like a shoot which grows on the trunk of an ancient tree; it is part of a formidable whole."[57] Yet to ears that only moments earlier had been soaking up Chopin's mellifluous phrases, the discordant opening music felt like an affront.

The audience's agitation quickly escalated as the curtain rose, revealing Roerich's garishly costumed dancers. Such a sight could not have been anything close to what the audience might have anticipated. And to exacerbate their discomfort, the dancers began their relentless jumping to the brutally repetitive "Augurs of Spring." Each one of Stravinsky's accented ostinato chords was driven downward into the stage, like so many implanted stakes, by feet-thumping peasants made to pass as ballet dancers. Rambert remembered that Nijinsky intended the thud of their stamping feet to give the sense of softening the earth so as to make it fertile; but the imagery was lost in the very un-balletic, earth-pounding gesture.[58] Both music and dance, acting as if co-conspirators, unapologetically shoved the mockery of tradition into the faces of an unprepared audience, precipitating their mounting disgruntlement. Choreographic gestures, if one could call them such, were intentionally distorted. The beauty of long white Taglioni dresses—seen only a moment earlier in Sylphides—stood in stark contrast to men draped in bearskins. The dancers, hunched over, shuffling, turned inward, angularly posed, and static, were completely void of any poise or balletic propriety.

The conclusion of the ballet, the "Sacrificial Dance," served as a dénouement to the evening. As André Levinson recalled, Marie Piltz, trembling throughout, just as the composer and choreographer had intended, faced "a hooting audience whose violence completely drowned out the orchestra." She stared trance-like, in a stupor, convulsive spasms obliterating the very tenets of classical dance. Her "primitive hysteria, terribly burlesque as it was, completely caught and over-whelmed the spectator," Levinson observed. The entire ballet was indeed "a crime against grace," and not only for the dancers but for the musicians as well. Instruments screeched in extreme ranges using special effects, leaving the audience hissing. Everything seemed upside down. Fifty years after the premiere, Stravinsky contended that it was not the music that had provoked the outburst so much as what the audience had witnessed on stage: "They came for Scheherezade, they came to see beautiful girls, [but] they saw Le Sacre du printemps, and they were shocked. They were very naïve and very stupid people."[59]

The reviews that appeared immediately after the premiere provided assorted truths, exaggerations, unsubstantiated claims, conflicting memories, and speculation. Some felt the riot had been better orchestrated than the music itself, given that several protestors had arrived at the hall with an agenda in hand. Diaghilev had perhaps gone too far with his salacious recent productions of L'Après-midi; and Jeux. Other adversaries harbored resentment over Fokine's forced resignation.

Vocal demonstrations broke out during the performance, balanced quickly by counter-demonstrations. Aesthetes voiced their disgust, while supporters shouted charges of philistinism. Stravinsky left the auditorium to stand next to Nijinsky, who according to the composer barked out the counting for the dancers from backstage, although Grigoriev recalled that "Nijinsky stood silent in the wings." Grigoriev further remembered that Diaghilev ordered the lights turned on and off in a futile attempt to help the police to disperse the warring factions though there is nothing to substantiate the involvement of the local gendarmes. Monteux persevered, as did the dancers, bulldozing ahead against the tide of catcalls hurled against them. Nijinsky claimed it was Stravinsky's cacophonous score that had incited the uprising, while Grigoriev, Rambert, and others maintained that the music had been barely audible amidst the chaos. Stravinsky argued that Nijinsky's choreography had triggered the disruption. Whatever the case, when all was played and danced, Diaghilev achieved precisely the splash he desired. More objective accounts were provided by composers such as Debussy and Ravel, dancers such as Nijinska and Rambert, and other artists such as Valentine Gross-Hugo, who sketched the dancers' poses on Stravinsky's score as a way of capturing Nijinsky's choreography.[60]

Years after the fervor subsided, Cocteau provided a more dispassionate commentary upon the scandal, attributing it to the inevitable conflict of "pitting a work of youth and force against a decadent audience" whose "super snobbism" was evident from the start. His account includes considerable detail regarding the strengths and weaknesses of Nijinsky's choreography, Roerich's costumes and sets, and Stravinsky's score—a score of "indispensable dynamite." Cocteau goes on to describe Stravinsky's *fauve* work as "a symphony impregnated with savage pathos" that produced a masterpiece caught in the "petty schisms and narrow formulas" that were then resisting the dawn of modernism; and Nijinsky as an artist willing to "reject grace, having known too well its triumph."[61]

In the end, history has accorded far too much weight to the scandal surrounding the premiere. Diaghilev was in the business of crossing thresholds and provoking reactions. The greater the controversy, the better his cause was served. What may have been lost amidst the hullabaloo was an uncompromising musico-choreographic assault upon the fossilized traditions of both arts. *The Rite* sounded a cry of emancipation intent on establishing new territory for those willing to accept the audacity of a genuine cultural sea change. The Parisian upper crust in attendance that opening night got what they bargained for: an inflammatory, sublimely unintelligible desecration to fuss over in chic conversation. Many walked away dazed by the incursion of sounds and sights upon their senses. They were offended, just as they were supposed to be. But for those who understood the implications of what they heard and saw, there was a piercing awareness that the Rubicon had been crossed. Nothing would ever be quite the same.

Only a few more performances were given in Paris after the premiere, and these were without incident. *The Rite* then moved on to London, where it was staged three times in July as part of the Ballets Russes season. It was performed as Stravinsky and Nijinsky had composed and choreographed it, although Diaghilev had briefly considered making cuts, perhaps to avoid another public skirmish. In the end, not only was the complete ballet performed without the outbursts that had greeted it Paris, but it even garnered a modicum of understanding.[62] Soon thereafter Diaghilev dismissed Nijinsky from the company. With his departure the original choreography would be lost; but the ballet's impact remained undiminished.

Word of the Paris premiere soon reached Russia. There were a few reports in the press, mostly focusing on Nijinsky's achievement rather than Stravinsky's score.[63] For the most part, however, the work slipped into dormancy during the war years. A new production would resurface in 1920 when Diaghilev asked Léonide Massine to prepare fresh choreography. Unsurprisingly, given his scholarly bent, Massine studied the work's ethnographic roots, consulting with Stravinsky often. The composer, having long abandoned any allegiance to Nijinsky's setting, praised Massine (who had never seen Nijinsky's version) for treating the music as an autonomous object, rather than as a score in need of narrative associations. Massine had freed himself from the strictures Nijinsky had brought to the choreography, the composer publicly noted. He had moved beyond "the tyranny of the bar line," which had dominated Nijinsky's approach.[64] Sokolova now danced the role of the Chosen One. The premiere of December 15, 1920, was given in the same theatre as the premiere of 1913, the Théâtre des Champs-Élysées, but this time the audience greeted the work with uninhibited enthusiasm. The reaction of critics, however, was mixed, some lamenting the loss of the primitivism of Nijinsky's original. Massine's successful revival nevertheless moved in and out of the Ballets Russes' repertoire for most of the 1920s. While Stravinsky still preferred to regard the score as a concert piece, Massine's version carried his imprimatur. *The Rite* traveled throughout Europe until Diaghilev's death in 1929. In 1930 it arrived in America, where it was staged in both Philadelphia and New York with Martha Graham in the role of the Chosen One.

Indeed 1930 marked the beginning of a profusion of new choreographic versions of Stravinsky's score. Because of the power of the music and its inherent challenges, *The Rite* became a crucible in which contemporary choreographers could test their mettle. There were well over one hundred new productions in the remainder of the twentieth century, and nearly fifty more have appeared since 2000. Among the most notable are Maurice Béjart's erotically evocative 1959 setting that culminated in an explicit mating ritual by a Chosen Couple, first performed in Brussels by the Ballet-Théâtre de Paris (the best *Rite* ever produced, according to Balanchine); Kenneth MacMillan's important 1962 version for the Royal Ballet, with clear connections to African dance; Glen Tetley's stunning treatment in which a Chosen Boy serves as the sacrificial victim, first performed in Munich in 1974; Martha Graham's provocative 1984 version, set not in pagan Russia but in the similarly barren, darkly haunting American Southwest and premiered at the New York State Theater; and more recently a setting by Heddy Maalem, created for his Compagnie Heddy Maalem in 2004 and revived in 2008 in Boston and at Jacob's Pillow. Nearly a century after Nijinsky's original, Maalem's powerful interpretation projects the primitivism of Roerich and Stravinsky's prehistoric conception, although set on a duskily lit stage with the bare-boned bodies of eight males and six females. Maalem's African dance idiom is at once both contemporary and eerily reminiscent of Nijinsky's primordial vision. Paradoxically, the dancers' visual counterpoint to the music may bring it as close to what Stravinsky had in mind, both instinctually and choreographically, as any production since the 1913 premiere.[65]

A historically important reconstruction of the original choreography was assembled in the late 1980s after nearly twenty years of research by dance historian and choreographer Millicent Hodson. First performed in 1987 by the Joffrey Ballet in Los Angeles and New York, the production was itself controversial—hardly surprising, given its attempt to recreate as closely as possible one of the most controversial cornerstones of twentieth-century art—setting off a firestorm of commentaries from dance historians and musicologists alike. Whether or not it is an accurate reconstruction of Nijinsky's lost choreography, Hodson's bold-spirited venture presents as close an approximation to the original as we are likely to see. In that sense it is no more or less historically flawed than the many recordings of *The Rite*, which likewise can never duplicate the performance Monteux conducted that spring evening in Paris.[66]

By August 1914, the world was plunged into a war of apocalyptic proportions, both physically and psychically. Diaghilev scrambled to keep the Ballets Russes afloat, touring constantly throughout Europe and America. Nijinsky would work for the impresario for a few more years, although their relationship would never be the same. From 1919 on, a deepening schizophrenia would force Nijinsky to spend his life in and out of various psychiatric asylums. Roerich traveled to America in 1920, increasingly absorbed by his interests in theosophy and peace studies. He would never again work with Stravinsky. The composer returned to

Ustilug for a brief summer residence, but by the winter had retreated again to Switzerland, where he would live in self-imposed exile for the duration of the war. From a distance he watched his homeland burst apart: the outbreak of the war, the murder of Rasputin, the revolution in Petrograd, the abdication of Nicholas II, and the establishment of the Soviet government. The orchestral score of *The Rite* would not be published until 1921, and those who came to know it did so largely through the release of the four-hand arrangement of 1913. The ballet itself went unperformed during the interim.

A century after its birth, *The Rite of Spring* has lost neither its artistic impact nor its broad historical reach, for it long ago transcended the worlds of music and dance to attain the status of a cultural landmark. More than any other work Stravinsky would create, *The Rite* immediately became a behemoth indissolubly synonymous with his name, to the point of becoming burdensome. Having conjured up such a cataclysm, what else could the thirty-one-year-old composer possibly write? When his 1928 ballet *Apollon musagètes* premiered in Washington, D.C., the audience fully expected a wanton, barbarically "Russian," *Rite*-like experience. As dance critic John Martin wrote wryly in his review, the American public arrived hoping to see a virgin sacrificed. Anything else would be a let-down.

The composer made every attempt to distance himself from the Russian ethnography that had initially sparked his imagination. What had once served as a liberating agent now seemed a strangulation. The ineffaceable images associated with the ballet persisted, from its darkly prehistoric evocation, as animated in Disney's 1940 *Fantasia*, to the physical and psychological ordeals of the Chosen One, as played out through the obsession-sacrifice-redemption drama of Oliver Hermann's 2003 surrealistic film *Le Sacre du printemps: A Silent Movie to the Music of Igor Stravinsky*. Indeed, *The Rite*'s cultural impact has become almost limitless, its music even serving as an intergalactic emissary. The composer's own recording of the "Sacrificial Dance" was loaded aboard NASA's *Voyager* spacecraft, launched in 1977, the only piece of twentieth-century art music to be included among the artifacts chosen to represent the achievements of human beings.[67] On the eve of the twenty-first century, virtually every millennial assessment of the great achievements of the previous one hundred years included Stravinsky's ballet. *BBC Magazine* crowned the work the best-known, most significant, and most influential composition of the twentieth century. Cultural historians spoke of it in the same breath as *Ulysses*, as T. S. Eliot did when he heard *The Rite* for the first time while reading Joyce's novel in 1922.

As we approach the centennial of *The Rite*'s premiere, one wonders if the pendulum has swung too far in an attempt to palliate the composition's imposing crudeness. Has our determination to uncover a unifying coherence become overstrained in explaining away the work's brutish physicality and grit? In cracking the code to its pitch vocabulary, plotting its rhythmic permutations, defending its unidiomatic orchestration, and unearthing its aboriginal folk tunes, have we succeeded in unlocking the secrets of its transformative, unparalleled influence as an iconic masterwork? For all the illuminating discoveries scholars have brought to the table, might we still be too hasty in underestimating Stravinsky's direct reliance, as he insisted, upon his ear as the guiding force in shaping this earth-shattering manifesto of sound? Yes, we have a better sense of the work's syntax—revealing in itself. Still, deciphering the work's overarching dynamism remains a challenge.

In a review of 1913, a critic remarked, "*Le Sacre du printemps* baffles verbal description. To say that much of it is hideous as sound is a mild description. . . . Practically, it has no relation to music at all as most of us understand the word."[68] Indeed, to say that *The Rite* forces us to reconsider what we understand by the word "music" perhaps best captures the work's essence. Stravinsky's ballet obligated its listeners to re-examine their fundamental thinking about musical meaning, just as Nijinsky's choreography obligated them to reconceive the compass of dance. More than anything, the ballet presented a gauntlet. Its demand for a sweeping reassessment of our perceptual limits cut penetratingly to the work's boldly momentous achievement in launching a new artistic order. In that sense alone, *The Rite* seems as compelling now as it did then.

CHAPTER FIVE

A New Approach — A New Collaboration

The Pathway to *Apollo*

WHAT WAS next? Would the notoriety the Ballets Russes had gained in Paris lead Diaghilev to engage Stravinsky for a fourth ballet—perhaps a ballet that would strive to push the envelope even further? Hardly. In the wake of *The Rite*'s impact, the bright light that had bathed Stravinsky over the preceding three years could not help but fade a little. Moreover, the composer had recently contracted typhoid fever, and this only augmented his mental and physical exhaustion. In addition to his personal fatigue, the escalating political tensions that were spreading throughout Europe loomed larger each day. Shortly after *The Rite*'s premiere, the Ballets Russes first moved on to a successful summer season in England, where the company "exchanged the frenzies of Paris for the peace and quiet of London," a relieved Grigoriev remembered.[1] Then on August 15 the troupe set sail from Southampton for Buenos Aires and its South American tour.

In 1914 events worsened, and with Russia's declaration of war on Germany the fortunes of the Ballets Russes darkened. Expectations of a short war, given what was thought to be the unassailable might of the Allies, quickly vanished. Stravinsky found himself hopelessly exiled in Switzerland. What had quickly become a dynamic relationship with the Ballets Russes was now necessarily placed in abeyance. Diaghilev nonetheless managed to scramble through the next two years, intent on keeping his company afloat. On January 1, 1916, the troupe sailed from Bordeaux for New York.[2] Performances in the United States caused a stir; especially works such as *Petrouchka*. Having never heard such odd "Russian" music, audiences were both curious and enthusiastic. An ocean away, Stravinsky struggled to finance his growing family, yet still managed to travel to Paris, London, Berlin, Warsaw, and Rome, where his earlier reputation as the Ballets Russes' star composer helped to enhance his international visibility.

With Diaghilev's company constantly on tour, the composer turned his attention to more modest compositions over the next few years. There were several song collections dedicated to his young children, some pieces for string quartet, a series of piano duets, and other modest projects undertaken in obvious contrast to the titanic *Rite*. Moscow's Free Theater commissioned the completion of his opera *Le Rossignol* (begun even before *The Firebird* had entered his life). Beset by intervening complications, the work was finally premiered in 1914. With little opportunity for performances or new ballet commissions during the war years, the composer returned to his roots, immersing himself in the study of folk music. His ethnographic interests, as well as his heartfelt nostalgia for his motherland, engendered several new compositions: *Pribaoutki* (1914), *Cat's Cradle Songs* (1916), *Renard* (1916), *Four Russian Peasant Songs* (1917), and the profoundly Russian *Les Noces*, a gargantuan work composed over several years during this same period.

At the same time, new interests emerged for the ever curious composer, including his fascination with jazz, especially ragtime. Rooted in the very real need to generate revenue, *L'Histoire du soldat* (1918) opened a new compositional path—one that would lead to a leaner, more "objective" approach, as critics adjudged. Given the clarity of contrapuntal textures and ostensibly unethnic spirit of subsequent works such as the 1923 Octet, the tag of neoclassicism began to attach itself to Stravinsky's compositions. Indeed, the Octet, a work for winds rather than strings, provided the composer with the opportunity to address this emerging style, in which "the emotive basis resides not in the nuance but in the very form of the composition."[3] A flowering of compositions bespeaking this new linear style appeared from 1918 through the 1920s. Stravinsky's interest in ballet was rekindled in accepting Diaghilev's offer to collaborate with Picasso and Massine on the ballet *Pulcinella*, premiered in Paris in 1920. With the war over and prospects remaining slim in Switzerland, Stravinsky moved to France in June of that year. Perhaps most relevantly in terms of the composer's renewed interest in dance, a young expatriated Russian would soon come into his life; together, the two would change the world of ballet.[4]

This fateful event occurred just as the composer was relocating his family yet again, this time to Nice, not far from Monte Carlo. Diaghilev once again served as a broker. The impresario and the twenty-year-old Giorgi Melitonis dze Balanchivadze first met in the autumn of 1924. Of Georgian descent, Balanchine (as Diaghilev would soon Anglicize him) had been raised by a father whose own musical interests instilled an appreciation for ethnic folk materials in his son. Such an interest would furnish one of several bridging agents in building a relationship with Stravinsky. Ten years before joining the

Ballets Russes, Balanchine enrolled in the Imperial Ballet School in Petrograd. Admonished by his instructors for a steely ambition regarded as improper, he also incurred the wrath of those who perceived a dangerous inclination to eroticize dance, one of many tarnishing contrarieties symptomatic of the evils of modernism. He became known as an instigator and was among a group of student petitioners who in 1919 drafted a "Program of Activity and Objectives of the Student Committee," demanding a broader exposure to the arts, not just ballet. He participated in experimental theater productions that took their literary cues from authors such as Traubeg and Yutkevich. There was also a distinctly American tinge to several plays Balanchine attended in Petrograd in 1923. Many adopted jazz idioms and comedic characters modeled on Charlie Chaplin (whom Stravinsky would later come to know in Hollywood). Balanchine organized his own Young Ballet troupe, in which his early choreographic efforts spoke to his "insolence," but an insolence, one reviewer commented, in which "one can see genuine creativity and beauty."[5]

While Balanchine was touring with a small ensemble of dancers during the summer of 1924, the opportunity to bolt free presented itself. In emigrating, Balanchine, like Stravinsky, could not help but carry with him indigenous folk dance as well as the grand tradition of the Maryinsky Theater in which he had been reared. Lenin's Committee on Education and the Arts was just then beginning to ban all artistic "deviations," meaning anything that did not conform to the communist precepts of what propagandistic art should communicate. By 1922, mass deportations had begun. The future looked bleak for creative thinkers, who realized that the expression of independent ideas would meet with staunch resistance by the ruling Bolshevik government. Even so, during 1922–24, and despite the considerable risks, Balanchine sided with avant-garde preconstructionists, who touched an inherently rebellious strain in the young dancer. Their works explored the realm of abstraction, particularly in terms of several cubist influences of the period around 1909–13. It was a lesson well learned, prompting Balanchine to contemplate fundamental geometric issues that included the pulling and pushing of symmetries with asymmetries, much like those so apparent in the Stravinsky scores he would eventually choreograph.

Branded as extremists, several of these renegade artists eventually surrendered to the utilitarian ideology of the Lenin regime in the early 1920s. Artistically, an obdurate Balanchine was compelled to leave. Yet he did not depart with the nostalgia that is evident in some of the folkloristic Russian fables that were set to music by Stravinsky during his homesick exile in Switzerland. Stravinsky and Diaghilev were for the most part comfortable in pre-revolutionary tsarist Russia. By contrast, Balanchine's earliest formative years were lived in a strikingly starker

Russia. His artistic schooling took place in a world of famine and terror under the martial law of a scorching civil war. The scars were indelible, both physically and psychologically. Eventually it all took a heavy toll on his health, including the loss of a lung. Remaining in Russia was no longer viable.

Billed as the principal dancers of the Russian State Ballet, Balanchine, Alexandra Danilova, Nicolas Efimov, and Tamara Gevergeva departed Russia in July 1924 for a summer tour. They performed wherever they could—in dance halls, beer gardens, even an asylum, enduring whatever was necessary to make ends meet. Just as their fortunes were waning, they were offered a contract for a month's engagement at the Empire Music Hall in London in October–November 1924. Luckily, the Ballets Russes' Boris Kochno attended one of the performances and immediately contacted Diaghilev. Shortly thereafter, in Paris, Balanchine and his small traveling troupe auditioned for the positions of director and company principals of the Ballets Russes. What many thought was Diaghilev's impulsive appointment of a very young and virtually untested choreographer sent out an unmistakable signal: the well-respected Bronislava Nijinska was about to be shunted from Diaghilev's male conclave. Balanchine joined the company in Monte Carlo on January 12, 1925, by which time the now expendable Nijinska had little choice but to announce her imminent departure. During the winter of 1924–25, when Stravinsky was touring as a pianist and conductor in the United States, Diaghilev needed not only fresh dancers and fresh ideas; he also especially needed an imaginative choreographer to breathe new life into his enterprise. And Balanchine, more simply, needed a steady job. Their mutual exigency hastened a contractual agreement in late 1924. In circumstances not unlike those in which Stravinsky had found himself fifteen years earlier, Balanchine was thus charged with choreographing for a company of international repute, known for its daring and standard-setting achievements.

His first test came in Monte Carlo, where the Ballets Russes enjoyed the patronage of the local opera company. It was an era in which grand productions of opera incorporated obligatory ballet scenes, for the sake of diversion. Choreographers such as Nijinska cranked out superficially engaging dances with ease. Whether Balanchine liked it or not, it was a job—and a familiar one at that. His own youthful performances in opera while still in Russia, including dance interludes in important productions of *Prince Igor*, *The Magic Flute*, and *Tannhäuser*, had provided a valuable insight. Moreover, in the fall of 1923, while still in Russia, Balanchine had prepared the choreography for a production of Rimsky-Korsakov's opera *Le Coq d'or*. He consequently declared himself ready to undertake the tasks Diaghilev assigned to him, as musically inane as they struck him ("He took . . . all the opera ballets as a huge joke,"

Ninette de Valois recalled).[6] During his first year with the company alone, he cursorily assembled a dozen lightweight ballets for opera productions.

Balanchine's sanguine approach perhaps endeared him to the company ranks rather too much, for Diaghilev, holding a tight leash as always, soon grew fearful of losing control. Not one to shy away from confrontation, Balanchine often questioned what he saw as Diaghilev's artistic deficiencies. A stand-off was inevitable. Would the impertinent neophyte be able to restrain his own views in bringing to the stage the wishes of his superior? Certainly Diaghilev was quick to appreciate Balanchine's raw and somewhat unfocused talent, but he also thought him undisciplined and culturally gauche. Their personal demeanor and artistic priorities could not have been more different. Balanchine, every bit as cocksure as the supercilious Diaghilev, was not about to submit to the role of an acolyte. He resented what he interpreted as Diaghilev's condescending bearing. Consequently, he wore his crudeness as a badge, while openly jeering at the uppity Riviera milieu in which Diaghilev pridefully moved.

To an appreciable extent, Stravinsky shared Balanchine's reservations. And the feelings of both composer and choreographer tugged in opposite directions. Like it or not, they were forced to succumb to Diaghilev's often unscrupulous whims and ploys. Obliged to adjust, they became victims of their own emotional black-mail. Moreover, they were unable to extricate themselves from equivocal feelings ranging from indebtedness to hostility. The toll was heavy. Perhaps most relevantly, their common plight drew them to one another. Beyond their professional affiliation, a personal rapport developed that united them for the rest of their lives. While Balanchine had come to know and in fact choreograph some of Stravinsky's music even before leaving Russia, his first meaningful contact with the composer took place in early 1925, soon after he joined Diaghilev's company. It marked the beginning of a friendship that would last almost half a century. Together, Stravinsky and Balanchine would explore the interaction of music and dance.

The 1925 *Chant du rossignol* was the first Stravinsky opus that Balanchine prepared for the Ballets Russes. Its genesis, however, is traceable to 1908, when Stravinsky, still studying with Rimsky, began composing what would be his first opera. It was to be a musical fairy tale to a story by Hans Christian Andersen entitled "The Nightingale." The composer's youthful friend Stepan Mitusov would write the libretto. Had Diaghilev not interrupted work on the first act by recruiting the composer for the Ballets Russes, Stravinsky may well have finished the opera then and there. But as fate would have it, an interregnum of nearly five years intervened, and two-thirds of the opera would remain uncomposed until after *The Rite of Spring*. Stravinsky was skittish about finishing the work. Given the rapid development of his musical language during 1909–13, he feared that adding a second and third act to pre-existing music would be to the detriment of compositional coherence. Moreover, his overall misgivings about opera germinated while composing his three Parisian ballets ("The artistic basis of opera is wrong . . . Opera is in a backwater," he had remarked in an interview of February 1913 for London's *Daily Mail*), and thus he welcomed Diaghilev's suggestion in 1916 that he should rework the opera into a ballet. He would prepare a concert piece based upon the music of the second and third acts, thus avoiding the potential mismatch between these and the earlier and by now stylistically dissimilar music composed for the first act. It was agreed, and the composer proceeded to finish the twenty-minute work in Morges during the spring of 1917.[7]

Stravinsky retained the essentials of the original opera scenario as a basis for Diaghilev's ballet production of 1920. With choreography by Massine, it was staged in early February, only a few months after the premiere of the symphonic version (which had encountered harsh criticism on account of its considerable dissonance). The story of the Nightingale's singing for the Chinese Emperor, and the enchanting bird's rescue of the ruler from the grasp of death, was just the kind of "oriental" mandarin exotica to resonate with Diaghilev's enculturated audience, as he well knew. The opening scene, "The Fête in the Emperor of China's Palace," finds the Nightingale singing sweetly, with bells ringing and flowers adorning the room. "The Nightingale is placed on a golden perch; and a Chinese March signals the entrance of the Emperor." The second scene, "The Two Nightingales," finds the Emperor of Japan bringing the gift of a mechanical nightingale also singing so beautifully that no one noticed that the real Nightingale "had flown away out of the open window." In "Illness and Recovery of the Emperor of China," the Emperor confronts Death, who has stolen his crown, sword, and other treasures. When all seems lost, the real Nightingale is heard singing outside the window. It convinces Death to give up the Emperor's possessions and spare him. Finally, in the closing "Funeral March," "The courtiers came in to look at their dead Emperor, and—yes, there they stood astounded, and the Emperor said, 'Good morning!' Meanwhile, the friendly Nightingale has flown back to the fisherman, who is heard singing his song once more."[8]

As soon as Stravinsky had sanctioned the use of the symphonic version of *Le Rossignol* as a ballet, Diaghilev approached Fortunato Depero, a young futurist painter then in vogue. Diaghilev commissioned Depero to design scenery and costumes for a 1917 production of the ballet—a clear indication of his interest in Italian futurism. Massine was eager to choreograph the work, although in the end Depero's staging would never be used. Henri Matisse served as the designer of the version that was eventually staged, for which Massine indeed furnished the choreography. The Ballets Russes premiered this version on February 2, 1920, at the Théâtre National de l'Opéra in Paris, with Stravinsky conducting. The dancers included Karsavina as the real Nightingale and Stanislas Idzikowski as the mechanical nightingale, with Lydia Sokolova as Death and Serge Grigoriev as the Emperor (the latter two also participating in the subsequent 1925 revival).

Stravinsky was unconvinced that the wholesale adaptation of operatically inspired music to a symphonic suite and then to a ballet would work: "I had destined *Le Chant du rossignol* for the concert platform," he wrote in his autobiographical account, "and a choreographic rendering seemed to me to be quite unnecessary. Its subtle and meticulous writing and its somewhat static character would not have lent themselves to stage action and the movements of dancing." His fears were well founded. The reviews were mixed, some praising the ballet as a watershed, while others denounced the music as "arthritic." When Diaghilev raised the prospect of reviving the ballet in 1925, the composer was skeptical. He sensed that Diaghilev was trying to "entice me—the lost sheep, so to speak—back into the fold."[9] Moreover, the composer had moved on. By the time Stravinsky first met Balanchine in 1925, the ornate music of *Le Chant* was notably different from the composer's developing devotion to a more athletic, neoclassical brand of writing. Compositions such as *L'Histoire du soldat, Ragtime* (1918), *Piano-Rag-Music* (1919), *Symphonies of Wind Instruments* (1920), and especially the Octet, as well as the Concerto for piano and wind instruments (1924), had charted a new course in which a formalist, leanly structured, abstract style prevailed.

According to Felia Doubrovska, Diaghilev mentioned to Balanchine in 1925 that he happened to have the score for *Le Chant* in his cellar. Would Balanchine, having just joined the company, like to choreograph the transformed work? Naturally the young choreographer accepted. Balanchine had for the most part greatly admired Stravinsky's music for over a decade. He had danced in a few productions of *The Firebird* and even played the walk-on role of a street vendor in a 1916 production of *Petrouchka* at the Maryinsky. Later in life, Balanchine recalled that he had choreographed the composer's 1918 *Ragtime* while still a student in Petrograd in 1922, though no record of the production survives. Balanchine not only knew Stravinsky's 1914 original operatic version of *Le Rossignol* but had played a small role in a 1918 production staged by Meyerhold in Petrograd: "In the *Nightingale* the soloists sang from scores, sitting on a bench [with] a lively pantomime unfolding around them. No one noticed Meyerhold's innovations . . . because by then no one had time for the theater; it was right after the Bolshevik uprising, there was nothing to eat. But I learned the music well, and so later, when Diaghilev asked me to stage Stravinsky's ballet *Le Chant du rossignol*, I was able to do it quickly."[10] Quickly, yes, but

Balanchine had also inherited the original 1920 Massine production along with the albatross of its history. He had to find a fresh tack in dealing imaginatively with a pre-existing ballet staged by the well-respected Massine.

The memories of Alicia Markova, who now reprised Karsavina's original 1920 role, are informative. Her eyewitness recollections provide a touchstone in framing the early Stravinsky–Balanchine relationship as the two men came to know one another personally for the first time. Markova had already watched Balanchine dance with his own company, the Russian State Ballet, before joining the Ballets Russes. She remembers her first meeting with him. In 1925, Diaghilev instructed Balanchine to audition her for the Stravinsky ballet. He asked her to perform several unusual extensions and positions, including some that seemed more acrobatic than balletic. Moreover, Markova remembers that the dancing was not so much classical as rooted in modern dance. While musicians, at least, are most likely to associate Balanchine with the classicism of the subsequent *Apollon musagète*, during the early 1920s Balanchine was essentially a modernist, and in sympathy with such progressive choreographers as Kasyan Goleizovsky, whom he admired above all others.

Diaghilev had, in fact, invited Goleizovsky to work for the Ballets Russes before turning to Balanchine. (Again one notes the similarity with Diaghilev's recruitment of Stravinsky when his earlier choices failed to materialize.) Diaghilev had become enamored with Goleizovsky's modernistic approach as a means to reinvigorate his company. During the 1920s, in fact, Diaghilev looked increasingly to younger dancers and faddish theatrics as a means of rejuvenating a company that some saw as being in decline. By casting the young Markova— at fourteen, Balanchine's first "baby ballerina"—in the principal role, the impresario thus created the buzz he desired. When an approving Diaghilev turned to Balanchine after Markova's audition to ask for the choreographer's opinion, one wonders if Balanchine had any choice but to agree. Like Stravinsky fifteen years earlier, Balanchine fully recognized the hands in which his future rested.

Markova recalled a patient, sympathetic Balanchine working tirelessly with her, as the very young ballerina prepared for the very daunting role. She remembered how deliberately Balanchine worked, devoting extra rehearsals to instilling confidence, especially in view of the considerable challenges of the score. She also recalled Stravinsky's advice in relation to learning the score: "You can't count, you must know the sound of every instrument," adding that she had to watch the conductor intently to catch the basic beat of each measure. The pulse served as a lifeline in negotiating some of the complex and purposely free rhythmic patterns. Kochno remembered that Balanchine would arrive at rehearsal as if he had nothing preconceived in mind. He gave the distinct impression that he would simply improvise as he went along (an impression reinforced by dancers with whom he worked throughout his career). Balanchine demonstrated the many "inventions" he was to incorporate into Le Chant—inventions that Markova claims later choreographers stole from him. Danilova added that Balanchine introduced chaîné turns, as they had never been seen in any previous ballet.[11]

Just as Stravinsky carefully monitored the way Balanchine choreographed in the studio (while dancers who were terrified of Stravinsky, because of his exacting demands, also looked on, reported Markova), so Balanchine learned from Stravinsky's physically demonstrative, kinesthetic approach to working with dancers. It was not in Stravinsky's nature to remain uninvolved. Balanchine, too, always participated in every facet of the production and understood this need for constant interaction in shaping the work on the spot. Stravinsky's insertion of himself into the creative process by physically doing something, either at the keyboard or in the rehearsal studio, impressed Balanchine. It stood in contrast to Diaghilev's often bloated sermonizing about the way art was created. Stravinsky, for his part, was equally impressed with Balanchine's physical approach, his understanding of music, his appreciation of artistic balance, and his refreshing thinking about movement. Indeed, the composer's interest in dance was renewed. He re-engaged the world of ballet—the world that only a few years earlier he had repudiated from religious conviction as "l'anathème du Christ."[12]

Not only did Stravinsky rehearse and conduct the new version of Le Chant, but as usual he exerted considerable influence on its restaging. He also shaped the production from the piano at several rehearsals. Matisse, too, played an important role in creating the scenery, as did Stravinsky's future wife, Vera Soudeikine, in preparing costumes. Stravinsky's exchanges with Balanchine were frequent. The composer was living in Nice, just a short distance from Monte Carlo, and as both Markova and Nabokov confirm, he regularly visited the rehearsal studio to watch Balanchine work. Filmmaker Tony Palmer captured an important memory in his 1982 biopic documentary Once at a Border. Here Balanchine, in one of his last interviews, recounts the first time he and Stravinsky met during rehearsals of Le Chant. The composer had come to the studio to check the ballet's tempi. As a dutiful young apprentice, Balanchine was following Diaghilev's directions in this matter. Stravinsky, however, found the tempi too slow and insisted on a faster pace. Complying with his wishes, Balanchine made the adjustment, as did the dancers. At a subsequent rehearsal, and in Stravinsky's absence, Diaghilev countermanded the composer's instruction, forcing the choreographer to reinstate the tempi he preferred. Balanchine found himself caught in the middle. In the end, perhaps the music that Stravinsky transformed from opera to symphonic poem to ballet, as well as the Massine ballet to which Balanchine fell heir, mainly provided an opportunity for the composer and choreographer to glimpse the future. Nothing would come of the work in terms of blazoning a new path—at least immediately. Something quite different, however, was about to consume their attention, and unite their artistic gifts.

Increasingly, classicism was in the air, especially among some of the Ballets Russes designers with whom Stravinsky and Balanchine became acquainted in the mid 1920s. André Derain (1880–1954), to name only one among Diaghilev's cohorts, doubtlessly made some impression in shaping Stravinsky and Balanchine's classical approach to dance at that time. Derain, as Roger Fry once commented, was an exponent of the "purest French classicism." His work with Diaghilev included sets and designs for such productions as *La Boutique* (1919) and *Jack-in-the-Box* (1926). Guillaume Apollinaire anticipated the essence of what Stravinsky and Balanchine would soon accomplish with *Apollon musagète* in describing Derain's achievement in the following terms: "With unequaled daring, Derain went beyond the most audacious forms of contemporary art in order to discover simplicity and freshness, the principles of art and the discipline which stem from such an exercise."[13] This would become the platform from which Stravinsky launched his own rediscovery of classicism.

Despite their growing friendship, there was no direct creative interaction between Stravinsky and Balanchine immediately following *Le Chant*, perhaps because Diaghilev feared that pairing the two would lead to a coordinated resistance to his authority. Over the next few seasons the composer and choreographer did not collaborate on a single project, although Stravinsky did continue to observe Balanchine's choreographic creations of other works as they unfolded in the studios of Monte Carlo and the theaters of Paris. It remained for the 1928 *Apollon musagète* to arouse Stravinsky's interest in the expressive possibilities of ballet. By then, Diaghilev's Ballets Russes, whatever the sum of its failures and successes, had performed an enormous service for Balanchine: it had provided him with a lifelong confidant. In Stravinsky, Balanchine found the artistic mentor Diaghilev originally set out to be. Their ensuing collaborations would confirm just how thoroughly Balanchine instinctively grasped, respected, and choreographically matched the musical aesthetic Stravinsky would set forth in his next ballet.

Apollon musagète—or *Apollo*, as the ballet came to be called—is an achievement of sheer visual beauty in its lyricism and classically steeped dancing. With his newest ballet, Stravinsky sought a melodic style that demonstrated pure beauty, free of ethnicity—"the taste for melody *per se* having been lost," Stravinsky commented in his *Autobiography*. "Melody *per se*" in this instance meant relying upon a more diatonic vocabulary ("It seemed to me that diatonic composition was the most appropriate for this purpose")—in effect, white music for a "ballet blanc."[14] Gone are all "superfluities," to use the composer's word, as well as the jutting three- and four-note cellular ideas of his earlier works, in which short motives underwent constant rhythmic and melodic variation and repetition as they frequently turned back upon themselves. Instead, there is a sense of calm created by the incorporation of longer, more contiguously constructed melodic lines—lines that unfold at a more unhurried, even casual pace. Rhythmically and metrically, the composer achieves an environment of steadiness, of dependability, in which continuity rather than disruption prevails. This is a new world, or perhaps better said, an imaginative revisiting of an old world. Recent Stravinsky scholarship has justifiably questioned the partitioning of the composer's works into distinct stylistic periods. *Apollo* nonetheless signals a remarkable shift; for while still retaining many of the underlying compositional techniques of earlier years, it sounds and looks different from anything Stravinsky had yet written. And despite some glimpses of the ballet's more restrained style in works such as the 1925 *Sérénade en la* (even more so than in *Oedipus rex*, written the year before *Apollo*), it is every bit as much a turnabout as *Petrouchka*. *Apollo* strikes a new path.

In addition to its overall eloquence, this 1928 Balanchine collaboration marks a memorable juncture. It is a historic merger of mind and spirit, the composer and choreographer's first genuine partnership in working on a project from beginning to end. While neither was very interested in publicly analyzing or explaining their works, each of the two men called attention to this ballet as a particularly significant moment in his individual artistic evolution. Balanchine spoke of selectivity as a purifying process, a filter in creating dance. He declared, uncharacteristically, that with this particular ballet he had come to realize that in choreography, as in music, he could better clarify his ideas by doing less rather than more. Economy suddenly became a virtue. Staying with an idea by exploring its potential fully, rather than moving on to another idea, absorbed Balanchine's attention. "It was in studying *Apollon* that I came first to understand how gestures, like tones in music and shades in painting, have certain family relationships. As groups, they impose their own laws. The more conscious an artist is, the more he comes to understand these laws, and to respond to them. Since this work, I have developed my choreography inside the framework such relations suggest."[15] Moreover, the new ballet boldly challenged the fashionable notion of novelty. As with so many of Diaghilev's productions, it presented risks. What would Parisians make of its somberness, its imperturbability, given the expectations that were roused whenever the impresario mounted a new work? Whatever the reception might be, Diaghilev insisted that while classicism formed the bedrock of all great works of art, its principles were not so rigid as to prohibit each artist from rethinking how these principles might be fashioned.

Viewed in this context, *Apollo* signifies classicism's melding of malleability and constancy—something that had been on Stravinsky's mind in recent years. Designated his own "U-turn," *Apollo* represents a redirection that would lead twenty years later to the limpid style of *Orpheus* (1948). He considered the ballet to be evidence of a new compositional approach. Yet this newness was rooted in something as old as *Mir iskusstva*. At the core of *Apollo* was the challenge of writing a ballet that valued austerity and homogeneity above all else. "I had specially in my thoughts," the composer wrote in his *Autobiography*, "what is known as the 'white ballet,' in which to my mind the very essence of this art reveals itself in all its purity."[16] Moreover, the tranquility of the ballet's music was autobiographical in itself, for it stems directly from a pivotal transfiguration in the composer's life.

Order in his music had always manifested the need for orderliness in his life. But now the composer sought more: he needed to find a sense of serenity, a spiritual deliverance through repentance. From 1926 through 1929, he again became a church communicant. His remarkably conciliatory letters to Diaghilev beg contrition for earlier sins, a reversal of attitude that could not have been imagined years earlier. The emotional turmoil in Stravinsky's private life caused by his love for his wife Catherine and his ongoing relationship with Vera Soudeikine also weighed heavily upon him, perhaps more than history has recognized. There is no question that the guilt he carried affected his thoughts—thoughts expressed not so much in words as in his music. His need to bring a measure of repose to his life becomes evident in most every score. Further, Stravinsky's change of heart and mind mirrored the god Apollo's own transmogrification. In the Homeric Hymn to Hermes, Apollo appears as a callous slayer intent on gaining spoils at any cost. Only later does he set aside his whip and arrows for the oracular lyre (the central symbol of Stravinsky and Balanchine's ballet).

The composer's self-scrutiny is also traceable to his intense study of Jacques Maritain's theological monographs. Deeply concerned with existence, being, and rationality, Stravinsky was struck by such cerebrations. Rooted in Aristotelian thought and the teachings of Thomas Aquinas, Maritain's "neo-Thomism" prized the efficacy of clarity, order, and proportion as eternal verities. Maritain's sense of reflexivity as a means of penetrating one's innermost self immediately appealed to the older, more contemplative Stravinsky. Moreover, the composer grasped the strong link between myth, religion, and ritual that was outlined in the philosopher's writings. One cannot appreciate the spiritual impetus for Stravinsky's "Greek" works without recognizing Maritain's behind-the-scenes influence. Indeed, Stravinsky's son Soulima remembers Diaghilev's inviting him to lunch then complaining bitterly about the elder Stravinsky's unhealthy interest in religion, and particularly his unqualified devotion to Maritain's writings.[17]

Unlike his opera-oratorio *Oedipus rex* (which immediately preceded *Apollo*), wherein the dramatic text explicitly provided the narrative voice for Stravinsky's personal identification with tragedy, the wordless *Apollo* offered a different challenge, and perhaps a greater one. Here was the perfect subject matter. Apollo, Greek mythology's most paradoxical figure, stood as the archetype of the gods' anthropomorphic dilemma as acted out in the confusing conflict between human weakness and godly omnipotence. Stravinsky, now a middle-aged man of forty-six, was engaged in a guilt-ridden, fatiguing, introspective struggle to find himself. Similarly characterized by polarities ranging from gentle to vehement, from compassionate to ruthless, and from guilty to guiltless, the passion of a younger Apollo's emotions was boundless. Yet he also personified antiquity's classical restraint, the need to look inwardly for truth and the perils of excess. "From a sea of blood and guilt, Apollo brings enlightenment, atonement, and purification."[18]

Stravinsky had reached a crossroads. *Apollo*'s solemnity reflects the composer's own need to pause and reflect upon his future, compositionally and personally. Through exploring the eternal power of myth, Stravinsky forced himself to confront his own vicissitudes and anxieties. He was fully aware that he was drifting. Composing *Apollo* would serve as a purgation. The plasticity of classical dance provided the ideal vehicle for such a cleansing reflection, he contended, for it expressed a beauty that could be achieved only through discipline—a process in which the composer believed deeply. Structure would always tame ambiguity, he argued. It was an eternal battle of timeless Apollonian and Dionysian principles, as he himself wrote in his chronicle; and the visibility of ballet, above any other art form, provided the "theater" for resolving such a fundamental conflict.

Stravinsky's music for the new ballet inspired a young, eager Balanchine. Although still in his early twenties, the choreographer was in a hurry. He needed to secure his own identity within Diaghilev's highly competitive company, where choreographers seemed especially vulnerable. Having joined the Ballets Russes only three years earlier, Balanchine was immediately exposed to Diaghilev's *faux pompier* productions (as Lincoln Kirstein labeled them), and soon withered under the humdrum stories and musically flimsy scores assigned to him during the 1926–27 season. Even then, his sharp musical instincts winced at the obvious banalities of the scores he was handed.[19] The uneven quality of the hodgepodge ballets produced during the waning years of Diaghilev's legendary company quickly exasperated an enterprising Balanchine; for he was not only ambitious but also astutely equipped to handle more challenging scores. He seemed frustrated by Diaghilev's taste for eclecticism, his willingness to take on such an odd batch of projects. As Nicolas Nabokov once remarked, such indiscriminate tastes reflected Diaghilev's desire to act "as a kind of director of a musical zoo, as someone who wanted to own every species of animal under the sun from the platypuses to the pandas."[20] But just as Stravinsky had endured Fokine's strictures during the composer's early years with the company, so Balanchine had to comply with whatever was asked of him. Now, however, Stravinsky's new ballet furnished an egress. The clarity of its classicism afforded the ideal crucible for the confidant Balanchine to display his abilities in complementing the composer's elegiac score.

Apollo constituted a revocation of the past for both men. As Balanchine broke free from Diaghilev's mannerist praxis, so Stravinsky shifted course, shunning the decadent fluff of nineteenth-century ballet scores. One must remember that in 1927 Balanchine was on the rise of an arc. He was not nearly as contemplative as Stravinsky. Twenty years younger, he viewed this juncture not as a crisis of conscience but as an exhilaration, a propitious opportunity to accelerate rather than to stop and ponder. When Stravinsky was Balanchine's age, he was virtually unknown, and in the eyes of his teacher Rimsky-Korsakov, no more than another naïve amateur. Now, in 1927, the internationally acclaimed composer looked back from a midlife plateau, a view the young Balanchine could not comprehend. How different their outlooks must have been. The oddity is that the confluence of shared artistic sympathies that led to *Apollo* could have emerged from such dissimilar perspectives. The self-assured young Balanchine, poised on the threshold of a breakthrough, was impatient to show what he could do. The pensive Stravinsky, standing at midlife, had reached a point where he was ready to renounce what he had already done.

The ballet's scenario consists of two scenes. The first, marked in Stravinsky's compositional sketchbook as "La Naissance d'Apollon," is adapted from Homer's Hymn to the Delian Apollo. The composer describes the mortal Leto's arrival on the isle of Delos in the Aegean Sea. With arms wrapped around a palm tree, she gives birth to Apollo. Two handmaidens blanket the child in swaddling clothes bound with a golden girdle. As the first tableau closes, the Muses present the young god with his magical lyre. The second tableau begins with a young Apollo, lyre in hand. The journey of the youthful god's maturation unfolds, leading to his final ascension to Parnassus, where he joins his father Zeus among the pantheon of the gods. Three Muses, as Balanchine stated, "were selected for their appropriateness to the choreographic art." Stravinsky described the trio in his *Autobiography*: "Calliope, receiving the stylus and tablets from Apollo, personified poetry and its rhythm; Polyhymnia, finger on lips, represents mime. . . . Finally, Terpsichore, combining in herself both the rhythm and eloquence of gesture, reveals dancing to the world and thus among the Muses takes the place of honor beside Apollo." Apollo's birth in the first tableau is followed by his first solo variation. Nearly six times the length of the introductory "Prologue," the second tableau consists of traditional solo and ensemble variations, a *pas de deux*, and a concluding apotheosis.

The composer's inclusion of the word "musagète" in the original title signi-fied Apollo's leadership of the Muses. Balanchine added that they were "goddesses . . . who derived inspiration from Apollo's teaching. . . . The Muses accept [Apollo's] gifts with delight and respect, form a line, and hop like pleased children to the side of the stage." But this is hardly a fair appraisal of the prominent place occupied by the Muses. Most mythologies have it the other way around. In Hesiod's *Theogony*, for example, the nine daughters of Zeus were empowered "with particular emphasis upon their ability to inspire the infallible revelation of the poet."[21]

Whatever literary license was taken, Diaghilev's production of the ballet was only a second chapter in the ballet's history. Although virtually forgotten, the actual premiere took place at the Library of Congress in Washington, D.C., on April 27, 1928. Understanding the American connection is essential both in defining the boundaries of the ballet's scenario and in establishing the ballet's musical and choreographic dimensions—dimensions that Stravinsky was obli-gated to follow in composing the ballet and that Balanchine would inherit and implement in Paris.[22]

The score of the ballet had been commissioned by American composer and benefactor Elizabeth Sprague Coolidge. Of particular relevance, the limited space for dancing allowed by the stage (which, having been designed for chamber music, was only thirty feet wide and twenty feet deep) would restrict the theatrical action. The opening program of the April 1928 festival during which *Apollo* was to be performed (which lasted three days and included several other ballets) promised "A program of dances under the direction of Adolph Bolm [that] will include the first performance of *Apollon musagète*, a ballet written by Igor Strawinsky for the Library of Congress."[23] Coolidge had invited her friend Adolph Bolm to design the production. Stravinsky had known Bolm in St. Petersburg, where, among other roles choreographed by Fokine, Bolm danced that of Petrouchka. Carl Engel, the head of the Library of Congress Music Division, found himself in the unenviable position of having to persistently (and often unsuccessfully) badger Stravinsky about the limitations imposed by the commission, especially regarding the issue of space. On July 11, 1927, Engel wrote to the composer describing the small theater and even including a picture of it, stating that the "sunken pit holds 20 people."[24]

The commission was first offered to Manuel de Falla, with the stipulation that no more than three characters could be cast. When Falla declined, Ottorino Respighi was approached. Nothing came of Engel's efforts to engage him either. Finally, in June 1927, Stravinsky agreed to terms. Anticipating performances beyond the American premiere, the composer's agent wrote to Engel on June 10, 1927, insisting on the right to offer the ballet Europe and South America immediately after Washington. That settled, Stravinsky's sketchbooks indicate that he began jotting ideas a few weeks later.

The staging of the production in Washington—without Stravinsky's usual on-the-spot presence—tested Engel's forbearance. Conductor Hans Kindler, choreographer Bolm, and the dancers constantly bickered. Engel feared a collapse: "If ever we get through this I shall do a dance of my own," he confessed to Coolidge.[25] In several unpublished letters, Engel and Coolidge exchanged complaints about the music's blandness. It was the exotic, Russian Stravinsky that Americans were expecting to hear, not the diatonic, innocuous-sounding "C-major" music of the neoclassical style (as some analysts have described it). The premiere was received tepidly. The composer downplayed the American reception, commenting that only the Paris premiere interested him. The ballet's American history might be tucked away in a footnote had the Coolidge commission not shaped the ballet's underlying structural dimensions.

As for Stravinsky's musical decisions, the *Apollo* sketchbook in Basel leaves a trail. The composer dated each sketch meticulously, enabling at least a partial retracing of the compositional process. For example, Stravinsky made much of his employment of a string orchestra:

My music demanded six [string] groups instead of the quartet . . . [or] to be more exact, "quintet," of the ordinary orchestra, which is composed of first and second violins, violas, violoncellos, and double bass. I therefore added to the regular ensemble a sixth group, which was to be of second violoncellos. I thus formed an instrumental sextet, each group of which had a strictly defined part. This requires the establishment of a well-proportioned gradation in the matter of the number of instruments for each group.[26]

Indeed it did, but the Basel sketches reveal that Stravinsky originally had a different instrumentation in mind, one that included both piano and harp. Given the centrality of the lyre in the Apollonian myth, the use of the harp makes sense. The extant sketches for piano are also unsurprising, especially since the keyboard was employed prominently in many of Stravinsky's works of this period, including the recently completed *Oedipus rex*.[27] The sketchbook further discloses that Stravinsky initially planned a complement of eighteen strings, and allowed space in his orchestration for the piano and harp, thus totaling the twenty instruments specified by Engel. But the two bulkiest instruments of his orchestra, the piano and harp, proved impractical for the auditorium's small orchestra pit. Once Stravinsky had conceded this, he began reorchestrating the strings, as his sketchbook shows, almost to the exact day. For the first time, the composer's sketches show strings written *divisi* as a functional solution, compensating texturally for the now forsaken harp and piano. As for Apollo's lyre, a solo violin would have to do. Had the Washington orchestra pit been larger, *Apollo* would certainly have been scored for a larger orchestra.

Apollo was performed only once during the festival. No matter, for Stravinsky remained uninterested in any American performance either on or off stage. The truth is that the composer's eyes had been focused on Paris from the start. After a single staged performance, and to the near erasure of any memory of the Washington premiere, Coolidge's *Apollo* instantly became Diaghilev's *Apollo*. And to Diaghilev's delight, no doubt, the composer's American commission of $1,000 paid substantial dividends for the Ballets Russes.

On January 21, 1928, Stravinsky telegraphed Diaghilev, inviting him and Balanchine to his home in Nice. Stravinsky played portions of the ballet at the piano, stressing the correct tempi. Long before Bolm received the completed score in Washington, Balanchine began rehearsing. Vera Stravinsky, who claimed that both the scenario and the staging were exclusively the composer's, recalled Diaghilev, Balanchine, and her then future husband regularly discussing *Apollo*. In an outtake from Palmer's biopic, Soulima Stravinsky remembered that because their home in Nice was so close to Monte Carlo, where the Ballets Russes wintered, his father often saw Diaghilev, who "would come very frequently and have meals with us and discuss business. I remember when father was composing *Apollo*, he played for Diaghilev as he was composing what he had already achieved." Once the composer had completed a section, Balanchine remembers Stravinsky clarifying exactly what he had in mind so that there could be no misunderstanding.[28]

While Diaghilev publicly praised the relevancy of the classicism that the composer was bringing to his newest composition, privately he seemed more ambivalent.[29] Moreover, he was growing more and more wary of his impious young choreographer's growing independence. Balanchine would be called upon to showcase Sergei Lifar in the role of Apollo, just as Fokine had been entrusted, seventeen years earlier, with featuring Nijinsky as Petrouchka. In a letter to Lifar of September 30, 1927, Diaghilev provides a description of a visit to Stravinsky in Nice that was surely meant to reassure the dancer of his centrality in the new ballet:

> After lunch he played for me the first half of the new ballet. It is of course an amazing work, extraordinarily calm, and with greater clarity than anything he has so far done; and filigree counterpoint round transparent, clear-cut themes, all in the major key; somehow music not of this world, but from somewhere above. It seems strange that, though the tempo of all this part is slow, yet at the same time it is perfectly adapted to dancing. There is a short fast movement in your first variation—there are to be two for you, and the opening is to be danced to an unaccompanied violin solo . . . The *Adagio* (*pas d'action*) has a broad theme very germane to us today; it runs concurrently in four different tempos, and yet, generally speaking, the harmony is most satisfactory. I embraced him and he said: "It is for you to produce it properly for me: I want Lifar to have all sorts of flourishes."[30]

Eager to establish his own style, how would Balanchine walk such a tightrope, made all the more perilous by Diaghilev's current intimacy with Lifar? While Diaghilev could not have compelled Stravinsky to compose a score entirely around the dancer, there is no doubt that he pressed Balanchine into playing up Lifar's notable strengths. Having choreographed four earlier ballets for Lifar, Balanchine was thoroughly familiar with the dancer's attributes as well as his shortcomings. Just as Stravinsky had had to deal with extreme spatial restrictions in Washington, so the choreography of Diaghilev's *Apollo* arose largely from Balanchine's accommodation of Lifar. Moreover, his breaching of traditional balletic concepts—imaginatively refigured in the cause of the work's avowed classicism—riled the ballet's critics.

In matters of costume, and especially of décor, a vocal Stravinsky was frequently at odds with Diaghilev. The composer proposed Giorgio de Chirico as designer, a reasonable choice given the artist's "obsession for classic architecture," as one reviewer commented. But Diaghilev instead chose André Bauchant, an eccentric gardener and occasional painter regarded by fashionable Parisian art dealers as a bright new star. Undoubtedly Diaghilev wished to capitalize upon Bauchant's current notoriety. Bauchant's aesthetic was quite unlike the thoroughgoing classicism of Derain or de Chirico. Consequently, the original sets and costumes were not at all to the composer's liking. He had specifically stipulated the short length of the tutus, a hotly contested topic of the 1920s ballet world, yet the Muses wore long white skirts. In the end, the costumes proved so unsatisfactory that Gabrielle "Coco" Chanel was asked to design new ones the following year.

Stravinsky conducted the premiere on the same program as his popular *Pulcinella* and *Firebird*, on June 12, 1928. Lubov Tchernicheva danced Calliope and Felia Doubrovska Polyhymnia, while Alice Nikitina and Alexandra Danilova alternated as Terpsichore. Whereas Stravinsky had displayed complete disinterest in the poorly reviewed Washington production, Paris was altogether different. The composer claimed that the "French" *Apollo* had succeeded marvelously. Lifar, Grigoriev, and Diaghilev bolstered what little praise they could find. Stravinsky had become an archaist, some critics scolded, a perpetrator of an ersatz classicism. Even Arthur Lourié, a frequent advocate of the composer's music, accused Stravinsky of abandoning the fundamental classical principles that had evolved over the last decade. He lamented the composer's dangerous tendency toward the excesses of Romanticism. For many, Stravinsky's score was dismally colorless, its melos exhibiting, as Asaf'yev criticized, "a dry and lifeless eclectic esperanto."[31]

Balanchine fared no better. His choreography employed gestures and movements that were deemed "horrifying." The reaction was inevitable: as Danilova remarked, the ballet was "revolutionary for the simple reason that at times we had to dance on flat fleet."[32] Reynolds similarly comments, "By introducing into a classical ballet such movements as shuffling on the soles of the feet, splaying the fingers of the hands, contractions of the torso, protruding hips, and elongated limbs," all within the "clarity and symmetry of the *danse d'école*," *Apollo* constituted "a new geometry."[33] Amidst all the criticism, the artistic cohesion that composer and choreographer had forged went unnoticed. It was a fusion that was even more impressive given the limitations of the American commission and Diaghilev's personal agenda. Balanchine had created a compatible, synergistic visualization of Stravinsky's classicism. The composer could not have hoped for more.

Stravinsky's rekindled interest in the ancient, enduring beauty of classicism sparked his imagination. Everything "Greek" captivated him, from medieval iconography and its embracement of the mysterious power of numbers and symmetry, to the Pythagorean view of beauty as "the reduction of many to one." Still, more than anything it was Stravinsky's study and adoption of classical literary models in creating *Apollo* that proved most meaningful, as source materials disclose.

Over one hundred pages of compositional sketches provide a window on the evolution of *Apollo*'s musical structure. To begin, Stravinsky did not compose the music in what was to become its ultimate order. He drafted eleven blocks of material, each carefully dated. Several internal passages were drafted before the opening measures of the "Prologue" were envisioned. Moreover, at a very early point, and amidst other sketches for the opening music, Stravinsky sketched his initial thought for the "Pas de deux," perhaps already anticipating the importance of such a crucial moment in the ballet. He notated the melodic line, descending in thirds, rather fully formed, although it was altered rhythmically in subsequent sketches. This simple, diatonic material eventually served as the main thematic material beginning in mm. 3–4 (see Example 3 (a)). Later

Example 3 (a) *Apollo*, "Pas de deux," mm. 1–9, transcribed sketch and score.

sketches begin to reveal other sections of the "Pas de deux," including motivic material first seen in mm. 4–5 and appearing elsewhere, such as at the final cadence (Example 3 (b)). At a later point in the sketching process, Stravinsky again returned to the "Pas de deux," this time sketching what was to become the thematic source for mm. 12–22 (Example 3 (c) and (d)). For example,

Example 3 (b) *Apollo*, "Pas de deux," mm. 34–39, transcribed sketch and score.

Example 3 (c) *Apollo,* "Pas de deux," mm. 12–15, transcribed sketch and score.

the composer eventually deleted the initial pitch c, and altered the rhythm. An iteration much closer to the final melodic and accompanimental material emerged in the second sketch, where the second violin pizzicato begins to take rudimentary form.

It is not unusual for the composer to jot an idea that ultimately functions in a subsidiary role. Frequently such a sketch is drafted at the same time as thematic material. In the first of Apollo's two variations, for instance, the composer began to draft a figure consisting of a dotted eighth note and sixteenth note—a central rhythmic motive for the entire ballet, as we shall see (Example 4). Then below this simple idea, he drafted a melodic figure that would become Apollo's main theme. It would be played by the two violin soloists, while the accompanimental figure would be assigned to the lower strings.

Example 3 (d) *Apollo*, "Pas de deux," mm. 12–15, transcribed sketch.

Stravinsky's sketching often proceeded along two lines: he would sketch rough ideas quickly, then return to working out some other section of the ballet more fully. Thoughts would be interspersed throughout the sketching, but once he had made decisions on the fundamental material, he then composed out the details.[34] Here, as in the earlier ballets, we can never know how much unrecorded searching went on at the keyboard. Whatever the pre-notational extent of the composer's thought process, however, it is clear that he composed short, two- or three-measure segments, only later assembling them into what would be their final sequence. At various points in the sketchbook, Stravinsky wrote in Russian, "insert," leaving no doubt that he added measures between previously composed segments. Remarkably, this seemingly scattershot approach did nothing to undermine the ballet's seamless nature. Indeed, it is the continuity of the music of *Apollo* that stands out as the work's signature.

Throughout the sketches another pattern emerges. Stravinsky would first craft a pivotally important musical idea, and would then compose up to that moment. Moreover, on the reverse side of virtually every sketch page, a very methodical Stravinsky tabulated the duration of each individual compositional unit, perhaps in this case because of the imposed time strictures of the Coolidge commission. (For its Washington audience, the ballet was merely one item in a gala evening, and as such its length had to be carefully controlled). Consider, for example, the "Pas d'action," where for the first time all three Muses join Apollo. Balanchine was particularly fond of this music's unusually serene melodic flow.

Example 4 *Apollo*, "Variation d'Apollon," mm. 2–8, transcribed sketch and score.

Indeed, the composer worked to attain its smoothness; for he sewed it together almost measure by measure from several short, separately conceived ideas.

The music begins at what is marked as Rehearsal 24 (m. 1 of the "Pas d'action") in the published score. It is assigned letter A in figure 6. Rehearsal 25 in the score (m. 6) is designated here by letter B, Rehearsal 26 (m. 13) by letter C, and so on. Each rehearsal number in the published score represents a separate compositional block—that is, one that the composer originally conceived of as a unit. Figure 6 provides a time-line summary of the sequence in which Stravinsky composed the music compared with the order in which the music appears in the published score. The difference is illuminating. The first music that Stravinsky composed, designated in figure 6 by letter F (Rehearsal 29), was not used until m. 38 of the score. The music that Stravinsky ultimately employed as the opening of the "Pas d'action," letter A (Rehearsal 24), did not appear until about midway through the compositional process. In fact only three sequences, represented by the underlined B–C–D (Rehearsals 25–26–27), J–K (Rehearsals 33–34), and the ending, N–O (Rehearsals 37–38), were composed contiguously. Every other unit was drafted independently, and then repositioned later, as the architecture of the piece unfolded.

Similar reconfigurations of separately composed modules occur throughout the ballet's sketches. In almost every case, the material that eventually served as the beginning of an individual dance (for instance, the separate variations of Calliope and Polyhymnia, and the second of two variations for Apollo) was not composed first. The pattern is consistent. Stravinsky worked with any number of non-sequential musical ideas as they struck him, then later forged a series of musical transitions to ensure overall coherence.

In declaring that *Apollo* was essentially about versification, an "exercise in iambics," Stravinsky provided perhaps the most important clue toward understanding the ballet's compositional riddle. The music's constant use of short–long and long–short rhythmic figures (such as an eighth note followed by a quarter note and vice versa) harkens back to fundamental classical rhythmic patterns in music and dance. Further, the composer commented, "I cannot say whether the idea of the Alexandrines, that supremely arbitrary set of prosodic rules, was precompositional or not . . . but the rhythm of the cello solo (at No. 41 in the

"Pas d'action"

Sketch Chronology and Final Compositional Order

Time-Line of Sketches by Block As They Were Composed	F, I, G, L,	B - C - D,	A, E, M,	J - K, H,	N - O
Rehearsal #'s in published score	#29	#25	#24	#33	#37-38
Measure #'s in published score	m.38	m.6	m.1	m.78	m.108

Figure 6 *Apollo*, "Pas d'action," sketch chronology and final compositional order.

Calliope variation) with the pizzicato accompaniment is a Russian Alexandrine suggested to me by a couplet from Pushkin, and it was one of my first musical ideas. The remainder of the Calliope variation is a musical exposition of the Boileau text that I took as my motto."[35]

Just so, the musical syntax of the ballet is inseparably tied to the Greek view of prosody as a basic grammatical device. Matters of textual nuance always intrigued Stravinsky. The meter of verse and the pure sound of the words themselves served as grist as he plumbed the natural rhythmic flow of syllabification. His sketchbooks consistently exhibit a manipulation of motivic ideas rooted in his affinity for linguistic sounds and rhythms. Whether the source was ethnic folk song or Greek prosody, Stravinsky's idiosyncratic style of instrumental writing frequently arises from the patterns of speech accent and dialect that he found constantly fascinating. This critical link helps to explain the fundamental linguistic roots of, for example, the distinctive string ensemble figurations of *Apollo*. Given the dramaturgy and classical tenets of the earlier *Oedipus rex*, the composer's projections of versification onto *Apollo*'s musical and choreographic structure might almost have been expected. Moreover, the composer's growing interest in the writings of contemporary French poets and intellectuals such as Apollinaire, Cocteau, and Valéry surely spurred him to embrace the ballet's classical message. Apollinaire and Valéry in particular advocated a return to the clarity of classicism. For Stravinsky, *Apollo* was a logical next step.[36]

The underlying bond between poetic meter and dance was an operative force. Particularly toward the end of the sixteenth century, with the establishment of such institutions as the Ballet Comique, the employment of measured verse provided a guiding principle. As music for the ballet required strict compliance with the metrical regulations of poetry, so too did dance. There was an axiomatic relationship linking specific dance steps with specific temporal durations at every structural level. Nowhere is such interfacing more evident than in Balanchine's setting of *Apollo*. Surely Stravinsky intended the dotted rhythms that permeate *Apollo* from the opening measures through the final cadence of the "Apotheosis" as explicit references to the court of Louis XIV.[37] It was through dance that Louis proudly exemplified the splendor of his monarchy in a very visible way. Stravinsky valued such civility and protocol. The dignity and clearly defined hierarchy of Versailles appealed to his sensibilities. He admired Lully's stature as a composer privileged to collaborate with Molière and Corneille in several acclaimed ballets. After all, dancing was understood as an important teaching tool—a means to acquiring social etiquette—designed to inform rather than merely to divert. Stravinsky's emphasis on iambic figures and his explicit reference to "the idea of the Alexandrines" warrant a closer look. Let us examine two examples: the first of the three Muse variations, and the concluding "Apotheosis."

The alexandrine is a twelve-syllable line, marked midway with a pause, or caesura. Originating in the Middle Ages, it experienced a revival in sixteenth-century France. At the time of *Apollo*, Stravinsky was reading the poetry of Nicolas Boileau (1636–1711). Revered for his staunch espousal of artistic discipline and restraint, Boileau authored the alexandrine-structured 1674 treatise *L'Art poétique*, acknowledged as the masterwork on classical principles. A friend of La Fontaine, Molière, and Racine, Boileau lampooned his contemporaries, taking aim at the often sermon-like bickering that divided ancients and moderns. In his *Moi et mes amis*, Francis Poulenc remembered visiting Stravinsky in 1927. With excitement, Stravinsky informed Poulenc that he had discovered Boileau. "I have found a verse in the *Art poétique* that is precisely what I needed to set an exergue for a variation of one of my muses."[38] Boileau was Louis's "royal historiographer." His alexandrines acquired the status of proverbs in extolling the sacred virtues of classicism. Indeed his *Art poétique* flowed straight from Horace's own *Ars poetica*. Yet Stravinsky adopted more than the broad spirit of Boileau's message. The musical language of *Apollo* frequently correlates directly to the poetic feet of Boileau's tightly measured verse. As the composer remarked to Poulenc, one particular alexandrine so interested him that he included the verse in the published score as an epigraph prefacing Calliope's variation:

Que toujours dans vos vers le sens coupant les mots,
Suspende l'hémistiche, en marque le repos

(May the intent of your verse always syncopate the words,
Suspend the pause, enhance its repose)

The rhythm of the opening twelve-note melodic figure replicates the duodecimal syllabification of the alexandrine. The composer is so rigorous in his musical transliteration that the "Suspende l'hémistiche" instruction, literally meaning a marking of the medial caesura, is fortified by Stravinsky's interruptive silence. Even the caesura's duration, occupying three silent pauses, contributes to an evenly paced tripartite symmetry of sound–silence–sound.

Not only does the sketchbook exhibit the regular revision of initial thoughts toward compliance with the poetic meter; the sketches also reveal attempts to stress the sixth pulse of each alexandrine by placing it at the highest point in the melodic contour, thereby emphasizing the medial caesura. In addition, Stravinsky entered precompositional scansion marks in pencil at those places where he considered altering the pattern's underlying regularity. Generally, the compositional process consisted of three distinct phases: the composer first drafted his primary compositional point, such as a particular melodic or rhythmic idea that would serve as the principal idea for a section; next he developed the materials, oftentimes by subtle variation; then finally he composed "around" the passage, writing additional music that functions in either a preparatory or a compensatory fashion. Each layer of this tripartite gesture was composed and timed separately.

Balanchine's own conception of the "Variation de Calliope" is just as sophisticated in its classical proportions. Following the composer's lead, the choreographer visually overlays the opening bars of the "Variation" with the alexandrine pattern. With each hemistich, Balanchine's Calliope haltingly approaches a seated Apollo. Just as the aforementioned medial caesura is reached in the music, Calliope both literally and figuratively "suspends" her *croisé-en-avant* gesture mid-motion, before continuing with the second hemistich. An important distinction must be made here: rather than terminating her movement in any stationary balletic sense, Balanchine's Muse unexpectedly disrupts what we are visually deceived into thinking is a continuous motion—just as Stravinsky's three-pulse silence also provides an abrupt interruption. Thus the impression of genuinely suspending the motion (as Boileau's verse advises and Stravinsky heeds), rather than statically dividing it without any sense of propulsion, is wonderfully achieved. Moreover, the choreographer's sense of musical "space," in which some lines appear and fade within the overall fabric of the music, is matched by the way the stage space is apportioned. Rather than replicating Stravinsky's musical segmentations, Balanchine's Calliope dances with her own visually classical symmetry. Where Stravinsky sometimes chooses to partition the twelve-pulse alexandrine into two equal halves, Balanchine slices the visual field into three parts. Both sonic and visual spaces share common terminal points as demarcated by clear compositional and choreographic gestures (the cessation of the musical phrase, the placing of the prop on the ground).

To continue with the "Variation," Stravinsky's sketchbook reveals that having completed the introduction, he next composed the principal theme, again modeling it as a strict alexandrine. As Balanchine describes the action, Calliope circles Apollo in a series of *chassés*. The sketches suggest that only after Stravinsky had drafted the melody did he forge a transition between the introductory passage and this principal melodic theme. In fact, Stravinsky for the most part composed the transition for each *pas* last. In this instance, the structural link is a single, arresting, one-pulse, *sforzando* D-minor chord. Its punctuating brittleness immediately catches one's attention. So emphatic is the jolt of the sonority that Balanchine could neither ignore nor disguise it. His solution has Calliope clenching her arms violently to her body while bending her knees each time the chord is struck. She directs her action inwardly. Then just as the alexandrine melody begins she rises *en pointe*, and quickly extending her arm and hand fully, suddenly opens her mouth, as if to speak—Calliope, "she of the beautiful voice," as the Greeks referred to the Muse.[39] Such Stravinskyan moments of compositional disjunction, whereby, without warning, the musical message is forcibly wrested in an entirely different direction, are frequent. In addition, Balanchine's boldness in confronting Stravinsky's startling sonority head-on with such a convulsive gesture was just the kind of brazen stroke needed to match the moment's impact.

According to Stravinsky, the ensuing B section (beginning at m. 24) originated in yet another alexandrine, this one by Pushkin, and here assigned as a solo for cello. The composer builds the B section entirely around this cello melody.[40] Stravinsky's scoring, consisting solely of a pizzicato string accompaniment, assures the cello's prominence. From a more traditional nineteenth-century balletic perspective, most choreographers would undoubtedly have set the cello's soaring melody with an equally eye-catching dance. Balanchine, characteristically, brushes off the obvious. Such a dance would have distracted from the cello's primacy, which Stravinsky took pains to emphasize by scoring the accompaniment so delicately. Rather than duplicating the cello's melody, Calliope, dancing *en pointe*, explicitly mimics the short–short–long pizzicato background accompaniment. Moreover, just as the composer marks off each occurrence of the three-beat rhythmic motive with a pause, so Calliope momentarily hesitates on the third pulse of each anapest as a means of punctuation.

The ballet's "Apothéose" provides a fitting summation in illustrating how Balanchine's choreomusical complexities align themselves in the service of clarity. The motto iambic motive first announced in the "Prologue" returns as an obvious cyclic element, bringing closure to the ballet. Apollo, followed by the Muses, ascends to Parnassus; and it is in these last moments of the ballet that Balanchine's instinctive equilibrium of aural and visual materials comes to the fore. Here again Stravinsky weaves elaborate rhythmic layers arising from the same fundamental principles of versification that integrate the entire ballet. Once more his motivic manipulation derives from partitioning the twelve pulses into various segments. The contrabass line, the second cello, the *divisi* violas and second violins—all of these orchestral lines display duodecimal divisions in patterns of two-, three-, and four-note clusters. An augmentation of note values is also evident as the passage proceeds, thus creating a *ritard*, or, in terms of psychological time, a gradual braking of the motion without actually changing the tempo. In fact, the composer refrains from marking any specific retardation of the tempo in the score, since it is built into the music. Because the pitch materials employed are so limited, often oscillating between just two or three notes, the motion seems even more static, providing a sense of resignation. There is a circular feeling of timelessness to it all, as the music moves in a loop, creating a beguiling sense of stasis. Most importantly, these concisely formed musical materials, constantly hovering within their confined boundaries, appear just at the critical moment where the balletic action depicts Apollo's departure from his earthly existence, as Zeus summons his son home.

Yet for all these interior structural intricacies, these instrumental parts collectively amount to no more than an accompaniment, supplying a stability above which the opening iambic motive returns in the first violins and first cellos.

Stravinsky repeats the violin and cello's four-note motive six times over the final music of mm. 19–24.[41] Each iteration of the by now familiar motive occurs at a different and aurally unpredictable point in the overall pacing of this closing passage. It is this unpredictability, this waiting to hear when the motive might reoccur, that holds our attention by heightening our expectation, thereby creating a sense of drive.

Rather than appending the dance to the musical accompaniment, Balanchine buttresses Stravinsky's structural scheme by having the dance element retreat from the final passage's musical action. The cornerstone of this passage is Balanchine's awareness of the fundamental pulse that serves as the foundation for this richly intricate music. At the very moment that the music of the final measures begins, there is an immediate surge of musical information simultaneously complemented by a withdrawal in the choreographic action. Indeed, as the music begins, all choreographic movement ceases, except for the most elegantly elementary movement of all: Apollo and the three Muses successively join in a grand promenade, walking slowly and stolidly across the stage, culminating in Apollo's final ascent.[42]

In a forgotten clip from A Stravinsky Portrait, a documentary shot by Hamburg's Norddeutscher Rundfunk in the 1960s, Balanchine rehearses some of his New York City Ballet dancers for an upcoming performance of Apollo. The camera catches Balanchine and Stravinsky bantering as the choreographer remembers that the ballet had moved too slowly for an irritated Diaghilev; there was simply not enough action for the anxious impresario, who feared that the audience would be lulled to sleep. Its placid deliberateness might have come as too much of a shock to those accustomed to the torque of the composer's more assertive, motor-driven pace. But now, nearly forty years later, Balanchine contends that the work has become so familiar that "people whistle it in the street." Stravinsky quips, "Not always in the street, maybe in the bathroom." He then offers Balanchine more to drink, saying, "Let's be drunk . . . you are not dancing, and I am not dancing."

In another segment, filmed in Stravinsky's absence, Balanchine listens to an audiotape of the ballet that had just been recorded by the composer and the Hamburg orchestra. Balanchine stands at a piano telling his dancers that the tempo of this new recording is appreciably faster than when he first choreographed the work—so fast that he will need to adjust some of the choreographic patterns (a comment somewhat reminiscent of Fokine's and Nijinsky's complaints about the frenetic tempi Stravinsky had demanded in Petrouchka and The Rite). Balanchine recalls how Stravinsky had sat at the piano in 1928 insisting on unhurried and very deliberately paced tempi. In an interview recorded nearly twenty years after the film, Balanchine recalled that when he first heard Stravinsky play the ballet for him in the 1920s, the composer "took the music quite slowly, more slowly than conductors do today. Stravinsky wanted it to sound sustained, endless. Most conductors take it too fast. It should give you the impression of an organ point. . . . It's like the ocean, continuous."[43]

The first staging of the work in New York took place in March 1937, as part of a Stravinsky festival produced by Balanchine at the Metropolitan Opera. Even then, the composer expressed concern over the appropriate tempo, urging Balanchine to heed the music's precise metronomic markings. While American reviews were again often lukewarm, Elliott Carter, who had actually attended the original Diaghilev production in Paris, found Balanchine's now slightly modified version more fluid in its "beautiful plasticity."[44] Thereafter, productions occurred more frequently, each involving changes in scenery, costuming, choreography, and at times even the music used. Balanchine's extraction of the entire "Prologue" in the late 1970s was surely the most controversial among cutbacks intended to bring even more austerity to the ballet's classicism. For musicians, this was a loss, since so much of the ballet's music flows from germinal motives introduced in the opening scene. The coherence that Stravinsky carefully built upon the early exposition of these melodic and rhythmic ideas is not nearly so convincing without the opportunity to follow their compositional evolution throughout the ballet. By the 1990s, at least some productions were restoring the uncut score.

Perhaps the greatest accomplishment of Apollo was the composer and choreographer's conveyance of a powerful artistic statement expressed not with pomposity, but with an economic, sotto voce fluency. Its subtlety washed away the grandiloquence of earlier times. The lost grace and classical elegance of a bygone stylistic idiom, stripped of artifice, deserved to be revived and rethought. It did not, however, deserve to be mummified. Stravinsky and Balanchine understood that classicism should not translate as the preservation of some sacrosanct relic. Balanchine, particularly, never saw his ballets, his "butterflies," as embalmed museum pieces. A ballet was always a work in progress. Stravinsky, likewise, continued to revisit and revive many of his works years after their inception. For both men, to deny change was to invite stagnation. In the forty years that followed *Apollo*'s premiere, Stravinsky and Balanchine were to collaborate often. While this 1928 ballet has changed in some respects, in others it has remained quintessentially the same. Even for a Greek myth, the journey of *Apollon musagète* has been a curious odyssey indeed. Stravinsky and Balanchine's unswerving devotion to the abiding principles of reason, balance, austerity, and order would serve them well in all of their future endeavors. Even today, *Apollo* deservedly remains one of the most frequently performed of twentieth-century ballets. Its combined underlying structural strength and gentle understatement continue to resonate tranquilly and timelessly.

CHAPTER SIX

AMERICA

APOLLO CONFIRMED the Ballets Russes' continuing capacity to make meaningful artistic statements. It proved that classicism was adaptive rather than brittle. Less than a year after the premiere, Diaghilev staged what would come to be seen as another masterpiece, *The Prodigal Son*, choreographed by Balanchine to a score by Prokofiev. It would be the impresario's last production. Diaghilev's death in Venice on August 19, 1929, would send ripples throughout the ballet world. For all its internal acrimony and divisive posturing, the Ballets Russes had furnished a safe haven for both accomplished and aspiring artists. The company was devastated, having realized the extraordinary achievement of Diaghilev's fostering of careers and forging of otherwise unexplored pathways. His demise lowered a curtain on the company's courageous experiment. Lincoln Kirstein wrote in his novel *Flesh Is Heir*, "It was the end indeed, the end of youth for a distinguished company of human beings, the end of power and endeavor, the end perhaps, of the first quarter of the twentieth century." The already declining company soon disbanded, touching off a balkanizing scramble for would-be successors, each attempting to assume Diaghilev's mantle and salvage the remnants of the troupe's once enviable reputation.[1]

Diaghilev's death shook Stravinsky severely. Although the composer's always conflicted relationship with the impresario had deteriorated after *Apollo*, their mutual affection was genuine. Stravinsky confided to his closest friends that his heart sank upon hearing of Diaghilev's passing. His friend pianist Arthur Rubinstein noted that Stravinsky seemed orphaned. Soulima Stravinsky recalled that "Diaghilev's death was hard on my father. It was as if it was a brother or more, even more." A letter to Walter Nouvel written on August 26, 1929, captures Stravinsky's own sentiments: "It is difficult for me to write these lines . . . as I prefer silence to a letter which expresses so inadequately what I feel. But I have summoned up courage to express my feelings . . . feeling the sharp pain which I have in my heart as a result of the sudden disappearance of Seriozha whom I loved so much."[2]

Only a few days earlier Manuel de Falla wrote to Stravinsky, "I was deeply moved by the death of Diaghilev and must write to you before anyone else. What a great loss for you! He did many wonderful things, but the foremost was to discover you. We owe that to him. Without you, moreover, the Ballet would not have been able to exist."[3] But perhaps it was the other way around. Without the catapult of the Ballets Russes, Stravinsky may not have become the composer history remembers. In collaborating with every major choreographer and set designer in Diaghilev's troupe, Stravinsky created more theater works for the company than any other composer, each of them absolutely distinctive. The success of his close collaborations with a cluster of artists and intellectuals grew out of a like-minded disdain for like-mindedness. The empirical lessons learned from the friendships cultivated within the Ballets Russes, predominantly the friendships of non-musicians, would sustain the composer throughout the remainder of his life. Benois, Bakst, Cocteau, Picasso, Roerich—the most dazzling faculty of theater artists imaginable—would later be succeeded in Los Angeles by Auden, Eliot, Huxley, Isherwood, Spender, and other literati. The denominator of these relationships came by way of a binding covenant: the quest for new expressive pathways. As Stravinsky remarked to Christopher Isherwood, "Diaghilev surrounded himself with people who were inventive, and inventions are the only things worth stealing."[4] Stravinsky's inventiveness, stolen or otherwise, took seed in the Ballets Russes, where the composer assimilated a broad sense of composition—not just music composition. Tension, release, architectural equilibrium, an overarching coherence, an understanding of physical movement, the rhythms of drama's structural pacing—this broad litany of supra-musical techniques filtered through the eyes of collaborating artists profoundly shaped Stravinsky's compositional approach. And as he contemplated these abstractions, there was the concrete praxis of the Ballets Russes right in front of him, heuristically serving as a working laboratory, an incubator, to test his ideas on the spot. How much progress would Stravinsky have achieved without the home Diaghilev provided? And would Diaghilev's company have traveled the adventurous road it did without Stravinsky's music? They had come to rely upon one another without daring to admit it. The fruits of their co-dependence ended in 1929. And by then, in fact, Stravinsky had already sought sponsorship elsewhere.

Le Baiser de la fée

In early December 1927, six months before the premiere of *Apollo*, Ida Rubinstein, who was just then launching a new ballet troupe in Paris, asked Stravinsky's agent if she might prepare her own production of the forthcoming *Apollo*. Diaghilev was not about to comply. Rubinstein quickly sought an alternative. As Stravinsky recalled, "Just as I was finishing the music of Apollo . . . I received from Mme Ida Rubinstein a proposal to compose a ballet for her repertory. The painter Alexandre Benois, who had done some work for her, submitted two plans, one of which seemed very likely to attract me."[5] Both plans focused on a "Tchaikovskyana" tribute, to use Benois's expression. Eighteen years earlier it had been a shared fondness for the music of Tchaikovsky that first brought the designer and young composer together as they collaborated on *The Firebird*. The plan chosen allowed Stravinsky to "compose something inspired by the music of Tchaikovsky," the composer recalled. He was to deliver the new work by summer's end—a tall order given his busy schedule of composing, conducting, recording, and concertizing in 1928 (Figure 7).

Rather than refurbish some of Tchaikovsky's popular ballet music, Stravinsky would employ several relatively minor works for piano or voice. Rubinstein and Benois had suggested a ballet that would be "inspired" by the music of Tchaikovsky. Given his long-held devotion to the earlier composer, Stravinsky now accepted the commission as a "compatriotic homage." He affixed a formal dedication to the score: "I dedicate this ballet to the memory of Peter Chaikovsky by relating the Fairy to his Muse, and in this way the ballet becomes an allegory, the Muse having similarly branded Chaikovsky with her fatal kiss, whose mysterious imprint made itself felt in all this great artist's work."

The real impetus in re-embracing Tchaikovsky is traceable to Stravinsky's felicitous involvement in orchestrating part of *The Sleeping Beauty* ("the most convincing example of Tchaikovsky's immense talent," the composer once commented). In the wake of the First World War, Diaghilev, in 1921, decided to remount this grandest of ballets, with Nijinsky and Karsavina. Stravinsky was delighted. For the neoclassically reinvented Stravinsky, Tchaikovsky—the most classically western of Russia's composers—rather than the once embraced kuchkists, was now seen as the soul of Peter the Great's Russia, and also as removed from the intellectual and musically misunderstood dodecaphonic advances of Vienna as one could imagine. Stravinsky took on the task of orchestrating some of the music that had been cut in the ballet's original production—music surviving only in piano score. Although Diaghilev's production was disappointing (Parisian performances were cancelled in the

Figure 7 Poster advertizing a typical Stravinsky program, with the composer as conductor, 1928.

wake of an unsuccessful London premiere), the composer's renewed contact with Tchaikovsky prompted his decision to accept Rubinstein's commission. Francis Maes remarks that *Le Baiser de la fée* (as the new ballet would eventually be entitled) was "a downright pastiche of *The Sleeping Beauty*. There is no question of stylization or disguise; it is a deliberate, calculated imitation."[6] Perhaps, but as with *Petrouchka*, Stravinsky's genius manifests itself not in the quotation of Tchaikovsky excerpts, but in the work's organic transformation of borrowed materials. From the opening measures, the composer seamlessly integrates his models into the ballet's thoroughly neoclassical texture.

Originally, Rubinstein intended to employ Fokine as the work's choreographer, but to Stravinsky's relief she eventually engaged Bronislava Nijinska.[7] Correspondence between Rubinstein, Benois, and Stravinsky ensued, and by mid January 1928, while laboring intensely on his forthcoming *Apollo*, Stravinsky had quietly, even stealthily, accepted Rubinstein's commission of $6,000 (six times the fee Coolidge paid him for *Apollo*) for the new ballet. A belligerent Diaghilev excoriated Stravinsky's acceptance of Rubinstein's offer. It was the final blow to their already flagging relationship. Diaghilev, as implacable as ever, was outraged at what he saw as Stravinsky's latest alliance beyond the Ballets Russes. Moreover, the fact that the composer would agree to work with Ida Rubinstein, whose history with Diaghilev was a tense one, surely irked him even more.[8]

While the Ballets Russes was on tour in 1928, Diaghilev absented himself to attend performances of Rubinstein's newest company at the Paris Opera. Since Rubinstein had enticed many of Diaghilev's principal artists, he was "somewhat disquieted," as Grigoriev reported. "However, his fears were soon dispelled; and he returned to us entirely reassured." Still, his accusations were invidious, and he remained "indignant that people such as Stravinsky . . . should deign to connect themselves with an undertaking so inferior."[9] He was equally dismayed that Benois would associate with Rubinstein. Further, he wrote to Lifar that upon seeing the Paris production of Stravinsky's ballet, he returned from the theater with "a fearful headache," complaining that the ballet was "tiresome, lachrymose . . . drab . . . and the whole arrangement lacked vitality. . . . The whole thing was still-born." Unable to suppress one final barb, Diaghilev concluded by telling Lifar, "Igor, my first son, has given himself up entirely to the love of God and cash."[10]

Based on Hans Christian Andersen's story "The Ice Maiden," Stravinsky's new work was eventually entitled *Le Baiser de la fée*. He had initially used Andersen's title, but changed his mind well into writing the work.

Although the composer later complained that the story had received too much credit as the ballet's source, Andersen's tales had long appealed to him. His early opera *Le Rossignol* (and subsequently the ballet *Le Chant du rossignol*) had also found inspiration in an Andersen parable. A note prefacing the published score captures the essence of *Le Baiser de la fée*:

Characters: A Fairy, a Young Man, his Fiancée, the Child's Mother, Creatures attendant on the Fairy, Villagers, Musicians at the fête, Friends of the Fiancée.

Argument: A fairy marks a young man with her mysterious kiss while he is still a child. She withdraws him from his mother's arms. She withdraws him from life on the day of his greatest happiness in order to possess him and preserve this happiness forever. She marks him once more with her kiss.

General Note: The strict and precise indications for the movements of the characters in this ballet as given in my score are intended to form *a fixed basis* for the producer. On the other hand, the vagueness and imprecision of my directions concerning the place and period of the action are meant to give designer and producer full freedom to construct a choreographic spectacle based directly on the character and style of the music.

The ballet unfolds in one act of four continuous scenes. Stravinsky conducted the premiere at the Paris Opera on November 27, 1928. Ida Rubinstein danced the role of the Fairy, although her name went all but unmentioned in several lackluster reviews. There were only two performances in Paris, followed by single perform- ances in Brussels, Monte Carlo, and Milan. Thereafter, the ballet virtually fell into oblivion (with the exception of a brief Nijinska revival in 1933) until Balanchine resurrected and refurbished the work in America.

Unlike the modestly sized *Apollo*, the forty-five-minute *Le Baiser*—longer than *The Rite*—utilized a full orchestra of strings, the harp originally planned for *Apollo*, winds (including a bass clarinet), brass, and percussion. The scenario seemed a far cry from the composer's recent Greek works; but Stravinsky heralded his new ballet as thoroughly classical: "Although I gave full liberty to painter and choreographer in the staging of my composition, my innermost desire was that it should be presented in classical form, after the manner of *Apollo*. I pictured all the fantastic roles as danced in white ballet skirts."[11] It struck others as classical, too, including Stravinsky's advocate Werner Reinhart. Writing in the fall of 1929, Reinhart commented, "Last spring, I had the oppor- tunity to hear your *Baiser de la fée* at La Scala. . . . and was deeply moved by your work, whose piano score you had so kindly given to me some time ago." Complaining that audiences seemed not to understand "the beauty of music that is so simple and pure," Reinhart added, "One must . . . go all the way back to Haydn to find a language whose richness is in its simplicity."[12]

In an appendix to his later conversation book *Expositions and Developments*, Stravinsky listed a handful of Tchaikovsky works that had been used as models, or at least as starting points.[13] For example, he quotes Tchaikovsky's familiar song "Berceuse de la tempête," op. 54, no. 10, but he reorchestrates, reharmonizes, and transforms the fundamental material both in the opening pages of the ballet (Example 5 (a) and 5 (b) and later in the first and last tableaux. From the very first measures, Stravinsky stretches the fundamental motive of Tchaikovsky's original melody, rhythmically extending its outline and carefully balancing a wonderfully

Example 5 (a) Tchaikovsky, "Berceuse de la tempête," op. 54, no. 10.

monophonic texture with filled in harmonic points of definition. The barren, open sound of this initial section beautifully matches the scenario, in which a mother calms a child during a storm. There can be no mistaking the treatment as Stravinskyan. The process continues at m. 6, where further development ensues. The composer uses a fragment of the same melody as a means of creating a

IGOR STRAWINSKY
1928, Revised 1950

Berceuse de la tempête

Example 5 (b) *Le Baiser de la fée,* "Prologue: Berceuse de la tempête."

transition into the next quotation (perhaps a reference to Tchaikovsky's Fifth Symphony, as some have suggested) at m. 13. This opening material serves as a unifying motive, returning toward the close of the first scene at m. 265, a dramatic juncture wherein the Fairy kisses the child on the forehead, thereby sealing his fate. Marked *Andante,* the motive is now inverted and also rhythmically transformed.

Whatever remnant of Tchaikovsky remains has been completely absorbed into Stravinsky's characteristic fragmenting and reassembling of the reprise's simple melodic material.

The ballet proceeds with numerous other Tchaikovskyan quotations, but the "Berceuse" returns at the beginning of the fourth tableau, appropriate to the dramatic action. The Fairy has wed the young man and transported him to the "Land beyond Time and Place." The original melodic motive, consisting of only four notes, is tossed from one section of the orchestra to the next, as Stravinsky once again fragments, rhythmically augments, and transforms the motive in this closing scene. The compositional pattern holds throughout the ballet, as several analysts have thoroughly discussed in addressing Stravinsky's adaptation of his Tchaikovskyan models.[14]

Stravinsky began work on the ballet shortly after the Parisian premiere of *Apollo*, composing from July through October 1928. Both the compositional sketches and the piano reduction are replete with directives. Moreover, in a letter to Benois, Stravinsky, rather adamantly, makes clear his desire for Alpine costumes, "from around 1850." He also identifies Interlaken as the location of the lake. From the very beginning, "pre-compositionally," Stravinsky also estimated the duration of each section of the planned ballet as he drafted the dramatic action. Even after he began writing, he continued to indicate the approximate length of each section. For example, at the top of the page for the "Pas de deux" sketches, Stravinsky writes, "Entrée 1½ minutes, Adagio 2 minutes, Variation I (*jeune homme*) 1 minute, Variation II 1 minute, and then the Coda." While sketches for the second variation exist, only the first variation would materialize. Stravinsky, as economical as ever, would employ some ideas from the scrapped variation in the final *scène*. Nor were these internal sections written in order, Variation I being composed after the Coda. The sketches include several early "nota bene" markings, to which Stravinsky would return later in the compositional process.

Throughout the final piano score used in rehearsal, the composer detailed his wishes, crossing out preliminary ideas and entering revisions, clearly indicating that he was in charge of the production. While there is no doubt that he preferred Nijinska to Fokine, still his usual suspicions surfaced, heightened now by his more recent and increasingly congenial association with Balanchine. Stravinsky recounted the circumstances surrounding the premiere in his chronicle:

> I was unable to follow the work of Bronislava Nijinska, who was composing the choreography in Paris bit by bit as I sent parts from Echarvines as completed. Owing to this, it was not until just before the first performance that I saw her work, and by that time all the principal scenes had been fixed.

I found some of the scenes successful . . . but there was . . . a good deal of which I could not approve, and which, had I been present at the moment of their composition, I should have tried to get altered.[15]

In several unpublished letters Stravinsky describes the final rehearsal process more bluntly. For example, in a letter written in October, only a month or so before the premiere, Stravinsky instructed Gavril Païchadze, director of the Éditions Russes de Musique, to withhold the piano score of the ballet from both Rubinstein and Nijinska. He insists that he himself must play the music for them, since neither dancer really understands musical matters, especially the setting of correct tempi. Three days later Stravinsky eased up a bit, now informing Païchadze that since the production would probably fall through unless rehearsals went forward without him, the rehearsal pianist could have the score, quickly adding that all the clearly marked tempi were to be followed without exception. He would, however, remain unsatisfied with Nijinska's staging.

The reviews of the performance were mostly drab. Henri Prunières, who was often sympathetic to Stravinsky's music, wrote in the *Revue musicale* in January 1929 that the work was an odd waste of the composer's time and nothing more than a feeble compendium of tuneful Tchaikovskyan models. On the other hand, Roland-Manuel celebrated the work's coherence and Stravinsky's ability to synthesize Tchaikovsky's music into his own style, writing to the composer, "*Le Baiser de la fée* is a success that surpasses success. . . . The powerful emotion that it inspires in me results from the unity of substance in the diversity of the objects."[16] But the comments of Roland-Manuel and other Stravinsky supporters aside, the work was hardly a public success. The ballet quickly vanished. Frederick Ashton presented a revised version at Sadler's Wells in 1935. It would, however, be Balanchine's restaging of *The Fairy's Kiss* (as it eventually came to be known) almost a decade later in New York, this time as part of the American Ballet's Stravinsky Festival at the Metropolitan Opera, that would meet with Stravinsky's approval. The composer conducted the premiere on April 27, 1937, in a program that included two of his other ballets. On the American side of the Atlantic, the reviews of Balanchine's production were overwhelmingly positive. It seemed that Stravinsky's being in the hands of Balanchine made all the difference. Increasingly their names were paired.

Jeu de cartes

After Diaghilev's death, Balanchine became a journeyman. He returned to arranging opera-ballets in Monte Carlo; served as a guest ballet master in

Copenhagen; staged dances to vaudevillian music in London ("the Diaghilev of the light-musical stage," as Vernon Duke tagged him); and in 1933, with the help of Kochno, Chanel, and Cole Porter, started his own ballet company, Les Ballets 1933. When the company folded within the year Balanchine remained rootless, but the short-lived experience provided a connection between the choreographer and the young, Harvard-educated balletomane Lincoln Kirstein. Within a few months, Kirstein arranged passage for Balanchine to New York. The choreographer, having grown increasingly disenchanted with Europe, would stake his future there. Within the year, Balanchine founded the School of American Ballet.

While Balanchine continued to acclimate himself to New York over the next few years, dividing his time between Broadway and the Met, Stravinsky remained in Europe, touring as a conductor and pianist. It was a disruptive period for the composer, leaving little time for creative work. There were to be no new ballets in his immediate future. Still, Stravinsky, Balanchine, and now Lincoln Kirstein remained steadfast in their shared beliefs about classical dance's mission. Having already weathered a barrage of criticism, Balanchine's young American Ballet grew more ambitious. The two-day Stravinsky Festival in April 1937 was unprecedented. The composer, just then touring in the United States, agreed to conduct both New York performances before returning to Europe. Held at the Metropolitan Opera, the Stravinsky Festival presented three of his ballets, including the first American performance of Balanchine's *Apollo*, nine years to the day after Bolm's already long-disregarded staging in Washington.

Most significantly, the company introduced *Jeu de cartes*, funded by Kirstein's financial partner Edward Warburg. The new work was expressly commissioned to showcase the vitality of the American Ballet's twenty-six young dancers. With some apprehension, given Stravinsky's reputation as an unforgiving collaborator, Kirstein and Warburg met with the composer in New York during his 1935 tour with the violinist Samuel Dushkin, to broach the idea of commissioning a ballet for Balanchine's new company. The ballet's action is traceable to the composer's lifelong enjoyment of playing cards. Characteristically, Stravinsky's memories are ambiguous. In an interview given a year after the premiere, he claimed that the idea of a card-game ballet occurred while he was riding in a fiacre, although he could not remember when. Thirty-seven years later, in discussing the work with Robert Layton, Stravinsky recalled things differently. He claimed that the idea "for a ballet in which the dancers would be dressed as playing cards" had come to him as early as 1920.[17] Nikita Malaieff assisted Stravinsky in drafting the synopsis and scenario for the ballet, although the composer eventually arranged his own libretto on the basis of a few verses of Jean de La Fontaine's apologue "Les Loups et les brebis" (The Wolves and the Sheep). It was La Fontaine's moralistic poetry that provided Stravinsky with the "argument" for *Jeu de cartes*.[18]

The characters proposed were cards in a poker game led by the duplicitous Joker, who weaves his chicanery throughout three separate deals. As his compositional sketches demonstrate, Stravinsky completed much of the work before being offered the commission. Initial sketches dating from December 1935 suggest that Stravinsky began the work without a clear balletic concept, although he may have had at least a basic storyline in mind. Writing to Balanchine six months into the composing process, Stravinsky expressed reservations about shaping his score for dance, not only because of his increasing qualms about ballet as an art form (qualms that had seemed to ebb and flow over the preceding fifteen years) but because a scenario was not yet settled. Consequently, how could he plan the music's architecture?[19]

The orchestral exuberance of the new work suggested that the score might have been intended for both the theater and the concert hall. Even before the composer toured America as a pianist and conductor, he had already arranged for several concert performances of it in London. Stravinsky often began a commissioned work before signing a contract. The choreographer originally suggested yet another Hans Christian Andersen story, "The Flowered Ball," as the basis for the scenario, but the idea was promptly rejected by Stravinsky, who thought it would be inappropriate if the ballet were to offer anything more than light fare. At the end of June 1936 Stravinsky drafted his own storyline, no doubt frustrated by stalled contract negotiations and a still undeveloped scenario. He also took it upon himself to determine the length of the ballet, the stage design, the size of the orchestra, even the number of dancers. The Basel archives retain both the original French synopsis of the ballet as prepared by Malaieff, as well as the very detailed scenario that Stravinsky drafted, complete with many choreographic directions already determined. The document offers a glimpse into the composer's initial thinking. For example, Stravinsky writes,

The characters of group Left discard their (blue) masks and dominoes one after the other and begin calmly to dance a waltz. In this dance they are joined by the characters of the two other groups who, however, remain in disguise. This dance finished, they take up their original positions. At this moment, the characters of group R., discarding their masks and dominoes, immediately attack group L., who after a desperate struggle realize themselves to be defeated and fly. The conquerors, chasing their foe, disappear with them off the stage.

Some of the compositional sketches already include notations that position the dancers. Other directions may have been added once the ballet was completed and rehearsal numbers were assigned. For example, Stravinsky instructs, "As soon as the Joker appears, the characters of the central group admit their defeat, and move off one after the other during the six measures of Rehearsal 20. From Rehearsal 21 to 33 bursts of challenge and helpless rage from the Joker against group L. During the five measures of Rehearsal 33 he leaves the stage." The Basel sketchbook reveals that Stravinsky often jotted down ideas for all three of the Joker's deals on the same day. The compositional process was thus far more scattershot than in *Apollo*. Yet even as he drafted *Jeu de cartes* much remained up in the air. Consequently, the sketches reveal quite a different evolution. Stravinsky often worked on isolated passages of several measures, then almost randomly, it seems, proceeded to sketch entirely unrelated music ultimately located in a completely different part of the ballet. The signature trumpet fanfare introducing each of the three deals, for example, was, as the Basel sketches attest, originally intertwined much more frequently at various internal points within each of the ballet's three large movements. The sketches also reveal that Stravinsky often changed his mind about the key in which the music would appear.

Example 6 illustrates the way the composer worked. The sketch shows an idea that is already fairly well developed both rhythmically and harmonically. A comparison of the sketch with mm. 27–37 of Variation V, where the Coda following this fifth variation begins, reveals just how much the composer does with the initial material. (The sketches here reveal that Stravinsky wrote the Coda before returning to write Variation V, just as he had composed the Coda before Variation I in *Le Baiser de la fée*.)

The composer regularly experimented with metric and rhythmic figurations, searching for the clearest way of notating his thoughts—something he often did even years after a score was first printed. The process can be observed in Example 7, which shows an early sketch of material eventually used in mm. 158–65 of the "Troisième donne," followed by the relative passage from the published score. This was an especially relevant juncture, as we shall see. In the sketch, the composer already assigns the lower treble-clef figure to the horns, while strings will eventually play the upper material. And as in sketches for earlier ballets, the composer inserts a letter to indicate his intention to repeat a block of material. A comparison of the sketch with the final version reveals the subtle changes the composer makes.

No work from the 1930s is more buoyant than this high-spirited musical romp. The composer admitted to having borrowed familiar tunes by Strauss,

Example 6   *Jeu de cartes*, mm. 27–37, transcribed sketch and score.

Ravel, and others. But even without the confession, they would be all but impossible to miss. Most familiar is the composer's thematic parody of the overture to *The Barber of Seville*. Rossini's well-known tune was one of the first passages that caught Balanchine's eye when he received the piano reduction in December 1936.[20] Creating an unadulterated pastiche was a clever way of quickly winning over listeners. Some, however, found the peppering of quotations not so much witty as downright slapstick. "Just why the musical setting of a poker game should quote from every musician from Rossini to Ravel is not readily apparent," groused John Martin in his *New York Times* review.[21]

Example 7 *Jeu de cartes*, mm. 158–65, transcribed sketch and score.

Here again the Basel sketchbook is instructive. The closing section of the Third Deal was finished on October 19, 1936. Only later, in November, did Stravinsky compose the passage leading up to this closing section. The Rossini quotation first appears in a transparent reference at m. 171 of the Third Deal, but Stravinsky actually composed in reverse order, just as he had in *Apollo*. He began with the material of mm. 158–65 as discussed above—all developed from what can now be seen as a rhythmic and metric variation of the Rossini material. Next, as the carefully dated sketches confirm, the composer abruptly abandoned the

Rossini materials that he had continued to develop for another 269 measures, choosing now to shape the final cadence beginning in m. 431. That accomplished, he returned to the Rossini parody, retreating even further back into the piece. He developed what would eventually be the rhythmic motive of m. 121, also clearly related to the Rossini tune—a tune that at that point remained unstated. In effect, motivic derivations anticipate their actual source until finally the source manifests itself. It is one of the composer's favorite ploys. Almost subliminally, the seeds of the Rossini quotation seep into our perception. When the tune finally appears forthrightly, and we recognize Stravinsky's game, the joke is all the more enjoyable. The composer wrote the entire passage in reverse, carefully assembling it not one measure and then the next, but rather one measure and then the one preceding it. Analysts eager to trace motive B from motive A in Stravinsky's music would do well to realise that it is often A that is derived from B.

Kirstein's illuminating 1937 essay "Working with Stravinsky" provides a rare eyewitness analysis of the rehearsal process.[22] He contended that *Jeu de cartes* was "a complete collaboration," although that was not the case. Stravinsky declared he was relatively unconcerned with detailing the action too specifically, although his sketches imply otherwise. With *Jeu de cartes*, he remembered that as he composed in France and Balanchine worked in New York, there was virtually no discussion about the choreography, although we know they discussed tempi, at least, when Stravinsky passed through New York on tour with Dushkin. Kirstein further recalled Balanchine plotting a sizeable portion of the choreography before Stravinsky's arrival. Once the composer entered the rehearsal studio that March, however, the dynamics changed. Kirstein claimed that Stravinsky had complete confidence in his partnership with Balanchine. Yet he was quick to add, in a curiously worded statement, that Stravinsky "treated Balanchine like a junior assistant, although on an absolutely equal footing as an expert, since there was a presupposed agreement that the spectacle would be governed by music rather than by any overall concept of stylized movement." Whatever the case, Stravinsky, irrepressibly it seems, participated in rehearsing *Jeu de cartes*, sometimes for as long as six hours at a time before "hauling the rehearsal pianist off to his hotel for more work." Whatever choreographic plan Stravinsky had envisioned while composing the work in Europe, it is clear that he modified his ideas once he saw Balanchine's dancers in action.[23] Kirstein found that the ballet adhered too restrictively to the "regulations of Stravinsky's very rigidly indicated libretto."

The composer physically demonstrated his instructions to the dancers. He would slap his knee, Kirstein described, keeping strict count and "gesticulating rapidly to emphasize his points"—much as he had been described by those who had observed him rehearsing *The Rite* twenty-five years earlier.[24] Stravinsky apparently refashioned the choreography. At the end of the first of the three deals, for example, he made alterations for the sake of simplicity. But he also showed flexibility whenever Balanchine requested additional music to allow the choreography to unfold. More than one witness remembers Stravinsky unhesitatingly adding music on the spot.

The Basel archives retain Stravinsky's sketch score—the score he finished in early December before shipping the piano reduction to New York. This primary source provides significant insight into whatever collaborative decisions were made. The score is a treasure trove in determining revisions completed in France, as well as clarifying what actually transpired in "real time" in Balanchine's New York rehearsal studio. Stravinsky often changed tempo markings from those he had originally planned, sometimes drastically. Several instrumental indications were added or rethought, dispelling the fiction that Stravinsky had the precise sound of the piece complete in his mind from the very start. Metric alterations often led to rebarring music in duple meter rather than the originally conceived triple meter. Indeed the score is copiously marked with arrows, inserts, and directions to repeat measures sometimes at distant junctures in the score. Such revisions point to the composer's willingness to reposition ideas as Balanchine visualized the ballet.

Illuminating too is the Basel manuscript copy of the piano reduction prepared by Erich Itor Kahn (with suggested revisions by the composer, who found the initial reduction too dense). Completed in the fall of 1936 and sent to Balanchine in early December, the manuscript also includes important tempo changes undoubtedly recorded in the rehearsal studio as choreographic adjustments were made to the music. For instance, Stravinsky added or relocated music at several junctures, as the piano reduction demonstrates. The opening tempo slows. Rehearsal numbers are added and adjusted. As a specific example of Stravinsky's modifying the pacing, the composer penciled in a directive to insert the already composed first five measures of Variation V, suggesting that Balanchine needed more time for his dancers. This was a very late adjustment. Once the insertion was made, Stravinsky changed all subsequent rehearsal numbers for the duration of the ballet. Taken together, the sketch score and annotated piano reduction illustrate just how fluid the process of composing and choreographing was, even during the final weeks before the April 1937 premiere.

While some expressed reservations about the ballet as a stage work, no one could deny that Stravinsky's orchestral score glittered. As Kirstein astutely observed, the scoring of the work "is almost too exquisite, rhythmic irregularities too finely delineated, subtle, sophisticated to ensure a crass success with choreographers . . . or with a public spoiled by successions of larger, harsher, or louder sounds."[25] *Jeu de cartes* immediately took on its own life as a remarkably accessible concert piece. As part of a 1938 French radio broadcast, Stravinsky responded to questions about the ballet posed by Les Six composer Georges Auric:

> Whatever may be the destination of a piece of music—whether intended for the theater, concert hall, or cinema—it is essential it should have its proper intrinsic value, its own existence, its *raison d'être*. . . . That's why, when I am writing for the theater, my first anxiety is to make certain my music has an independent existence and to guard it from the danger of subjecting itself to the demands of the other theatrical elements involved. . . . My later scores are conceived and constructed as separate musical entities, independent of their scenic purpose; and because of that I attach as much importance to their concert performance as to their stage presentation.[26]

Danses concertantes

Balanchine's Stravinsky Festival brought only a temporary reunification of composer and choreographer, although now with the munificent support of Lincoln Kirstein. By Kirstein's own admission, however, the festival was at best a modest step leading nowhere. Just as the better part of a decade had separated *Apollo* and *Jeu de cartes*, so another ten years would pass before the composer and choreographer's landmark collaboration on the 1948 *Orpheus* came to fruition. A week after the festival, Stravinsky sailed back to France, where he continued to work on several compositions, including the Symphony in C for the fiftieth anniversary of the Chicago Symphony Orchestra. The next few years would prove particularly trying for him, both personally and professionally. He was informed of his sister-in-law's death shortly after the 1937 premiere of *Jeu de cartes*, and tragically his daughter Lyudmila passed away in 1938. The next year both his wife Catherine and his mother died. All the while Stravinsky became increasingly disheartened by France's decreasing attention to his music, and by the tepid reception of performances of his scores in neighboring countries.

Moreover, it became increasingly difficult to tour a Europe enveloped by the threat of war. Neville Chamberlain agreed to Germany's annexation of the Sudetenland in the fall of 1938: Hitler invaded Poland a year later, and within days Britain, France, Australia, and New Zealand were plunged into a world war. The bright prospects Paris had offered twenty-five years earlier had now run their course. Stravinsky knew it was time to leave, and having become familiar with America, he knew where he wanted to go. The opportunity to emigrate material-ized in the form of the Charles Eliot Norton Chair of Poetry at Harvard University, which he held during the 1939–40 academic year. His archives show that his six Harvard lectures, later compiled as the *Poetics of Music*, interested him far less than completing the Symphony in C. By contract, Harvard allowed him to continue touring during the academic year, and as a consequence Stravinsky came to know Los Angeles, where he would soon reside. Finally, in the spring of 1940, he married Vera de Bosset (Soudeikine), with whom he had now had a relationship for almost two decades (he had been introduced to her by Diaghilev). The composer wanted the peace and order of an uninterrupted routine that would allow him to continue working. For the better part of the rest of his life he found at least some measure of a regular schedule in California, despite his continuing travels.

Like so many other composers and writers at this time, Stravinsky attempted to find a niche in the lucrative Hollywood film industry. His efforts, however, proved largely unsuccessful. In 1941 he completed about half of the music for a new, unspecified work. Eventually entitled *Danses concertantes*, it had been commissioned by Werner Janssen as a chamber orchestra piece for his Los Angeles ensemble. Although just another commission, Stravinsky felt obliged to defend the lighthearted work's compositional style. His close friend Sol Babitz (a knowledgeable violinist who played in Janssen's orchestra) remarked that *Danses concertantes* revisited the ballet music of the nineteenth century "noting all its charm and all its fatuity as well."[27]

The work was cast in a typical balletic design. An opening "Marche" is followed by a "Pas d'action," then a "Thème varié" with four variations. A "Pas de deux" and concluding "Marche" end the twenty-minute work. *Danses concertantes* premiered as an orchestral work in Los Angeles on February 8, 1942, with Stravinsky conducting. Yet given the ballet notations evident in the earliest sketches, it is likely that the composer envisioned choreography from the first. Stravinsky probably discussed the music with Balanchine, who was involved in the Hollywood film industry, in early 1942 if not earlier. If Stravinsky had no thoughts of a possible ballet, it is difficult to reconcile Balanchine's reply to an interviewer who asked if the choreographer had ever requested that Stravinsky specifically write ballet music for his use: "If he had free time, I would ask him to write something. Once he said, 'Yes, I have time. What would you like?' I said, 'Just start with something—a variation—anything . . .' so he wrote *Danses concertantes*."[28]

The lively composition immediately appealed to Balanchine. He found its "volatile" rhythms (to use his word) challenging but danceable, and its plotless music in perfect keeping with his own developing balletic notions. Reynolds suggests that the ballet's physical challenges indeed "foreshadowed some of [Balanchine's] most important later work," given that "it was almost deadly in the precision with which it dealt with a score of extreme rhythmic complexity."[29] In

1944, with scenery and costumes by Eugene Berman, Balanchine choreographed the work for the Ballet Russe de Monte Carlo at New York's City Center of Music and Drama.

The composer and choreographer met often in April 1943, even rehearsing the ballet at Balanchine's apartment. In fact, in preparing *Danses concertantes* the composer and choreographer convened more frequently than in any previous collaboration. Stravinsky also often attended performances of the work, whenever programmed in Los Angeles over the next few years. He and Balanchine continued their bicoastal meetings, discussing music in Los Angeles whenever Balanchine was in town, as well as in New York, where Stravinsky—still concertizing—would often practice piano at Balanchine's apartment. Berman showed his set design sketches to Stravinsky in July, but the composer expressed dismay. Within a week the sets were redesigned to the composer's satisfaction. The dancers included principals from the old Diaghilev days, such as Alexandra Danilova, as well as some of Balanchine's own young School of American Ballet ballerinas, among them his future wife Maria Tallchief.

The festive music exuded "the Italian spirit of the *commedia dell'arte*," as Balanchine remarked in his famous essay "The Dance Element in Stravinsky's Music." He spoke of his affinity for Stravinsky's dance music, and Stravinsky reciprocated with his own approbation, commenting that Balanchine approached *Danses concertantes* "architecturally and not descriptively." The composer added that Balanchine "went to the roots of the musical form, of the *jeu musical*, and recreated it in forms of movements." Stravinsky contended that his music needed to "live side by side with the visual movement, happily married to it, as one individual to another."[30]

The composer was in Los Angeles when the ballet premiered in New York on September 10, 1944. John Martin's vituperative *Times* review upbraided both the music and the ballet's "abstract" character: "Stravinsky's music is gravely *démodé*, belonging to that avant-gardisme of about 1925 which is now as quaint as grandmother's antimacassar . . . It is also as completely antagonistic to movement as any score within memory, lacking the sustained dynamics, which are the very basis of dance. Mr. Balanchine has done a clever, somewhat mathematical, job of choreography, almost totally devoid of dancing. It is extremely difficult . . . and most ungrateful to dance."[31]

Scènes de ballet

1944 also marked Stravinsky's only Broadway excursion with his newly composed *Scènes de ballet*. The work was written for Billy Rose's *Seven Lively Arts*, although Rose used only a few fragments of the seventeen-minute, $5,000 score (the composer having in fact asked for $15,000). Busy with conducting engagements, Stravinsky entrusted the piano score to his friend Ingolf Dahl. The work premiered on November 27 as part of the Philadelphia preview of Rose's show, which moved to the Ziegfeld Theatre in New York on December 7 for a five-month run. Classically patterned, the ballet included eleven dances for a *corps de ballet* (four boys and twelve girls) and two soloists. The composer had originally worked through a possible scenario with Anton Dolin (since Rose stipulated that Dolin was to dance and choreograph the work) on June 16, 1944. Later the same day Stravinsky met with Balanchine and the two finalized a different scenario. In the end, Balanchine provided the choreography for this second scenario, although Stravinsky characteristically claimed afterward to have outlined the dance itself: "The choreography was my own, in the sense that I conceived the sequence, character, and proportions of the pieces myself and visualized the dance construction of this plotless, 'abstract' ballet as I wrote the music. In fact, no other score of mine prescribes a choreographic plan so closely."[32]

Knowing what Rose wanted (and what Broadway audiences expected from a classical ballet composer), Stravinsky wrote music that was recognizably beholden to nineteenth-century balletic conventions. That is not to say that the composer's by now familiar rhythmic manipulation of thematic material is absent. The choreographic dialogues between a principal male dancer and prima ballerina were built into the music itself, and conspicuously so, as if the ghosts of *Giselle, Coppélia,* and *Swan Lake* were hovering in the wings. Lawrence Morton's description of the music is unforgettable: "In *Scènes de ballet* . . . there is a trumpet tune of almost incredible sentimentality. . . . Remove from it the marks of genius, make it four-square, give it a Cole Porter lyric, and you have a genuine pop-tune. As it stands, however, it is a solemnization of Broadway, a halo for a chorus girl, a portrait of Mr. Rose as Diaghilev."[33]

Despite the less-than-successful abridged version of his ballet that had been used in Rose's show, Stravinsky pictured a more important balletic future for his seventeen-minute score. Almost immediately after the Broadway production he declared his desire to see it staged again, but with more consideration given to his original conception.[34] Having made certain that his contract with Rose allowed him control of the "symphonic domain," he wasted no time in bringing the work to the concert stage, conducting it himself with the New York Philharmonic in early February 1945 (along with some of his other recent works, including the *Ode* and *Norwegian Moods*—both salvaged from aborted Hollywood film scores). In June 1946, the composer met with Berman and Balanchine to discuss staging the work. Earlier that spring, in fact, negotiations had begun with Oliver Smith in California, with a view to mounting a production during the next season, but these had failed, as Balanchine's various demands, which included the employment of his own dancers as well as certain financial considerations, had not been met.

None of these ballets of the late 1930s and 1940s entered the mainstream, and music analysts have never known quite what to make of them. Stephen Walsh comments that *Jeu de cartes* "has the slightly souped-up Beethoven sound of the Symphony in C," adding that such lightweight ballets "are the products of the 'lingua franca' phase of Stravinsky's neo-classicism."[35] It is as succinct a description as one is likely to find. As for specific techniques evident throughout these works, one might add that the musical vocabulary of this often disregarded cluster of ballets reveals no genuinely new advances. The orchestrations are charmingly bright, although they merely rely upon techniques traceable to Tchaikovsky's antiphonal exchanges betweens strings and winds. The pitch materials are neither strictly diatonic nor strictly octatonic (although a case can be made for octatonic figurations in a number of chromatic passages). Syncopated figures rhythmically energize Stravinsky's by now familiar metrically diverse landscape. More-or-less tonally oriented areas quickly come and go. Discrete passages often discontinuously transit from one key to another, frequently by the half-step movement that is commonly found in popular theater music. Harmonic progressions turn more functional as cadences are approached. And formal designs mainly stem from the simple reprise-based divisions that are so often employed in classical dance compositions.

In one way, these ballets have more significance for the annals of dance history than for those of music history. They speak to the widely divergent and often appallingly pernicious opinions that muddled the New York dance scene in the early 1940s. Stravinsky and Balanchine were now considered Russian partners in crime, and as such could not avoid the emotionally charged fracas in which such artists were inevitably caught up. The political fallout of the war had an enormous impact on the artistic life of America, the network of émigré artists extending from Hollywood to New York. Like other Americans, Stravinsky sat nervously through West Coast blackouts and air raids, while reports of Japanese warplanes attacking Los Angeles caused mass hysteria. Tracking the military movements of the Allied forces in Europe, Stravinsky placed pins on a map to mark their advance. He registered for defense work, participated in gas rationing, and took part in broadcasts for the U.S. War Department—all the acts of a "patriot," as he liked to think of himself.

On the East Coast, ballet companies competed with one another for survival in this turbulent atmosphere. The conservative Ballet Russe staged Agnes de

Mille and Aaron Copland's wildly popular *Rodeo* in 1942 and 1943 only because, as de Mille herself put it, "it was wartime and they wanted an American ballet on an American theme by an American."[36] Lucia Chase's new company, Ballet Theatre, hitched its wagon to the young Jerome Robbins and Leonard Bernstein, who in 1944 produced the jazzy, stylishly quintessential American ballet *Fancy Free*, a perfect wartime scenario about three rollicking sailors on shore leave in New York. Still, other successful companies preserved the great *Coppélia* tradition. Predictably, not everyone was comfortable with attempts to break free from nineteenth-century European traditions. Americanizing the dance was fine; but so too was the retention of the inviolable classics. It was not a propitious time to rock the boat with experimental ideas.

Yet beginning with *Jeu de cartes* and extending through much of the 1940s, the Stravinsky–Balanchine partnership pursued the very path the American press so jingoistically renounced. With the addition of nonconformist designers like Tchelitchev and Berman on top of Balanchine's ostensibly misguided ventures with the plotless ballet and Stravinsky's "démodé" music, the critics bristled even more. For some, collusion was in the air. Besides, why would Stravinsky and Balanchine so willingly participate in a faddish, sugarcoated mélange of Broadway shows, Hollywood films, and other popular endeavors, and then be so cheeky as to think they could mount serious ballets for the urbane New York audience? For some, such impudence smacked of contempt.

Orpheus

In 1943 Lincoln Kirstein joined the army—a setback for Stravinsky and Balanchine's belief in a musico-balletic equilibrium. Without his ministry, and without an established company to visualize the principles of their shared devotion to classicism, the Stravinsky–Balanchine partnership stalled. Stravinsky became the most sought-after prize in an inter-city war over the future of ballet. Reviewing the January 11, 1940, debut of Lucia Chase's Ballet Theatre for the *New York Times*, John Martin proclaimed that the city had now acquired "for the first time in its life a cosmopolitan ballet company of its own, comparable in its field to the opera house and the art gallery." There was no room for skepticism, he added. Ballet Theatre "was no less than a brilliant success." Shortly after returning from his military service, Kirstein announced the formation of Ballet Society. During the 1940s, Kirstein and Chase actively campaigned for an exclusive affiliation with Stravinsky. Kirstein's Ballet Society created a membership-supported company standing just beyond the reach of critics. The press would buy tickets to performances like everyone else. The original brochure proclaimed, "The Ballet Society will present a completely new repertory, consisting of ballets, ballet-opera and other lyric forms. Each will have the planned collaboration of independent easel-painters, progressive choreographers and musicians, and employing the full use of advanced-guard ideas, methods and materials." The brochure also previewed commissions for the next season (1947–48), which included *Orpheus*, with "Book and Music by Igor Stravinsky." As early as the summer of 1945 Balanchine began planning for the new enterprise. He and Stravinsky met often in early 1946 as plans for Ballet Society ambitiously went forward.

Kirstein had long envisaged an epic ballet trilogy based upon the Greek myths. On the opening night of the 1937 Stravinsky Festival he and Balanchine had "begged a sequel" to *Apollo*. "The composer confirmed," Kirstein recalled, that "this must inevitably involve Orpheus, Apollo's Thracian son, whose dam was eloquent Calliope, [and] a decade later, after another world war, Stravinsky gave us his 'second act.' "[37] Kirstein and Balanchine had in fact staged an *Orpheus and Eurydice* at the Metropolitan Opera in 1936, during Balanchine's American Ballet's residence, with music based upon Gluck's 1762 opera *Orfeo ed Euridice*. Even earlier, in 1931, Balanchine had staged Offenbach's *Orpheus in the Underworld* in Paris. The Orphic eschatology, with its pursuit of morals, judgment, perdition, and the afterlife, thematically parallels Stravinsky and Balanchine's earlier depiction of Apollo's odyssey from birth to Parnassus. Most obviously, Orpheus's command of the lyre—said to be so powerful as to move inanimate objects—furnished a ready-made, tangible symbol that would provide coherence for Kirstein's "second act" coupling to Apollo himself.

Kirstein officially commissioned *Orpheus* in the fall of 1946. The publicizing of *Orpheus* became big business for a composer who was becoming increasingly adept at American marketing. To promote his score, Stravinsky agreed to answer six questions posed by RCA's Allan Kayes during a radio broadcast of November 1, 1949. A transcript of these questions and the composer's answers (which had been prepared in advance) is preserved in the Sacher Stiftung. Stravinsky's unedited lengthy reply is instructive: "I did not use the whole story of Orpheus in my ballet. When Balanchin [*sic*] spent the summer of 1946 in Hollywood, we settled the main lines of the legend. We decided also the exact length of the music or rather the exact duration of each movement." And a little further into his response, "Precision of timing and the physical capabilities of the dancers are primary factors which I have always considered in constructing the proportions of my ballets." That conviction alone clarifies the many care-fully timed durations found throughout the sketches for the composer's ballets.

A final section of Stravinsky's script replies most directly to many of Kayes's six questions:

I visualized the character of this music as a long, sustained, slow chant, composed independently of any folkloristic elements, concerning which we know almost nothing. But even if I knew ancient Greek music, it would be of no use to me. The sophisticated painters of the Rennaissance [*sic*] painted the stories of ancient Greece or the Bible in the European landscape and costumes of their own time without attempting to reconstruct the scenes of Greece or Palestine with historical accuracy. I have also avoided all unessential ethnographic details for the sake of a higher symphonic reality.[38]

Both composer and choreographer insisted that their concept of *Orpheus* was meant as a broad setting of a universal story. As for the work's visualization, Kirstein chose Isamu Noguchi—no stranger to the dance world, having collaborated with Martha Graham as early as 1929. In discussing the transformation that unfolds in the ballet, Noguchi displays his own spiritual kinship with Stravinsky and Balanchine's emphasis on ritual: "Eurydice follows Orpheus because he is the artist entranced with his own vision. He doesn't care about reality very much—he doesn't see it because he's blinded by his imagination. . . . So it's an ever-recurring story which, I think, we are all subconsciously aware of. . . . It's the ritual of recurring spring and the immortality of art. It's a kind of ritual dance."[39]

In early April, several months before the commission, Stravinsky and Balanchine met for several concentrated sessions in Los Angeles spread over two days, during which they drafted the entire scenario of *Orpheus*.

Balanchine's colorful memory of the working process is revealing:

I would visit [Stravinsky's] home in California and we'd talk. "What do you want to do?" he'd ask, and I'd say, "Supposing we do *Orpheus.*" "How do you think *Orpheus* should be done?" "Well," I'd say, "a little bit like an opera . . ." And Stravinsky said, "I'll write the end first; I sometimes have an appetite to write the end first." And that's what he did, with the two horns—it's a beautiful thing, sad, hair flowing. We couldn't have a river on stage, but it suggests something like that. Then he asked, "Now, how to begin?" And I said, "Eurydice is in the ground, she's already buried, Orpheus is sad and cries—friends come to visit him, and then he sings and plays." "Well," Stravinsky asked, "how long does he play?" And I started to count [Balanchine snaps his fingers], the curtain goes up. "How long would you like him to stand without dancing, without moving? A sad person stands for a while, you know." "Well," I said, "maybe at least a minute." So he wrote down "minute." "And then," I said, "his friends come in and bring something and leave." "How long?" asked Stravinsky. I calculated it by walking. "That will take about two minutes." He wrote it down. And it went on like that.[40]

Thus Balanchine remembered the scenario's creation and the durational precision of the ballet's musico-choreographic planning. These telling notations, all in Russian except for the French titles of the ballet's individual sections, are in Stravinsky's hand. The composer sketched this preliminary *ordonnance* on both sides of two separate sheets of paper, taping them together. Referring to these work sheets, Stravinsky later recalled that he and Balanchine set the action in three scenes covering twelve separate episodes with the help of "Ovid and a classical dictionary in hand."[41]

The ballet begins with Orpheus at the grave of Eurydice, whereupon the Angel of Death masks the minstrel and leads him to the underworld. In the second tableau's opening "Pas des furies," set in Hades, Orpheus magically quells the Furies' "agitation and their threats" (Stravinsky writes in the published score) as he plays his lyre. The Furies are so moved by Orpheus's "Air de danse" that Pluto allows a blindfolded Orpheus to lead Eurydice back to earth.

To this point at least, the composer and choreographer follow Book 10 of Ovid's *Metamorphoses* faithfully. As the "Pas d'action" of the second tableau ends, Orpheus breaks his vow. As given in Ovid:

And as they neared the surface of the Earth,
The poet, fearful that she'd lost her way,
Glanced backward with a look that spoke his love—
Then saw her gliding into deeper darkness,
As he reached out to her, she was gone;
He has embraced a world of emptiness.[42]

In Book 11, Ovid describes the death of Orpheus, who is rent by the Bacchantes, "Tearing his body with blood-streaming hands." Or as Stravinsky and Balanchine's scenario states at the beginning of the turbulent "Pas d'action," "The Bacchantes attack Orpheus, seize him and tear him to pieces." However, in the third tableau of the ballet, "Orpheus's Apotheosis," the composer and choreographer seem to have either concocted a suitable ending themselves, or perhaps relied upon other, non-Ovidian interpretations of the Orphic myth. Apollo now appears at Orpheus's graveside, grieving for his son. At Apollo's command, Orpheus's lyre miraculously rises from the grave, "entwined in a long garland of flowers. The lyre rises higher and higher, carrying with it for the ages the tenderness and power of his song."[43]

The choreography is an imaginative mixture of two-dimensional pantomime and abstract movement with no more than a trace of classical technique. *Orpheus* explores choreographic space and time. The opening curtain rises on Orpheus, his back to the audience and his lyre resting on the back of his right leg. This is a mournful man whose physical attitude—static, motionless, crestfallen—defines the empty space around him. The music's tranquility is reminiscent of the closing moments of *Apollo,* where time has detached itself from the ballet's characters. In fact the earliest compositional sketches for *Orpheus* reveal the same unifying rhythmic motive that pervades *Apollo.*[44] Only at a later sketching stage did Stravinsky choose to soften the dotted rhythm. The six measures of one of the earliest sketches for the opening, for example, dated October 20, 1946, stand in marked contrast to the final version (Example 8). The iambic motive originally used to prepare the cadential

Example 8 *Orpheus,* opening, transcribed sketch and score.

A-major chord at the conclusion of the brief first scene disappears. The entire "mournful" (to use Balanchine's own description) rhythmic fabric of the ballet's opening scene completely eschews dotted rhythms in favor of a more hypnotic, slowly unfolding processional flow of the descending scales.

The Basel sketches further disclose that it was not the haunting modal descent of the harp that was conceived first, but rather the interruptive wind music at m. 8, where the curtain rises and, as written in the score, "Some friends pass bringing presents and offering [Orpheus] sympathy." Once Stravinsky had settled this crucial dramatic juncture, he then composed around it. As we have already seen, such a retrogressive approach to composition can be seen as a thread running throughout his sketchbooks. Moreover, the sketches for the material eventually used at m. 14 of the closing "Orpheus's Apotheosis" show that the composer initially planned a much more elaborate passage, with the harp and French horn in a contrapuntal interplay (Example 9). In the end, the composer deleted the entire horn line, making for a simpler, subtler passage more in keeping with the prevailing serenity of the dance.

The deliberateness of the music matches the unfolding promenade of the dancers, who enter unrushed, passing by Eurydice's grave without taking notice, oblivious to any notion of time. There is a resignation to the music and to the trio of "friends" consoling Orpheus, as they acknowledge his grief, gently touching him before exiting. Nicolas Nabokov's well-known "Christmas" memory of Stravinsky's walking him through the score for *Orpheus* underlines the significance of the harp, both musically and symbolically:

> Then, coming to a passage in the Epilogue where a harp solo interrupts the slow progress of the fugue, he would stop and say, "Here, you see, I cut off the fugue with a pair of scissors. . . . I introduced this short harp phrase, like two bars of an accompaniment. Then the horns go on with their fugue as if nothing had happened. I repeat it at regular intervals, here and here again. . . . You can eliminate these harp-solo interruptions, paste the parts of the fugue together, and it will be one whole piece." I asked him why he introduced the harp solo. "What was the point of cutting up the fugue this way?"
>
> He smiled maliciously, as if he were letting me in on one of his private secrets. "But did you hear?" He turned the pages to the middle of the score. "It is a reminder of this—the Song of Orpheus." And he added thoughtfully: "Here in the Epilogue it sounds like a kind of . . . compulsion, like something unable to stop . . . Orpheus is dead, the song is gone, but the accompaniment goes on."[45]

Example 9 *Orpheus*, "Orpheus's Apotheosis," mm. 13–16, transcribed sketch and score.

Allusions to *Apollo* are apparent throughout Orpheus's "Air de danse." Just as Apollo picks up and begins to pluck his lyre in the 1928 ballet, so too does Orpheus, as a duet of bassoons signals a call to action with rising scales. He displays the ballet's central symbol in sweeping gestures, while the orchestra provides a pizzicato accompaniment similar to that of the first "Variation d'Apollon" in the earlier ballet. From a dancer's perspective, his body opens and closes alternately, sometimes pulled in as he bends toward the earth, then arching outwardly, as the music also opens. He even plucks the instrument gently from his prone position, where the music and action slow just before m. 38. It is here that Stravinsky introduces a brighter hue in D major (as opposed to the darker, more bereaved music up to this point).

The first tableau of *Orpheus* closes with the "L'ange de la mort et sa danse." The Angel of Death emerges from the shadows accompanied by four French horns, whose muted sound enhances the vaporous atmosphere of the scene. Orpheus is masked and led to Hades as a solo trumpet, again muted, sounds at m. 46. It is with this dramatic gesture that Balanchine's Angel places the golden mask over Orpheus's eyes. Numerous sketches for the fifty-nine measures of this dance disclose that Stravinsky initially paired French horns with trombones, but ultimately thinned some of the lines by cutting doublings and assigning melodies to solo instruments. This helps to preserve the fragility of the entire ballet, whose volume seldom rises to *forte*.

The first "Interlude" follows, depicting the descent of Orpheus and the Angel of Death in front of the billowy curtain used to separate Orpheus's earthly existence from the underworld. Orpheus and the Angel of Death reappear "in the gloom of Tartarus" (m. 13) as the curtain lifts on a darkened stage to reveal the second tableau. The "Pas des furies" is unexpected in its thoroughly jazzy rhythms. The "Air de danse" of Orpheus that follows now prominently employs the harp. The Angel of Death constantly cajoles Orpheus to evoke the sweet sounds of his music as the emblematic lyre literally, physically, joins them. The composer's sketch sheets reveal that he struggled with this dance, constantly reworking the material, and even discarding several versions of individual passages.

There follows the brief five-measure "Interlude," wherein "The tortured souls in Tartarus stretch out their fettered arms towards Orpheus and implore him to continue his song of consolation." Stravinsky obliges with a resumption of the "Air de danse" for another ten measures. The "Pas d'action" follows. An eight-measure introduction serves as a transition to Eurydice's solo. As is typical in Stravinsky's writing, it is much more than an introduction, presenting important musical figures that support the structural basis for the dance itself. A reversed dotted rhythm reminiscent of Apollo's iambic motive appears in the first two measures (in the violin and viola). Its iteration is so subtle that it is hardly audible. But it will become Eurydice's signature motive once she commences her dance at m. 9. During these eight measures the stage space expands, in preparation for Eurydice's all-important entrance. The Furies clear the stage while the Angel of Death ushers Orpheus to the side. Balanchine and dance author Francis Mason describe the ensuing action: "In the dark recesses of the stage a strange shape begins to turn toward [Orpheus]. It is Pluto, God of the Underworld. Standing before him, her hands resting on his shoulders, is Eurydice."[46]

Orpheus's disconsolate wife now emerges from the shadows, slowly moving forward during four darkly scored measures of viola and cello music (mm. 9–12). Then an unexpected soft but bright trumpet entry heralds the beginning of Eurydice's suppliant dance, as she now springs to life. Toward the end of this "Pas d'action," Orpheus, the Angel of Death, and Eurydice join hands, again tied literally and symbolically by the lyre. The three dancers merge in a conjunction that gradually unfolds during four measures of music (beginning at m. 32) written for flutes and clarinets, a timbre that contrasts dramatically with the preceding string music and trumpet solo. The subtle music keeps turning back onto itself in a loop, ending on a bright D-major chord. It is a crucial moment, reminiscent in sound and dramatic power to the second "Variation d'Apollon," where Terpsichore finally joins Apollo with an equally symbolic touch of their fingers.

The Angel of Death now leads Eurydice and Orpheus back to earth, again in front of the curtain, as the "Pas de deux" unfolds. Stravinsky scores the radiant F-major music entirely for strings, casting it in three distinct divisions. Eurydice urges Orpheus to remove his blindfold during the central section. Here again the compositional sketches reveal numerous insertions, repetitions, and adjustments that were no doubt a consequence of what unfolded in the rehearsal studio. The five concluding measures (mm. 80–84) were composed before the music leading to the ominously silent measure in which "Orpheus tears the bandage from his eyes [and] Eurydice falls dead." Then, as usual, Stravinsky composed toward that climactic moment.

Balanchine persuaded Stravinsky to extend certain passages, including the concluding section of the famous "Pas de deux," where the extension occurs just at the moment Eurydice dies. The sketches for mm. 67–84 reveal that Stravinsky labored in reapportioning the passage according to Balanchine's durational demands. Ten separate drafts reveal that Stravinsky altered rhythms, rethought meters, and modified melodic motives. Moreover, the sketches reveal that the extension was fashioned in both directions: Stravinsky reworked the architectural structure of the entire passage by revising the music not only after the four-beat measure of silence marking Eurydice's death, as Balanchine requested, but also before the fateful event. Clearly he was concerned with the music's overall structural balance.

Following the next "Interlude" (featuring a "Veiled curtain, behind which the décor of the first scene is placed") a second "Pas d'action" begins. Here, as the Bacchantes dismember Orpheus, Stravinsky writes some of the most propulsive, theatrical music of the ballet. The highpoint is articulated at m. 56 (marked triple *forte*, it is the loudest music in the ballet), where the full orchestra literally shrieks Orpheus's impending death. The final tableau ensues, with the harp again intoning the plaintive music heard at the ballet's opening. Noguchi best encapsulates the ballet's final two episodes: "The Furies are like time, they come and destroy everything; but even if time destroys, something else survives. Time and decomposition of things are, in a sense, contested by another factor, which is not affected by time at all. A musical composition does not die."[47]

By determining the durations of the ballet before the commission was settled, Balanchine and Stravinsky established its blueprint from the outset. Their working notes reveal how they plotted the temporal architecture of the individual episodes right along with the story. For example, they originally allotted a half minute for the music of Orpheus's lyre at the ballet's haunting opening, then another one and a half minutes to complete the scene—a total of two minutes. Their preliminary 1946 estimates of the ballet's temporal design were modified very little as the score evolved over the next two years. Throughout their frequent meetings later in 1946 and in 1947, and even as the choreography began to come together in the rehearsal studio in 1948, they deviated only slightly from their initial temporal ideas. Maria Tallchief recalls that Balanchine and Stravinsky worked "side by side in the rehearsal studio. Ordinarily, when George was choreographing, Stravinsky kept his distance. But this time was different. He was always making suggestions, and was exacting about what he wanted."[48]

The preliminary compositional sketches for *Orpheus* are difficult to assemble chronologically. They nevertheless reveal the same compositional methodology evident in Stravinsky's other sketchbooks. The composer frequently added measures at the bottom of a sketch page in red and blue brackets, with arrows pointing toward an insertion point, suggesting that these last-minute addenda were incorporated for choreographic reasons. Moreover, most of these ostensibly new measures are not new at all, but rather literal repetitions or slight modifications of pre-existing material, thereby assuring that the organic flow of the passage would not be disrupted. For example, the Basel sketches show that mm. 22–24 of the "Air de danse" were added (obviously derived from material at m. 7) at a very late moment, perhaps even in the rehearsal studio. Surely this stems from Balanchine's need for a few more seconds of music.

With the much anticipated premiere of *Orpheus*, Morton Baum, chairman of City Center's executive committee, invited Ballet Society to become the resident ballet company of the City Center of Music and Drama, thereby joining the New York City Opera and the City Center Orchestra. Thus the New York City Ballet was born. Even John Martin begrudgingly conceded in his *New York Times* review of April 1948 that *Orpheus* was a ballet that deserved attention, "an extraordinarily beautiful work, realized in a rare theatrical synthesis. . . . Balanchine has treated it with the utmost simplicity. . . . It is undoubtedly not for everybody, and will never be anything like a popular favorite, but it is a notable work nonetheless, with great distinction and a rich beauty for those who can find it." In a May 1948 review for *Musical America*, however, Robert Sabin raised a concern. Although he, too, conceded that Stravinsky's music was a "masterpiece," he not only found Balanchine's choreography "confused and unconvincing," but grumbled about "very little actual dancing." This became the most common reproof of a ballet that is now too seldom performed.

At the root of the criticism was Balanchine's decision that dance should be but one of many contributing elements in the production, along with the dramatic sets, the costumes, the message of the myth, and the serenity of the music. It is true that *Orpheus* is not so much ballet as what some see as a hybrid of modern dance and theater. By 1948, harangues against Balanchine were fully anticipated. Perhaps he was too much of a musician for his own good. Kirstein pre-empted such criticism in a piercing article published in December 1947. "Critics seem to assume that Balanchine actually wishes he were a musician. It is true that few choreographers share Balanchine's intense musical preoccupation. However, to claim that he is musical as if it were an accusation of a one-track mind is like saying that a painter draws too well, or that his single interest is in paint texture alone, color alone or formal composition alone."[49] The ballet is entirely constructed upon the grounds of restraint. Stravinsky, like Balanchine, had once again placed himself at risk. *Orpheus* was a dignified, gracious work, a far cry from the bombastic, stylized Russian scores that critics still longed to hear. No matter, composer and choreographer were of one mind. Reflecting their serene confidence, the score made a powerful, expressive statement.

On April 29, 1948, the day following the premiere, Kirstein wrote to Stravinsky, thanking him for the ballet. He expressed gratitude that Ballet Society had been able to work with Stravinsky, certainly recognizing how such an association had credentialed his fledgling enterprise. More importantly, Kirstein was moved to re-engage the composer immediately, while firmly reasserting his own vision of a Greek trilogy: "*Apollo* gave me confidence in the line of the academic classic dance, and on it our school has been founded. To me *Orpheus* is the second act of a great lyric-drama. Which leads me, on the day after the second act, to ask you to write a third act."[50] But at that moment Stravinsky already had another composition in mind, one that he had in fact been contemplating for years. For the foreseeable future, he would devote his time almost exclusively to what would become *The Rake's Progress*, working with W. H. Auden and relying increasingly upon a young Robert Craft for assistance. The opera would premiere in 1951, marking both an end and a new beginning. Kirstein's request for a third ballet would have to wait, and by the time Stravinsky obliged, his compositional world had changed dramatically.

CHAPTER SEVEN

A COUNTERPOINT OF MINDS
Agon

H ISTORY HAS doggedly attempted to portray *Agon* as the final chapter of a grand classical Greek trilogy neatly packaged by Stravinsky and Balanchine. The tidiness of it all is appealing. But the 1957 ballet was not to be a dramaturgical culmination of what had begun nearly thirty years earlier with *Apollo*. Moreover, *Agon* stood a world apart from *Orpheus*, written nearly a decade earlier. The creation of Stravinsky and Balanchine's last complete balletic collaboration evolved over a protracted period that witnessed significant transformations in each of their lives. Following *Orpheus*, Balanchine turned his attention to the practicalities of establishing his new ballet company. With his restaging of Stravinsky's perennially popular *Firebird* in 1949 (much less embroidered than Fokine's original version), the New York City Ballet began to assume an artistic presence. Meanwhile, impatiently waiting for Stravinsky's "third act" to develop, Kirstein successfully produced a number of the composer's less popular neoclassical works. And while competing companies in both America and Europe trotted out the old Diaghilev favorites, Balanchine's young, muscular New York City Ballet soon became synonymous with definitive interpretations of Stravinsky's newer, leaner, and less romantically inclined works. City Ballet became a vehicle for championing the composer's later works in much the same way as the Ballets Russes had served as Stravinsky's pulpit in his early years.

While Balanchine's productivity traveled several routes from Broadway to television, the late 1940s found Stravinsky laboring to find work. He often conducted programs of his own recent ballet suites and symphonic compositions, although audiences mainly wanted to hear the old warhorses of earlier days. He completed a Mass for chorus and winds in 1948, although parts of it were finished even before *Orpheus*. He focused most of his attention from 1948 through the spring of 1951 on completing the two-and-a-half-hour *Rake's Progress*, to a libretto by Auden and

Chester Kallman. The 1951 Italian premiere of the much anticipated opera was, however, less than the success Stravinsky had envisioned—and it bothered him. Criticism of the opera's "obsolescent neoclassic language" gave him pause to rethink his future, as he had done so many times throughout his career.

The compositional rethinking that transpired during that period of reflection cuts to the core of *Agon*. Cast for strings, winds, harp, mandolin, piano, timpani, tom-toms, xylophone, and castanets, the work would be dedicated, appropriately, to Kirstein and Balanchine, who had co-commissioned the work through funds that City Ballet had received from the Rockefeller Foundation in 1954. Between the time the ballet was first contemplated and its final composition, Stravinsky produced several important works, including the Cantata (1952), the Septet (1953), *In memoriam Dylan Thomas* (1954), and the *Canticum sacrum* (1955) written for the Venice Biennale. Each work pushed the composer progressively further down a new road quite distinct from the dozen or so works completed in the 1940s. Each incrementally advanced the forging of a new compositional tack that could not have been anticipated. Each successively explored alternatives to the diatonicism that was still quite evident in the *Rake*. And each evinced an increasing interest in the exploration of intervals and their capacity for development.

Ballet would once more provide the testing ground for a new direction. In 1952, Stravinsky, now a septuagenarian, was back in Hollywood. In February he attended several rehearsals and a performance of Arnold Schoenberg's Septet-Suite. Returning from dinner a few weeks later, the uncharacteristically disheartened composer disburdened himself to his wife and Robert Craft. He had reached an impasse, he confided, fearing he had nothing else to offer compositionally. Indeed, with what would prove to be Craft's providential arrival in the Stravinsky household in 1948, Schoenberg's death in the summer of 1951 (and subsequently the more frequent performances of his music), the apathetic reception of *The Rake* a few months later, and Stravinsky's own 1952 admission of feeling adrift, the composer exhibited an unforeseen inquisitiveness about Schoenberg and his younger disciples. Craft openly admits both his intercession and his influence at this pivotal moment: "I say in all candour that I provided the path and that I do not believe Stravinsky would ever have taken the direction he did without me. The music that he would otherwise have written is impossible to imagine."[1]

Certainly Craft was instrumental in leading the composer out of the cul-de-sac in which he found himself. Moreover, given that Stravinsky always thought of himself as an "interval" composer, there was surely a predilection to explore the serial literature that so many young composers had embraced. Anton Webern's music was of particular interest, and as Stravinsky's archives establish, he

studied the Viennese composer's scores closely, often marking them, no doubt
with Craft's own insight as a guide. There seemed to be a natural affinity with
Webern, as Stravinsky began listening to and studying his music, which was just
then being performed frequently in Los Angeles. He saw the degree to which
Webern's music was concerned with temporal pacing. Both composers were
economists in search of small musical cells capable of building a sense of structural unity. Both were texturalists, too, and their sense of silence, sparseness,
color, and orchestration helped to define and clarify the multiple layers of their
intricate contrapuntal lines.

Balanchine seemed to share Stravinsky's blossoming interest in serialism.
The choreographer visited Schoenberg's widow Gertrude in 1953 while City
Ballet was on tour in California. Suggesting that it was time to choreograph a
work by her husband, he asked her for permission.[2] He specifically spoke about
his fascination for Webern's music, adding that Stravinsky had introduced him
to it. Balanchine's ballet to Schoenberg's music, *Opus 34*, premiered on January
19, 1954, Kirstein recalling, "Some would see it as a first sketch for *Agon*."[3]

It was at about this same time that Stravinsky grew increasingly curious
about another repertoire, the music of the Renaissance (although he had always
exhibited a general interest in music of the past). The melding of his interests in
serialism and the sixteenth century proved pivotal. Both literatures imposed
strict limits, an economy of materials, and a rigorous contrapuntal discipline.
Stravinsky himself embraced these principles explicitly: "The rules and restrictions of serial writing differ little from the rigidity of the great contrapuntal
schools of old. At the same time they widen and enrich harmonic scope; one
starts to hear more things, and differently than before."[4] The composer's extant
library includes an impressive collection of scores and scholarly books ranging
over several Renaissance topics. Without question, *Agon*'s deepest roots stem
from the composer's immersion in these studies. Among the sketches for *Agon*,
for example, the composer writes out a section of Gesualdo's "Illumina nos,"
one of many instances in which he took the time to copy sections of a
Renaissance work for voice or lute.[5]

Stravinsky also attended many of the legendary Monday Evening Concerts
in Los Angeles that regularly featured a mix of early music and contemporary
literature. As always, Stravinsky listened attentively. In February 1952 he
composed the "Westron Wind" section of his Cantata. Here, notably,
Renaissance verses are set extensively to imitative and canonic techniques that
presage his serial music, including the multiple canons that permeate *Agon*. The
lessons learned in hearing and intensely examining these two literatures fueled
his imagination. The convergence of their pathways leads directly to *Agon*'s

composite design. Typically, the composer would look to the past as a guide to the future, but in the case of *Agon* the resources from which he would draw were enormously rich, given the diversity of his models. It remained for Stravinsky to fuse the divergent musical styles and compositional techniques that would shape his path. While all of this was unfolding, it fell to Kirstein, Balanchine, and others to keep the still indistinct prospect of a new ballet alive.

Between 1948 and 1957, Kirstein repeatedly approached the composer about a sequel to *Orpheus*. In the summer of 1950 he alerted him that T. S. Eliot had declined to suggest a scenario to complete Kirstein's envisaged trilogy, but was interested in collaborating with Stravinsky on a ballet based upon the two fragments of his poem *Sweeney Agonistes*. On February 16, 1951, Kirstein formally offered the composer a $5,000 commission for the new ballet. A perhaps over eager Kirstein again contacted Stravinsky on November 28, urging him to meet with Balanchine "about plans for *Terpsichore*: I hope we can present it a year from now. Is this too early to make plans for it? I want to ask Pavlik [Tchelitchev] to redesign *Apollo* and *Orpheus*, and do the new ballet, as a consecutive three-act spectacle." Kirstein even took it upon himself to include a draft of the suggested *Terpsichore* scenario, outlining seven individual sections.[6] Nothing came of the proposal. Despite Kirstein's good intentions (and his realistic need to plan the upcoming seasons), Stravinsky was not about to be pinned down. His letters to Kirstein and others quietly but forcefully imply that efforts to circumscribe his thinking were distracting.

While it would be expedient to believe that Stravinsky eagerly endorsed Kirstein's concept of a Greek triptych, the truth is that he never warmed to the idea. Out of Kirstein's hearing, he wrote to his publisher, "I plan to compose my music without any blueprint for a plot. I will compose a kind of symphony to be danced."[7] Between 1948 and 1953, Stravinsky rejected each scenario that Kirstein and others presented. It was Stravinsky's interest in literary models— perhaps even more than musical ones—that informed his thinking as he considered his pre-compositional ideas for his new ballet. The *Sweeney Agonistes* proposal was no exception, even though Eliot envisioned its balletic conception beyond Kirstein's trilogy. In truth, the connection between *Sweeney Agonistes* and *Agon* is closer in spirit than history has allowed, and in tracing the roots of the ballet, Eliot's influence should not be underestimated.[8]

Agon owes its title to Eliot's poetry. Craft confirms that it was after reading Eliot's poetic fragments as well as "the great *agon* between Aeschylus and Euripides in Aristophanes' *Frogs* [that Stravinsky] became interested in the 'contest' concept, and it stuck."[9] The Greek definition of an "agon" encompasses many nuances, even though we are inclined to translate it simply as a contest or struggle, or as it has sometimes been defined, as combat. In reality the agon stood at the center of Greek life. The term also applied to a debate among citizens in a public forum, as well as elections in Athenian democracy. Stravinsky certainly knew the tragedies of Euripides and the comedies of Aristophanes. Moreover, the notion of any form of contest appealed to him. In a compositional context, it immediately allowed the existence of a protagonist (from *agonizesthai*, meaning to compete) and thus some type of contrasting, competing action.

The Sacher Stiftung retains a typed letter from Stravinsky to Kirstein dated August 8, 1954, in which the composer left a blank to fill in the title of the new ballet. Only after the letter was finished did he fill in "AGONE" in pencil. He also inserted an asterisk after he filled in the title, and at the bottom of the page, in a handwritten note, he provided the translation "contest." Beyond adapting Eliot's title, the composer's study of his two "agon" poems, first published in 1926–27, suggests a deeper influence. Originally decried as symptomatic of jazz-age profanity and insouciance, the quirkiness of *Sweeney Agonistes* surely tantalized Stravinsky. Eliot's poetic probing of Sweeney's psyche has much in common with the sharp contrasts of the ballet. Sweeney finds himself in a contest that both questions and celebrates the concept of difference. Eliot's vivid poetry dwells on starkly black and white dualities, including powerfully sensual male and female tensions. Sweeney must confront his internal demons and reconcile the discordant claims of humanness, animalism, and spirituality. Eliot's agones were products of self-consciousness, something Stravinsky understood as well as he understood any of antiquity's classical metaphors. Such reflection became a preoccupation during the 1950s, as the composer once again held up a mirror to his past while contemplating the ambivalence of an uncharted future.

At another level, Eliot's words deeply influenced the temporal rhythms of *Agon's* music, even if, as was typical of Stravinsky's reliance upon literary models, the influence was oblique. A devoted student of linguistic morphology, the composer once again heeded the flow of language, syllabification, accent, meter, and inflection, just as he had with Boileau's alexandrines thirty years earlier in *Apollo*. Nor was his curiosity about English prosody—including *Sweeney's* much criticized sleek, unidiomatic speech rhythms—any less fervent. One must remember that while reading the linguistic twists and turns of Eliot's fragments, the composer was just then immersing himself in Auden's text for *The Rake*. Finally, Eliot's own Aristotelian analysis of drama as a "ritual consisting of a set of repeated movements [which] is essentially a dance" was also something with which Stravinsky would have concurred.[10] All of this was surely churning in the composer's mind as he mulled over the ideas Kirstein shared with him in the early 1950s.

With the arrival of a letter from Kirstein on August 31, 1953, opportunity's window opened. Kirstein presented Balanchine's clear vision of a new ballet— an extraordinary vision in its ambition and scope:

> What [Balanchine] wants is a ballet-ivanich. He would like a ballet which would seem to be the enormous finale of a ballet to end all the ballets the world has ever seen, mad dancing, variations, pas d'action, pas de deux, etc., with a final terrific and devastating curtain when everyone would be exhausted. He suggested a competition before the gods; the audience are statues; the gods are tired and old; the dancers re-animate them by a series of historic dances, the correct tempi of which you can quite ignore, but they are called courante, bransle, passepied, rigaudon, menuet, etc. etc. It is as if time calls the tune, and the dances which began quite simply in the sixteenth century took fire in the twentieth and exploded. It would be in the form of a *suite de danses*, or variations, numbers of as great variety as you pleased. I am sending you a book which may possibly interest you along these lines.[11]

Interest him it did. It was nothing less than the kind of epiphany that frequently ignited Stravinsky's thinking. The composer now had an external, tangible starting point to spark his imagination. As Balanchine later recalled, Kirstein's timely gift of this critical volume became *Agon*'s "point of departure."

The gift was in fact François de Lauze's *Apologie de la danse* (1623), one of the most substantive dance treatises of the seventeenth century. Kirstein's August 1953 letter included the recently published 1952 British edition of the book rather than a copy of the original publication. Greatly supplemented by its editor, Joan Wildeblood, de Lauze's manual addressed the instruction, history, and function of several period dances. Most relevantly, Wildeblood offered detailed explanations of several popular dance patterns. Given Stravinsky's immersion in the music of the Renaissance, Kirstein could not have sent the manual at a more propitious time. Although the *Apologie* dates from the 1620s, its spirit is more of the sixteenth than of the seventeenth century, just as *Agon*'s musical roots are directly traceable to the Renaissance rather than the Baroque.

De Lauze's treatise provided a lexicon of protocol. His writings affirmed the inviolable virtues of classicism that Balanchine, Kirstein, and Stravinsky revered. His call for order and deportment was fundamental to a composer whose personal code of conduct embraced comportment and deference. Equally important were the tenets of logic and reason associated with the courts of Louis XIII and XIV (and leading to the establishment of both the Royal

Academy of Dance in 1661 and of Music in 1669). Order and proportionality were part of *la belle danse,* just as they are basic to *Agon's* tightly conceived structure. For the Greeks, proportion was the principal cohesive force in all the arts. And for Descartes, the perfect proportion was 2:1—a ratio visually reflected in *Agon's* eight female and four male dancers and in its many trios (two females, one male, or two males, one female), and aurally evident in the ballet's pervasively employed short–short–long rhythmic values related to the short–long syllabic division of Greek prosodic meter.

Balanchine claimed that Stravinsky "hit upon the idea of a suite of dances based on a seventeenth-century manual of French court dances—*sarabandes, gaillards, branles*—he had recently come across."[12] However, the kernel of the idea was surely also in Balanchine's mind before Stravinsky ever received de Lauze's treatise. Balanchine's original vision of a grandiose ballet, unbound in scope, did not sit well with a composer who demanded boundaries. Stravinsky replied to Kirstein on September 9, 1953, that "the idea you and George have of doing a 'ballet to end all ballets' may prove a limitless affair," adding that "limits are precisely what I need and am looking for above all in everything I compose. The limits generate the form." More relevantly, Stravinsky thanked Kirstein for sending the treatise, adding, "I am studying it 'poco a poco.' "[13]

"Little by little," indeed. In fact the composer studied the manual assiduously. Although, as was his custom, he disavowed any close examination of it, his copy of the *Apologie* reveals the extent to which he relied upon the dance patterns outlined by de Lauze and expounded by Wildeblood. Several illustrations reproduced in the Wildeblood edition furnished important resources in molding both the ballet's sound and its look. For example, the second "Pas de trois" (Bransle Simple), which Stravinsky scored for a trumpet duet engaged in a musical canon, took its cue from the illustration entitled "A Nobleman Leading a Bransle," in which two trumpeters perform from a balcony, as if calling the proceedings to order. Moreover, the two male dancers choreographically mirroring each other to the canonic music is only one of many such contrapuntal exchanges in *Agon.* The canon was a characteristic feature of Renaissance music as well as a frequent serial technique, as many of Stravinsky's earlier works from the 1950s demonstrate.[14] The same illustration undoubtedly inspired the initial measures of the opening "Pas de quatre," consisting of the famous fanfare-like announcement of the two trumpets. As the sketches for the fanfare reveal, Stravinsky did not begin by composing what eventually became the initial measures. Rather, he began by drafting and then sculpting the clarion call to the dance, revising the signature rhythmic motive and adjusting the number of motivic repetitions. Other engravings in the manual also caught Stravinsky's attention. The snapping of fingers in

Agon's double "Pas de quatre," for example, has its origins in the plate entitled "Lady Snapping Her Fingers in Dancing" (Figure 8).

Stravinsky underlined various portions of the treatise, adding marginalia and highlighting particular passages in red. Such annotations reveal a fully engrossed composer educating himself in French choreographic conventions a full year before he and Balanchine first met in August 1954 to chart the ballet's course. By the time Balanchine and Stravinsky sat down together, the composer knew de Lauze's treatise thoroughly, just as he knew what he pictured on stage. In *Agon*, as in virtually every ballet he wrote, the composer was immersed in the choreographic conception from the outset, often notating specific dance patterns as he worked through his initial compositional sketches.

Figure 8 François de Lauze, *Apologie de la danse* (1623), "Lady Snapping Her Fingers in Dancing."

Several passages of the treatise that Stravinsky highlighted in red reveal his particular interest in the bransle as a dance form. Significantly, Wildeblood spoke of a ritualistic connection: "The world-wide use of this form of the dance is well known . . . it may be of interest to record that this salient feature of pagan festivals was preserved in the clandestine rituals of the dying religion in Western Europe for many centuries." The composer also underlined a few sentences that Wildeblood quotes from Margaret Murray's *The Witch-Cult in Western Europe*: "The ring dances were usually round some object, sometimes a stone, sometimes the Devil. The round-dance was . . . essentially a witch dance."

Stravinsky's affinity for the bransle can be seen fifteen years earlier in a movement of his 1940 Symphony in C, where one hears the same fundamental rhythmic pattern as is employed in *Agon*'s "Bransle gay." Wildeblood also summarized de Lauze's explanation of the dance. Stravinsky once again marked the entire passage:

In 1623, de Lauze's *Suite* consists of five *Bransles*, which he names the *Bransle Simple, Bransle Gay, Bransle de Poitou, Bransle Double de Poitou,* the "Fifth" *Bransle*, and lastly, the *Gavot*, which made the sixth dance in the *Suite*. . . . Finally, we have Mersenne's *Suite*. Though the date of his book is 1636, he had obtained the King's Privilege in 1629, six years later than the date of de Lauze's book. As the names and the order of the *Bransles* he gives are identical with those of de Lauze, one may conclude they were speaking of the same dances. He writes, "There are six kinds (of *Bransles*) which are danced now-a-days at the opening of a Ball, one after the other, by as many persons as wish; for the entire company, joining hands, perform with one accord a continual *Bransle*, sometimes forwards, sometimes backwards; it is done with divers movements to which are adapted various kinds of steps, according to the different airs which are used. They dance round very sedately at the beginning of the Ball, all with the same time and movements of the body. The first of which is named the *Bransle Simple* . . . the second is called the *Bransle Gay* . . . the third is named *Bransle-à-Mener*, or *de Poitou* . . . the fourth *Bransle Double de Poitou* . . . the fifth is called *Bransle de Montirande*, and the sixth is *La Gavot*." . . . Arbeau explains there were four divisions of dances in his day, as in ancient Greece. There were the *Grave*, the *Gay*, and a combination of the two, *Grave-and-Gay*.[15]

Wildeblood's mention of Marin Mersenne is critical. Stravinsky wrote on the title page of his copy of the *Apologie*, "with some musik by Marin Mersenne (1636)"—acknowledging the important inclusion of Mersenne's melodies in

Wildeblood's edition. A renowned French theorist, mathematician, theologian, and musician, Mersenne was admired greatly by Stravinsky. His thirteen-hundred-page *Harmonie universelle* (completed in 1636 and liberally quoted in Wildeblood's edition) constitutes a major contemporary thesis on seventeenth-century music and instruments.

According to Mersenne, "The poets, musicians, and composers of dances and ballets . . . would benefit by studying the ancient Greek rhythms in order to apply them to songs and dances which they composed." Stravinsky understood that while the temporal divisions of Mersenne's tunes carried a French coating, their roots were Greek. Similarly, the underlying rhythmic structure of *Agon's* courtly dances is as profoundly Greek as the mythologies upon which *Apollo* and *Orpheus* are based. Stravinsky knew firsthand the connection that Mersenne stressed throughout his discourse:

> The most excellent metrical feet, which have given name and birth to the rhythm of the Greeks, are practiced in the *air de Ballets*, in dance songs, and in all the other actions that serve as public or private recreations, as will be proven when the [metrical] feet that follow are compared to the airs one sings or that one plays on violins, the lute, guitar, and other instruments. Now these feet can be called "[rhythmic] movements" according to the manner of speech of our musicians and composers of airs. This is why I will use this term from now on, to join theory and practice.[16]

The composer marked yet another of Mersenne's Greek admonitions, which Wildeblood stressed: once a melody is chosen, "one must join it to its proper movements, which the Greeks called Rhythm." It is a sentiment clearly reminiscent of Eliot's *Sweeney*. Stravinsky noted such passages one by one throughout his copy of the dance manual, paying special heed to the bransles reprinted from Mersenne's Suite. It is significant that he marked in particular Wildeblood's own editorial emphasis that Mersenne "writes at some length on this subject, and includes a 'Table of the movements or measured feet' of 'Twelve movements Simples.' . . . These rhythmic feet are based on the long and short syllables of Greek rhythms."

Without question, Mersenne's Suite of bransles served as the model for *Agon's* second "Pas de trois." Wildeblood provided several tables illustrating the dance patterns that clearly shaped the composer's initial thinking and the choreographer's eventual realization. In describing one of the bransle types, Wildeblood remarked, "Take the Left foot forward and outward to the side, so that it describes a semi-circle in moving, with the toe turned well out, and step on to the whole foot." Moreover, the true genesis of *Agon*'s trio of bransles becomes apparent in examining a few of the Mersenne melodies that Stravinsky bracketed in his copy of the dance manual and to which he added the same type of scansion notations that are found thirty years earlier in his *Apollo* sketch-book. These "divisions" reveal the ballet's fundamental rhythmic fabric. Stravinsky's marking of Mersenne's melody no. 3, "Bransle gay," for example, is directly imported into *Agon*'s own "Bransle gay", where it appears as the famous castanet rhythm mimicked by the two male dancers flanking the female soloist (Example 10).

Similarly, the composer segments Mersenne's "Bransle à mener ou de Poitou" and the "Bransle double de Poitou." The fundamental patterns of these

Example 10 (a) and (b) Mersenne's "Bransle gay" with Stravinsky's markings, and *Agon*, mm. 1–6.

two bransles also find their counterparts in *Agon*. The *Apologie* holds that in the "Bransle de Poitou"—shortened to "Bransle double" in *Agon*, although in his first sketches the composer actually used the same "Bransle de Poitou" title— "the rhythm is counted in five beats whilst the measure is triple." As marked by Stravinsky, Mersenne's bransles display the same five-beat grouping that is evident in *Agon*.

Moreover, the composer employed melodic as well as harmonic pitch materials closely related to the Mersenne examples he studied. Mersenne's melodies were the wellspring for *Agon*'s first "Pas de trois," a reservoir from which Stravinsky drew many compositional ideas, not just rhythmic ones. Stravinsky often transmuted melodic lines beyond the point of recognition. He would retain the essence of the original, but transform it rhythmically, harmonically, contrapuntally, and texturally in refurbishing it toward serving his compositional needs. In the end—and not surprisingly—he utilized Mersenne's melodies as a catalyst to kindle his own imaginative thinking, rather than as untouchable models beyond the reach of reconstruction.

Likewise, Stravinsky replicates the tune for Mersenne's "Bransle gay" in the opening measures of its counterpart in *Agon*. He marked in red and boxed the relevant passage of the *Apologie*: "The second (bransle) is named 'Bransle Gay', which is composed of four steps and in order to get the cadence better begins with the last (of these) by bending knees a little so as to join both heels in rising on the toes." Stravinsky highlighted the expression "rising on the toes," confirming his interest in choreographic implications. He further marked "one must set aside the left foot, and make the other follow it . . . let it go gently to the side, in sliding on the heel." Moreover, his early sketches for the dance show that he sometimes inserted specific choreographic directions directly on the page. Vera Stravinsky remembers that her husband "had little dancers posed the way he thought they should be." In a draft for the "Bransle gay," the composer wrote on his sketch, "Dancer only turning her head to meet the male dancer," marking an arrow at the exact point in the score where this gesture was to occur.[17]

Finally, *Agon*'s "Bransle simple" employs two males engaged in a brisk catch-as-catch-can canon, matching Stravinsky's trumpet duet music. In describing this specific bransle, de Lauze observed, "Young men who have an excess of agility make these divisions at their pleasure." It is an appropriate portrait of the "agile" choreography created by Balanchine. Furthermore, de Lauze explained those divisions as a dance of eight definable steps, also reflected in *Agon*'s choreography. Musically, the Mersenne example studied by Stravinsky allows six measures of double time for these same eight steps in setting the bransle.

Although he ultimately deviated slightly from Mersenne's rhythmic pattern, the alteration was important enough that he first copied the temporal divisions at the top of his sketch page as a preliminary guide—a procedure followed in several of *Agon*'s sketches (as in those of *Apollo*). Only later did he graft his serially organized pitch materials onto these pre-existent rhythmic patterns, which by that stage of the compositional process had given way to his own concept of Mersenne's model.

Stravinsky marked virtually every passage of the *Apologie* describing the bransle; but he did not stop there. Further annotations reveal close study of the history of other dance forms too. Just so, the dances of *Agon*'s first "Pas de trois" also have their origins in de Lauze and Mersenne. Although the sarabande goes unmentioned in both Arbeau and de Lauze, Mersenne addresses the form in his *Harmonie universelle*, suggesting that Stravinsky's researching of courtly dances was broader than many have allowed. Wildeblood's edition included an example by Mersenne of one common sarabande rhythm (there were several), and it is upon this rhythmic scheme that Stravinsky bases his conception of the dance in *Agon*. Mersenne wrote, "a Sarabande is danced to the sound of the guitar and castanets—its steps are composed of tirades or glissades." Both instruments appear prominently in *Agon*—the distinctive clacking of the castanets in the aforementioned "Bransle gay" and the "mandolino" in both the "Gailliarde" [*sic*] and Coda of the first "Pas de trois." Mersenne had also referred to "all the little bones—or knuckle bones—and little sticks of wood or other matter, which are held in the fingers." The rattling tremolos of the xylophone employed in the *Agon* version give an aural approximation of such an effect, especially the rapid figurations typical of the instruments and sounds listed by Mersenne. Stravinsky's desire to bring a measure of choreographic authenticity to *Agon*'s sarabande is further demonstrated by several markings written directly into his compositional sketches, including, "Sarabande Step (male dancer)—Five Steps forwards and Three Steps backwards." Finally, as if we needed further evidence of his borrowing, under Wildeblood's explanation of the sarabande in the *Apologie*, Stravinsky underlined, "sometimes forwards, sometimes backwards."

Agon's "Gailliarde," choreographed for two female dancers, follows. While the dance form was traditionally cast in some form of triple meter, Stravinsky's treatment was much more elaborate, employing a crosscutting metric and rhythmic scheme that intentionally blurred the division of pulses. In fact, it is precisely the alternation of duple and triple divisions that marks the galliard's long history. The concept of dividing six pulses into two groups of three or three groups of two creates an aurally perceivable internal temporal division. Wildeblood summarized the diverse explanations of the galliard by Arbeau, de

Lauze, and Mersenne. Arbeau's description of the dance as containing six steps and six notes played in triple time finds its analogue in Balanchine's choreography and Stravinsky's music. Here again, Stravinsky focused on the Mersenne example, which provided the obvious architectural plan for *Agon*'s "Gailliarde." Further, Stravinsky widened his study, consulting additional sources as he studied the musical and choreographic components of the dance. In his earliest sketches, the composer notated what appear to be several samples of pre-existing galliards on the manuscript page itself, clearly to serve as a guide.

Stravinsky was just then studying the music of several sixteenth-century lute composers, including the well-known vihuela player and composer Luis de Milán. He was also perusing the important galliards of the lutenist John Dowland. His acquaintance with such Renaissance music accounts for the rather unusual use of a mandolin (the lute itself might have been inaudible) in *Agon*'s "Gailliarde." Finally, de Lauze's manual states, "From the Italians come the Gaillarde; or Romanesque," and Stravinsky wrote at the top of his compositional sketches, "*Gaillarde* (Garliarde) Saltarello, Romanesca," suggesting that he was methodically exploring such dances. He even consulted lexicographer Paul-Émile Littré's celebrated *Dictionnaire de la langue française*, published in 1874 (a coffee-stained p. 1816 confirms that he familiarized himself with the definition of the dance specifically). The composer copied Littré's definition on a small index card, stapling it to his compositional sketches as another crib to guide him.

Between 1953 and 1957 Balanchine and Stravinsky intermittently discussed *Agon*'s development. Balanchine claimed that it was he who decided on twelve dancers, but that the 2:1 ratio of eight females to four males was Stravinsky's idea. He also recalled the composer offering specific choreographic suggestions from the outset. The notation of stick figures and spatial diagrams throughout Stravinsky's sketches reveals a constant attentiveness to the ballet's choreographic demands.[18] Balanchine recalled discussing each dance's character and tempo: "We discussed timing and decided that the whole ballet should last about twenty minutes. Stravinsky always breaks things down to essentials. We talked about how many minutes the first part should last, what to allow for the *pas de deux* and the other dances. We narrowed the plan as specifically as possible. To have all the time in the world means nothing to Stravinsky. 'When I know how long a piece must take, then it excites me.' "[19]

Once he received de Lauze's manual, Stravinsky promised Kirstein the ballet by the end of 1954. The earliest rough sketches are dated December 1953. He assured Kirstein in August 1954 that he and Balanchine had already "established the whole structure" while Balanchine was in California. It was then that the two men determined *Agon*'s architecture. These summer sessions yielded one of the most revealing documents to have emerged from all of the Stravinsky–Balanchine collaborations. An enlightening record of their exchanges, in the form of a detailed summary chart, plots each component of *Agon*'s planned action. Stravinsky drafted his initial thoughts on several single leaves of paper that track his evolving ideas. This in-progress document, reproduced in a number of sources, delineates the three main sections of the ballet. The document also includes the titles of individual dances; the specific temporal durations for each section; and several stick figures illustrating the various male and female configurations for each dance.[20] As useful as this remarkable document is, it represents the end product of Stravinsky and Balanchine's summer exchanges, not the original version, as is often claimed. Several earlier unpublished leaves reveal that the composer and choreographer often changed their minds. Thus the often reproduced facsimile shows where their thought process ended as of mid August 1954, not where it began.

Stravinsky and Balanchine initially conceived a different balletic order. What now stands as the ballet's "Prelude" was added later. Originally, the composer and choreographer planned a "Quartet for Girls" just after the "Pas de deux" (Stravinsky sketches four skirted dancers in a straight line), probably to balance the ballet's opening "Pas de quatre" for boys. Another discarded sheet exhibits a boxed area with four couples in a line ("Dance of the Four Duos," as it was originally entitled), and underneath Stravinsky writes "SINFONIA," a movement never used. Below that, he draws four groups of two females and one male each ("Dance of the Four Trios"). Further down the sheet he sketches another boxed area with four males in a line, adding the word "EPYLOGUE" [*sic*] in the center of the box and to the left and right drawing four females, one in each corner. On the reverse of this discarded sheet is a detailed sketch for the final scene, assigning specific positions for all twelve dancers. He appended the titles for several of the court dances sometimes months later. Other annotations appear in red and blue pencil, a sure tip-off (as in *Orpheus*) that these are indeed revisions rather than first thoughts.

At a luncheon in January 1955 Balanchine and Kirstein agreed to postpone the ballet's premiere until 1957 so that Stravinsky could accept a new commission from the Venice Biennale Festival for his *Canticum sacrum*. Stravinsky continued working on the ballet with Balanchine during the late summer of 1956, while awaiting the premiere of *Canticum*. The choreographer first heard parts of the score even as Stravinsky was composing them; because of health problems, however, the composition of *Agon* again halted. Over eighty sketch pages survive, some dated, but most unordered. The composer notated ideas on loose-leaf sheets, some of them dated. An assortment of index cards record everything from a short pitch series that the composer methodically charted, to a subtle rhythmic change offered as an alternative to a passage already composed. Stravinsky completed the ballet in late April 1957. Balanchine flew to Los Angeles on June 16 to attend the orchestral premiere the next day, Stravinsky's seventy-fifth birthday.

The composer's conversion to dodecaphony startled many. But his manipulation of small motivic cells was not so new. The fundamental compositional procedures of serialism and twelve-tone writing are essentially the same: a twelve-tone row or "series" is conceived and submitted to the operations of retrograde, inversion, and retrograde-inversion. Throughout the sketches, the composer generated other forms of the basic twelve-tone row through rotation and transposition. In every case, it was the segmentation of a row into smaller units that seemed to intrigue Stravinsky most. Moreover, he continually rethought the internal ordering of each dance's musical materials, often first working through materials that would eventually stand as the middle, climactic, or closing passage of the movement. Only later did he conceive the opening passage, often as the very last phase of the compositional process. The *Agon* sketches also show that he struggled most with transitional passages, sometimes laboring over them in multiple drafts as he created just the right link. The sketches also reveal Stravinsky's adoption of the serialist's vocabulary, especially the technique of pitch rotation, which serves as an overarching force throughout the ballet. Several compositional scraps disclose the composer's systematic efforts to mine the properties of a limited number of compactly constructed pitch configurations. He often sketches short motivic ideas, especially three-, four-, and six-note segments—all divisible subsets of *Agon*'s numerically magical twelve.

Among the sketches is a $4'' \times 2''$ remnant on which Stravinsky constructed one of the ballet's fundamental four-note cells (Example 11 (i)). The cell constitutes a symmetrical set $(0,1,3,4)$ disposed in such a way that Stravinsky surrounds a minor third by outlying half steps. There is nothing new here, for the set is plainly traceable to a larger, frequently relied upon octatonic collection. Stravinsky first writes out and numbers the tetrachordal pitch collection abstractly (without any rhythmic character, as is typical throughout his sketches), and then writes the same series backwards, constructing the retrograde version. Next he works out the inversion of the original four pitches, a kind of mirror image in which an intervallic leap will move down where it originally jumped up and vice versa. He then notates the retrograde-inversion in which the original series unfolds both backwards and upside down. That done,

Example 11 *Agon,* transcribed sketches of symmetrical sets: basic set and transformations; linked segments of basic set.

and after several intervening sketches had been drafted, he notates a line linking four overlapping iterations of the set (Example 11 (ii)). Stravinsky himself includes the stemming to indicate the segmentation. The original four-note set is elided with the retrograde-inversion, which is linked to the transposed form of the inversion, which is in turn joined to the original retrograde. The composer makes extensive use of these transformed sets in several later sections of the ballet.

For example, Stravinsky employs the symmetrical set and its permutations throughout the "Pas de deux." In an early sketch he bracketed various forms of the original tetrachord, now rhythmically shaped (Example 12 (i)). This set and its transformations appear in the opening measures of the Coda of the Pas de Deux (m. 495), sometimes distinctly segmented, but occasionally overlapping (Example 12 (ii)).[21]

As with earlier works, Stravinsky consistently timed individual sections of *Agon* with temporal precision. He fastidiously marked the duration of individual passages in total seconds, sometimes every few measures. The chart that he and Balanchine settled upon during their 1954 summer discussions served only as an

Example 12 *Agon*, "Pas de deux," Coda, mm. 495–98, transcribed sketch and score.

initial guide. Once he began composing, Stravinsky modified the ballet's internal division. For example, consider again the "Pas de deux," nearly six minutes in total length (including the Coda) and divided into six choreographically identifiable sections. On an index card, Stravinsky noted the specific durations for each of six divisions, though these do not coordinate exactly with the six choreographic sections actually labeled in the printed score. He then taped the card to a summary sheet on which he had already recorded the durations of the ballet's earlier sections (a total of 12′ 15″, Stravinsky carefully recorded).[22]

The sketches of the "Saraband-Step" reveal other aspects of Stravinsky's sketching habits. In drafting the earliest nub of an idea, he sometimes sketched only a line's basic contour, without any specific rhythm, pitch, harmony, or texture. Just so, in mapping out the beginning of the "Saraband-Step," Stravinsky initially outlined what amounts to no more than a skeletal figure, doubtlessly based upon some of the sarabandes he was then studying. The sketch reveals that he originally drafted four pitches that rose in one direction together with five pitches that descended, the two lines converging in a chord. The final version of what ultimately becomes the dance's m. 148 (as numbered in the score) exhibits a much more embellished version of the chord in keeping with the character of the stylized dance. Here part of the original figure appears in the violin solo, while the two trombones fill in what was the basic descent of the lower line. Stravinsky retains the final chord of the original draft. The sketches also demonstrate that he considered four separate openings, each with a different instrumentation and all progressing toward the overall duration of 1′ 15″ that he and Balanchine had stipulated. The most distinctive sound of the dance, the xylophone, is nowhere present in any of these early sketches. This suggests that Stravinsky added it later, perhaps to help simulate the sound of Arbeau's and Mersenne's instrumental recommendations. Again, Stravinsky was aware of the dance's original choreographic structure. He also marked on the sketches themselves, "Male dancer, Five Steps forward, and three steps backwards"—just as in the *Apologie* he had underlined the section of Mersenne's Suite that specifies, "sometimes forwards, sometimes backwards."

While numerous drafts are devoted to a methodical forging of a cohesive pitch structure, other sketches reveal Stravinsky's reliance upon the models provided by de Lauze and Mersenne. This is especially true of his efforts to govern the rhythmic and metric underpinnings of the first and second "Pas de trois." While de Lauze's dances provided a departure point, they came at a cost, for the composer now needed to reconcile such pre-tonal models with a post-tonal environment. In many sketch scraps he systematically graphed Mersenne's rhythms on one side of the paper, while charting pitch rotations and transpositions superimposed onto Mersenne's scheme on the other.

Adding to what could easily have become a hodgepodge of colliding ideas and conflicting techniques, the composer adopted a full-blown Webernesque twelve-tone approach. His use of the technique first appears in the Coda of the first "Pas de trois." It marks a sea change. In one of the Coda's first sketches he wrote out the row, then constructed its inversion, retrograde, and retrograde-inversion—all clearly marked by the composer and without rhythmic shape. Here, as in many preliminary sketches, Stravinsky took the time to write in his analysis of individual rows. Using colored pencils, he marked one form of the row in red, another in blue. He often marked each individual note in the row as the pitches weave through the orchestration. Moreover, he frequently indicated which form he was employing: original, inversion, retrograde, and so on. In the Coda's first draft, Stravinsky sketched the music of what would become mm. 198–200 as based upon this series.

Sometimes Stravinsky broke the twelve-tone row into two hexachords, exploring the various possibilities of the first hexachord for one half of a piece and those of the second for the other. In an early sketch for the "Bransle simple," Stravinsky notated a hexachord in the treble clef, and then in the bass clef immediately sketched its inversion. Ultimately, he used this single hexachord (with one exception) rather than a complete twelve-tone row as the pitch material for the entire bransle. He drafted the second half of the next dance, the "Bransle gay," first (beginning with m. 321). A week later, he composed the beginning of the dance, writing mm. 310–20. Here he employed a new hexachord. In terms of twelve-tone techniques, the hexachord of the "Bransle gay" is the complement to that of the "Bransle simple." A complete row comprising all twelve pitches results from a combination of the two. The "Bransle double" used both hexachords, taking full advantage of the complete twelve-tone row for the first time.[23] In essence, this final bransle is a culmination of the earlier two dances.

The sketches may prove even more insightful for dancers. In tracking these internal operations, one begins to discover Balanchine's coordination of Stravinsky's score with his choreographic techniques—a synergistic achievement if ever there was one. Balanchine was far too perceptive to illustrate every pitch rotation and every retrograde-inversion with a matching physical gesture. Still, there is no question that he understood the basic compositional principles at work. Armed with that knowledge in a way no other choreographer could be, he fashioned a ballet that would provide a fitting match for the music. It was a choreographic parallel that could be grasped only through understanding the complex interior network of Stravinsky's intricate score.

The choreographer himself described the work in the New York City Ballet Playbill of November 25, 1957, as something akin to "an IBM electronic computer. It is a machine, but a machine that thinks." Stravinsky had his doubts about just how successful the "machine" would be, skipping the premiere in New York. But to his surprise, perhaps, Agon was an instant hit. Marcel Duchamp attended, comparing the moment's excitement to that he had experienced at the premiere of The Rite forty-four years earlier. Indeed, the work's energy entranced both the audience and the dancers. Kirstein spoke of the fundamental musico-choreographic connections: "No dance work has been more highly organized or is so dense in movement in its bare twenty minutes. Clock time has no reference to visual duration [and] there is more concentrated movement in Agon than in most nineteenth-century ballets. . . . Agon was by no means 'pure' ballet, 'about' dancing only. It was an existential metaphor for tension and anxiety." Walter Terry wrote in the New York Herald Tribune,

"For sheer invention, for intensive exploitation of the human body and the designs which it can create, *Agon* is quite possibly the most brilliant ballet creation of our day."[24]

From various socially conscious perspectives, the ballet could not have been timelier. *Agon* erupted onto the New York ballet scene during the late autumn of 1957, hardly a month after the Soviet Union launched *Sputnik*, marking the dawn of the Space Age. Quickly tagged a "futuristic" ballet, *Agon* was bound to invite interstellar comparisons. The ballet was "like travel in outer space," Edwin Denby wrote, a work that pushed the envelope of the dance universe with its "jetlike extensions," "soundless whirl," and "intent stillness." Just as the Russian space shot redefined our earthly limits, Stravinsky and Balanchine's newest collaboration challenged the artistic conception of musico-balletic time and space. Balanchine's comparison of the ballet to an IBM electronic computer seemed right: "a measured construction in space," he observed, "demonstrated by moving bodies." Those bodies appeared in the blackness and whiteness of practice clothes, thus revealing, as Nancy Reynolds observes, "the raw mechanics of the body as propelled by a score so naked it was almost brutal."[25] The work's computer-like temporal exactness was emblematic; its techno-precision, both musically and choreographically, presaged the spirit of a new era.

Moreover that bold new spirit audaciously asserted itself in the ballet's "Pas de deux," in which Arthur Mitchell was paired with Diana Adams. In one of the most visually insinuative dances Balanchine ever conceived, the partnering of a black male dancer and a white female dancer appeared at a racially volatile moment in U.S. history. Balanchine, his dancers attest, was acutely aware of the contrast and inevitable controversy, but rather than shrink away he exploited it fully. Melissa Hayden remembered, "The first time you saw Diana Adams and Arthur Mitchell doing the pas de deux it was really awesome to see a black hand touch a white skin. That's where we were coming from in the fifties."[26] But Balanchine had no desire to use dance as a public soapbox. Rather, he delighted in creating jarring visual impacts. More than anyone, he realized that such a stark contrast would viscerally intensify the visual polarity that *Agon* often sought. It was just one further aspect of the "contest" that was at *Agon*'s core. As Mitchell himself recalled, "There was a definite use of the skin tones in terms of Diana being so pale and me being so dark, so that even the placing of the hands or the arms provided a color structure integrated into the choreographic one."[27]

Balanchine seemed more anxious about the audience's reaction to the work's choreographic challenges than about any perceived racial overtones. Indeed some of the images portrayed in the "Pas de deux" were erotically suggestive,

giving rise to another level of risk. Like never before, the female dancer participated in explicitly shaping the sexuality of the action, no longer demurely
playing the manipulated, submissive respondent. To a far greater degree than
the women of *Apollo* and *Orpheus, Agon*'s eight women symbolized a new level
of empowerment. In terms of both gender and sexuality, not only does the
ballet "celebrate strong, independent women and present triangular partner-
ships dispassionately," suggests Sally Banes in *Dancing Women*, but it offers a
"modernist" view of love.[28] It bids us pause to question the virtues and limitations of cultural traditions, just as Mitchell and Adams's integrative dance
compels us to question what are too often deeply ingrained biases.

As always, Balanchine's approach to the ballet began with study of the score.
As an able musician, there is no question that the choreographer was keenly
aware of the work's cryptography. He worked especially hard to decipher its
many puzzles, for only by solving them could he, as the musician-choreographer
that he was, conceive a synchronous visual complement. He heard the rhythmic
implications of *Agon*'s many musical canons and visualized them inventively, not
just imitatively. He recognized that the basic serial procedures of pitch inversion
and retrograde could find a choreographic correlation in the many mirror
images permeating the ballet. Most importantly, he understood that *Agon*'s spirit
demanded a new approach that would produce a "visual equivalent which is a
complement; not an illustration." Moreover, he realized that divisions of the
whole were more important than the whole itself; and that subsets, not sets,
furnished the bonding agent that would tie together *Agon*'s multiple sources and
models. The substructure mattered most, especially when it came to expressing
choreographically the musical form of a dance.

While in Los Angeles for *Agon*'s June 1957 orchestral premiere, Balanchine
attended at least one rehearsal. He also obtained a copy of the orchestra
tape that Stravinsky had made just after the first performance. For Balanchine,
acquainting himself with Stravinsky's orchestration was especially crucial. The
use of harp, mandolin, castanets, and the chamber-like reduced orchestra of the
middle third of the work were intimately tied to his choreographic concept. It
comes as no surprise, for example, that choirs of instruments were associated
with gender depictions. The trumpets of the ballet's opening fanfare and
"Bransle simple" that accompany the males and the harp and flutes of the
Gailliarde that attend the females are obvious matches, particularly given the
composer's explicit references to the many instrumental associations outlined
by Arbeau, Mersenne and de Lauze.

Stravinsky had sent the piano reduction to Balanchine in April 1957; thus the
choreographer was already familiar with the music by the time he heard the

orchestral premiere in June. We know that Balanchine would constantly consult the piano score, darting back and forth from the dancers to the piano in an effort to match what he was seeing with what he was hearing. Sometimes he did more than that. According to Melissa Hayden, he often sat at the piano playing the score. In the "Bransle Gay," he demonstrated to the dancers the different layers of rhythmic activity that Stravinsky had built into the music. He clapped individual lines, constantly counted the beats of a pattern, marked the accents, described the Spanish flavor of the rhythms, and played various melodic ideas at the piano. He choreographed the first part of the dance without piano, but the second section evolved at the keyboard, in about thirty minutes. Finally, Hayden recalls that Balanchine instructed her to dance the same bransle a bit faster than he first conceived the tempo, but that ultimately Stravinsky wanted it even faster, "jazzier."[29] The music's newness challenged the twelve dancers in unprecedented ways. Diana Adams remembered, "We used to have hilarious rehearsals in the first part of *Agon* because we were in three groups and at the end of one section when we cross and go to a different position we were always getting there on a different count."[30]

Although Stravinsky's numerous suggestions furnished a general outline, Balanchine realized the specific details back in the Manhattan studio. Stravinsky did not see any of the ballet until November 10, 1957, only a few weeks before the premiere. Balanchine confided to Davidova that he was worried about the validity of his concept: "I don't even know whether I'm on the right path or not. Would you do me a favor," he beckoned Davidova. "Bring him to rehearsal so that I can know his reaction."[31] Roy Tobias, remembered for his dancing in *Agon*'s bransles, recounted his memory to Richard Buckle: "Hitherto, in the opening pas de quatre the four boys had faced the audience. The composer suggested that they should turn their backs. This was agreed. In Melissa's variation [the Bransle gay, central section of the second pas de trois], Balanchine made me beat on the stair rail with a stick to represent the castanets. While we were working on the Bransle double . . . [Balanchine] made the boys enter together rather than in canon."[32]

Balanchine's conception invigorated the composer. Of the several suggestions volunteered by Stravinsky, none proved more brilliant than turning the four males away from the audience as the ballet begins, though in fact the original chart that he and Balanchine had constructed years earlier specifically directed the men to face toward the back of the stage. According to Balanchine's biographer Bernard Taper, also an observer that day, Stravinsky changed not only the ballet's beginning, but also its ending, stipulating how the males were to position their arms during their closing movements. There also seems to have been discussion about tempi, particularly in relation to Balanchine's suggestions about slowing down certain sections (the previously mentioned Bransle Gay notwithstanding), with which Stravinsky generally agreed.[33] Moreover, Paul Horgan remembers Stravinsky and his wife, as well as Robert Craft, returning from several studio rehearsals "full of praise for the choreography devised by Balanchine. . . . Stravinsky spoke of Balanchine's musicianship, making the point that he could talk with him in purely musical terms, not in dramatic or balletic analogies."[34]

Sections of the ballet are available on several commercial videos, including *The Balanchine Celebration*, part 2, which offers a complete performance of *Agon*'s middle section. Of particular interest are the first "Pas de trois" and the three bransles of the second "Pas de trois," since these constitute the de Lauze archetypes that Stravinsky studied.[35] The videotape begins with the "Prelude," in which the structure of the dancing reflects the score's clearly delineated halves. Trumpets and timpani announce the first section (mm. 121–31), as the two females and male rush center stage with widely extended arms and legs stretching upward. The instrumental register also rises steadily higher, until the trumpet sounds a climactic *sforzando* in m. 131—a dramatic peak for both the orchestra and the trio of dancers. The incessantly driven motivic rhythms of the trumpet, timpani, and tom-toms provide the foundation for a dynamic contrapuntal exchange among the woodwinds and strings. The second half of the "Prelude" features woodwinds (mm. 136–45) in a dramatically slowed *meno mosso* section. Whereas the brassy opening section was frenetic, here a mood of stasis prevails. There is a stately Renaissance feel to the dotted rhythms and embellished figures of the flutes and bassoons. The two females stand on either side of the male in a mirrored arabesque. The courtly bow performed by all three ushers in the de Lauze dances of the first "Pas de trois," as the women depart and the man prepares for the ballet's first solo variation.

The "Saraband-Step" retains many of the characteristics normally associated with its sixteenth-century model, though detection of any historical connection upon first viewing is unlikely. In keeping with the original form's binary nature, the dance divides into two eight-measure halves (with a two-measure codetta). Its triple meter and rhythmic accents are also consistent with historical models. The meter is unarticulated, however, thus disguising any recurring patterns. Likewise, Balanchine avoids recurrent strong beats too, choosing instead to add a separate layer of dance that ostensibly contravenes Stravinsky's compositional divisions, camouflaged as they often are. A series of *glissades*, as well as a continual cutting back and forth, up and down stage ("sometimes forwards, sometimes backwards," as Stravinsky underlined in the manual), are evident.

The pervasive contrapuntal dialogue of music and movement is reminiscent of so many imaginatively asymmetrical overlays found in works as early as *Apollo*.

The "Gailliarde" is cast in ternary form (A = mm. 164–70, B = mm. 171–78, A = mm. 179–84). This time the two female dancers proceed mostly in mirrored gestures, demarcating each musical division. Moreover, these mirrors should not be separated from the movement's pervasive use of canon. In this instance, the dancers/strings, working together, serve an accompanimental function. The interior layer of the music emerges centrally. The harp and mandolin solos proceed in a strict canon that, as usual, is not immediately obvious unless one is made aware of it. Nor was it particularly important to Stravinsky that the canon be heard. As in so many other instances, the canon served as a substructural means of organizing his musical materials—similar, in fact, to the wonderful (but for most listeners inaudible) canon employed nearly thirty years earlier in the "Pas d'action" of *Apollo*.

The middle section carries repeat signs in the score, and upon its repetition, Balanchine, following his custom of setting previously heard music to new choreography, alters the dancers' movements. He now includes three hand-claps by the women to help stress the prevailing musical pulse. In the final A section (mm. 179–84), Balanchine's female dancers mirror the flutes of the orchestra (mm. 179–80). More extensively, the canon between the mandolin and harp proceeds; this time, however, the mandolin takes over the melody sounded by the harp in the original A section, with the harp now assuming the role of the follower. Balanchine was keenly aware of the need to continue physical movement during longer note values in the music. Stravinsky ends the last measure of the "Gailliarde" with a sustained final harmony, eschewing any other musical activity in this multi-layered, texturally variegated dance. Balanchine reciprocates, having the two dancers assume a stationary, mirrored pose at the final cadence. With graceful hand movements, they articulate each of the final chord's interior pulses.[36]

We have seen that the Coda of the first "Pas de trois" marks Stravinsky's fateful turn to twelve-tone writing, and an equally memorable dance was needed to match the moment. Balanchine's choreographic divisions parallel Stravinsky's row segmentations. The Coda has an A–A′–B design: an opening statement (A = mm. 185–210); a slight variation (A′ = mm. 211–33); and finally a contrasting closing section (B = mm. 234–53). As so often in the ballet, Stravinsky utilizes specific instrumental colors to signal important structural junctures. In the opening A section, for instance, he snakes his first twelve-tone row statement through a harp and cello solo. At the same time, the trumpets sustain and the mandolin strums an open-fifth harmony that has nothing to do with the row. One has the impression that the composer is holding onto the tonal world of the tonic–dominant c–g pitches in the trumpets and mandolin while simultaneously abandoning it in the two dodecaphonically conceived solo lines (mm. 185–90). Balanchine directs the two females to stand to the side of the male but then immediately engage in their own canon as he comes to the foreground and then retreats, as if to announce the inauguration of an important event. His welcoming front-kick gesture (used so often by Agon's males to mark a new musical idea) ends just as the first iteration of the row comes to a close.

The composer disassembles the next row statement texturally, punctuating individual notes between the piano and two bass trombone parts. The percussive sound of the piano and edginess of the trombones effectively highlight the progressively unwinding statement of the row. At the same time, the double-stops of a solo violin outline a succession of very tonal, very non-twelve-tone-like intervallic sixths. The dodecaphonic world, expressed by piano and brass, and the tonally oriented world of the solo violin are texturally partioned, although both proceed together throughout the passage. Balanchine responds to the music's textural division with a completely new choreographic design. As the row begins in the piano (m. 191) the male dancer is pressed into solo action, while the two females perform as a separate unit, thus producing a male-female duality analogous with the score's dodecaphonic-tonal duality.

Choreographic articulations occur in the other two sections of the Coda as well. The reprise of the A section begins in m. 211 with the statement of the original twelve-tone row in the piano and trombones. Since the music is essentially the same, Balanchine creates a different design, combining the man and two women in new configurations. Finally, the B section introduces another statement of the original row, this time for the solo violin, trumpet, and mandolin (mm. 234–41), while at the same time the three flutes combine in playing the inverted and retrograde forms of the same row. Balanchine's dancers now participate in a new canon, echoing the increased activity. Perhaps most dramatically, when Stravinsky introduces another row statement in m. 242, he does so with a textural sparseness closer in spirit to Webern than ever before. The music is now pointillistic, with notes strategically positioned across the full orchestral register. The solo violin performs *sul ponticello*. Other vaporous-sounding "bleeps" join a parade of instrumental devices, including pizzicati, glissandi, and *con sordino*. All add to the singular sound of the passage.

Balanchine met the challenge by building equally new, counter-classical visual images. Here, for the first time, all three dancers converge, collapsing upon themselves, touching shoulders, standing abruptly erect, and generally engaging in angular motions that are as spatially diffuse and unanticipated as the music's pointillistic style. Finally, as the last musical gesture unfolds with sustained chords beginning in m. 249, an even more complex retrograde-inversional statement of the row begins. To match the intricacy of these final row presentations, Balanchine choreographically marks the passage as another structural pivot. The two females each perform two classical pirouettes in succession, forming a revolving line. The male attends both of them as they rotate through his support; and as the Coda concludes, there is yet another courtly bow.

The "Bransle simple," cast in a straightforward three-part design (A = mm. 278–87, B = 288–97, A′ = 298–309), opens the second "Pas de trois." Stravinsky's marking of Mersenne's bransle model reflects his conscious adaptation of the same long–short–short accent patterns. Choreographically, the two males replicate the musical canon of the dueling trumpets throughout the A section, but with one important difference. Stravinsky's canon unfolds at the time interval of a half note, while Balanchine's dancers chase at the distance of a quarter note—in effect twice as fast. A contest of aural and visual layers ensues, each proceeding along its own time-line, though always in perfect temporal harmony. The B section's fragmentary phrases, now vertically constructed as opposed to the canon's earlier horizontal line, are tossed between instruments. The dancers abandon the regimented canon and engage in a long mirrored passage over the entire ten-measure central section.

The female soloist's "Bransle gay" is also cast in a tripartite design (A = mm. 310–20, B = mm. 321–31, A = mm. 332–35), with the two men now standing to the rear and miming the sound of the clacking castanets. The castanets' underlying 3/8 rhythmic pulse once more has its origins in the Mersenne model studied by Stravinsky. The fact that the composer constantly shifts his notated meter between 7/16 and 5/16 does nothing to compromise the powerful 3/8 pull of the ostinato. As in *Agon*'s earlier dances, Stravinsky marks the tripartite structure's interior divisions texturally. The B section, for example (noting that this central section was actually composed first), stands alone in its contrapuntal layering of solo flutes and clarinets. On four occasions, the composer also uses a measure of solo castanets as a formal marker: to introduce the dance, to separate the two phrases of the A section, to divide that entire section from the B section, and finally to close the dance. In the first two instances, the female soloist dances "through" the ostinato with an independent gesture, while replicating the rhythm with her arm movements in m. 320 (dividing A from B) and again in the final bar. The initiation of virtually every one of these various choreographic patterns coincides with Stravinsky's hexachordal divisions.

Mersenne's "Bransle de Poitou" served as the rhythmic and metric model for *Agon*'s "Bransle double." While the opening violins play a clearly articulated triple meter, emphasizing each strong beat, the trumpet and tenor trombone engage in a duet consisting of duple divisions. Balanchine realized the choreographic possibilities of this crosscutting meter. As the dance begins, the female is tossed between the two males. She also performs a series of splits supported by the two males, again creating the sense of splitting the texture and meter into competing levels. As for pitch, the composer employs a complete twelve-tone row for the first time in the second "Pas de trois," combining the two hexachords of the previous two bransles. Balanchine marks the divisions with choreographic gestures that help define the structure. The Coda, which commences in m. 373, consists of a series of interwoven twelve-tone transformations. It represents the most elaborate intersection of row forms to this point in the ballet. There is a shift to duple meter, the steady half-note motion establishing clarity of pulse while signaling an important change. The music now moves more slowly and deliberately. The choreographic movement also shifts to a slower pace, the three dancers joining hands at the exact moment the Coda begins. As the complex interweaving of the twelve-tone row transformations gets underway, so the trio embarks on a series of movements in which the arms cross underneath one another while the dancers are stationary. The final leap of the woman from the arms of one male to the other provides a choreographic accent, just as Stravinsky halts the musical motion with a single pizzicato chord on the last beat.

Despite the innovative qualities of the "Pas de deux," its roots are classical. This is evident in its traditional design—a formal entrance, followed by a supported *Adagio*, individual male and female variations, and finally a return to partnering in the Coda. Stravinsky meticulously calibrated each of these sections abstractly before composing the music. Temporal pacing, as ever, was uppermost in his mind. As noted earlier, the basic pitch cell employed throughout the "Pas de deux" consists of a symmetrically constructed tetrachord: the first two notes of the cell divided by a half step, then an intervening interval of a whole step, and finally the final two pitches divided by a half step. It one of Webern's prototypical four-note patterns. The pitch contours of this cell stretch in the same manner that Balanchine stretches the choreographic gestures—for instance, in the female's constant extensions of arms and legs, lunging in every direction. Moreover, the choreographic equilibrium of the dancers' gestures, often mirroring one another, replicates the symmetrical structuring of Stravinsky's pitch materials. Balanchine continues to articulate major intersections in the score. For example, the first point of musical repose occurs at m. 427, where violins, violas, cellos, and basses participate in a long, sustained cadence. At this exact moment Balanchine elevates the female for the first time, stretching legs and arms to the limit, supported by the male who gently and gradually lowers her back to the floor. The entire section repeats, but now with completely new choreography exuding some of the ballet's most provocatively sensual gestures.

The brief ten-measure male variation beginning at m. 463 emphasizes the same split intervals. Another canonic treatment at the temporal distance of one measure prevails, now scored for piano and three horns in stark contrast to the earlier string writing. The solo male's leaps and hand gestures accord with the suddenly brighter music. Since the male soloist alone cannot portray a two-line canon, Balanchine fashions an independent counterpoint with the piano and horn trio. He moves at a slower, more deliberate pace, in effect adding an additional layer to the texture. We now hear and see three intersecting strata of music and choreography. The female initiates her eleven-measure solo at m. 473, with a duet of flutes supported by the strings. Stravinsky employs three- and four-note segmentations for the flutes' melodic material, material first seen in the earlier *Adagio* but now set in a very un-Webernesque way. Balance prevails as the woman takes center stage, engaging in the most classically oriented gestures of her duet. Both musically and choreographically, these brief eleven measures provide a respite before the male's refrain recommences at the *Istesso tempo* of m. 484, where the canon of the piano and horns returns.

The Coda, beginning at m. 495, combines strings and brass. The male grabs the female aggressively, pulling her to him as they begin a series of linked movements, each one briefly starting and stopping wherever Stravinsky segments the tetrachordal pitch material and marks a pause. The *Doppio lento* at m. 514 marks a critical juncture, a return to the music's *adagio* mood and a resumption of the more pointillistic texture. For the first time in the entire composition, the ballet's disparate styles now fuse. The two soloists renew all of the suggestive, sensual tensions of Balanchine's choreography. Just as the "Bransle double" concluded with a string pizzicato, snapping the music's last moment, here too the cello's final, punctuating pluck draws the ingeniously conceived "Pas de deux" to a dramatic close.

Stravinsky used his historical models as powerful creative springboards. They should not be dismissed as quickly as the composer would have us do. In which direction would his imagination have led him without Kirstein, Eliot, and Mersenne? Likewise, Balanchine's choreographic setting is intimately tied to the composer's study of de Lauze's manual in particular. Nor can one hope to understand the structural network that Stravinsky assembled without addressing the composer's new approach to pitch collections. That Balanchine so beautifully visualized *Agon*'s multiple musical layers, clarifying its many sophisticated serial and dodecaphonic segmentations, signifies his full understanding of Stravinsky's score and his appreciation of its complexities. More than ever, these two artists had achieved a counterpoint of minds. Ultimately, however, *Agon* is not only, nor even primarily, about pitch, but about the temporal flow of rhythm. It is about symmetry and "architectonics," to use the composer's own term—concepts Stravinsky had been exploring in works leading directly to the ballet, especially the 1955 *Canticum sacrum*. *Agon* is the musico-choreographic exemplification of the idea that the beauty of architecture grows in splendor the more it is regulated and even restricted by the discipline of classical templates. Stravinsky, the indefatigable classicist, turned to pre-existing models that would provide the structural foundation he needed to construct his "futuristic" creation. As he stated in his *Autobiography*, quoting Verdi, "Let us return to old times, then we will progress." Balanchine was the most sympathetic of collaborators. He could wondrously visualize what the composer wanted to say. That this innovative work owes its genesis to sources as distant as the Renaissance is befitting. For in both Balanchine's and Stravinsky's estimate, the pathway of the future was inseparable from the achievements of the past. *Agon* takes us down a "path of mystery marked by the most restrained of means," as Horgan wrote upon attending the premiere.[37] Much the same could be said of all the Stravinsky–Balanchine collaborations. And in the end, this may be the fairest, most poetic measure of their shared achievements.

CHAPTER EIGHT

TERPSICHOREAN HYBRIDS

Compositions incorporating dance in a rich variety of guises, many of which could hardly be classified as traditional ballets, appear throughout the entire Stravinsky literature. Depending upon how strictly one applies the label, some of the eleven works discussed in detail to this point would qualify as bona fide classical ballets. In this chapter, six other compositions incorporating dance are addressed. Together they form an unorthodox collection of works that occupies an equally important place in Stravinsky's more broadly defined theatre oeuvre. In fact, several are performed more often than the ballets heretofore discussed, and in various ways break new ground. As a group they combine dance elements of varying dimensions with music for chamber ensemble, symphonic music, music with words, narrators, actors—all aimed toward transcending the boundaries of fixed forms, and all conceived as hybrids created in the broader interests of modernist theater.

Taking full advantage of the opportunies provided by Diaghilev, Stravinsky seemed eager to question the precepts of structural design almost from the start. *Les Noces, Oedipus rex, Renard, Pulcinella,* and other hybridized compositions created during the Ballets Russes years resist convenient categorization. Throughout the composer's life, the expression of content overrode the arbitrariness of hermetic, prefabricated models. It was not so much a conceit to create new, archetypal structural designs, as it was an artisan's need to customize templates toward resolving discrete compositional problems as they presented themselves. As he contended throughout his career, each new composition presented a new problem to be solved. Process was more important than production, he maintained. Once a task was accomplished, Stravinsky was prepared to move on to a new challenge. In his Norton lectures at Harvard he spoke of the value of limits: "Let us take the best example: the fugue, a pure form in which the music means nothing outside itself. Doesn't a fugue imply the composer's submission to the rules? And is it not within those strictures that he finds the full flowering of his freedom as a creator? Strength, says Leonardo da Vinci, is born of constraint and dies in freedom."[1]

A classicist through and through, the composer was able to balance the value of limitations with the artist's need to exceed those same limitations as warranted. "The moment you cheat for the sake of beauty," wrote Max Jacob in his 1922 *Art poétique*, "you know you are an artist." Post-Diaghilev works by Stravinsky such as the choreographic melodrama of *Perséphone*, the *Symphony of Psalms*, the pantomimic theater of *Orpheus*, and the peculiar alchemy of *Agon*—these and other works took their cue from a composer who possessed a taste for "radical individualism," to invoke a familiar *Mir iskusstva* exhortation. The specific compositional techniques Stravinsky applied after the Ballets Russes may have changed a bit, but the desire to identify or invent the most effective structural form to solve whatever challenge was currently in front of him remained essentially the same. And make no mistake, the greater the challenge, the greater the constraints imposed, the more Stravinsky's imagination was unleashed.

Renard

Of the six works addressed here, perhaps none is more anomalous than *Renard*. Completed in 1916 in Morges, it is a barefaced burlesque, full of bawdy ethnic humor and bombast. Surely, it captured the composer's nostalgic longing for his homeland, evident throughout the Swiss years. In this case, the humorous exploits of Afanas'yev's barnyard characters—a rooster, a cat, and a goat, every inch stereotyped and all would-be victims plotting the eventual undoing of a cocksure fox—furnished just the right material for a theatrical retelling. The idea of an allegorical tale, fatuously spun by animals who wear their moralizing message lightly, appealed to Stravinsky. The production included these four comically etched characters, four solo singers, and a small orchestra featuring a comically obstreperous percussion battery. The chamber-sized nature of the work may be partly attributable to the modest performing forces available during the war, and partly to the work's financial patron, the Princesse Edmond de Polignac, who was just then commissioning compositions intended to counter the bloated works of Germanic origin that were still in favor. She may also have envisioned soirée-like chamber performances in her salon, even though in this case such a performance did not materialize. The premiere of this twenty-minute, eccentrically scored theater work had to wait until May 1922, when it was finally produced in Paris by Diaghilev.

While there is a full complement of strings, the brass and woodwinds play particularly prominent roles in emulating the raucous sounds of the principal characters as they bark and bellow their way through a delightfully crude piece of street theater. As Asaf'yev observed, it was about time. "Buffoonery—or Russian grotesque art, which had been suppressed by hundreds of years of every kind of hypocrisy, had sooner or later to manifest itself in our lyric theater . . . Throughout their history, Russians have always expressed these attitudes in 'masks' of song, dance, and music that portray the measure of mockery, insolence, cunning, and irony which they find in life."[2] Such mockery is captured in the form of the metallic crackling of a cimbalom, an instrument meant to ape the Russian gusla, a type of goat-string balalaika that by then was all but impossible to find. (Early sketches indicate that Stravinsky had planned to use either the piano or the harp in its place.) It was the plinking and plucking sounds of the instrument, first heard by the composer in 1915 in a Geneva bar, that prompted him to enlist the Hungarian cimbalom in an effort to "imitate the cries of animals," as he recounted in his chronicle. The clangorous instrument took on a concertante role, requiring a performer of considerable proficiency. Moreover, the cimbalom added a harsh element of rawness to the orchestral mix, emphasizing the earthy vulgarity of the piece. The vocal texture is reminiscent of simple Russian folk songs in the style of *Pribaoutki*, here melodically expanded to include unwieldy leaps doubtlessly intended to emulate the animal-like braying of the four characters. Stravinsky had become enthralled with the idea of textual settings. He strove to accent, distort, and generally utilize the rhythms and declamation of Russian words as an integral, even driving compositional agent (figure 9). The ungracious melodic jumps and asymmetrical rhythmic construction underscored the bigger-than-life histrionics of the work—histrionics enhanced by the equally acrobatic gesticulations of the dancers.

Diaghilev was in no hurry to mount the work. His travels to America as well as his need to continue staging the more spectacular ballets of a few years earlier took precedence over *Renard*. When he did finally get around to staging it, Michel Larinov provided the costumes and set designs (Figure 10). Ernest Ansermet, one of Stravinsky's trusted friends at that point, directed the orchestra. Most importantly, Nijinska provided the choreography in just the right "spirit of its mountebank buffoonery, and even danced the role of the Fox in the original production."[3] The loss of her choreography is regrettable, especially given the indispensable role played by dance in this multi-faceted theatrical piece of Russian folk art, to which dancing was so essential.

The premiere of May 18, 1922, was less than a success, although Larinov's and Nijinska's contributions were noted. While the work has occasionally been

Figure 9 *Renard*, sketch showing Stravinsky's setting of Russian words.

restaged, it has failed to find a secure footing in the theater or dance repertoire. In the years immediately following the original production, the work appeared twice in Germany and even once in Leningrad, where its Russian roots still resonated within the climate of social realism. Yet the work's satire did not fare well in what one might have guessed would be an important remounting by Diaghilev and Lifar in 1929. By then Stravinsky was at odds with both men, and criticized the revival. Thereafter, only a few now almost entirely forgotten revivals ensued. It was not until Balanchine offered a new version as part of Ballet Society's adventuresome 1947 season, with costumes and scenery by Esteban Francés, that the work succeeded, at least modestly.

Given his dissatisfaction with Lifar's staging of almost twenty years earlier, as well as his confidence in Balanchine, the composer's excitement and expectations must have been high. He made a point of attending rehearsals, and as always,

Figure 10 *Renard*, costume design by Michel Larinov, 1922.

actively participated. Craft recalls that during one rehearsal, after instructing the orchestra about tempi, the composer went on stage and "mimed movements for the dancers."[4] Balanchine in fact employed mostly mime and demi-character steps for the dancers. Yet once again, the odd mixture of theater and dance, singing and playing, seemed a bit too jumbled for audiences expecting to witness a more classically styled ballet. John Martin's *New York Times* review of February 16 reflected the ambivalence shared by many who attended the production: "*Renard* was an important event, for here is a work extremely difficult to produce [and] destined always to be unpopular. . . . It was composed in 1915 and marks Stravinsky's transition from a merely progressive force in the lyric theatre to a radical one." Martin concludes that it is easy to see why earlier productions of the work had been unsuccessful, while halfheartedly recognizing that nevertheless "it is a kind of historical milestone in the modern ballet."

Todd Bolender, who played the Fox in Ballet Society's 1947 production, provided one of the most interesting reconstructions. An accomplished choreographer, Bolender recreated the work during the 1950s in Boston and San Francisco. Then in 2001—over half a century after the Balanchine staging—Bolender's razor-sharp memory enabled him to reconstruct the 1947 choreography for the Kansas City Ballet during a city-wide Stravinsky festival. This brilliant production only confirmed that while Stravinsky's music is quite marvelous, it remains conspicuously incomplete without the choreography—choreography that helps to articulate the boisterous nature of the work. Asaf'yev perceived the interdependence of music and dance early on. He saw and heard the asymmetry of Stravinsky's music spring to life through physical motion, commenting that "the motion of *Renard* fully meets the requirements of precision demanded by pantomime, dance, and acrobatics," adding that "gesture, not description," is the work's fundamental point of departure.[5] It is regrettable that few companies today include this important composition in their repertoire.

L'Histoire du soldat

Written in 1918, *L'Histoire du soldat* traveled a similar theatrical path to that of *Renard* of a few years earlier. And like *Renard*, Stravinsky's newest opus hardly provided the kind of highbrow music that was thought fitting for the staid concert halls of Paris and Vienna. *L'Histoire*'s cautionary tale, and especially its rhythmic piquancy, would have an exoteric appeal beyond the circle of devotees of the Ballets Russes. While the decimation of the First World War may have only nipped at the margins of a nonaligned Switzerland, its hostilities consumed the rest of Europe. Stravinsky's musico-dramatic parable of a naive "Everyman" soldier who falls prey to the Devil's treacherous grip resonated immediately. As shopworn and pontificating as this familiar moralistic tale was, it was the nevertheless right moment to retell the story, now framed by the tensions of 1918. *L'Histoire* confronted its audience with the age-old quandary of individuals victimized by the forces of war's devastation. How do they react? How do they survive? And with whom are they willing to barter? For Europeans, the war had become a nightmarish intrusion, closing in on them with each passing day. An increasingly disconsolate Stravinsky was virtually cut off from St. Petersburg, Paris, and the scenes of his earlier artistic triumphs. Moreover, the Bolshevik insurgency could only have intensified the composer's ambivalence about having fled his homeland.

Struggling to remain solvent, the Ballets Russes was in no position to commission works from the composer during his Swiss exile; nor did Diaghilev provide any royalties from his earlier ballets. The scoring of Stravinsky's recent compositions reflected the harshness of the times. As mentioned earlier, he wrote mostly nostalgic miniatures speaking to a happier era. His plight worsened, and necessity interceded. Living in "a position of the utmost pecuniary difficulty," as he laments in his *Autobiography*, Stravinsky met with Charles Ferdinand Ramuz, a local friend and author who had recently provided him with the Russian translations for several texts, including those of *Renard* and *Les Noces*. They would collaborate in concocting a small, mobile theater production, "to be read, played and danced"—a "théâtre ambulant," as they first envisioned it. With *L'Histoire* they hoped to reach an unsophisticated public of villagers and locals wishing merely to be entertained. They would transport the show from place to place, setting up this portable art work without the garniture or pretension of classical theater. The readily collapsible sets and small ensemble of musicians and actors could travel easily from hamlet to hamlet. Assembling the production in a small theater or village square could be done easily. Or so they first thought.

Stravinsky's score was so rhythmically complex, however, that only skilled players could handle the musical challenges. Moreover, the demands of mounting, transporting, directing, and marketing a full-scale theater piece proved more burdensome than Stravinsky and Ramuz had first imagined. Initially entitled "Le Soldat, le violon et le diable" in the composer's sketchbook, *L'Histoire* is traceable to a single Afanas'yev text, despite Stravinsky's claim that several stories had been cobbled together. Ramuz assembled the libretto from the tale entitled "The Runaway Soldier and the Devil."[6] Ramuz and Stravinsky's adaptation unfolded over six separate scenes in two large divisions, the music playing an integral part in the dramatic action throughout. Occasionally it serves as background commentary, embellishing the Narrator's storytelling. Sometimes it enhances the dialogue between characters. The music often rises to the forefront during the story's mimed sections. At other moments, it commands the listener's full attention, as in "The Little Concert" of Scene 4, where there is no stage action and only a few lines of text.

Stravinsky originally considered scoring the work for a solo instrument with "polyphonic qualities," such as the piano, but he quickly abandoned the idea. If *L'Histoire* was to be a truly portable work, the piano obviously constituted a problem. Ansermet recalled that Ramuz had suggested a guitar, accordion, or harmonica to support the important and frequent solo violin passages.[7] Instead, the composer opted for a chamber-sized orchestra of seven instruments, all used strikingly: clarinet, bassoon, cornet, trombone, a fiddle-like violin, double bass, and a prodigiously virtuosic battery of percussion instruments that included an array of drums, a triangle, cymbals, and a tambourine. Three instrumental choirs, distinctly contrasting the high and low tessitura of winds, brass, and strings, grouped the players. Stravinsky's scoring made great demands upon the instrumentalists. For many, the music was dynamic, brashly setting a new and unanticipated course. From the start, Stravinsky recognized that a concert suite would be financially beneficial. Nor was it unusual for the always enterprising composer to envision his theater music as an independent score, even as he worked on fleshing out the narrative and staging with his collaborators. Besides, the truth is that for the most part he and Ramuz worked separately as the piece evolved. As an immensely popular concert suite, *L'Histoire* surely stands as the composer's most successful hybrid work.

It is nonetheless important to realize that Stravinsky envisioned *L'Histoire*'s musicians not as mere background support but as participating actors in their own right. The orchestra, seated to one side of the stage, would invite spectators "to see these instrumentalists each playing his own part in the ensemble," he explained in his *Autobiography*. "I have always had a horror of listening to music with my eyes shut, with nothing for them to do. The sight of the gestures and movements of the various parts of the body producing the music is fundamentally necessary if it is to be grasped in all its fullness." He further acknowledged the visual nature of musicians actually making music. Why deny it? he argued. "Why shut the eyes to this fact which is inherent in the very nature of musical art?" *L'Histoire* would connect the coequal elements of narration, dramatic action, and music in a triangular unity symbolized by their spatial placement on the stage.[8]

Much to the composer's delight, the costumes and scenery were prepared by René Auberjonois. Stravinsky helped select the costumes, including the Soldier's Swiss Army uniform as it appeared in 1918. All of the story's characters were stereotypically defined in the familiar story of crossroads, confrontation, temptation, and its consequences. The role of the Narrator, however, surpassed that of a neutral reader describing the action. This character would be crucial in tying together the story's layered meanings as the wandering Soldier and the opportunistic Devil traversed the work's six scenes. The Narrator served as a go-between, facilitating the dialogues between the actors, as well as commentating on the action. Often the Narrator assumed the role of an admonisher. At the end of Scene 5, for example, comes his somber homily: "No one can have it all, for that is forbidden. You must learn to choose between," he declaims over Stravinsky's Lutheran-styled music, the "Great Chorale."

L'Histoire was dedicated to its financier Werner Reinhart, an amateur clarinetist who championed the production.[9] The first performance, conducted by Ernest Ansermet, took place at, the Théâtre Municipal de Lausanne on September 28, 1918. Those in the audience who were familiar only with

Stravinsky's earlier Diaghilev ballets must have sat up. While pragmatism may have been the catalyst for the work's chamber scoring, its jaunty sound sent up a flare. Stravinsky's statements during his Swiss exile increasingly imply a downgrading, even denigrating of theater as an expressive enterprise—at least of traditional theater as associated with opera and ballet. Perhaps as a consequence of his forced embracement of an artistic frugality during these years, he grew suspicious of theater's "distractions," as he now adjudged them. Scenery, costumes, props of any kind carried the audience away from rather than toward the music. The composer appeared to reject the spirit of collaborative integration espoused by *Mir iskusstva*—a spirit he now pronounced "mistaken." He openly denounced the coupling of music with movement and words as "bigamy." By 1921, only a few years after *L'Histoire*, he pronounced ballet bankrupt as an expressive art form. The composer now turned to a Francophile intellectualism that would suffuse his thinking in the years ahead. For him, it was the era of "objectivity," of emotionless beauty. Yet the seeds of what appeared to be a volte-face were for the most part unapparent and certainly unrealized in *L'Histoire*.

How important was the element of choreography to the story? The work's sprightly trio of dances appears at the opening of Scene 5, wherein the Soldier, playing his magical violin, fiddles the life back into an ailing Princess. As a token of his gratitude, the King offers the Soldier his daughter's hand in marriage. Yet there is nothing in the original Afanas'yev tale linking the revival of the Princess with dancing. Why then did the composer include the suite of three contemporary stylized dances that were then popular, the "Tango," "Waltz," and "Ragtime"? Perhaps because they would have been familiar to the audience while simultaneously providing a diversion, as the incorporation of dance into theater was often intended to do. In later years, Stravinsky contended that the dancing had been inserted simply to prevent monotony, adding that there had in fact been too much of it.[10]

Nor was it the first time that Stravinsky had demonstrated an interest in these currently fashionable dance forms. We find it several years earlier in a series of short piano duets written for his children, such as the "March," "Waltz," and "Polka" of the Three Easy Pieces for piano of 1914–15, or the nationalistic-flavored "Española" and "Napolitana" of the slightly later Five Easy Pieces, both composed after trips to Spain in 1916 and 1917.[11] Moreover, Stravinsky's fascination with ragtime was evident even before his collaboration with Ramuz. He had completed most of his *Ragtime* for eleven instruments by the spring of 1918, months before *L'Histoire* was on his mind. In addition, he sketched the fundamental ideas for his important *Piano-Rag-Music* (not published until 1920) well before he began working with Ramuz.

For the most part, the pitch vocabulary employed throughout *L'Histoire* was familiar. Clearly sculpted pitch cells often arise melodically from major and minor thirds, while harmonic figures consist of combined fourths and fifths, as in the "Music to Scene 1." While chromatic inflections replicate some of the semitone shading found in ragtime, a strong sense of diatonicism and functional harmony provides the anchor, especially at cadential moments. That said, at the heart of *L'Histoire*'s identity is the inventive approach to rhythm that had continued to develop rapidly in Stravinsky's writing around 1918. Popular music had come to imbue his thinking, and its inherent energy now fueled his already well advanced predisposition toward syncopation and asymmetrical rhythmic figurations. Fitful, jagged rhythms, disrupting halts, and unanticipated starts permeate the work from the opening "Soldier's March," with its punctuating silences and jarring offbeat entrances of the woodwinds and brass. Here and elsewhere rhythmically charged instrumental exchanges, often interrupting one another, are bandied about over a stabilizing ostinato. The unidiomatic writing for the violin—the soul of the piece both literally and figuratively—is as idiosyncratically brilliant as anything the composer had yet written. The Faustian overtones of the original Afanas'yev tale hover over Ramuz and Stravinsky's adaptation at every point. What choice could there have been other than to exploit the Devil's own virtuosic fiddle, as had Tartini, Paganini, and others in earlier centuries?

Historians often have contended that *L'Histoire* has its roots in American jazz. But is this a fiction? Stravinsky claimed not to have heard any jazz at that time. Yet he admitted that he had relied heavily upon its techniques as evident in "sheet music" that he was studying. "I borrowed its rhythmic style not as heard but as written." Moreover, years later the composer declared that *L'Histoire* signaled his embracement of American jazz, as well as his "final break with the Russian orchestral school."[12] The veracity of this late statement (which perhaps too conveniently draws a line in the sand) and the extent of Stravinsky's reliance upon American jazz as the rhythmic wellspring from which he drew his ideas have recently come into question.[13] Whatever the source of his inspiration, however, there can be no doubt that *L'Histoire* signaled a novel, rhythmically buoyant spirit that would typify what some heard as a new Stravinskyan style.

Ramuz and Stravinsky cast the production, Ramuz auditioning students from the local university for the roles of the Narrator, the Soldier and the Devil. One of the student-actors, Jean Villard-Gilles, who played the Devil, remembered Stravinsky during the preliminary rehearsals. The composer was "always in a frenzy of enthusiasm, inventiveness, joy, indignation, headache; leaping on the piano as if it were a dangerous foe that had to be subdued by a bout of fisticuffs, then bounding on to the stage, swallowing glasses of kirsch."[14] The two collaborators mapped the on-stage movements to accommodate the dimensions of the small theater. Moreover, both fully invested themselves in these early rehearsals, although George Pitoëff ultimately assumed the role of director in finalizing the staged production.[15] Pitoëff's wife, Lyudmila, danced the role of the Princess. Stravinsky claimed that he and Mme Pitoëff worked together to develop the choreography for the three dances. It made little difference that Pitoëff had never studied classical ballet, let alone choreography, since she simply had to emulate the characteristic movements of the highly stylized dances. Beyond her contribution as the Princess, Pitoëff bequeathed a wonderfully colorful description of Stravinsky visiting her home in Geneva in the months before L'Histoire was completed: "He pounced on the piano and percussions, while imitating other instruments with his voice. Fireworks seemed to be exploding in our little salon, and Stravinsky reminded me of a devil in a Byzantine icon, so red, so black, so resonant. . . . The fracas at the end tore the atmosphere to shreds."[16]

The complexity of the Devil's part required splitting acting and dancing duties into separate roles. Stravinsky, perhaps jokingly, considered dancing the role of the Devil himself. In a letter written only a few weeks before the premiere, Ramuz reported to Auberjonois that the composer was actually considering dancing the final scene, and that this intriguing possibility should be encouraged. A cajoling Ramuz wrote to the composer that if he were to dance the Devil, he would "do so with rhythmic vitality and save the day."[17]

Diaghilev remained uninvolved in both the sponsorship and the production of L'Histoire. No doubt he was offended by the composer's willingness to accept Reinhart's funding—just as he was unnerved by later ballet commissions funded by Elizabeth Sprague Coolidge and Ida Rubinstein. Still, Diaghilev knew the value of concession. By 1920, he was eager to stage whatever the internationally known composer wished, no doubt swallowing hard and suppressing his own value judgment in favor of the work's broadly based marketability. The composer recalled that Diaghilev, having harshly criticized L'Histoire, changed his opinion, expressing eagerness to stage the work. Moreover, plans were afoot to jettison Ramuz's story while retaining Stravinsky's score. Massine would provide the choreography and Picasso the scenery and costumes—the same collaborators who would successfully stage Pulcinella a few years later. Ramuz was not about to accept an absentee role in such an arrangement. The principals involved in the ensuing negotiations failed to reach agreement, and Stravinsky, reluctantly it seems, turned his attention elsewhere.

Tucked away in Lausanne, *L'Histoire*'s premiere was a far cry from earlier Parisian first nights. *La Suisse* deemed the work so "bewildering" as to have confused the audience. Another local paper questioned the composer's arbitrary attempt to hybridize an art form, to break free from perfectly good conventions. "The authors wanted precisely and deliberately to break with all norms, all tradition, to create something absolutely spontaneous without attachment to the past." The reviewer dismissed the ovations that had greeted the production—a production the reviewer heard as a mishmash of unblended drama, music, and choreography. For some *L'Histoire* seemed neither fish nor fowl.[18] A decade after the premiere, Boris Asaf'yev provided a rich perspective on what he saw as Stravinsky's achievement in contemporizing Afanas'yev's story, and especially the rhythmic vitality that has become the work's signature:

> Don't forget that *Soldat* was written during a period of frightful carnage when there was plenty of justification for pessimism. But there is no pessimism in *Soldat*. . . . I see in *Soldat* the affirmation of life. . . . The primary law of all life is rhythm. Rhythm proceeds from movement and controls all movement. All our senses are rhythmic, and especially our sense of hearing, for outside of rhythm it is difficult to conceive the nature of the material of sound; without rhythm, that material remains scattered and unordered. Since rhythm is most directly perceived through motor-muscular sensations, the most abiding intonations are those that have been most closely connected with such sensations—through gesture, movement, and dance, and finally through the sound of words. Dance is the primary agent of form and movement in Stravinsky's art.[19]

Of the many productions of *L'Histoire* that included dance, a few are historically notable. In 1927, Lydia Lopokova, long associated with Diaghilev's Ballets Russes, staged the entire work in London, dancing the Princess herself. Stravinsky's wife-to-be, Vera Soudeikine, collaborated on the design. Maurice Béjart choreographed the work in 1966 (Italy) and 1982 (Belgium). A remarkable production was mounted at Lincoln Center in 1966 as part of a Stravinsky festival, with Aaron Copland as the Narrator, Elliott Carter as the Soldier, and John Cage as the Devil. More recently, *L'Histoire* has caught the attention of several contemporary choreographers, such as the always provocative Bill T. Jones, who staged the work at the Kennedy Center in 1997.[20] Performances of the concert suite have been even more frequent. In any of its popular versions, *L'Histoire* remains not only one of Stravinsky's most successful and popular hybrid works, but one of his most luminous and enduring compositions.

Pulcinella

The same may be said of the effervescent *Pulcinella*, first produced by Diaghilev in the spring of 1920 at the Paris Opera. Stravinsky referred to the work as an "action dansante"—presumably because the work's inclusion of mime and song exceeds traditional balletic dictates. Historically significant, the thirty-five-minute hybrid marks Stravinsky's official rapprochement with Diaghilev and the Ballets Russes after years of separation from the troupe and constant squabbling with its director. The 1919 commissioning of *Pulcinella* prompted Stravinsky to end what many considered his ill-advised Swiss exile during the war years. Both financially and artistically, *Pulcinella* furnished the impetus needed to escape the provincialism of his "Alpine colleagues," as Diaghilev commented derisively. Eagerly, Stravinsky returned to the center-stage spotlight of Paris. The composer pronounced *Pulcinella* both the "swan song" of his Swiss years (written while he was still residing in Morges), as well as the "epiphany through which the whole of my late work became possible."[21]

Just how much of an epiphany it was remains arguable. Some consider the 1920 work to be pivotal, suggesting that it immediately propelled the composer onto an entirely new and unexpected compositional trajectory. For others, it was much less of a harbinger than Stravinsky grandly proclaimed. One needs to turn to the *Symphonies of Wind Instruments*, *Mavra*, and the *Octet for Wind Instruments*, all written within the next three years, to track more clearly the composer's advance toward what historians think of as his neoclassical style. Still, the commission presented an opportunity for the omnivorously inquisitive Stravinsky to explore several pieces of unfamiliar music of the past—music that Diaghilev literally laid in front of him. Stravinsky, typically, would later confer landmark status on his own contribution to *Pulcinella*. But it was largely Diaghilev's embracement of incongruity—an admixture of past and present—that pointed the way to an emerging new ingredient in the evolution of modernism. To some extent, Stravinsky simply went along for the ride.

The world of the Ballets Russes that Stravinsky re-entered in 1919 was considerably different from the one of his earlier triumphs. The composer now found Diaghilev to be drawn more than ever to European culture. His love of Spain was evident, but he was above all attracted to Italy, both to that country's rich musical heritage, including the music of the eighteenth century, and to the artistic predilections of its imaginative, paradigm-breaking futurists. In Diaghilev's mind, Italy's classical past had wed its avant-garde—a peculiar wedlock to be sure, but one that significantly affected the troupe's artistic course over the next ten years. Lynn Garafola addresses the merger that ushered in Diaghilev's new approach: "Simultaneous with his discovery of Italy's artistic present came a second major breakthrough, a revaluation of its pre-romantic past. . . . Leaping over the nineteenth century, he discerned in the lost music of Domenico Cimarosa, Giovanni Pergolesi, and Domenico Scarlatti the forgotten choreographies of Feuillet and Rameau, and the popular art of the *commedia dell'arte*, expressions of Latinity's authentic tradition."[22] In many ways *Pulcinella* is more about Diaghilev than about Stravinsky. It was his eureka rather than the composer's that fueled the creation of the ballet, together with Stravinsky's own revitalization of classicism as a compositional tool that would serve him well in the coming years.

Although the war had taken its toll on his company, Diaghilev continued to recruit new artists to his roster, including Léonide Massine, whose own Italianate affinities ripened through frequent sojourns with Diaghilev to Venice, Naples, and elsewhere. Their shared love of Italian culture became manifest in several popular Diaghilev ballets, beginning with the 1917 *Good-Humoured Ladies*, which featured music by Scarlatti orchestrated by Vincenzo Tommasini. Two years later came Massine's *La Boutique fantasque*, with music by Rossini orchestrated by Respighi. The choreographer's interest in vernacular art had emerged as early as 1914, when he became "charmed by *commedia dell'arte* street performers in Naples; and that same year [he] had come across a manuscript, circa 1700, entitled *Les Quatre Polichinelles semblables*. He was beginning to see how a ballet based on Pulcinella might work."[23]

Massine's curiosity swelled with each expedition to the libraries of Naples. He wished to merge the idioms of folk dancing with classical ballet, a seemingly incompatible combination, but one that resonated with Diaghilev's own current devotion to the built-in friction created by the fusion of disparate artistic styles. Massine described the evolution of the ballet:

> I began to do some extensive researches into the *commedia dell'arte*, for I had an instinctive feeling that this Italian type of folk-theatre, with its emphasis on mime and its use of extempore acting, based only on a scenario, might hold the key to my artistic dilemma. . . . I decided that the character of Pulcinella would best lend itself to balletic treatment. Pulcinella, who was something of a local hero in Naples, typified the Neapolitan personality, witty, eccentric, a composite creature. . . . During that summer [1917], I went often to watch the puppet-plays in which Pulcinella played the chief part. I delighted in his ever-changing gestures, his dangling legs, and his hooked-nose mask, with one side of the face laughing and the other crying. From an old Italian actor I bought an

authentic Pulcinella. . . . I put it on and began trying to reproduce Pulcinella's gestures and movements.[24]

He further recalled his portrayal of Pulcinella as "a bit of a rogue," adding that he added "every possible flourish, twist and turn to suggest the unscrupulousness and ambiguity" of the character.[25] Moreover, inclining toward academicism in balletic technique, Massine thoroughly understood the vocabulary of classical training. Like Stravinsky, however, he also knew that following its precepts too rigidly could become constrictive.

Even as Massine's conception developed, Stravinsky monitored the fortunes of the Ballets Russes throughout the war years from his remote vantage point in Switzerland, traveling as much as he could. He attended rehearsals in Monte Carlo and performances in London. He could see for himself the turn in the road engineered by Diaghilev and Massine, and he took special notice of the choreographer's work. Diaghilev refashioned the company, moving it toward lighter, more farcical works intended to satisfy an enervated public that was weary of war and desirous of some escape. He invited Stravinsky to rejoin the flock—not by providing a full-throttled primitivistic score to another ritualistic story such as *The Rite* or *Les Noces*, but by "orchestrating" sections of some rather formulaic, texturally sparse, conservatively styled chamber music. In effect, Stravinsky was charged with rehabilitating several virtually unknown scores for yet another Italianate theatrical work already fully formed in Diaghilev's and Massine's minds. It was the first time since *The Firebird* that Stravinsky would write music—and derivative music at that—made to order. The composer was not being asked to prepare a new score for *Pulcinella*. Rather, he was charged with recomposing—some would argue simply rearranging—passages of several pre-existing scores (figure 11). Some of the music, but not all, was Pergolesi's. How much Stravinsky warmed to what must have first appeared a menial "compositional" task is questionable.

There were, however, extenuating circumstances, and Diaghilev was ready to capitalize on these.[26] Surely Stravinsky could not deny the guileless charm of the scores Diaghilev had retrieved from Italy, and the chance to renew his affiliation with a major ballet company was undoubtedly too tempting to decline. Moreover, he respected Massine. The real seduction, however, must have been the opportunity to team with Diaghilev's chosen designer, Pablo Picasso. "The proposal that I should work with Picasso, who was to do the scenery and costumes and whose art was particularly near and dear to me," wrote Stravinsky in his chronicle, was certainly appealing.[27] By 1920, the flamboyant Picasso commanded a level of Parisian esteem that Stravinsky himself had enjoyed a

Figure 11 *Pulcinella*, sketch consisting of an eighteenth-century manuscript score of Pergolesi's opera *Il fratello innamorato* with annotations by Stravinsky.

decade earlier. The painter had become a mischievous *bon vivant*, gracing the most elegant soirées in the city, while at the same time projecting a supercilious mystique very much in keeping with Diaghilev's sense of a marketable haughtiness. The impresario now offered Stravinsky the chance to collaborate with the city's most talked about and controversial artist. How could he resist?

The familiar character of Pulcinella (or Punch in the English tradition) was to the *commedia dell'arte* what Petrouchka was to Russian folklore. To use his full name, Pulcinella Cetrulo (from "citrullo," meaning "blockhead"), with his beak-like nose, was an affable buffoon who first appeared in the seventeenth century. Most closely associated with the burlesque of Neapolitan puppetry, Pulcinella proudly symbolized the working class, liberated by poverty from both pretension and politeness. His contempt for the privileges of the aristocracy was played out through calculated albeit bungling attempts to thwart those in power. Whimsical at one moment and doltish the next, Pulcinella was both loveable and pitiable. While in Italy, Diaghilev came upon several collections of the eccentric puppet's exploits. He was particularly struck by one episode from a book of Neapolitan comedies dated 1700, entitled *The Four Pulcinellas*, although it may have been Massine who initially brought the book to Diaghilev's attention. The story would provide their scenario. In addition to Pulcinella himself, the other principal players, Il Dottore (originally danced by Cecchetti) and Tartaglia, were both well-known characters who appeared frequently in Italian comedies. Massine originally played and danced the role of Pulcinella—a formidable task calling for the actor–dancer to command the stage throughout most of the production. The distinction between true dancing and mime became blurred, in the cause of doing whatever was necessary to impart the storyline. Mistaken identity, disguise, *double entendre*, and unadulterated silliness prevail throughout the nonsensical, quickly paced action. In the end, Pulcinella's ingenuity naturally wins out, as he foils his upper-crust detractors and marries his beloved Pimpinella (originally danced by the elegant Karsavina). The on-stage action included out-and-out slapstick performed by a cast of thirteen characters. Yet the production was not simply a loosely assembled farce. As Cyril Beaumont observed, the ballet was "much more than a *pastiche*, [as] it breathes the very spirit of the *Commedia dell'arte*, so far as it can be assimilated from a study of the plays and engravings of the period."[28]

Stravinsky divided the small body of strings into concertino and ripieno ensembles, consistent with eighteenth-century orchestral practice. Woodwinds, and especially the brass, play prominent roles. Stravinsky captured the jocularity of the action as choreographed by Massine through inventively scored orchestral combinations, one being a wonderfully bumbling duet for double bass and trombone. Additionally, the composer chose several pre-existing vocal pieces, mostly but not exclusively by Pergolesi, whose short life (1710–36) was distinguished largely by his operatic and choral works. Consequently, the ballet featured several operatically styled movements for soprano, tenor, and bass soloists. As in the earlier *Renard*, however, the soloists were intended chiefly to enhance the broader sound palette of the orchestra as one particular color. The vocal texts had nothing specifically to do with the characters on stage, nor were they meant to advance the dramatic action. Stravinsky completed his score in April 1920, less than a month before the first performance. The premiere was once again conducted by Ernest Ansermet.

The collaboration posed challenges. Still living in Morges, Stravinsky traveled regularly to Paris for conferences with his artistic colleagues, later recalling meetings fraught with disagreement. For Diaghilev, working with Picasso proved to be just as nettlesome as working with Stravinsky. They argued over the style of the costumes and contested the merits of historically accurate reproductions as opposed to more contemporary dress. As the composer remembered, "Picasso's first designs were for Offenbach-period costumes with side-whiskered faces instead of masks. When he showed them, Diaghilev was very brusque: 'Oh, this isn't it at all,' and proceeded to tell Picasso how to do it."[29] To no one's surprise, neither man gave ground. Deciding upon the décor was equally contentious. At one point Picasso hoped to design a puppet theater within a theater—not unlike the opening scene of *Petrouchka*. In 1917, Stravinsky and Picasso met for the first time, the composer being in Italy to conduct performances of his early ballets. He and Picasso attended puppet shows together in Naples, as well as "music-halls and probably the San Carlo Opera House."[30] Picasso's cubist preferences met with Diaghilev's immediate fury. White summarizes Jean Cocteau's memory of the process: "The theatrical framework was scrapped and only the Neapolitan scene remained—the entrance to a narrow, moonlit street, with a glimpse of the Bay of Naples and Vesuvius in the background. As for the costumes, they seem to have been more or less last-minute improvisations."[31]

Stravinsky dug in his own heels as Diaghilev pressed the composer, requiring him to forward each refurbished portion of the score for suggestions and final approval.[32] He did, however, send the recomposed movements of the work to Massine as soon as he completed them. Diaghilev appears to have anticipated much more elaborate dancing with a fuller orchestral sound, even going so far as to inform Massine that Stravinsky's orchestra would include two harps. To the contrary, the composer's orchestration was modest, as was immediately evident to Massine, who regularly received, studied, and choreographed the music from Stravinsky's piano reductions. Attending rehearsals in Paris, the composer was surprised by the look of the production as it evolved: "It often happened that when I was shown certain steps and movements that had been decided upon I saw to my horror that in character and importance they in nowise corresponded to the very modest possibilities of my small chamber orchestra." Adjustments followed in the interests of striking the right musical and visual balance. "The choreography had, therefore, to be altered and adapted . . . and that caused [Diaghilev and Massine] no little annoyance."[33]

Just how much of *Pulcinella* was composed rather than rearranged or reorchestrated has provided considerable fodder for debate. Stravinsky began by making a few small alterations directly onto some of the manuscripts Diaghilev provided. But the process quickly became more proprietary, as the composer changed pitches, adjusted pacing, and added his own orchestral colors. He paid special attention to the rhythmic fabric since, by his own admission, he was writing for dance. Most importantly, he eschewed a perfunctory reworking of Pergolesi's scores as well as those of Domenico Gallo, Unico Wilhelm Graf von Wassenaer, Alessandro Parisotti, and Carlo Ignazio Monza.

In Stravinsky's view, altering only a note or two would have amounted to no more than a "forgery."[34] *Pulcinella* was not merely a shopworn refurbishing of existing music, the composer explained, as if to pre-empt criticism. The composer recalled that Diaghilev initially recoiled at the orchestral version. Stravinsky's treatment of the music constituted a fresh, "satirical" approach that would break free from the stylistic strictures that had burdened him in the past.[35]

Knowing he would be attacked for his overtly imitative approach, Stravinsky offered a lengthy apologia in the journal *Comoedia* on the day of the premiere. He spoke of refashioning "the very foundation of the sound material" he had inherited by "juxtaposing" antipodal orchestral colors. He proclaimed his indifference to the conventionally scored sonorities typical of chamber music. Rather, he purposefully sought a "disequilibrium of instruments" that ran completely contrary to one's expectations. Puffing up his chest, he claimed that this was unprecedented, and that his aim in writing *Pulcinella* was to reorient our conception of which orchestral textures were and were not congruous. "Nobody has ever tried it in music. There are some innovations which cause surprise. But the ear becomes bit by bit sensitive to those effects which are at first shocking. There is a whole musical education to be undertaken."[36]

For some, however, *Pulcinella* seemed merely a facelift of Pergolesi and his contemporaries. What was one to make of such an amalgamation of old and new? Constant Lambert's comments were blunt: "In Stravinsky's adaptation the expressive element is treated in a mechanical way, and purely conventional formulae of construction are given pride of place. Like a savage standing in delighted awe before those two symbols of an alien civilization, the top hat and the *pot de chambre*, he is apt to confuse their functions." Lambert took particular exception to Stravinsky's bowdlerized treatment of melody, cobbling together pre-existing ideas and adapting them synthetically. "One cannot create a creature of flesh and blood out of fossil fragments," he complained.[37]

The work's curious conflation of old and new played out in the reviews that immediately followed the 1920 premiere. André Levinson's prose was every bit as purple as Stravinsky's, observing a "sarcastic harmonic scheme, where the trombone utters insolent persiflage and the bassoon hiccoughs asthmatically." Reynaldo Hahn, writing of the premiere in *Excelsior*, concluded his review by stating that the composer's imagination "was never greater than in *Pulcinella*, nor of a surer taste in audacity."[38] One thing was certain: with Diaghilev's help, Stravinsky was again positioned exactly where he wanted and needed to be. Once more, he was the talk of the town, and *Pulcinella* went on to be one of his most performed works.[39]

Les Noces

The first performance of Stravinsky's *Les Noces* marked the end of a long journey. Talk of a premiere began as early as 1916, but this proved premature. Diaghilev next planned a first night for the Paris Opera in 1919, and certainly no later than the 1920 season. When those dates failed to materialize, 1922 seemed a certainty. Contractual disputes and other mitigating factors intervened, however. Finally, on June 13, 1923, to an irritated Diaghilev's disappointment, the Ballets Russes mounted the production at the Théâtre de la Gaîté-Lyrique, a far less prominent venue than the Opera. The premiere's delay was at least partially attributable to Stravinsky himself, for the protracted history of *Les Noces* also reflects the odyssey of an exiled composer working his way through a reconciliation of his past with the pathway ahead. From its inception in 1912, even as Stravinsky was still working on *The Rite*, to its Parisian premiere, *Svadebka*—or *Les Noces* as it soon became known—occupied Stravinsky on and off through a decade of metamorphosis.

Spanning the years 1912–23 (bookend years for Stravinsky's two most massive and deeply ritualistic Russian compositions), the work developed during a historically pivotal decade that saw Russia and Europe changed forever. Though often described as a neonationalist ballet, *Les Noces* is not in fact so easily categorized. Of all the works discussed in this chapter, this thirty-five-minute composition stands as Stravinsky's most complex hybridization. The composer devoted a large part of his energy to identifying the precise orchestration that would best project the blunt and barren sound he wished to capture in portraying an ancient peasant wedding ceremony. Almost ten years after he first envisioned the setting, he settled upon soprano, mezzo-soprano, tenor, and bass soloists, an SATB chorus, four pianos, and a large percussion battery.

Bronislava Nijinska's choreography, added relatively late, would prove every bit as imaginative as Stravinsky's score. Her conception was far more sympathetic to the composer's thinking than her elder brother Vaslav's had been for *The Rite*. How could it have been otherwise, given Nijinska's frame of reference for *Les Noces*? "In bringing several musical measures together into a whole, I was creating a choreographic measure, which, while not necessarily corresponding in its beat to the musical one, responded to the sonorities of the music. For the choreography appeared to me to have its own 'voice,' being an independent score within the full score and an integral part of the overall synthesis of the work." Nijinska's approach is breathtaking in its anticipation of Balanchine's *Apollo*.[40]

As is true of the composer's other hybrid works, determining the nature of *Les Noces* is far from straightforward. Stravinsky referred to it in a variety of ways: it was a dance cantata, a divertissement, a masquerade, or in Nijinska's words, a choreographic concerto. The work's eventual subtitle, "Russian Choreographic Scenes with Song and Music," perhaps best captures the symbiosis of sound and sight in balancing dance and song in this ritualistic composition.

In early July 1914, on the eve of war, Stravinsky traveled from Switzerland to Russia. This brief pilgrimage to his family estate in Ustilug, where he searched his father's library, as well as a quick visit to Kiev, created a channel through which his creative thoughts would soon flow. "I had been thinking of a grand *divertissement*, or rather a cantata depicting peasant nuptials," he wrote, adding that he returned to Salvan with several "collections of Russian folk poems," once again setting aside the fiction that questions of ethnography and the enlistment of folk materials as sources of inspiration were unimportant to his compositional approach.[41] Among these collections were poems, stories, and folk song anthologies by Afanas'yev, Kireyevsky, A. V. Tereshchenko, and others. They would soon be put to good use in the many nostalgic Russian compositions produced during Stravinsky's Swiss years. Kireyevsky's wedding songs and Tereshchenko's *Everyday Life of the Russian People* would become particularly useful in furthering the composer's interest in one particular ritual. His reliance upon such source materials only underscores his lifelong desire to situate his works within historically accurate contexts. Nevertheless, unlike *Petrouchka*, in which extant folk melodies were either quoted in full or slightly varied, and even unlike *The Rite*, in which numerous folk songs provide the basis for transmuting melodic material, *Les Noces*, with the exception of a quoted factory worker's song, does not rely upon specific models.

No score is more profoundly steeped in the eternal power of tradition. For many, *Les Noces* is Stravinsky's signature work, piercingly probing and entirely without embellishment. Its spirit begins and ends with a consciousness of ritual's timeless beauty, disencumbered of personal persuasions, subjective hopes, and individual sentimentalities. Originally entitled *Les Noces villageoises*, the work expresses the ennoblement of the Russian village community, whose imperishable history remains oblivious to the notion of present or future tense.[42] In this case, the tradition in question is the sanctity of wedlock, whose solemnity springs in part from the somberness of loss—the bride's predetermined loss of virginity, the loss of her family, the loss of free will. Her sudden passage from peasant girl to womanhood embodies a sacrifice that seems even more unendurably mournful than that of *The Rite*'s Chosen One. Indeed, *Les Noces* resurrects—to a far greater degree than the mythically based *Rite*—the pure Russia, a proudly Slavic Russia lost in the sweep of Peter's avaricious embrace of Europeanism. *Les Noces* rejects that embrace, and with it the supposed inferiority with which the Russian people had long been saddled.

Little wonder that when the composer played some early sketches of the work for Diaghilev in 1915 the impresario wept, remarking that "it was the most beautiful and the most purely Russian creation of our Ballet."[43] For both men, *Les Noces* rebuilt a bridge to an enduring heritage whose grip could never be released. Its uncompromising clarity and elemental force are overwhelming, and neither Stravinsky's music nor Nijinska's dance makes any apology for its coarseness. Its sheer assertion insists upon an asceticism far more illuminating than many of the prettified European works that would find favor across a war-ravaged continent during the 1920s.

Primary sources indicate that Stravinsky initially intended to enlist an unconventional array of instruments, including, somewhat oddly, guitars and harpsichord. In his chronicle, the composer claims to have begun the score with "a mechanical piano and an electrically driven harmonium, a section of percussion instruments, and two Hungarian cimbaloms" (the last of these, as we have seen, engaging the composer's interest when he was scoring *Renard*).[44] By 1918, his devotion to the pianola had moved beyond what might first have been perceived as an infatuation. He not only included it in the score, but added saxhorns and flugelhorns. Three years later he determined that an orchestra of four pianos and percussion was sufficient to emphasize the brittle sound he desired. A number of revisions were added in France from 1921 onward until the final score was completed in Monaco on April 6, 1923. By then, and with time running short, Nijinska, now in Monte Carlo, had already moved the rhythmically intricate work into rehearsal. Stravinsky was often present, offering the choreographer his suggestions. The production progressed gradually through May.

The score's rhythmic asymmetry prompted familiar accusations: guttural, barbaric, primitive. Here again was the bestial Stravinsky pounding away in a convulsion of unintelligible rhythms and disjointed melodies. Constant Lambert charged the composer with adopting a "peculiarly African use of rhythm . . . [and] antiphonal use of melodic phrases reminiscent of primitive African singing."[45] Such gratuitous inferences abounded in attempts to explain away the short bursts of helter-skelter hiccupping that erupted as rhythmic motives and melodic cells went their separate ways. For many, *Les Noces* was one long paroxysm. But nothing could be further from the truth. More cohesively structured than anything Stravinsky had composed previously, the work derives its unity not from a musical source but from a linguistic one.

Stravinsky's fascination with versification, and specifically with the rhythmic-melodic flow of Russian folk poetry about this time, constituted nothing less than a "rejoicing discovery," he later proclaimed.[46] It was not simply the verse itself that interested him, but its individual components. What of its prosody, inflection, and declamation—and even more particularly the accentuation of individual syllables? Where did such accents naturally flow? How might they be altered? And how could the intentional distortion of versification prove useful as part of a compositional transmogrification? As he wrote in his chronicle, "the sequence of the words and syllables, and the cadence they create" supplied him with a new fountainhead of rhythmic figurations. More to the point, he stressed, it was the morphology of verse that intrigued him, without regard for its expressive content. Each element became a potentially useful item—a predicate more than a subject—as part of a musical vocabulary that demanded no further meaning. This might be all well and good as a compositional approach, but it was hardly comprehensible to his audience. He wondered if the work's intent could "ever completely reveal itself to a non-Russian. In musical versification of this sort a translation of sound-sense is impossible and a translation of word-sense, even if possible, would be through a glass darkly."[47]

The scenario of Les Noces is built upon one of the most established rituals in Russian folklore, that of a village wedding. "Wedding plays" had been set by Russian composers as early as the eighteenth century, the ritual's oppositional elements of melancholy and joy providing ideal material for operatic drama.[48] Part 1 of Les Noces consists of three scenes: the "Benediction of the Bride," the "Benediction of the Groom," and the "Departure of the Bride from the Parental Home." A single tableau constitutes Part 2: the "Wedding Feast," which moves from the religious bonding of the couple in the eyes of God to their physical bonding. The "play" ends with the peeling of bells, as the couple enter the bedchamber to consummate their union.

Yet Les Noces is far more than a fertility ritual. While Asaf'yev's analysis pounces upon the "instinct for procreation" as the work's nucleus, Stravinsky insisted that he had had no such idea. "Better to forget, because this has no bearing," he protested. "I meant nothing of the kind. [Asaf'yev] has a great desire to find an orgiastic tendency that simply is not there."[49] Procreation was merely one aspect of marriage. More broadly, matrimony effected a merger of families negotiated by a matchmaker. The bride had no say in a contract that coerced her into becoming a member of her husband's family. More to the point, she was nothing more than a chattel. Her lamentation, mirrored so poignantly in Stravinsky's vocal incantations, expresses submission rather than assent. The marriage represents the symbolic death of her past as she accepts this rite of passage, surrendering what she has known and loved to a servility she must bear for the remainder of her life. Whatever new joys may eventually come, they are at this moment muted. As for her husband-to-be, his nearly extraneous role in the ritual receives mostly only passing mention. For him, the union is not initiatory, and certainly not a milestone. Unlike his wife, he loses virtually nothing.[50]

The ritual itself draws strength from its changelessness. Its regularity is mechanistically dependable. Stravinsky's orchestration, with the black and white clarity and cold precision of its pianos, supplied the musical analog for which he had searched for so many years. "One day in 1921 . . . I suddenly realized that an orchestra of four pianos would fulfill my conditions. It would be at the same time perfectly homogeneous, perfectly impersonal, perfectly mechanical."[51] That impersonality characterizes the vocal writing as well, in that none of the four soloists is associated with a single character. Rather, the quartet of singers switches from one role to another. Similarly, Nijinska's choreography also pedestaled the custom itself, not the soloist—a clear departure from convention. Missing the very essence of the ritual, André Levinson denounced such an approach, branding Nijinska's dance "Marxist" in its sublimation of the individual dancer.[52]

Of course Nijinska knew exactly what she was doing. She shared with the composer a bittersweet longing for Russia, the authentic Russia that was uncorrupted by westernized adaptations. Just as Stravinsky visited Kiev in 1914, a passionately patriotic Nijinska returned from the same city in 1922, having experienced the tumult of revolution. Throughout her memoirs, she recorded a cultural intensity that was contagious. When Diaghilev invited her to choreograph Stravinsky's work that spring, they visited the composer's studio together, where she first heard the score. She immediately felt the connection. By her own admission, the work of her famed brother, with whom she had collaborated on earlier Stravinsky ballets, influenced her own ideas. But Stravinsky's extraordinarily dynamic, unembellished music demanded a new approach. Whereas Nijinsky had shaped the gestures of the sacrificial virgin in *The Rite* from a male perspective, Nijinska brought a different insight to *Les Noces*.[53] Perhaps more than any other choreographer, she understood the wedding ritual as being "of the nature of tragedy," and one that stressed the centrality of loss. "The young girl knows nothing at all about her future family nor what lies in store for her," Nijinska later commented. "Not only will she be subject to her husband, but also to his parents. . . . The soul of the innocent is in disarray—she is bidding goodbye to her carefree youth and to her loving mother."[54]

The choreography of *Les Noces* is unlike anything seen in the composer's earlier ballets. There is a sense of serenity, and lingering. Nijinska's dance reveals a resignation empowered by antiquity's durability. Gestures move down, grounded to the earth, rather than breaking free in the stylized leaps of grand ballet intended to symbolize freedom. Her emphases on *pointe* work (initially contested by Diaghilev) are notable in their exploration of static gestures, just as Stravinsky's repetitive rhythmic and melodic gestures constantly turn back on themselves without any hint of impatience or impulse to expand too hastily. For example, Diaghilev prescribed a very specific action wherein several young girls were to comb and plait the bride's hair—a traditional act of the wedding ritual. Nijinska protested, however. She imagined much longer plaits (ten feet, in fact), with the bride's friends "holding the tresses" as they gathered around her. Rather than combing the plaits, as Diaghilev wished, Nijinska argued, "Their dance on pointe and hers will express the rhythm of plaiting." Doing so would "elongate the dancers' silhouettes and make them resemble the saints in Byzantine mosaics." Throughout the work she treated the traditional vocabulary of classical ballet unconventionally, often lingering on an especially poignant idea. The choreography of *Les Noces* (and for that matter its music too) is a harbinger of neoclassicism, with its focused clarity, chiseled gestures, and sharp edges. Nijinska's portrayal of women is rooted in a stark realism far more expressive than had heretofore been seen.[55]

In his 1936 chronicle, Stravinsky complained that the stage production did not comply with his original vision. Still, nothing indicates that he gave much thought to the work's staging over its long evolution, even though he implied that he had helped to shape the choreography. "I wished to place the orchestra on the stage itself, letting the actors move on the space remaining free. The fact that the artists in the scene would uniformly wear costumes of a Russian character while the musicians would be in evening dress not only did not embarrass me, but on the contrary, was perfectly in keeping with my idea of a *divertissement* of the masquerade type."[56]

The initial sketches for sets and costumes made by Natalia Goncharova, who was involved with *Les Noces* from as early as spring 1914, missed the target, reflecting the colorful, ornamental design associated with the Ballets Russes in a style reminiscent of *Le Coq d'or*. Like Stravinsky's instrumentation, Goncharova's ideas about stage and costume design evolved over time. She first prepared a décor appropriate for a wedding ceremony associated with a privileged Russian social class—a class marked by "enjoyments, abundance and happy vitality." Later, however, she changed her mind: "I decided to place the action in a setting close to that of the peasant—the lower middle class in suburbia," she later wrote. "I came to know the reason for these country weddings—marriages of necessity, without love, where the religious rite and the benedictions of the parents take the place of the bond of love."[57] In truth, Goncharova was forced to alter the costumes and scenery at Nijinska's insistence. The dramatic shift from colorful sets and costumes to the achromatic look of the stage and the purposely drab, brown and white peasant garb was attributable to Nijinska's vision, and much more in keeping with what the composer had in mind. Upon seeing Goncharova's sketches in 1922, Nijinska immediately recognized the conflict. "The sketches of Goncharova seemed to me to be diametrically opposed to the music of Stravinsky," she remarked, "and also to my conception of the choreography of the ballet." After a few scuffles with Diaghilev, Nijinska got her way. "*Les Noces* was the only ballet in which he allowed the choreographer to have a deciding influence over the entire production."[58]

The opening night reception was as expected. Those who lamented Stravinsky's more recent forays into rag music, frivolous Italian masquerade, drably impassive pieces for winds, and chamber-like opera buffa were surely relieved. The wayward sheep had apparently returned to the familiar Diaghilev fold. *Les Noces* may not have elicited the same stupefaction as the mythical *Rite*, but at least the composer's newest work sounded reassuringly primal—indeed, contentedly uncultured. Émile Vuillermoz noted the beauty of the work's harsh impersonality as captured by the composer's "metallic" orchestration. He praised the "ill-treated pianos, the hallucinating cry of the castanets whipped at every blow, the rippling of the xylophone, and the muffled detonations of kettledrums," all of which engulfed "the melodies and the cries of the singers with a rhythmic atmosphere that is marvelously exact and sharp."[59]

Diaghilev presented eight performances that June of 1923 at the Théâtre de la Gaîté-Lyrique. The following year Stravinsky conducted the work at the Théâtre des Champs-Élysées. Two years later, in 1926, *Les Noces* was mounted in London, with Georges Auric, Francis Poulenc, Vittorio Rieti, and Vladimir Dukelsky at the four keyboards and Eugene Goossens conducting. The British press assaulted the work with a barrage of particularly rancorous diatribes. A "hideous" composition, commented Ernest Newman in the *Sunday Times*, adding that all of Europe "is already more than a little tired of the moujik and his half-baked brain." Rising to the composer's defense, H. G. Wells responded with an open letter to the tabloids, those "guardians of culture," remarking that he could find no other ballet "so interesting, so amusing, so fresh or nearly so exciting. . . . The ballet is a rendering in sound and vision of the peasant soul. In its gravity, in its deliberate and simple-minded intricacy, in its subtly varied rhythms, in its deep undercurrents of excitement, that will astonish and delight every intelligent man or woman who goes to see it."[60]

Les Noces remains one of Stravinsky's most frequently revived stage works. Merce Cunningham, Ludmilla Chiriaeff, Maurice Béjart, Léonide Massine, Heinz Spoerli, Paul Mejia, and dozens of others have either attempted to restore Nijinska's original choreography or designed their own. Jerome Robbins's 1965 production remains a landmark.[61] Although Stravinsky was never particularly fond of new productions of old works, he seems to have warmed to Jerome Robbins's proposed restaging of *Les Noces* for La Scala in 1954. (Robbins had also tried to convince Stravinsky to allow him to remount *The Rite*, but without success.) Robbins sought the composer's advice in 1953, asking a series of questions based upon Victor Belaiev's famous 1928 descriptive analysis of the work.[62] The choreographer's questions were informed and pointed, expressing, for example, a specific concern about staging the second tableau. Stravinsky, for whom Robbins was second only to Balanchine among contemporary choreographers, responded, entering his corrections on the copy of the analysis that Robbins had included. Specific matters of accentuations and rhythmic patterns were pursued—all indicative of Robbins's desire to comply with the composer's wishes. He even flew to California for further discussions. In the end, however, the Milan performance fell through. The work was eventually staged in 1965 by Lucia Chase's Ballet Theatre, with starkly monolithic sets by Oliver Smith, Leonard Bernstein proclaiming it the best Stravinsky performance since the 1957 premiere of *Agon*. On May 20, 1998, shortly before his death, Robbins revived the work (using Dimitri Pokrovsky's controversial recording of the score) for the New York City Ballet. A decade later, as part of a festival of Robbins's work, *Les Noces* was produced once again, this time with the full complement of performance forces on stage, as Stravinsky had always wanted.

Perséphone

Composed in France, Stravinsky's 1934 *Perséphone* marked a renewed lyricism, even as his mood darkened with the gathering storm clouds of war. His newest work echoed the quietude of the 1928 *Apollo* while anticipating the simplicity of the 1948 *Orpheus*—both neoclassical ballets arising out of the composer's devotion to Greek mythology. Yet designating *Perséphone* as this or that kind of work is unfruitful. Its creators could never quite agree upon what this protean opus was exactly. Since it was neither an opera nor a symphonic work, and was clearly not a full-fledged ballet, the somewhat arbitrary tag of "melodrama" seemed sufficiently indistinct to describe its hybridized design. André Gide, whose symbolist roots are everywhere manifest in his forging of the work's original concept, described *Perséphone* to Stravinsky as a "symphonic ballet." Yet in his later years, the composer, who himself struggled with the work's characterization, preferred to think of it as a "masque or dance-pantomime coordinated with a sung or spoken text." Into whatever pigeonhole we attempt to squeeze the work, it is evident that the supportive element of dance is an essential component.[63] Unfortunately, like *Renard*, this nearly one-hour composition seldom finds an appropriate performance venue. Written for a solo tenor, narrator, chorus, children's choir, and a rather large orchestra (including two harps and piano), and incorporating dance and mime, this elaborately scored work does not easily lend itself to production.

Stravinsky had known Ida Rubinstein since his arrival in Paris in 1910. Eighteen years later, they worked together on the aforementioned *Le Baiser de la fée*, the ballet that helped to launch Rubinstein's new company while simultaneously severing Stravinsky's always fragile relationship with Diaghilev. Now, in 1934, her Ballets de Madame Ida Rubinstein continued to make waves in Paris with its sometimes peculiar but often innovative productions. Rubinstein, whose perseverance was not to be denied, would provide the impetus in pulling together the many collaborators needed to mount Stravinsky's complex, theatrically inspired new work.

Rubinstein's interest in Gide's poetry long predates the 1933 commissioning of *Perséphone*. Moreover, Rubinstein stood as an uncompromising nonconformist, an entrepreneur inclined to mount hybrid works that others were likely to shun. Like Stravinsky, she relished testing the sometimes prescriptive boundaries of dance. When Rubinstein first approached Gide about furnishing her company with a new work, Gide spoke of "a small ballet" entitled "Proserpine", which he had worked on years earlier. In fact, he had resurrected thoughts of completing and staging the ballet over a long period, although nothing had ever come of it. Extant sketches are traceable to at least 1909, and correspondence in which Gide refers to the work appears as early as 1894. Originally, the poet had drafted a Parnassian setting of the story of Persephone. According to the Greek myth, Persephone was the daughter of the fertility goddess Demeter. Condemned to an existence wandering between earth and Hades, she was compelled to join Pluto each winter.

Now, nearly forty years later, Rubinstein endorsed the project as worthy of her staging, and worthy of enticing Stravinsky to collaborate with Gide. In earlier years Gide had in fact considered collaborating with other composers, including Florent Schmitt and Paul Dukas, in a production under the aegis of Diaghilev. At Rubinstein's urging, Gide wrote to Stravinsky in February 1933, asking if he might consider collaborating. The composer knew Gide slightly from his days with the Ballets Russes. Upon receiving Stravinsky's positive reply, Gide declared, "I am thrilled by the ballet proposal I just submitted to [Rubinstein]." Stravinsky's response was equally enthusiastic. And as was typical of him, he wasted no time in issuing directives: "I am having a new edition of the *Odyssey* sent to you. The last of the hymns (to Demeter) was my inspiration. . . . In two days I will send the first draft of the first scene, which has a recitative, some dances, and some songs. Madame Rubinstein tells me that it is impossible to have choristers dance or dancers sing," an indication perhaps that the composer initially envisioned an even grander infusion of dance.[64]

The opportunity to set a new Greek story intrigued Stravinsky, especially given his decade-long preoccupation with the power of mythology as expressed in *Oedipus rex* and *Apollo*. The challenge here would be the actual setting of words, or more precisely the matter of syllabification—a matter Stravinsky addressed at some length in an article in *Excelsior* of April 29, 1934, the day before the premiere. "For *Perséphone*, I wanted only syllables, strong, beautiful syllables, and then movement," the composer declared.[65] Moreover, setting the words in French added another welcome challenge, since Stravinsky had never undertaken a large-scale setting of French prosody.

His collaboration with Gide began smoothly enough, but soon frayed. There were several points of contention, the most troublesome being their disagreement over the actual text setting, especially with regard to the words' rhythmic flow. Gide wanted a strict, syllabic articulation of each word, whereas Stravinsky saw text and music in a productive opposition, as layered partners or complements. The music was not intended as a subsidiary element, underscoring the text. The composer purposely wrote against the grain, willfully distorting the natural accentuation and stresses of language. Such overt textual-musical discordance abraded Gide's poetic sensibility. He feared his words would become the victim of contortion in an unhealthy competition between text and music. Rubinstein's hopes for a genuine collaboration soon vanished. Composer and poet worked separately and almost at cross-purposes right up to the premiere, which Gide refused to attend.

The role of Perséphone is demanding. The actor must speak, mime, and dance. Rubinstein welcomed the role as a vehicle to display her own talents. She appeared in the premiere of April 30, 1934, conducted by Stravinsky at the Paris Opera. The production featured costumes by André Barsacq and scenery by Jacques Copeau, although Stravinsky had hoped that his own son, Theodore, would prepare the work's design.[66] The well-respected German choreographer Kurt Jooss provided the choreography, having fled his country in 1933 as Hitler rose to power. Jooss was familiar with Stravinsky's ballets, having staged

Pulcinella only two years earlier. Stravinsky complained that he had no say in appointing any of his collaborators. He did, however, manage to squash the suggestion that Fokine serve as choreographer, adding that Massine and Balanchine were the only artists capable of creating the dance. Rubinstein nonetheless selected Jooss, and Stravinsky reluctantly agreed.

Years later the composer addressed the importance of dance as a theatrical element lost in concert performances. He recalled that Rubinstein had "declaimed the text at the premiere, but she did not dance, which was as it should be." In the end, he concluded that the work was best served by having two performers share the role. Moreover, he later described how the work should be mounted in very specific terms, including the clear separation of the various performing forces throughout the action. "The resulting separation of text and movement would mean that the staging could be worked out entirely in choreographic terms," he explained, going on to comment, "Balanchine would have been the ideal choreographer, Tchelitchev the ideal decorator."[67]

The choice of choreographer was the least of various problems that beset the 1934 production from the start. The premiere was less than successful. Rubinstein, unwisely it turns out, had placed herself at the center of the performance. Critics intent on embarrassing the freewheeling Rubinstein scorned her portrayal of Perséphone. She was neither a dancer nor an actress, the *Nouvelle Revue française* complained. Gide, unhappy with the subordination of his text, remarked that Rubinstein's beauty, so notable in earlier productions, had withered in the role of Perséphone.[68] Such criticism must be viewed within the context of a role that perhaps asked too much of its interpreter, including quick adjustments between miming, vigorous dancing, and the need to narrate the text. It is little wonder that Stravinsky later suggested that the duties be split between two interpreters.

Only three performances followed the 1934 premiere, and the complexity of staging the work conspired against subsequent revivals. *Perséphone* was virtually relegated to the status of a concert work. There were a few fully staged productions in the 1930s and 1940s, but none of lasting merit. A 1956 restaging in Minneapolis by Vera Zorina, for which Antal Dorati both prepared the design and conducted the orchestra, held promise. Zorina, known not only for her dancing but for her acting skills on Broadway and in Hollywood, was particularly notable. Indeed, Stravinsky had originally pictured her as the ideal Perséphone. Five years later, in 1961, Stravinsky conducted a concert performance in what was then one of his favorite venues, the Santa Fe Opera. Soon thereafter, the young company prepared a production with the guidance of Zorina and the composer. It was, the composer rhapsodized, "the *Perséphone* I had always dreamed of and never saw until now."[69]

Twenty-one years later, in 1982, New York City Ballet offered a new production as part of a centennial celebration of the composer's birth (see chapter 9). Balanchine, Zorina, and John Taras shared the task of preparing the choreography, although Balanchine's contribution was limited by his declining health. Zorina again portrayed Perséphone with speaking and limited movement, while Karin von Aroldingen (one of Balanchine's most trusted ballerinas by that point) played the Spirit of Perséphone and served as the principal dancer. The production, conducted by Robert Craft, honored some of Stravinsky's later suggestions regarding how the work should be performed. Even so, it did not prove to be an enduring success. Echoing comments made nearly fifty years earlier at the 1934 premiere, *Comoedia* pointed to the conflict between the simplicity of Gide's poetry and the "complexity of form and means, both aural and visual, in the profusion of elements (dance, chorus, solo singer, spoken narration and orchestra)."[70] In the end, this may be the inherent paradox of this much maligned opus that continues to confound audiences.

The Flood

When seven million American viewers tuned in on June 14, 1962, to watch Stravinsky's first composition written expressly for television, expectations were high. A media blitz proclaimed *Noah and the Flood*, as it was first advertized, a cultural milestone. It was produced by Robert Graff and directed by Kirk Browning, both experienced veterans who were eager to shape television's experimental early years. Stravinsky's name carried weight, and television wagered that Americans would immediately accept the conventions of his newest compositional style. They did not. The reviews were devastating. "From its pompous beginnings to its tiresome and witless conclusion, *Noah and the Flood* was a bitter disappointment," wrote Emily Coleman for *Dance Magazine*. The verdict was clear: Stravinsky's "dance-drama," as he referred to it, had done nothing to refute the charge of the chair of the Federal Communications Commission, Newton Minow, that television was nothing more than a "vast wasteland." Had the composer failed to understand the limits and possibilities of the new medium? Was he simply indifferent to its challenges? Did he really have anything left to say?

Stravinsky scored the biblical tale for orchestra and chorus with dance. Unsurprisingly he asked Balanchine to provide choreography for the twenty-three-minute work, although the network broadcast lasted a full hour. Balanchine agreed to collaborate, but really as a favor. The perceptive choreographer, who always harbored reservations about music and dance written for television, immediately sensed that *The Flood* was doomed from the start. Still, he agreed to choreograph two sections for his New York City Ballet. The cast included Laurence Harvey as the Narrator, Sebastian Cabot as Noah, Elsa Lanchester as Mrs. Noah, and Robert Robinson as Satan. Two actors were used to portray the Voice of God, John Reardon and Robert Oliver. The work was cast in six large sections: a "Prelude," the "Building of the Ark" (choreographed), the "Catalogue of the Animals" (Paul Tripp reading the part of the Caller), the "Comedy," the "Flood" (choreographed), and the "Covenant of the Rainbow".

Television's early efforts to bedazzle the audience with visual trickery suffocated the production. Angels tumbled from the heavens, silhouetted male and female hands simulated the procreative act, figurines were used to represent Noah's menagerie of beasts, dancers emerged from a huge rippling blanket representing the flood itself—all of this smacked of technological legerdemain. Frequent shampoo commercials completely splintered the production's flow. The broadcast had opened with a homily delivered by Laurence Harvey. He spoke of flood myths, of Zeus purging the earth's transgressions, of Noah's unquestioned faith in God's cleansing of a sinful world and in life's renewal. Harvey warned us of "the Bomb" and the fragile times in which we lived. *The Flood* was intended to impress the gravity of the situation on a public already terrified by the prospect of a nuclear winter. Harvey then faded to black, from which emerged a visibly solemn Stravinsky telling us that it was more important to hear the music than to describe it; and with that the first, and last, televised performance of *The Flood* began.

The composer's feelings about television vacillated. "A televised concert is a great bore," he confided to the choreographer during an interview for *Saturday Review* published the week the work aired. Yet two weeks later he remarked, "I feel that television is the greatest medium for a new musical form, and if I decide to write another opera myself, I know that it will be for the electronic glass tube. . . . The one 'specific' of the medium that guided me in my conception of *The Flood* [was that] visualization can be instantaneous."[71] Still, given his equivocation, why did Stravinsky involve himself in a project over which he would have little control? It would not be an opera or a ballet, "perhaps not a theater piece at all," he stressed to his publisher in April 1961. He would only confirm that he was composing explicitly for television, and that Balanchine would stage some ballet fragments. But it was Stravinsky who envisioned choreography from the beginning. Balanchine had been involved in a variety of television shows from the late 1940s. His frequent exchanges with Stravinsky throughout the 1950s, as he became increasingly involved with television productions such as the *NBC Opera Theater* and the immensely popular *Bell Telephone Hour,* sensitized the composer to the potential landmines of the new medium. Balanchine complained that television impeded dance, inevitably leaving viewers with a distorted impression. He felt obliged to preface any of his televised choreography with a stern caveat: "What you're going to see is really going to be pretty awful." The screen image simply failed to do justice to the beauty of dance and of his dancers, he lamented.[72]

Balanchine actively attempted to dispel the notion that *The Flood* was a ballet: "This is a miracle play more than a masque. As I see it, it's a church play or a choreographed oratorio. Most importantly, it's *not* a ballet . . . Our version is a *musical* composite. It's all done in gesture by dancers and objects. The most important thing about it is that it's Stravinsky." Balanchine offered his appraisal to Arthur Todd during the taping of the choreography. As Todd reported, "Quite naturally [Balanchine] envisaged the movement only to enhance and enliven the score, but never to illustrate it." Todd, who witnessed the process as it unfolded, spoke of Balanchine always having the camera in mind, and by extension, of course, his concern for the viewer.[73]

The producer of the project, Robert Graff, originally suggested W. H. Auden as a librettist, but Stravinsky wanted T. S. Eliot. By 1959 Eliot and the composer were discussing the idea of collaborating on an opera. Stravinsky suggested they develop an "alternative" kind of theatrical piece. The composer wrote to Eliot in August, outlining the origins of what would become *The Flood*. His unreleased correspondence shows that he fully expected Eliot to accept the collaboration, but as subsequent exchanges reveal, Eliot gradually retreated from the idea. By September it had become clear that Stravinsky needed to seek another partner. He turned to Robert Craft. The well-known "Working Notes for *The Flood*" published in Stravinsky and Craft's *Dialogues* summarizes the discussions between the composer and Balanchine. But Craft's contribution to the work's basic scenario was more significant than first thought.

After Stravinsky's death, Craft divulged just how central his role had been.[74] At Eliot's suggestion, Stravinsky obtained a paperback edition of *Everyman and Medieval Miracle Plays*, which Craft then employed as the basis for the libretto. An examination of the book, which is held in the Sacher Stiftung, confirms that Craft studied the text carefully, underlining certain sections that eventually became part of the scenario. The libretto would draw on passages from the Chester Miracle Plays as well as the York Mystery Play cycle. In addition, an unpublished transcript in the Stiftung records a lengthy exchange between Craft and Graff in New York during the spring of 1960. Craft outlines everything from the specifics of the scenario to the style of the music that would be written, suggesting that the work would be contemporized to address the day's issues. He also assured Graff that the work would be conceived with television in mind.

In March 1962, Balanchine joined Stravinsky in California, where they assembled the final scenario. CBS Studios recorded and taped the work in Hollywood two weeks later. Craft conducted the orchestra for the sound recording while the dance segments were shot in New York in early June. As Todd reported, "The choreographer's deep involvement was obvious, whether in studio rehearsal or during the taping with director Kirk Browning. Camera angles, placement and timing were all planned in sympathetic collaboration between choreographer and director."[75] On April 15, Stravinsky and Balanchine sent a jointly authored cable to Graff: "We are now absolutely clear in our minds that nothing should be changed, cut, or repeated and that the work should be heard exactly as it now stands." They reassured the still very much in the dark producer that the work would take twenty-five minutes, but that this could be achieved only "by lengthening of pauses . . . not by the repetition of unrepeatable music." Whereas Stravinsky had previously argued that the work was not a ballet piece, he now backpedaled, saying, "We have worked out a choreographic visualization . . . and your earlier publicity releases about *The Flood* calling it a Stravinsky–Balanchine ballet are now more precise than we at that time thought."[76]

Several compositional sketches reveal how late in the day decisions were made. Measures were added, deleted, shifted, and repeated. Stravinsky taped some passages into the score at the last moment, especially in the dance sequences. Typically, the composer carefully timed every fragment. Durations marked as precisely as "seventeen seconds" are common. The sketches also establish that the composer did not complete the music until March 14, the afternoon Balanchine arrived in Los Angeles to begin blocking the stage action. The performance script is heavily marked with suggestions for revising the wording of sentences, advice on textual enunciation, and specific inflections for the delivery of lines. The actual pacing of the narration (including how quickly characters should make entrances and exits) was all carefully regulated to insure that the program would run neither over nor under the allotted broadcast slot. Craft was the guiding force in all of these technical issues, and Stravinsky seems to have listened to his advice.

By the time the creators of this commercially designed show viewed the tape, it was too late to pull the program from the network schedule. Fortuitously, as it turned out, Stravinsky was touring Germany as part of his eightieth birthday celebrations, so he did not see the telecast. As reviews came in, it became evident that the reception was almost unanimously negative. Sponsorship had gambled on the lure of Stravinsky's and Balanchine's names, but the outcry following the broadcast was overwhelming. Critics railed that television was no place for such artistic dada, and no place for Stravinsky's sermonizing about the world's impending nuclear calamity. Others denounced Balanchine's choreography as "restricted and dark." A barrage of pre-telecast commercials had led viewers to expect more dancing. Edward Villela, Jillana, Jacques d'Amboise—popular young stars in Balanchine's galaxy—were touted as having important roles; but their parts were so small as to be all but missed. The sets, props, and electronic gimmicks appeared contrived. The *Baltimore Sun* critic could not resist the obvious metaphor: "*Noah and the Flood* . . . was less like a deluge than a leaky faucet. It's now painfully obvious that in television [Stravinsky] is a whale out of water."

Balanchine voiced his general frustration with "what always happens on American television." Given the sponsorship's good sense in commissioning Stravinsky, he had hoped that they would "have the taste to put it on in a way that does justice, or at least not to mess it up." The problem, as Balanchine rightly perceived, was that "the producers had sold the work to the network as a one-hour package," even though the piece itself was only twenty-three minutes long. The network had "smothered the work by a whole goulash of other things they dumped into the package to fill it up." The choreographer complained that the package had been "sickening and patronizing" in its browbeating of the public over the intrinsic value of "high art." Just so, for Balanchine, certainly more than Stravinsky, understood the fine line one must walk in dealing with the paying public.[77]

Successful artistic programs of the day such as *The Voice of Firestone* tended to showcase opera divas or beautiful ballerinas in the elegant white-tutu tradition of *Swan Lake*. This was just the kind of accessible, entertaining fare American television audiences looked for as they settled back for their weekly dose of Saturday-night culture. Consequently, they were unprepared for a canting miracle play set to music in a still unfamiliar and to them craggy, "unmelodic" compositional style. "What did they expect," asked Stravinsky, "sea chanties?"[78] Of course that is precisely what they expected. Moreover, audiences did not relate to some of the work's theatrics: the dual bass voices of God, the abnormally high voice of Lucifer, the masks of Noah and his family, the miniature figurines meant to represent animals, the undulating gossamer blanket symbolizing the flood—all of this seemed patronizingly artificial in its abetting of the work's preachy tone. In the end, *The Flood* succumbed to its own homiletics, and while he would never admit it, the work's very public castigation hurt Stravinsky personally. Fifty years earlier, the young composer was just completing the youthfully virile *Rite*, a work that would mold the course of music history. Now, when the venerable octogenarian commanded a global notoriety as the world's greatest living composer, his most recent work seemed devitalized—"an inglorious flop," as the *Los Angeles Times* jibed.[79]

Balanchine, more tough-skinned by nature, had less at stake. As always, he remained loyal to the composer, defending *The Flood* as an artistically meaningful composition, and even restaging it (with the help of Jacques d'Amboise) as part of the 1982 Stravinsky Festival at Lincoln Center. Rouben Ter-Arutunian's provocative sets and costumes, designed for the original 1962 television broadcast, were retained with only a few changes. John Houseman now took the important role of the Narrator, Adam Lüders and Nina Fedorova were Adam and Eve, and Francisco Monicon played Noah. Balanchine retained most of the original choreography. Whereas Balanchine's miniature figurines had been photographed as part of the original filming, now students of the School of American Ballet paraded across the stage carrying huge cardboard representations of the Ark's animals. Some felt that the restaging was more successful than the original telecast, confined as that had been to television's "small screen." But others thought the work still ineffectively staged, and as one critic suggested, in need of "computer graphics to achieve a density equivalent to the music."[80]

While both Stravinsky and Balanchine welcomed the freedom bestowed by boundaries, in this one instance both the restrictions imposed on them and their inability to control the final production created too great a stranglehold. In the nearly fifty years since its television broadcast, and with the notable exception of Balanchine's revival in 1982, the work has been only infrequently mounted. For better or worse, because of its composite nature—and hodgepodge of media—this unusual work has yet to enter the repertoire. Of the six hybrid works incorporating dance discussed in this chapter, *The Flood* remains, sadly, the least likely to be remembered.

CHAPTER NINE

DANCING A LEGACY

Balanchine and Beyond

*T*HE *FLOOD* would prove to be the last of Stravinsky's hybrid compositions incorporating choreography. Seven additional works followed through the fall of 1966, the last year in which Stravinsky completed new music. Thereafter came a few sketches for projects contemplated, as well some orchestrations of pre-existing works. The composer died in the spring of 1971. Over his final five productive years to 1966, his continuing interest in twelve-tone composition inspired several substantial orchestral and vocal scores, among them *Abraham and Isaac* (1963), *Variations* (1964), and the remarkably vigorous *Requiem Canticles* (1966). But his interest in writing pure ballet music had come to a halt ten years earlier with the score for *Agon*.

Stravinsky's work on *The Flood* marked another milestone: it was the last time he and Balanchine would actively collaborate on a new composition intended to include choreography from an early point in the work's inception. From Balanchine's 1925 conception of *Le Chant du rossignol* to their March 1962 discussion of *The Flood*'s dance element, the partnership flourished for the better part of four decades. Of the numerous theater collaborations in which Stravinsky had been engaged (beginning with his 1909–28 association with the Ballets Russes and extending through *The Rake's Progress* in 1951), his partnership with Balanchine proved the longest, and also the closest. As the two worked together throughout their years in France and America, a genuine friendship grew. Grounded in a deeply rooted Russian ethnicity, it was a friendship impossible to disentangle from their prolific achievements. Any appraisal of Stravinsky's impact upon the world of twentieth-century dance must take full account of Balanchine's contribution.

Balanchine knew Stravinsky's music years before he knew the composer himself. As a young student at the Imperial Theater in Petrograd, he was immediately drawn to Stravinsky's high-spirited works. At age eighteen he choreographed the composer's very un-Russian *Ragtime*. He intended to stage *Pulcinella* in 1922, but the project fell through. By the time of his death sixty-one years later, Balanchine had choreographed more of the composer's works than anyone else. Slow or fast, vocal or instrumental, subtle or intense, Stravinsky's music pulsated with a danceable exuberance that Balanchine found irresistible. By its very nature, the music almost craved physical motion, even— and perhaps especially—in its punctuating silences. To some the music frequently appeared non-developmental, even "static," as Adorno criticized. But that was never the case. No matter what the piece, the genre, the instrumentation, Balanchine was able to grasp the music's intrinsic propulsion, declaring, "Every measure Eagerfeodorovitch ever wrote is good for dancing."[1]

The success of their partnership stemmed from a melding of several ingredients, perhaps chief among them Balanchine's well-developed and exceptionally sensitive musicianship. Although Stravinsky had worked productively (if often fractiously) with all of Diaghilev's choreographers during his years with the Ballets Russes, none of them, he asserted, fully understood the intimate contrapuntal interplay of dance and music as much as Balanchine. It was the dialogue of eye and ear that formed the basis of their approach. The composer adamantly proclaimed the integrity of music and dance as independent entities, refuting any notion that either art should be regarded as subsidiary, let alone accompanimental. As separate art forms, their strength derived from a necessary, beneficial disconnection from one another, rather than from any dependence upon one another. Years before he found a sympathetic partner in Balanchine, Stravinsky had appeared nearly evangelical in preaching that his music, at least, would not stoop to abet the choreographer in privileging the dance, even in such an overtly programmatic score as *The Firebird*. "I have never tried, in my stage works, to make the music illustrate the action, or the action the music," he asserted. "I have always endeavored to find an architectural basis of connection."[2] Yet years after he and Balanchine had collaborated on the neoclassical *Apollo*, Stravinsky's frequently espoused homily on the autonomy of music and dance seemed to soften a bit. In a public statement of 1934, he allowed that the two arts could co-exist, and maybe even live happily together under the right circumstances: "Music and dance should be a true marriage of separate arts, a partnership, not a dictatorship of one over the other.[3] A year later, in an article for the Parisian journal *Candide* of June 6, 1935, he served up yet another variation: "What are the connections that unite and separate music and dance? In my opinion the one does not serve the other. There must be a harmonious accord, a synthesis of ideas. Let us speak, on the contrary, of the struggle between music and choreography."

It was only through acceptance of this separate-but-equal relationship of the two arts that the unexploited potential of such disconnectedness could transform dance into a powerfully expressive art form. Conversely, dance that merely replicated music—let alone dance that claimed to translate music visually—was illusory. Such an assumption could not have been further from the truth, both men asserted. Moreover, to a far greater extent than any other choreographer, Balanchine employed his choreography as a conduit through which the message of Stravinsky's music could be clarified and strengthened. This urge to illuminate the score became particularly important in the composer's later works, beginning with *Agon*. For many, Balanchine's attitude was heretical: it turned the dance–music pyramid on its head. Music was still best cast in an ancillary role, his critics charged. Yet Balanchine was fully prepared to sublimate dance in the service of music whenever he felt it appropriate. His counterintuitive notion that at times dance literally had to get out of the way of the music was tantamount to blasphemy. Such an inverted equation still remains controversial for many aficionados.

Stravinsky and Balanchine's shared goal of a coherent, symbiotic dance-music composition also arose from a common working method. Unity could be achieved only by setting in motion a sequence of work leading from the discipline of order, to precision, to a beauty attainable only through the daily grind of hard work. Neither man was willing to wait for the muse to pay a visit. Both saw themselves as artisans, and the process of reaching down into the earth and making something out of nothing ran very much to their *homo faber* core. They simply felt the need to put things together—to "assemble," as Balanchine said. The limitations of boundaries were viewed as liberating rather than impedimental.

Stravinsky's embrace of serialism in the 1950s reflected a desire to write new music by adopting more contemporary compositional techniques. With astonishing acuity, he quickly adapted the fundamental precepts of Webern (as we have seen in *Agon*) for his own purpose. And while others, including once loyal disciples such as Nadia Boulanger, cast a cold eye toward what they considered Stravinsky's nearly treasonous capitulation to the dodecaphonists, Balanchine leaped to endorse the composer's rebirth. His affirmation of Stravinsky's ambition to explore another new pathway should have come as no surprise. As mentioned earlier, the choreographer had himself already gained a familiarity with and affinity for Schoenberg's music, having set the *Accompaniment for a Film Scene* as a ballet entitled *Opus 34* in 1954.[4] Then in 1959, with Martha Graham, Balanchine choreographed the aphoristic orchestral works of Webern in the ballet *Episodes*. As always, he withstood the criticism of those unable to appreciate the beauties of such music. In City Ballet's sold-out "twelve-tone nights" programs the choreographer introduced a new style of dancing altogether. Such "high-protein ballets, with more 'grip' per measure than anything that had been seen up to that time," as Arlene Croce wrote, provided a platform for avant-garde scores that other orchestras in New York and elsewhere were reluctant to program.[5]

Unswervingly, Balanchine remained one of the composer's staunchest advocates during the 1960s. Although Stravinsky had foregone writing ballet, or even hybrid works incorporating dance elements, the choreographer remained committed to his friend's music. He now turned his attention to the composer's concert works, especially the newest and thorniest. Always on the lookout for pre-existing, non-balletic Stravinsky scores that he might transform and bring to City Ballet, Balanchine seized several opportunities to stage some of the composer's recent serial music—music that was mostly unappealing to concert audiences. Many of the major scores that Stravinsky composed after *Agon* owe a large measure of whatever visibility and dissemination they received to Balanchine's intercession. Stravinsky now freely consented to Balanchine's requests to choreograph some of his most complex orchestral and vocal works. The composer recognized that the platform provided by his friend in the soon to be opened State Theater at Lincoln Center would place his music in front of audiences that otherwise might have completely ignored the music alone. It was a wise decision. Several of the composer's eight concert works undertaken by Balanchine in the years 1960–68 have found a permanent home in the dance repertoire.

In the spring of 1960, for example, two years before the bedeviled television production of *The Flood*, Stravinsky completed his *Monumentum pro Gesualdo di Venosa ad CD annum*, a collection of three Renaissance madrigals rewritten for instruments to commemorate the four-hundredth anniversary of Gesualdo's birth. Balanchine produced the ballet that same fall (with the simpler title *Monumentum pro Gesualdo*). Each of these brief instrumental madrigals is choreographed separately, the entire ballet lasting seven minutes. Stravinsky's instrumental arrangement of the three madrigals is not nearly as expansive as the wholesale renovation of Renaissance models evident in the earlier *Agon*. In the Gesualdo set, everything is closer to the original, and more akin to the fairly modest tweaking seen in *Pulcinella*. In keeping with the courtly manner of the Renaissance, there is more restraint in *Monumentum*'s approach. It is no more or less than an imaginative reconstitution of a repertoire the composer had come to love.

Balanchine's *Ragtime (I)* appeared a month later, in December 1960. Using the music of Stravinsky's 1918 *Ragtime* (written for eleven instruments, including winds, brass, percussion, and cimbalom), this brief duet was part of a larger, jointly choreographed ballet entitled *Jazz Concert*, which set a quartet of short twentieth-century scores that included another Stravinsky composition, the 1946 *Ebony Concerto*, originally written for Woody Herman (and here choreographed not by Balanchine but by John Taras).[6] Although Balanchine's *Ragtime (I)* was unenthusiastically received, the choreographer found the music and dance possibilities sufficiently fertile to prepare a new version of the score, *Ragtime (II)*, which was produced as part of a festival of Stravinsky's music ("A Festival of Stravinsky: His Heritage and His Legacy") held at Lincoln Center's Philharmonic Hall in 1966. It would be the first of three important festivals featuring Stravinsky's dance scores to be organized in New York over the next seventeen years.

In the spring of 1963, Balanchine presented one of his most innovative ballets to a concert work by Stravinsky. Composed between 1958 and July 1959, *Movements* for piano and orchestra is a compact nine-minute work originally intended as a Concerto for piano and groups of instruments. Stravinsky, however, revised the title, mainly because of the prominent but still chamber-like concertante piano part. He pronounced the five-movement opus his most intricately conceived serial composition to date. Indeed, the compositional distance traveled in the two years since *Agon* is remarkable. Audiences seemed unable to keep up with the seventy-eight-year-old Stravinsky's intellectual pace. The composer of the evocative *Firebird* (as, regrettably, audiences continued to think of him) had embraced what was seen as the height of arcane abstraction. The reviews of the New York premiere, conducted by the composer on January 10, 1960, were tepid at best. It is quite likely that Balanchine rescued the work from a path headed toward oblivion. From 1966, and in the choreographer's hands, *Movements* came to be danced in tandem with *Monumentum*—a wonderfully congruous coupling for many reasons. Stravinsky's well-known interests in the literature of the Renaissance and in Webernesque compositional techniques blended seamlessly.

While *Movements* did not constitute a genuine collaboration in the same way as *Agon*, surely Balanchine discussed the score with the composer, who attended a rehearsal of the work in 1963, as Balanchine was setting the music. Moreover, several German and Canadian television producers and filmmakers tracked Stravinsky's every move around that time, hoping to capture something sufficiently audience-worthy to include in their documentaries. Frequently Balanchine is seen in conversation with the composer, asking questions about how a work is put together. Stravinsky replies with explanations about the work's pulses, rhythms, and structural relationships. The work's intent had always entailed the emphasis of textural contrast. Unsurprisingly, therefore, Stravinsky later characterized Balanchine's balletic approach as a double concerto in which the male and female soloists are "identified" with the piano solo that filters through all five concise movements. The very young and "rubber-spined" (as one review put it) Suzanne Farrell premiered as the female soloist, while the *corps de ballet* represented the full spectrum of the orchestration's colorful timbres.[7] Moreover, it was *Movements* that prompted the composer to speak more glowingly of Balanchine's illuminative powers than ever before:

> Balanchine's visualization of the *Movements* exposed relationships of which I had not been aware in the same way. Seeing it, therefore, was like touring a building for which I had drawn the plans but never completely explored the result. He began by identifying familiar appendages of my musical style, of which I myself became conscious only through his eyes. And as I watched him fastening on the tiniest repeated rhythmic figure, I knew that he had joined the score to my other music faster than it could ever get there by way of the concert hall. Beyond that, he discovered the lyricism of the piece; his dramatic point is a love parable—in which ballet is it not?—and his coda has a suggestion of the ending of *Apollo*.[8]

How much of *Apollo* the everyday viewer sees in the work is debatable. More evident, as Reynolds argues, is Balanchine's "most absolute statement of the reductive principle."[9] Both music and dance are streamlined, producing an arresting leanness. Yet within the compression of Stravinsky's music, the same fundamental compositional principles of tension, release, and architectural balance are apparent. In essence, Balanchine treats the score just as he had earlier works by Stravinsky, tonal or serial. Texture, instrumentation, the division between pianist and orchestra—all were enlisted to help define the music's economic structure choreographically. Balanchine's setting was not only musically sympathetic—it was stunning.

Farrell would be featured in another work by Stravinsky, *Variations*, premiered on March 31, 1966. Like *Movements*, *Variations* was originally conceived as an orchestral work. Dedicated to Stravinsky's close friend Aldous Huxley, who had died four months earlier, the score was cast as a set of symphonic variations. Once again, critics rushed to label the work "space-age" music—a convenient way of obviating the need for any rational explanation of its compositional principles. To a far greater extent than *Agon*, *Variations* was based upon manipulations of "twelve," in terms of formal divisions (twelve-part variations) and instrumentation (twelve solo violins at one point in the score).

Without direct collaboration, Balanchine once again made it his business to familiarize himself with Stravinsky's latest creation. He analyzed the work's internal structure and accordingly constructed the choreography around the music's duodecimal patterns. He provided choreography that called for three complete iterations of the brief score, the first set for twelve women, the second for six men, and the last featuring Farrell's solo. On the same 1966 program (part of the Stravinsky Festival at Philharmonic Hall), Farrell also danced a newly choreographed solo to another of the composer's pre-existing concert works, the 1944 *Élégie* for solo viola.

Another new work, the overtly romantic blockbuster *Jewels*, was premiered in the spring of 1967, featuring Farrell and Jacques d'Amboise. The now acclaimed couple danced the final "Diamonds" section to the music of Tchaikovsky, while the first section, entitled "Emeralds," was set to music by Fauré. The central section of this plotless, full-length ballet, "Rubies," was based on Stravinsky's brilliantly orchestrated *Capriccio* for piano and orchestra of 1929—originally written for his own use while touring as a pianist. Stravinsky had composed the work just after finishing *Le Baiser de la fée*, and the dance-like quality of that Tchaikovskyan score shines through in sections of the *Capriccio*. Balanchine understood the intrinsic dance character of the original piano work and caught the spirit of its neoclassical adaptation of jazz, a style with which the composer had been so absorbed at the time of its composition.

Balanchine would set just one other Stravinsky work while the composer was still alive. Now in declining health, Stravinsky was still able to at least discuss matters with the choreographer. *Requiem Canticles*, written for vocal soloists, chorus, and orchestra, was finished in August 1966. It would be the last major composition Stravinsky completed. This thoroughly serial work is based upon two twelve-tone rows and is symmetrically constructed in six vocal movements, framed by an instrumental prelude, interlude and postlude. The text is based upon portions of the Latin Requiem Mass. Fifteen minutes in length, it is one of Stravinsky's most intensely moving compositions, truly a crowning achievement for the eighty-four-year-old composer, whose music remained as vibrant as ever.

Two years later, in the spring of 1968, Balanchine created a balletic arrangement of the score as a memorial for the recently assassinated Martin Luther King. Although there seem to be no surviving sketches, Stravinsky apparently began to draft an additional instrumental prelude intended for the choreographer's staging two weeks before the scheduled premiere, but was unable to complete it.[10] The original score was danced on the same program as the premiere of the dramatically contrasting *Slaughter on Tenth Avenue*, another tour de force for Arthur Mitchell and Suzanne Farrell. As a ballet, *Requiem*

Canticles was presented only once. With costumes by Rouben Ter-Arutunian, the dancers—or rather processional celebrants—appear in white robes, walking in bare feet, each bearing with great dignity a three-stemmed candelabrum as they move about in the dark of the stage. During the poignant "Lacrimosa" section, one woman, portrayed by Farrell, futilely searches among the others, looking but never finding. At the end of the score, Mitchell, dressed in purple robes, is raised high, representing King himself.[11]

Arnold Newman's collection of photographs *Bravo Stravinsky* includes several wonderful pictures of Stravinsky and Balanchine discussing *Requiem Canticles* as the choreographer demonstrates some of his ideas, the two men having just listened to a recording. Stravinsky was in California when Balanchine's production was given its one performance, but as the photographs demonstrate, he was still interested in having some say in the ballet. As ever, Balanchine was concerned with the look of the production, even though he certainly realized this would not become a repertory piece. And ever sensitive to his friend's music and opinions, he made a point of familiarizing him with the staged work as best he could.[12]

The last few years of Stravinsky's life were compromised by failing health. He composed only a few relatively minor works and arrangements—nothing substantial enough for Balanchine to undertake. By the late 1960s it was clear that Stravinsky could not continue much longer. Although the creative appetite remained, the composer turned what energy he had left to orchestrating the music of others. He died in New York on the morning of April 6, 1971, at the age of eighty-eight. For many, his physical decline was unbearable to witness. Yet long after others had abandoned the failing composer in those final years, Balanchine faithfully visited him, dined with him, and conversed with him in Russian, even during the week of the composer's death. To the end, the choreographer remained one of Stravinsky's most loyal and genuinely caring friends.

For well over half a century the incisive pulse of Stravinsky's music had furnished Balanchine with what he once called the dancer's "floor." The music's boundless energy was hypnotic. Occasionally the music so fascinated the choreographer that he took up the same score more than once, or turned to non-balletic scores, sensing they were easily convertible to the stage. Throughout his life, Stravinsky grumbled that his concert scores were not intended to be danced, that dancers tended to draw the listener away from the music. In actuality, however, this was not always the case. Given the right circumstances, and in the right choreographer's hands, the composer's objections were silenced. Moreover, more than many choreographers, Balanchine was at the top of his game when choreographing concert music—whether of Stravinsky, Mozart, Tchaikovsky, Ravel, or any other composer. Balanchine admitted to feeling hampered by the imposition of a preconceived scenario. Too frequently, he contended, the dance was unable to rise above the role of visual appurtenance. A story generally demanded illustration in exacting choreographic detail. "A plot is a very difficult thing for the dance," he wrote. "You cannot dance a story."[13] Concert music liberated the musically astute Balanchine. It stripped away the unneeded layers of narrative, allowing physical movement to speak fully on behalf of the score. In an interview of June 1972, and to the chagrin of his critics, he proclaimed what his detractors thought a distorted view: "You do not go to the ballet only to see, but also to hear."[14] Nowhere would the choreographer's beliefs become more evident than in the opulently presented New York City Ballet Stravinsky Festival mounted that same month.

Balanchine began thinking about a celebratory event shortly after Stravinsky's death. Plans took shape quickly. Vera Stravinsky and Robert Craft were consulted about repertoire. The choreographer envisaged the 1972 Stravinsky Festival as a bacchanalia (as Lincoln Kirstein described it) rather than a memorial. The one-week "banquet" would offer a jubilant retrospective of a man whose music had literally brought about a new order in the worlds of music and ballet. The festival included some of the composer's most important ballets, as well as significant non-staged works (including the early 1908 *Fireworks* and the 1930 *Symphony of Psalms*, which solemnly closed the seventh and final program on June 25). Of the three dozen works programmed, thirty were ballets. Most were premieres prepared by various choreographers: Todd Bolender, John Clifford, Lorca Massine, Jerome Robbins, Richard Tanner, and John Taras. Robbins was especially busy, remounting his ballet *The Cage* (to Stravinsky's 1946 Concerto in D) and working with Balanchine on a jointly choreographed version of *Pulcinella*. He also created new ballets to four other Stravinsky scores: the 1908 *Scherzo fantastique*, the 1938 Concerto in E-flat (known as "Dumbarton Oaks"), the 1942 *Circus Polka*, and the 1966 *Requiem Canticles*.[15] Nine newly choreographed works by Balanchine formed the event's centerpiece. As Clive Barnes wrote his *New York Times* review of July 2, "There has never been as creative an outburst as this in the history of ballet." Three of Balanchine's ballets warrant particular mention.

Balanchine had first choreographed Stravinsky's 1931 Concerto in D for violin and orchestra (which had had limited success as a concert work) in 1941, in a ballet entitled *Balustrade*. Expressly choreographed for Tamara Toumanova, it was premiered in New York by the Original Ballets Russes. The popular ballerina later described Balanchine and Stravinsky's collaboration during rehearsals: "When Balanchine and Stravinsky were together, they were like two incredible teachers." The deferential Balanchine would always agree with Stravinsky on whatever points the composer raised, she recalled. She also reported that

Stravinsky was "absolutely enchanted" with Balanchine's creation: "George, I think this is the epitome of what I thought."[16] While it is hard to determine the degree of Stravinsky's "ecstasy," as Toumanova described it, it is clear that Stravinsky was pleased to see his seldom performed violin concerto take on balletic life. Balanchine's abstract choreography won little praise from the critics, however, who were deeply divided over the Balanchine–Tchelitchev–Stravinsky clique. Almost anything Balanchine created met with mixed reactions.

Balanchine had felt encumbered by Tchelitchev's restrictive costumes and scenery. Such burdensome visual contrivances could only draw one's attention away from Stravinsky's music. Thirty years later, the ballet was entirely reconceived for the 1972 festival. It quickly became one of Balanchine's greatest plotless ballets. "Stravinsky never wrote *Balustrade*," Balanchine insisted, "he wrote *Violin Concerto*," as the work was retitled. "The ballet should be announced as what it is." He continued, "Then the musicians can come, the young people who love music and who want to hear the composition—they'll know what they're getting. They don't have to look at the ballet if it bores them, they can just listen to the music. And that's fine with me, that's wonderful."[17] In an even greater tribute, Balanchine once more retitled the ballet in 1973, as *Stravinsky Violin Concerto*. As such it remains one of the New York City Ballet's most ebullient offerings. More than this, *Violin Concerto* marked the sixty-eight-year-old choreographer's first opportunity to stage one of the composer's works without his guidance, input, collaboration, requisite approval, and perhaps even his intervention. After nearly fifty years of unwavering devotion to Stravinsky, Balanchine was finally on his own.

The equally impressive *Duo concertant* was presented in Balanchine's now familiar practice-clothes look. Balanchine first heard the 1932 *Duo concertant* for violin and piano in France shortly after it was written. The two instruments contribute equally to the interchange: there is no piano accompaniment here. In this ballet more than any other, Balanchine affirms the music's primacy in the most stunning way. What stronger homage could he pay to Stravinsky than to have the male and female soloists stand by the piano during the opening "Cantilène" (the first of the five movements) listening attentively to the musicians. It is a statement ballet, expressing Balanchine's convictions about music and dance more clearly than any words could do.

Stravinsky's *Symphony in Three Movements* dates from 1942–45. Balanchine discussed the music with the composer during a visit to Hollywood in this period. He was struck by the athletically jazzy score and immediately began looking for an opportunity to stage it. The twenty-five-minute composition was more programmatic than most any other piece of concert music Stravinsky had written. The composer even directly referred to it as his war symphony, as it depicted in unusual pictorial detail various scenes of battle, suffering, and death. The first movement includes a concertante piano part, while the *Andante* that follows showcases harp writing every bit as important as the keyboard, also featured in this second movement. Both instruments, described by the composer as "protagonists," are highlighted in a dialogue that takes place during the closing *Con moto*.

Like so many works by Stravinsky in which conventional musical forms are customized to serve content, all three of these scores challenge the traditional interaction of solo instruments and ensembles. The Concerto in D sets aside the Mozartian classical concerto model, and unsurprisingly so, given Stravinsky's qualms regarding the traditional notion of a concerto. The composer's long-held misgivings about the elusive balance between creator and interpreter were well known. Balanchine, too, was wary of the egotistically motivated star dancer. The *Duo concertant* also breaks free from tradition. Stravinsky often treats the piano and violin percussively, although at moments there is a wonderful lyricism, as in the plaintive "Dithyrambe." For the most part, the soloists go their separate ways with a purposeful independence. The *Symphony in Three Movements* has always resisted categorization in its synthesizing of concerto and symphony. Stravinsky's deliberate blurring of identifiable musical designs and instrumental roles parallels Balanchine's ever shifting treatment of soloists and the *corps*.

This powerful trio of ballets proved to be the festival's most successful productions. Forty years later, all remain repertoire staples. Who more than Balanchine understood the basic tenets of theater and inherent drama of conflict evident in all three works? As he often argued, the dynamics, ritual, and rival polarities of the male-female "dance" (both literally and figuratively) provided the only plot ballet needed. This itself was sufficient to hold an audience's attention, so why dilute dance's elemental power with unneeded storylines?

In reviewing the 1972 Stravinsky Festival for *The New Yorker*, Andrew Porter remarked that ballets like *Violin Concerto, Orpheus,* and *Agon* seemed "almost to flow from a single mind, an entity called Stravinsky–Balanchine." A few critics dissented, suggesting that with the single exception of *Agon*, "very little outcome of their collaboration was top-drawer Balanchine," his "generic" approach to Stravinsky's music lacking the "sophisticated choreography" with which we associate the Balanchine name.[18] Other theories speculated that Balanchine was uneasy with the composer's insistence that the music must always come first, implying that the choreographer silently harbored some pent-up resentment. Balanchine's drastic revision of *Apollo* a few years after the composer's death, in which the choreographer provocatively deleted important passages of the score, was adduced as evidence. Such an excision would never have been contemplated while working with the composer.[19]

Whatever the warring opinions within the world of dance, the week-long 1972 festival marked a historic moment: not since the old Diaghilev days had Stravinsky's achievements as a dance composer received so much attention. With the conclusion of the festival, Balanchine mostly turned his attention to other composers. He did, however, mount a second homage to the composer, the Stravinsky Centennial Celebration, in June 1982. More than two dozen works were prepared not only by Balanchine (who contributed a relatively small number of ballets by comparison with the 1972 festival), but also by Peter Martins, Jerome Robbins, John Taras, and others. Productions included early compositions such as *Fireworks* (Peter Martins), neoclassical works such as the Concerto for piano and wind instruments (John Taras), and later compositions including *Monumentum/Movements*.[20]

Balanchine died on April 30, 1983. The choreographer had positioned Stravinsky's music in the public eye whenever and wherever he could. Just as the Ballets Russes had widely disseminated the composer's music over its spectacular twenty-year history, ending in 1929, so Balanchine took up the Stravinsky torch immediately upon his arrival in America in 1933. His New York City Ballet became synonymous with the Stravinsky-Balanchine repertoire, eventually standing as the foremost promoter of the composer's ballets internationally. Indeed, City Ballet continues to stage his works season after season. Moreover, Balanchine's own dancers, several of whom have become choreographers and now lead their own companies, continue to spread Stravinsky's ballets throughout the world. In one form or another, Balanchine astonishingly choreographed nearly 40 percent of Stravinsky's published oeuvre, much of this work still being regularly performed.

In the twentieth-century pantheon of collaborative artistic achievements, the Stravinsky-Balanchine partnership represents a landmark. Not only do the ballets it produced emit stamina and vitality, but most have become so exclusively linked with the choreographer as to suggest almost a copyright identity.[21] When one thinks of *Agon*, one thinks primarily of Balanchine. Balanchine's embracement of Stravinsky's music serves as a choreographic gold standard, such was his unparalleled devotion and success. Yet other distinguished artists have found and are still finding inspiration in choreographing many of the composer's ballets and abstract instrumental scores. Several have been mentioned in earlier chapters; but there are literally hundreds of others. *Agon*, for example, prompted several alternative choreographies almost immediately, such as Tatiana Gsovsky's 1958 setting for the Städtische Oper Ballet, first presented in Berlin less than six months after City Ballet's New York premiere. Although Balanchine first mounted the 1944 *Danses concertantes* with the Ballets Russes de Monte Carlo, Kenneth MacMillan provided a new version for the Sadler's Wells Theatre Ballet in 1955. And, as mentioned earlier, although *Scènes de ballet* also premiered in 1944 as part of a stage revue, Frederick Ashton most successfully choreographed it in 1948, again with the Sadler's Wells Ballet.[22] Even earlier, while the fame of the original Ballets Russes was still at its zenith, thirty-seven different choreographies for *Firebird* and *Petrouchka* were created in addition to the well-established Fokine settings.

Inevitably, several of Balanchine's dancers became Stravinsky advocates through their first-hand familiarity with his music. Others who had established reputations in choreographing romantic and narrative repertoire quite unlike much of the composer's post-Diaghilev writing also demonstrated an eagerness to undertake Stravinsky's music. Choreographers who have shaped the world of twentieth-century dance, as well as younger, contemporary choreographers, continue to be drawn to works ranging from *The Rite* to the composer's serial compositions. In the case of *The Rite*, for example, music history will admit the importance of Nijinsky's 1913 choreography, and perhaps even of Massine's 1920 version. Beyond these, there may be a passing mention of *The Rite* as set by Maurice Béjart (1959), Kenneth MacMillan (1962), Glen Tetley (1974), or Martha Graham (1984). Yet over two hundred choreographies for *The Rite* have been created, each, it seems, attempting to view the music through a prism of one kind or another. Boston Ballet's 2009 centennial celebration of the Ballets Russes' founding, for example, brought forth a new version, which, as one reviewer unkindly put it, "seemed determined to arouse mindless sensationalism."[23] From a musicologist's—and even more broadly, a cultural historian's—viewpoint, some of these versions might surely warrant study. Certainly Béjart's thirteen Stravinsky choreographies evince a devotion to the composer that is worthy of examination. But the work of less well known artists also deserves study. For example, Soviet choreographers Natalia Kasatkina and Vladimir Vasilyov's 1965 production at the Bolshoi Theater—the first staged performance of the historic ballet in Russia, coming over a half-century after the Parisian premiere—holds much merit.[24]

Viewed as a whole, the corpus of Stravinsky choreographers exhibits a remarkably diverse array of stylistic approaches: Alvin Ailey, Tatiana Baganova, Pina Bausch, Todd Bolender, Lew Christensen, Merce Cunningham, Anna Teresa De Keersmaeker, Agnes de Mille, Aurel Milloss, William Dollar, Marian Horosko, Bill T. Jones, Kurt Jooss, Jiří Kylián, José Limón, Lydia Lopokova, Peter Martins, Mark Morris, Jerome Robbins, Heinz Spoerli, Hannah Spohr, John Taras, Paul Taylor, Richard Tanner, Christopher Wheeldon, Mary

Wigman—these represent but a small, arbitrary sampling of the more than seven hundred choreographers listed in Stephanie Jordan and Larraine Nicholas's extensive database "Stravinsky the Global Dancer."[25] As one example, the Hungarian-Italian choreographer Aurel Milloss, while relatively unfamiliar to musicians, is second only to Balanchine in his devotion to Stravinsky, reports Jordan, having staged no fewer than eighteen of his works, including most of his ballet scores.[26] Even a signature work such as *Apollo*, again often exclusively associated with Balanchine, has generated thirty different choreographies by established companies in such countries as Australia, Belgium, the Czech Republic, Germany, Italy, Ireland, Japan, and New Zealand.

Indeed, as the new century unfolds, the volume of performances of Stravinsky's ballets, as well as the number of choreographers, some prominent, some obscure, who have been attracted to his scores, continues to expand rapidly. More than ever before, these ballets have acquired an international prominence. Jordan and Nicholas's database records performances in nearly fifty countries from Argentina to Zimbabwe. It would in fact be easier to list those works that have not been choreographed (including works not originally intended as ballets). Of Stravinsky's approximately one hundred published compositions and arrangements, nearly 90 percent have been set to dance—an extraordinary proportion, surpassing that of any other major composer. At last count, the database records nearly thirteen hundred different choreographic settings of Stravinsky's music.

So what do these statistics tell us? It is evident that creative artists around the world continue to be unendingly intrigued by the composer's music, no doubt for a variety of reasons—certainly and perhaps chiefly the music's rhythmic energy, but also the clarity of individual lines, the colorful orchestrations, the separable textural layers that lend themselves to choreographic divisions, and surely an almost instinctual desire to try one's hand at the music of a composer whose sheer historical weight as a dance composer is unmatched. Yet any comprehensive database can provide only so much in charting, or in this case quantifying, such a history. Many of the choreographers included saw their works performed only once. And some choreographers and productions listed in the interest of inclusiveness are inevitably more distinguished than others.[27]

In one sense, Balanchine's almost proprietary settings could prove stultifying to those courageous enough to tackle Stravinsky's music. Some who have taken up the Stravinsky–Balanchine repertoire have produced nothing much more than prosaic, "anemic echoes," as Reynolds rightly describes them.[28] But these disclaimers do nothing to compromise the fundamental message. In the end, the raw numbers reveal more about the music's longevity, its enduring richness, and its intrinsic power to captivate than does any single effort, successful or mediocre, to set one of Stravinsky's scores to dance. Such an overwhelming appetite to engage the composer's music speaks to its ability to inspire a vast array of choreographers. Whether well established or not, those who wish to create dance are magnetized by Stravinsky's music to a degree unequalled by any other composer in the history of western classical music.

From the *Firebird*'s neonationalist mimicry of Rimsky, through the purifying neoclassical clarity of *Apollo*, to the serially constructed *Agon*, Igor Stravinsky's dance works serve as a barometer. Collectively, they track a fifty-two-year development from its beginning to its end. To some extent these ballets provide a looking glass into Stravinsky's compositional evolution in the same way as other comprehensive musical monuments such as Beethoven's quartets. Each provides a glimpse of an evolutionary process, allowing us to trace an ever expanding journey step by step. And each is replete with observable stylistic changes, discrete turns in the road, and overarching commonalities that speak to matters of unity and coherence.

Moreover, if longevity is a factor in reckoning the import of great works of art, then the ballets discussed in these pages surely meet at least that criterion. From every angle, they have proven uncommonly durable. Masterpieces beckon us to return to them time and again. They coax us to reconsider our earlier and sometimes crystallized perceptions. Such works are confident and pliable, contemporary and timeless. As with all enduring musical monuments, they demand reflection, patience, and open-mindedness. Musical masterworks ask us to rehear, reinterpret, and constantly reassess their illuminating treasures. And in continuing to stir our imagination, Stravinsky's ballets invite us to do just that.

Notes

CHAPTER 1: From St. Petersburg to Paris

1. Geoffrey Hosking, *Russia: People and Empire* (Cambridge, Mass.: Harvard University Press, 1997), 276. For those wishing to trace Russia's history from 1552 through the 1917 Bolshevik Revolution, Hosking's text provides a far-reaching survey, consistently framing the arts within a nation's complex evolution.
2. *Newsweek*, May 21, 1962. The comment is reprinted in an article by Boris Schwarz, "Stravinsky in Soviet Russian Criticism," *Musical Quarterly* 48/3 (July 1962): 340–61, in which the author summarizes the U.S.S.R. reception of the composer's works from the "Parisian" ballets forward.
3. Prince Peter Lieven, *The Birth of the Ballets-Russes* (New York: Dover Publications, 1973), 55–56. Lieven's book was first published in 1936 and later translated by L. Zarine. Born in Moscow in 1887, Lieven witnessed the evolution of ballet around the turn of the century. He was also a confidant of Alexandre Benois, whose role in the development of the Ballets Russes was central. Lieven admits that much of what he conveys in his observations relies heavily upon Benois's remembrances. The dancer Istomina studied with Didelot and became one of the prima ballerinas of the early nineteenth century. Immortalized in Pushkin's *Eugene Onegin* ("Forth from the crowd of nymphs surrounding / Istomina the nimbly bounding"), she appeared in several ballets and operas including *Ruslan and Lyudmila.*
4. Hosking, *Russia: People and Empire*, 294.
5. The Table of Ranks remained in force until the 1917 Revolution. Painters and actors were entitled to the status of "free artist" long before musicians. In addition to social status, there were financial implications, including exemption from certain government-levied taxes.
6. Igor Stravinsky and Robert Craft, *Memories and Commentaries* (1960; reprint, Berkeley: University of California Press, 1981), 33. In recent years, the reliability of Stravinsky's comments has come under scrutiny. The essence of the composer's thoughts is generally preserved, although one should be wary of depending too heavily upon these still valuable conversation books. For further discussion of Craft's editing of Stravinsky's remarks, see the introduction to Richard Taruskin's *Stravinsky and the Russian Traditions*, 2 vols. (Berkeley: University of California Press, 1996); Charles M. Joseph, "Boswellizing an Icon: Stravinsky, Craft, and the Historian's Dilemma," in *Stravinsky Inside Out* (New Haven: Yale University Press, 2001); and Stephen Walsh's *Stravinsky: The Second Exile: France and America, 1934–1971* (New York: Alfred A. Knopf, 2006), the second volume of Walsh's biography of Stravinsky, wherein Craft's representation of the composer's thoughts is queried.
7. Roland John Wiley, *Tchaikovsky's Ballets* (New York: Oxford University Press, 1985), 1.

8. Wiley, *Tchaikovsky's Ballets*. See especially his introduction, "Composer and Balletmaster," which addresses the extent of Petipa's authority, and how Tchaikovsky thought of himself as a "spectator." See also Lincoln Kirstein, *Thirty Years: Lincoln Kirstein's "The New York City Ballet"* (New York: Alfred A. Knopf, 1978), 99, for more on the Petipa–Tchaikovsky collaboration.

9. Lieven, *The Birth of the Ballets-Russes*, 69–70. Tamara Karsavina, *Theatre Street: The Reminiscences of Tamara Karsavina* (London: Readers Union, 1950), 131.

10. Lynn Garafola, *Diaghilev's Ballets Russes* (New York: Oxford University Press, 1989), 6.

11. Robert C. Ridenour, *Nationalism, Modernism, and Personal Rivalry in Nineteenth-Century Russian Music* (Ann Arbor: UMI Research Press, 1981), 3.

12. See Francis Maes, *A History of Russian Music: From Kamarinskaya to Babi Yar*, trans. Arnold J. Pomerans and Erica Pomerans (Berkeley: University of California Press, 2002), 31–32, for a brief summary of opera's highly regarded place "at the center of the musical life" of St. Petersburg. Maes quotes Faddey Bulgarin, the diplomatic spokesperson for Nicholas I: "Let's admit it: without an Italian opera troupe it would always seem as if something were missing in the capital of the foremost empire in the world! There would seem to be no focal point for opulence, splendor, and cultivated diversion. . . . [Italian opera] not only satisfies our musical cravings but nourishes our national pride." Given such official praise, it is easy to imagine the esteem that accrued to Stravinsky's gifted father—and whether Igor would admit it or not, the doors such esteem would open.

13. See Stephen Walsh, *Stravinsky: A Creative Spring: Russia and France, 1882–1934* (New York: Alfred A. Knopf, 1999), 30. In this first volume of Walsh's biography, mention is made of Stravinsky keeping a notebook that included comments on Wagner's operas, including *Parsifal* and *Tristan und Isolde*. See also Lieven, *The Birth of the Ballets-Russes*, 69, for his comparison of opera and ballet.

14. Ridenour, *Nationalism*, 217. The author states that Rimsky doggedly struggled to learn the disciplines of fundamental music theory and counterpoint. "Nearly in a panic, he undertook to teach himself these subjects by intense reading and writing hundreds of exercises, managing to stay a week or two ahead of his pupils." For a fuller account, see Taruskin, *Stravinsky and the Russian Traditions*, vol. 1, 29ff., wherein the author quotes extensively from Rimsky's own autobiographical account.

15. Joseph, *Stravinsky Inside Out*, 181. In addition, this material includes a rare outtake in which Stravinsky speaks candidly of his parents, especially his father. His demeanor is more somber than the more telegenically friendly image that was most often projected in the film clips included in the numerous documentaries that were actually aired. He speaks of a "severe and unappreciative" father, one with whom he was never on good terms. "I could say many things about my father but I wish to forget them. I will never speak about it."

16. Igor Stravinsky, *An Autobiography* (1936; reprint, New York: W. W. Norton, 1962), 26.

17. Stravinsky and Craft, *Memories and Commentaries*. See the section "Diaghilev and His Dancers," 31–53, for additional comments on the composer's relationship with Pavlova, Fokine, Nijinsky, and others. See also Lieven, *The Birth of the Ballets-Russes*, 56.

18. Guyau's thoughts about morality must have intrigued Stravinsky, although one wonders how intensely the young composer might have interrogated Guyau's exegeses. Still, the basic principles articulated—morality needs no coercion, humans are predisposed to lead an intensive life, struggle and risk are innately rewarding, intellectual postulations come naturally—all of these comport with much of Stravinsky's own thinking as articulated in so many of his later Francophile declarations about pursuit, discovery, imagination, inspiration, and creativity.

19. Igor Stravinsky and Robert Craft, *Expositions and Developments* (1962; reprint, Berkeley: University of California Press, 1981), 66. Stravinsky's affection for St. Petersburg seems sentimentally reconstructed in his conversations with Craft (28–35). See also Simon Volkov, *St. Petersburg: A Cultural History* (New York: Free Press Paperbacks, 1995), xii, where the author presents an equally warmhearted portrait of the city: "In Petersburg, the inanimate excitingly came to life, palaces and monuments moved onto the pages of prose and poetry or were reflected in the spellbinding music, only to freeze once again on the granite banks of the river and along the open squares but now enriched and elevated, like magically enticing symbols."

Exciting as the city surely was, these touchingly wistful remembrances surely arise from a deeply emotional source. Stephen Walsh counters, "The Petersburg of the last two or three decades of the nineteenth century (and the first of the twentieth) was one of the most overcrowded and without rival the dirtiest, most diseased capital city in the whole of Europe. . . . Dirty and stinking, the Petersburg streets were also often excessively crowded [bringing] poverty and homelessness." In fact several members of the Stravinsky family, including Igor himself, suffered from scarlet fever, diphtheria, and tuberculosis. His parents' letters regularly express health concerns (*Stravinsky: A Creative Spring*, 23–24).

20. Garafola, *Diaghilev's Ballets Russes*, 5. Karsavina vividly recounts the tensions surrounding the strike: "I was going home from a political meeting which we artists had held that day. I chose a roundabout way avoiding pickets. That artists, so conservative at heart, usually so loyal to the Court . . . should have succumbed to the epidemic of meetings and resolutions seemed to me like treason. Meetings were being held everywhere; autonomy, freedom of speech, freedom of conscience, freedom of the printed word—even children at school were passing these resolutions." Karsavina, *Theatre Street*, 122–24.

21. *Memories and Commentaries*, 27.

22. See Walsh, *Stravinsky: A Creative Spring*, 84, for elaboration, as well as the curious omission in Stravinsky's writings of the events of 1905, which surely affected him more than he cared to disclose.

23. Walsh, *Stravinsky: A Creative Spring*, 30.

24. Perhaps the most beneficial role Glazunov played in Stravinsky's future was in his capacity as the eventual director of the St. Petersburg Conservatory, a post he assumed following Rimsky's support of the 1905 student protests in the wake of Bloody Sunday. In 1919, Glazunov admitted a fifteen-year-old pianist, George Balanchine, as a music student, even though Balanchine was also studying dance at the Imperial Ballet School. Balanchine's musicianship would, as will be explored, become the nexus of the Stravinsky–Balanchine collaborations.

25. See Taruskin, *Stravinsky and the Russian Traditions*, vol. 1, especially chapter 3, "Fourth-Generation Belyayevets," for details of Stravinsky's heavy dependence in each of his early works on an abundance of models, including Balakirev, Borodin, Glazunov, Glinka, Mussorgsky, Rimsky, Scriabin, Tchaikovsky, Wagner, and others one might expect. The op. 7 Four Studies for piano of 1908, for example, are egregiously Scriabinesque. A comparison of Stravinsky's first Etude in C Minor with Scriabin's own Etude in F-sharp Minor, op. 42, no. 2, immediately divulges a flagrant measure-by-measure lifting of exact rhythmic and melodic motives, as well as harmonic vocabulary and structural pacing. See Charles M. Joseph, *Stravinsky and the Piano* (Ann Arbor: UMI Research Press, 1983), 45–54. While some reliance on other composers is to be expected in such early works, Taruskin's particularized analysis of virtually every work written during Stravinsky's early years reveals how comprehensively such influences took hold.

26. Stravinsky, *An Autobiography*, 21.

27. The sixty-four-page autograph manuscript of the *Scherzo fantastique* is held at the Morgan Library and Museum in New York, on deposit as part of the Robert Owen Lehman Collection, and signed and dated by the composer March 30, 1908. Even in what was intended as the final version of the work, Stravinsky has altered several passages. The harp parts are sometimes changed, metronomic markings are altered, and orchestral details are occasionally reconceived.

28. Stravinsky, *An Autobiography*, 24.

29. Lieven, *The Birth of the Ballets-Russes*, 125.

CHAPTER 2: *The Firebird*

1. John Drummond, *Speaking of Diaghilev* (London: Faber and Faber, 1997), 21. Fokine remembers that he was with Diaghilev, and perhaps Benois, when he heard *Fireworks*, although he gives no date. He claims that the audience was indifferent but the music was "afire," and just what he needed for *The Firebird*. Perhaps so, but it was the *Scherzo* not

Fireworks that originally turned Diaghilev's head. Michel Fokine, *Memoirs of a Ballet Master*, trans. Vitale Fokine (Boston: Little, Brown, 1961), 160.

2. See Ada Raev, "Working for Diaghilev—An Introduction," in Sjeng Scheijen, ed., *Working for Diaghilev* (Schoten: BAI, 2004), 8.

3. For a discussion of the early issues of *Mir iskusstva*, which includes a translation of Diaghilev's first and fourth essays, see Joan Acocella, "Diaghilev's 'Complicated Questions,' " in Lynn Garafola and Nancy Van Norman Baer, eds., *The Ballets Russes and Its World* (New Haven: Yale University Press, 1999), 71–93.

4. Quoted in John E. Bowlt, "Diaghilev and the Eighteenth Century," in Scheijen, ed., *Working for Diaghilev*, 14.

5. Karsavina, *Theatre Street*, 147. For a detailed look at Russia's distorted image as projected through the lens of the Ballets Russes, see Hanna Järvinen, " 'The Russian Barnum': Russian Opinions on Diaghilev's Ballets Russes, 1909–1914," *Dance Research* 26/1 (Summer 2008): 19. Järvinen argues that in rushing to praise Diaghilev's company, westerners have neglected several pertinent Russian perspectives. Did Paris truly appreciate dance as an art form? Yet for all their "laudatory clichés," the author remarks, "the Russians also saw through all the superlatives and realized that in the [Ballets Russes], ballet was quite secondary" (22). Concluding that Russia was depicted as "some sort of Oriental backwater inhabited by naturally dancing barbarians," Järvinen claims that a fundamental "irrevocable racial (i.e. biological) divide" (25) only deepened the Russian stereotypes Diaghilev rather shamelessly exploited. Moreover, authenticity was sacrificed for effect. *The Firebird*, as we shall see, was a sewn-together hodgepodge of stories (often completely unrelated) rearranged for the audience's benefit—something to which even Stravinsky explicitly objected.

6. Lieven, *The Birth of the Ballets-Russes*, 56.

7. Aspects of orientalism were continually associated with Stravinsky's early works, including his opera *Le Rossignol*, begun in 1908, and the short song set *Three Japanese Lyrics*, composed in 1912–13. The fascination with Russian orientalism (traceable to Nicholas I) has a history, especially among the French but also for Americans, as Diaghilev discovered upon the Ballets Russes' tour of the United States in 1916. In reviewing a February performance in Boston, Olin Downes observed that the company was "the last word in all that is gorgeous and intoxicating in Oriental art." See Maes, *A History of Russian Music*, 80–83, for a short summary. "Orientalism," writes Maes, "was able to fulfill several functions. It could . . . serve as a safety valve for subjects unmentionable in one's own culture. Thus it helped to disguise political themes in the eighteenth century, and erotic fantasies in the nineteenth."

8. John E. Bowlt, *The Silver Age: Russian Art of the Early Twentieth Century and the "World of Art" Group* (Newtonville, Mass.: Oriental Research Partners, 1979), 186.

9. The ballet had originally been choreographed by Fokine in 1907, and was premiered at the Maryinsky that winter. Glazunov had prepared the orchestrations, although he had transcribed several of the Chopin works even earlier.

10. Stravinsky may also have orchestrated a work entitled *Danse siamoise* by Christian Sinding for Nijinsky's performance on February 20. Garafola lists the work in *Diaghilev's Ballets Russes*, 386. If such a work existed, it has vanished, as has "Kobold."

11. Stravinsky, *An Autobiography*, 25.

12. Cherepnin was closely associated with Diaghilev from 1908, and often conducted concerts in conjunction with Diaghilev's appearances in Paris. He was so aligned with French music that he earned the nickname "Debussy Ravelevich Cherepnin." The music Cherepnin began to compose for *The Firebird* became a short orchestral work entitled *The Enchanted Kingdom*, op. 39, whose title page indicates that the story derives from the Firebird fairy tale. As Donald Street points out, the similarity between this music and Stravinsky's score is too close to ignore. Cherepnin's composition premiered in St. Petersburg in March 1910, a few months before *The Firebird*. Given their friendship at that point, Stravinsky may well have heard Cherepnin's score that spring. See Donald Street, "A Forgotten Firebird," *Musical Times* 119/1626 (August 1978): 674–767.

13. Lieven reprints a portion of Diaghilev's letter to Lyadov in *The Birth of the Ballets-Russes*, 107.

14. Serge Grigoriev, *The Diaghilev Ballet, 1909–1929*, trans. Vera Bowen (London: Constable, 1953), 29.

15. Diaghilev had originally used the title "The Firebird" in the ballet *Le Festin*, offered in Paris in May 1909 during the previous season. In one of the sections Karsavina had danced the Firebird and Nijinsky had portrayed a Hindu prince, in keeping with the ballet's oriental bent. The music was actually Tchaikovsky's, originally used for the "Blue Bird" *pas de deux* in *The Sleeping Beauty*. In advance publicity Diaghilev had promised the Parisians a Firebird ballet in 1909. The Tchaikovsky-Petipa *pas de deux* would buy him time to prepare *The Firebird* for the next season. Moreover, it would be difficult to identify a culture without a Firebird-like mythology, such mythologies being found in Africa, Arabia, Britain, Germany, Greece, Hungary, Israel, Ireland, Mexico, Swahili, Sweden, Turkey, the United States, and countless other countries. Titles include *The Golden Bird, The Golden Nightingale, The Nunda, Eater of People, A Prince, a King, and a Horse, The Jeweled Cage and the Evil Sister*, and so on.

16. Igor Stravinsky and Robert Craft, *Conversations with Igor Stravinsky* (1959; reprint, Berkeley: University of California Press, 1980), 96. Stravinsky remarked that Diaghilev chose Golovin because his "orientalism conformed to the ideals of the academic orientalism then so popular." Fokine had been intrigued by eastern dance since his school days, visiting museums and observing turned-out heels and straight backs. See Fokine, *Memoirs*, 36.

17. Stravinsky's comments were made in a 1933 interview with Edwin Evans. In the same interview Stravinsky further stressed that "Russian legends have as heroes characters that are simple, naïve, sometimes even frankly stupid, devoid of all malice; and it is they who are always victorious over characters that are clever, artful, complex, cruel and powerful." Portions of Evans's interview appeared in Eric Walter White's *Stravinsky: A Critical Survey, 1882–1946* (Mineola, N.Y.: Dover Publications, 1997), 25–26.

18. Fokine, *Memoirs*, 164. The author details the story on pp. 163–65.

19. Fokine, *Memoirs*, 165.

20. Karsavina, *Theatre Street*, 165–66. Lieven remembers that during rehearsals "there was great difficulty in staging the passing of the two horsemen, Night and Day, by the footlights. It could not be managed at all, though the music was very appropriate with the suggestion of the mysterious stamping of hoofs. In the end, the horsemen had to go on foot, pacing slowly across the stage to this 'equestrian' music." Lieven, *The Birth of the Ballets-Russes*, 108.

21. Grigoriev, *The Diaghilev Ballet*, 31.

22. Tamara Karsavina, "A Recollection of Stravinsky," *Tempo* 8 (Summer 1948): 8.

23. Grigoriev, *The Diaghilev Ballet*, 32.

24. Stravinsky and Craft, *Memories and Commentaries*, 32. See also Stravinsky, *An Autobiography*, 29, in which he implies that he had some say in the casting. Stravinsky told Craft that Pavlova had not liked his *Scherzo fantastique* and *Fireworks*, dismissing them as "horribly decadent." Even so, the composer reports that he had hoped she would dance the Firebird and Karsavina the role of "the captive princess."

25. Alexandre Benois, *Reminiscences of the Russian Ballet* (London: Putnam, 1941), 302.

26. Brussel's comments appear in White's *Stravinsky: A Critical Survey*, 25. Diaghilev often invited friendly critics to rehearsals. Brussel frequently previewed productions in *Le Figaro*, helping to ensure Diaghilev a sympathetic audience. For more on Diaghilev's marketing strategies, see Garafola, *Diaghilev's Ballets Russes*, chapter 10, "Paris: The Cultivated Audience."

27. Grimm's collection of fairy tales includes the story of "The Twelve Dancing Princesses," which was choreographed by Fokine in 1909 and performed by Bakst and others informally in St. Petersburg in March of that year. See Taruskin, *Stravinsky and the Russian Traditions*, vol. 1, 569–70.

28. Bronislava Nijinska, *Bronislava Nijinska: Early Memoirs*, trans. Irina Nijinska and Jean Rawlinson (New York: Holt, Rinehart and Winston, 1981), 299–301. Diaghilev often involved himself with lighting. "No one who saw him 'light' a ballet could agree that he was not a creative artist. Under his direction a drab, commonplace stage became a décor come to vivid life." W. H. Haddon Squire, "The Mantle of Diaghilev," *Tempo* 5 (Autumn 1947): 30.

29. Fokine, *Memoirs*, 72.

30. Karsavina, *Theatre Street*, 131.
31. Stravinsky and Craft, *Memories and Commentaries*, 35
32. Stravinsky and Craft, *Expositions and Developments*, 129.
33. The composer accurately describes the dances in *Memories and Commentaries* (33), although in fairness to Fokine, the constant, demure covering of the princesses' faces and the Cossack-like kicking of legs in the "Infernal Dance" were surely intended to further enhance the folkloristic "Russianness" of the ballet.
34. Stravinsky, *An Autobiography*, 30. The composer fondly remembered Golovin's "magnificent setting." See Taruskin, *Stravinsky and the Russian Traditions*, vol. 1, 638, for Benois's comments. Lieven, *The Birth of the Ballets-Russes*, 108.
35. Precedents include Rimsky's *Christmas Eve* (1895) and Ravel's *Rapsodie espagnole*, the latter published in 1908. (Ravel actually attended the premiere of *The Firebird*, as did other *culturati* including Marcel Proust and Sarah Bernhardt.) Certainly Stravinsky was familiar with Rimsky's opera, at least. The young composer studied whatever orchestration texts he could find. In 1910 he purchased a copy of Charles M. Widor's 1904 treatise *Technique de l'orchestre moderne*, a lexicon for the would-be orchestrator, its examples including many extracted from Wagner's operas. Now held by the Paul Sacher Stiftung in Basel, Switzerland, Stravinsky's copy of the book is heavily marked, showing how often he questioned Widor's wisdom. He commented upon harmonics for the double bass, trills for the trombone, and when the use of the harp was appropriate. He also wrote a chart of possibilities for multiple string stops. His copious marginalia resonate with orchestral effects present in *The Firebird*. Exactly when Stravinsky studied the treatise cannot be determined, but it is clear that he was thinking hard about orchestral possibilities, as manifested in *The Firebird* and the two other Ballets Russes scores that followed it. Stravinsky's interrogation of established orchestration conventions—and an inclination toward counterintuitive orchestrating at times—is evident throughout his life.
36. For possible models for this and other dances in the ballet, see Taruskin, *Stravinsky and the Russian Traditions*, vol. 1, chapter 9. As is only to be expected, Stravinsky's ideas frequently originated in precedents by Rimsky, Glazunov, Tchaikovsky, Scriabin (as in this example), Balakirev, and Lyadov.
37. Fokine, *Memoirs*, 167–68.
38. Quoted in Lincoln Kirstein, *Dance: A Short History of Classic Theatrical Dancing* (Princeton: Dance Horizons, 1987), 273.
39. Grigoriev, *The Diaghilev Ballet*, 32.
40. In 1963 Arthur Berger observed, "Anyone who undertakes an investigation of the essential relationships of tones in the works of Stravinsky may find himself somewhat at a disadvantage as a result of the fact that no significant body of theoretical writing has emerged to deal with the nature of twentieth-century music that is centric . . . but not tonally functional." See Berger's pioneering "Problems of Pitch Organization in Stravinsky," *Perspectives of New Music* 2/1 (Autumn/Winter 1963): 11. With these words Berger unleashed a deluge of ratiocinations on the riddle of Stravinsky's pitch materials. From Pieter van den Toorn's *The Music of Igor Stravinsky* (New Haven: Yale University Press, 1983), which broadly addresses Stravinsky's music, to Allen Forte's *The Harmonic Organization of "The Rite of Spring"* (New Haven: Yale University Press, 1978), focusing on that specific masterpiece, virtually every aspect of Stravinsky's treatment of pitch has been and continues to be scrutinized. Historical musicologists have frequently cited Stravinsky's reliance upon Rimsky-Korsakov's adoption of symmetrical scales. These "artificial" or "synthetic" scales, as once described, seemed explanation enough for many years. Finally, octatonic scales (as Berger first coined them), in which whole tones and semitones alternate symmetrically, are central in understanding Stravinsky's *The Firebird*, and earlier works as well. That Stravinsky relied so heavily upon Rimsky, and Rimsky in turn on earlier composers such as Liszt, comes as no surprise. To the contrary, it would have been peculiar had he not adopted the models with which he was familiar. For an excellent pitch-class set study of *The Firebird*, see Allen Forte's "Harmonic Syntax and Voice Leading in Stravinsky's Early Music," in Jann Pasler, ed., *Confronting Stravinsky* (Berkeley: University of California Press, 1986), 95–129. Forty years after Berger's initial article, exchanges about

Stravinsky's octatonicism continue. For a more recent colloquy, see Pieter C. van den Toorn and Dmitri Tymoczko, "Stravinsky and the Octatonic: The Sounds of Stravinsky," *Music Theory Spectrum* 25/1 (Spring 2003): 167–202.

41. Boris Asaf'yev, *A Book about Stravinsky*, trans. Richard French (Ann Arbor: UMI Research Press, 1982), 19.

42. Stravinsky and Craft, *Expositions and Developments*, 128.

43. For a more complete exploration of these examples and others, as well as the reproduction of several additional pages from the March 21 piano score, see Joseph, *Stravinsky and the Piano*, 252–70. The manuscript is held at the Morgan Library in New York.

44. Even a few measures earlier, at m. 20, the arpeggiated thirds immediately preceding Ivan's smashing of the egg—played by two clarinets, just as in *Petrouchka*—seem to presage another famous passage from the composer's next ballet. Stravinsky himself calls attention to the similarity in *Expositions and Developments*, 132.

45. See Robert Craft, *Stravinsky: Selected Correspondence*, vol. 2 (New York: Alfred A. Knopf, 1984), "*Firebird*: A Publishing History in Correspondence," 219–58. On p. 223, Craft reproduces the title page of Stravinsky's original draft of the complete orchestral score, dated autumn 1909, where the work is described as a "Ballet fantastique" in one act with an apotheosis. It was not at all unusual for Stravinsky to mark such drafts—sometimes copiously— with notes to himself regarding the scenario, the orchestration, and other matters, as they continued to evolve.

46. For an especially useful analysis, see Pieter C. van den Toorn, "Will Stravinsky Survive Postmodernism?" *Music Theory Spectrum* 22/1 (Spring 2000): 104–21. Van den Toorn takes issue with Taruskin's comment that the recitative-structured music of the ballet, rather than the more popular diatonic dances including the "Finale," is the only harbinger of the future Stravinsky (Taruskin, *Stravinsky and the Russian Traditions*, vol. 1, 588). His analysis explores Stravinsky's use of "block" structures, "the technique of slicing up thematic statements into smaller units and of repeating those units separately and independently of each other." Indeed, such compositional segmenting (and irregular repetition) is fundamental to understanding Stravinsky's music, including all of his later ballets.

47. The New York City Ballet occasionally programs the 1949 Balanchine version— significantly revised in 1970—in both New York City and Saratoga Springs, using Stravinsky's reduced 1945 score (almost twenty minutes shorter than the original 1910 score). A number of commercially filmed versions are now available on DVD. The Royal Ballet's production of the 1950s, released in 1959, stars Dame Margot Fonteyn in the title role (as coached by Karsavina) and surely comes closest to the 1910 Diaghilev production. Unfortunately, there are a few cuts in the score, resulting in the loss of several important musical leitmotivs. It is a live performance, and consequently Stravinsky's brilliant orchestral writing is largely obscured by the poor audio. More recently, the BBC released a 2001 televised performance of the ballet performed by the Royal Ballet and the Royal Opera House orchestra conducted by John Carewe. This version restores Fokine's choreography as much as possible. Leanne Benjamin dances the Firebird and David Drew portrays Kashchei. The DVD includes rehearsal footage and an interview with Drew. In 2002 the Bolshoi Ballet and the Bolshoi State Academic Theater Orchestra, conducted by Andrey Chistiakov, offered a film-fantasy version of the ballet, in which Nina Ananiashvili portrayed the Firebird and Andris Liepa tripled as Ivan, the film's director, and the screenwriter. Complete with special effects, brilliant lighting, and all the advantages that a production expressly shot for film at the Mosfilm Studios allows, this controversial recreation recasts much of the dancing (except for that of the Firebird, although her leaps are occasionally filmed in slow motion), especially for the corps. Gone are all of the folkloristic gestures of the "Infernal Dance," the covering of women's faces and the men's kicking feet, while both the dancing and the acrobatics are much more violent and earthy. The production is an odd mixture, taking liberties with certain aspects of the original while retaining much of it—even reinstating the two horses representing Day and Night at the beginning and close of the ballet.

48. Stravinsky, *An Autobiography*, 29–30.

49. Henri Ghéon, "Propos divers sur le Ballet Russe," *Nouvelle Revue française* 4 (1910), 210. For an important review by the critic Michel-Dmitri Calvocoressi, in which the author praises *The Firebird* as appealing "not only to our taste for the weird and to our sense of physical pleasure, but also to our higher emotional faculties," see "A Russian Composer of To-Day: Igor Stravinsky," *Musical Times* 52 (1911): 511–12.

50. Taruskin reprints several critical reviews in his study, 641–42. Stravinsky made several arrangements of the ballet, beginning in 1911 with a suite of five dances. While living in Switzerland, he prepared, in 1919, an arrangement of the five most popular parts of the ballet ("The Firebird and Its Dance," "The Princesses' Khorovod," the "Infernal Dance," the "Lullaby," and the "Finale"). This slimmer version is still often played (as in Disney's *Fantasia 2000*). The third and final suite, prepared in 1945, is considerably shorter than the original ballet. It too is written for a reduced orchestra, and was later used by Balanchine. Stravinsky also arranged sections of the ballet for piano and violin during the late 1920s and early 1930s, using these arrangements while touring as a concert artist for several years. For two important articles addressing an available facsimile of the autograph orchestral score of 1910 and recent critical editions of the it, see John Shepard, "L'Oiseau de feu: fac-simile du manuscrit Saint-Petersbourg, 1909–1910," *Notes* 44/4 (June 1988): 804–7; and Joni Lynn Steshko, "L'Oiseau de feu [1910]," *Notes* 54/5 (June 1998): 997–1002.

51. Järvinen, " 'The Russian Barnum' ": 19.

52. The letter appears in Vera Stravinsky and Robert Craft, *Stravinsky in Pictures and Documents* (New York: Simon and Schuster, 1978), 24.

53. Ironically, *The Firebird* eventually became Stravinsky's biggest albatross. The "destructive popularity" of the music, as he once dubbed it, vexatiously perpetuated his early compositional style as the defining feature of his career. Moreover, he received no royalties for performances; Diaghilev and he quarreled constantly over remuneration; the composer later became involved in a bitter lawsuit over a published arrangement; and orchestras often wanted him to conduct nothing else, or at least to make sure that the work would be included on programs.

CHAPTER 3: *Petrouchka*

1. Diaghilev's quip appears in Grigoriev, *The Diaghilev Ballet*, 52.

2. Diaghilev's last opera before *The Firebird*, Alexander Serov's 1909 *Judith*, appeared in the same theater as the premiere of *Petrouchka*. Four years would pass before he staged another opera, on May 22, 1913, only a week before Paris was stunned by *The Rite of Spring*. During the interim, fifteen new ballets appeared. While living close to Monte Carlo where the Ballets Russes wintered, Stravinsky frequently attended rehearsals and performances of these new productions. For example, he attended Fokine's 1911 *Le Spectre de la rose* only a few months before the premiere of *Petrouchka*.

3. Lincoln Kirstein, *Four Centuries of Ballet* (Mineola, N.Y.: Dover Publications, 1984), 194.

4. Not only did the composer always work at the keyboard, but he remained active as a pianist from his earliest days, regularly serving as a rehearsal pianist for his own ballets (including *Petrouchka*), and often accompanying singers and instrumentalists. Beyond his youthful piano compositions, Stravinsky incorporated both the piano and the celesta in orchestral works, including an early unpublished cantata, the *Scherzo fantastique*, *Fireworks*, the orchestrated Chopin works for *Les Sylphides*, and of course *The Firebird*.

5. Stravinsky, *An Autobiography*, 31–32. In an interview with Florent Fels published some years before his autobiography, the composer spoke of a "combat between the piano and orchestra," in which the soloist "sat himself at the piano and rolled incongruous objects on the keyboard, while the orchestra burst out with vehement protests, with sonic fisticuffs." Taruskin includes a part of this 1928 interview, which first appeared in *Les Nouvelles littéraires*, in *Stravinsky and the Russian Traditions*, vol. 1, 664. By the time Diaghilev and Nijinsky heard Stravinsky's sketches, most of the second tableau was complete—certainly the most pianistic section of the ballet. Although the piano plays no role in the final two

tableaux in the 1911 score, Stravinsky did assign important passages to the instrument in his 1947 revision. In addition to a pianola version, pianists will be familiar with Stravinsky's pyrotechnical transcription of portions of the ballet for Arthur Rubinstein in 1921, which included the music of most of the final tableau as well as the "Russian Dance" and "In Petrouchka's Room." The manuscripts for both the 1911 and the 1947 version of the ballet are held by the Morgan Library and Museum. The 1911 manuscript is particularly instructive in tracking Stravinsky's revisions. The score is dated (in Russian) "Rome 13/26 May, 1911." The hundreds of modifications to it include numerous changes in string markings, including single notes for the entire violin section eventually marked *divisi* in the final published score; a thinning of passages for the two harps; stage directions such as those indicating where the curtains occur; adjustments to dynamics (for example, several crescendos that did not make their way into the published score); tempo changes and directions such as *meno mosso, stringendo*, most of which do not appear in the published version; and frequent rescoring of instrumental parts, including instances where single lines are ultimately scored in octaves. More specifically, additions seem to have been made after the manuscript was completed, perhaps in the service of the drama. For example, the transition to the second tableau ("In Petrouchka's Room") originally included neither the short oboe duet nor the drum roll leading into the next scene. Rather, the 1911 manuscript indicates that the tableau was to have begun immediately after the brief passage for two clarinets in mm. 140–41.

6. Stravinsky and Craft, *Conversations*, 15.

7. For some informative anecdotes about the importance of Stravinsky's pianistic "imprints," see Jeffrey Kresky, "Urban Legends for Music Theorists," *Music Theory Spectrum* 25/1 (Spring 2003): 121–25. Kresky reports, for example, that in discussing the opening signature sonority of the 1930 *Symphony of Psalms*, Claudio Spies recalls, "it is undoubtedly true; it was an imprint of [Stravinsky's] hand" to which the shape of the chord is traceable. Moreover, the present author can remember Soulima Stravinsky speaking of his father seated at the keyboard, constantly searching for novel spacings of chords, which were often based upon the unusually large size of his hands. See Joseph, *Stravinsky and the Piano*.

8. The often revealing octatonic pitch analyses offered over the last three decades may occasionally tend to overshadow other aspects of Stravinsky's compositional approach. Even Arthur Berger, the "founding father" of octatonicism, lamented that the symmetrical pitch collection had become overused as an analytical tool in explicating Stravinsky's music, adding wittily, "I wish I had never mentioned it." Robert Craft, *An Improbable Life* (Nashville: Vanderbilt University Press, 2002), 393.

9. Benois, *Reminiscences*, 325. For one explanation of the convoluted history of the *balagani*, see Andrew Wachtel's essay "The Ballet's Libretto," in Wachtel, ed., *Petrushka: Sources and Contexts* (Evanston: Northwestern University Press, 1998), 11–40. "Petrushka" theatre was an art form in itself, and as familiar to Russians as a "Punch and Judy" show was to Europeans. It often included clowns, dancing bears, gibing comedians, and other revelers associated with the raucous nature of carnivals, such as those held during Shrovetide celebrations. Wachtel contends that the "authentic prototypes" of a typical Russian puppet show have little in common with those found in the Stravinsky-Benois adaptation. Historians also often point to Serov's opera *The Power of the Fiend* (1871) as a precursor, citing its Shrovetide Fair setting and the inclusion of carnival characters traceable to the early *balagani*. As with *Petrouchka*, moreover, Serov's opera relies greatly on Russian folk song as a fundamental element of coherence.

10. Nijinska, *Early Memoirs*, 31–33.

11. Benois, *Reminiscences*, 325. Benois goes on to describe the addition of the third principal, the "Blackamoor," discussed later in this chapter.

12. Wachtel, ed., *Petrushka: Sources and Contexts*, 130–38. Wachtel's Appendix B consists of translations of letters between Stravinsky and Benois regarding *Petrouchka*, including musical examples and stage sketches that they exchanged.

13. Yet later in the same letter Benois again suggests a more felicitous ending, with the crowd discovering that Petrouchka has fallen victim only to a harmless, cardboard knife, which

relieves and delights them. "We have to do it so that the whole theater dances along," he urged. See Wachtel, ed., *Petrushka: Sources and Contexts*, 130–31.

14. Stravinsky and Craft, *Expositions and Developments*, 136.

15. Lieven, *The Birth of the Ballets-Russes*, 142.

16. For an account of the troupe's unaccommodating stay in Rome, see Nijinska's *Early Memoirs*, 358–64. Karsavina's memories are recorded in "A Recollection of Stravinsky," 8.

17. Lieven, *The Birth of the Ballets-Russes*, 143. Such last-minute turmoil was not in fact unusual for such productions. And indeed Stravinsky's new score was still encountering hostility two years later in Vienna, where, as Grigoriev again reports, the Vienna Opera Theater Orchestra (one of the finest ensembles of the era) found the music "dirty" and unworthy of a performance. Neither Monteux nor Stravinsky (who attended the first rehearsal and requested a larger orchestra) could do anything to convince the orchestra otherwise. It was only through Diaghilev's forceful intercession that the musicians agreed to rehearse.

18. Kirstein, *Four Centuries of Ballet*, 194. *Esmeralda*, to a score by Pugni, was premiered in London and revived (with several musical alterations) by Petipa in St. Petersburg in 1886.

19. The description appeared in the *Souvenir Serge de Diaghileff's Ballet Russe*, distributed to audiences during the troupe's 1916 appearances at the Metropolitan Opera House in New York.

20. Taruskin provides an illuminating summary of folk song transcriptions and recordings known to Stravinsky at the time of the composition of his new ballet. This ethnographic material was certainly essential to the composer's concept of the work. For example, recordings of peasants singing several different songs simultaneously correspond to the layered techniques of *Petrouchka*'s first tableau. See Taruskin, *Stravinsky and the Russian Traditions*, vol. 1, 722–35.

21. The following description is based on *Paris Dances Diaghilev*, a video of performances of *Petrouchka*, *Les Noces*, and other works by the Paris Opera Ballet, filmed in 1990 and commercially available through the Electra Nonesuch Dance Collection. Its value lies in the restoration of Fokine's original choreography and Benois's scenery and costumes, as restaged by Nicholas Beriosoff. Michel Tabachnik conducts the Paris Opera Orchestra. Other more recent DVD and video performances are available, including *Tribute to Nijinsky* (1998), from Warner Home Video, and *The Magic of Russian Ballet* (2004), from Philips.

22. Garafola, *Diaghilev's Ballets Russes*, 22.

23. Fokine, *Memoirs*, 189–91. How successful he was in individualizing the characters and dances is arguable. See Tim Scholl's essay "Fokine's *Petrushka*," in Wachtel, ed., *Petrushka: Sources and Contexts*, 47: "[Fokine's] group dances are . . . staged as unison events. Nurses and coachmen enter the stage, identically dressed, and dance identical steps."

24. Janet Kennedy argues that once Fokine became involved with the production toward the end of the process "he was given considerable latitude in creating the three main characters." See her essay "Shrovetide Revelry: Alexandre Benois's Contribution to *Petrushka*," in Wachtel, ed., *Petrushka: Sources and Contexts*, 54. But one wonders. Stravinsky and Diaghilev were already at odds with Fokine's inflated ego, and though Fokine implied that he was given the scenario as Stravinsky and Benois were developing the story, the truth is that he received it only after its completion. He clearly played a much lesser role in the evolution of *Petrouchka* than he had in that of *The Firebird*. Certainly he was ultimately responsible for the gestures that came to define the principal characters, especially Nijinsky's Petrouchka, but one must be wary of thinking of him as a genuine collaborator. As Fokine himself commented, "The 'freedom from Fokine' movement had already begun." *Memoirs*, 202.

25. Asaf'yev, *A Book about Stravinsky*, 23. The prescient author saw the ballet as a portent. "In order to give music the capability and the strength to express a new living content, in order to give it back its basic energies, one had first to pull out by the roots the choking weeds of academic dogma that flourished in a culture of security and prosperity and self-satisfied Philistinism. That Stravinsky did, and he thereby opened the way directly to *Sacre*" (23). Indeed in 1929, the year in which Asaf'yev's book was published in Leningrad, Boris de Schloezer (in his own *Igor Stravinsky*, Paris: Éditions Claude Aveline) similarly remarked that one should consider *Petrouchka* rather than *The Rite of Spring* as the truly revolutionary

work that set Stravinsky on a new course. Understandably, it was the ballet's unprecedented, jagged rhythms and dissonantly layered tunes that so appalled the highly respected humanist and dance critic Akim Volynsky: "Torrents of aural and visual impulses flow between two equally low levels of musical sensation. . . . Added to these shortcomings . . . is a kind of malleability of the melodic design that the frivolous spurts and disruptive jolts of certain poorly coordinated motifs invariably violate." Akim Volynsky, *Ballet's Magic Kingdom: Selected Writings on Dance in Russia, 1911–1925*, trans. and ed. Stanley J. Rabinowitz (New Haven: Yale University Press, 2008), 74.

26. Bronislava Nijinska danced the role of the street dancer at the premiere. Fokine choreographed the part specifically for her, asking, "Do you know any tricks? Can you do the splits and whirl around on one leg while holding the other foot stiffly, high in the air?" as Nijinska recalled in her memoirs. Moreover, she based her movements upon a character from an earlier Petipa ballet that had found favor with Benois and other members of *Mir iskusstva*. "I started to imitate Mathilda Kshessinska, her *cabrioles* and her *relevés* on toe from the last act of *Le Talisman*." See Nijinska, *Early Memoirs*, 363. The beating of the triangle proved costly for Stravinsky: he had quoted a popular tune familiar to him entitled "Elle avait un' jambe en bois" ("She had a wooden leg"), the composer of which, Émile Spencer, would thereafter collect royalties for it on the grounds that Stravinsky had violated his copyright.

27. Lieven, *The Birth of the Ballets-Russes*, 137.

28. For a useful summary of these folk song sources, see Taruskin's essay "Stravinsky's *Petrushka*," in Wachtel, ed., *Petrushka: Sources and Contexts*, 70–71.

29. Stravinsky continues to employ bits and pieces of folk song. For example, much of the music of mm. 9–96 arises from his quotation and transformation of the "Song for St. John's Eve," first transcribed in the 1880s. The piano retains its original prominence in the orchestral score, quoting the tune in full, uncharacteristically, at m. 59. The detail of this unusual folk song is given in Frederick W. Sternfeld's "Some Russian Folk Songs in Stravinsky's *Petrouchka*," reproduced in the Norton Critical Score of the work edited by Charles Hamm, 208–10.

30. See Nijinska, *Early Memoirs*, chapter 47, "The Ballerina Doll in *Petrouchka*," especially 422–26.

31. Kirstein, *Four Centuries of Ballet*, 195.

32. Fokine wrote at length of the music's rhythmic complexity, again declaring vehemently, "I emphasized the total freedom of the composer of the music to express whatever he feels and however he feels it." *Memoirs*, 186. He asserts that he never asked Stravinsky to add or delete measures (as had been the case in *The Firebird*). He could not resist protesting, however, that he wondered if the ballet, which "suffered from mathematics," as he put it, could not have been written with simpler rhythms. "Are all these rhythmical difficulties necessary which the present-day dancer encounters working with modernistic music. If the difficulty is justified by artistic necessity, then of course I cannot deny that it is essential. But is this always the case?"

33. Nijinska, *Early Memoirs*, 373–74.

34. Benois, *Reminiscences*, 337–38.

35. See Scholl, "Fokine's *Petrushka*," in Wachtel, ed., *Petrushka: Sources and Contexts*, 47, for a summary of the unconventional techniques Fokine employed in depicting Petrouchka's character, and his fears. "Petrushka's tendency to quasi-fetal positions violates every principle of the balletic body. . . . Even when Petrushka raises his arms, they are pulled up through the line of the torso, rather than extending outward and upward in an arc."

36. The portrait engendered another conflict between Benois and Diaghilev. The impresario disliked the depiction and requested that Benois revise his conception; but he refused. When Benois missed the dress rehearsal, so the story goes, Diaghilev instructed Bakst to repaint the picture. Benois became enraged. According to Grigoriev, Valentin Serov successfully restored the original, "but all to no purpose." Grigoriev, *The Diaghilev Ballet*, 53–54. In his own *Reminiscences*, Benois denounced Diaghilev's directive as "an unpardonable outrage against me as an artist, and my whole plan for the ballet" (334).

37. Garafola, *Diaghilev's Ballets Russes*, 37.

38. Wachtel, ed., *Petrushka: Sources and Contexts*, 131. The letter also reveals Benois's thinking on the other tableaux.

39. This seems not to have been Stravinsky's original conception, having thought of the Moor as much more dastardly, "a brutal savage monotonously padding up and down the sides of his cell like a caged tiger and occasionally interrupting his pacing with an outburst of vicious snarling." White, *Stravinsky: A Critical Survey*, 36. Benois contended that the "Blackamoor" was an afterthought, but added to "serve as the embodiment of everything senselessly attractive, powerfully masculine and undeservedly triumphant." See Benois, *Reminiscences*, 326.

40. Grigoriev, *The Diaghilev Ballet*, 52.

41. Quoted in White, *Stravinsky: A Critical Survey*, 36. Lieven confirms this, suggesting that Benois conceived the entire scene as an interlude of the sort found in the Russian *guignol* (puppet show), where often two moors would chase each other around the stage with sticks. He eventually substituted the coconut as the object of the on-stage action. "Gradually," writes Lieven, "the religious significance of the coconut took shape, and finally the Blackamoor's fury was invented, his wild desire to discover the secret of his idol, to look inside the nut." Lieven, *The Birth of the Ballets-Russes*, 139–40.

42. Fokine, *Memoirs*, 192.

43. Fokine, *Memoirs*, 186.

44. The melodic material introduced by the cornet four measures into the waltz, and by the flutes sixteen measures later (at the striking key change from E-flat major to E major), derives from folksy waltzes written by the Austrian composer Joseph Lanner in the early 1840s.

45. See the Norton Critical Score, 210–11, for a brief history and the song's translation. The song was a particularly well known one, first published in a Tchaikovsky folk song collection in 1868, but used ten years earlier in Balakirev's 1858 *Overture on Three Russian Themes*.

46. Lincoln Kirstein attributes many of the gestures to Fokine's knowledge of the work of Charles-Louis Didelot, who had been instrumental in establishing ballet techniques in St. Petersburg a hundred years earlier. Didelot had employed native Russian themes in his early ballets such as *The Prisoner of the Caucasus* (1823). He had also employed Persian and Tartar dances for Caterino Cavos's opera *The Firebird* (1815). Kirstein adds, "Earlier Russian-born ballet masters adapted folk steps and arm positions from the provinces—from Christmas or Shrovetide peasant festivals." Kirstein, *Four Centuries of Ballet*, 166. Ivanushka, the principal character from Didelot's 1864 ballet *Koniok Gorbunok* (The Humpbacked Horse) was "the ancestor of the agonized puppet-clown-hero of *Petrouchka*" adds Kirstein.

47. The quoted tune is a Russian love song about a newlywed wife, familiar to many, including Tolstoy, who refers to the song in *War and Peace* (see the essay by Sternfeld in the Norton Critical Score, 211).

48. Lieven contends that Diaghilev had a greater role in some of the staging and choreography than has been suggested. "The coachmen and grooms were Diaghilev's suggestions. He demonstrated to Benois the gestures of drivers beating their hands on their sides to keep themselves warm." Lieven, *The Birth of the Ballets-Russes*, 139.

49. Fokine recalls this as being the most problematic section to choreograph, especially because "the 5/8 count [at Rehearsal 121] is played at a very rapid pace. This was so difficult that my rehearsal changed into a lesson in rhythmics . . . Was this obstacle an absolute necessity to the composer? I doubt it. I believe that Stravinsky could have achieved the same musical result with a more natural rhythm for this dance." Fokine, *Memoirs*, 188.

50. Although there was much discussion of the quizzical ending in the correspondence between Benois and Stravinsky, Benois recorded in his memoirs his reconsideration toward seeing things Stravinsky's way. "The composer reached the height of tragedy in the final few bars expressing Petrouchka's agony, his piteous goodbye to life. To this day I cannot listen to it without the deepest emotion." Benois, *Reminiscences*, 329.

51. Stravinsky and Craft, *Expositions and Developments*, 136–37. The composer added that just as he had conceived of the second tableau's bitonal music as "Petrouchka's insult to the public," so he had wanted the trumpets of the closing measures, also in two keys, "to show that [Petrouchka's] ghost is still insulting the public."

52. Benois, *Reminiscences*, 330.

53. Nijinska, *Early Memoirs*, 374. For a part of the Tugenhold review, see Taruskin, *Stravinsky and the Russian Traditions*, vol. 1, 759–60.

54. Debussy's comments on Stravinsky appear in a letter to Robert Godet. See *Claude Debussy: Correspondance, 1884–1918*, ed. François Lesure (Paris: Hermann, 1993), 296–97. Debussy's letter to Stravinsky (dated April 1912) is reprinted in Stravinsky and Craft, *Stravinsky in Pictures and Documents*, 64.

55. Quoted in Malcolm Brown, "Stravinsky and Prokofiev: Sizing Up the Competition," in Pasler, ed., *Confronting Stravinsky*, 42.

56. Stravinsky and Craft, *Expositions and Developments*, 135.

57. Stravinsky's lengthy epistle has been translated and reprinted in several sources, the most complete version appearing in Taruskin, *Stravinsky and the Russian Traditions*, vol. 2, 972–74.

58. Taruskin, *Stravinsky and the Russian Traditions*, vol. 1, 661.

59. Asaf'yev, *A Book about Stravinsky*, 20.

60. *Souvenir Serge de Diaghileff's Ballet Russe*, 1916.

CHAPTER 4: *The Rite of Spring*

1. Richard Taruskin, "*The Rite* Revisited: The Idea and the Source of Its Scenario," in Edmond Strainchamps and Maria Rika Maniates, eds., *Music and Civilization: Essays in Honor of Paul Henry Lang* (New York: W. W. Norton, 1984), 201.

2. See Shelly C. Berg, *Le Sacre du printemps: Seven Productions from Nijinsky to Martha Graham* (Ann Arbor: UMI Research Press, 1988), 10.

3. Kirstein, *Four Centuries of Ballet*, 206.

4. Modris Eksteins, *Rites of Spring* (Boston: Houghton Mifflin, 1989), xiv.

5. Eksteins, *Rites*, xiv.

6. Maes, *A History of Russian Music*, 228. Not everyone endorsed such a notion. Maes also reports that Jacques Rivière, in reviewing the ballet, worried that Stravinsky's score represented a time when humans were not yet considered as individuals. For more on the Rivière review, see Taruskin, "A Myth of the Twentieth Century: *The Rite of Spring*, the Tradition of the New, and 'The Music Itself,' " *Modernism/Modernity* 2/1 (1995): 15.

7. Lieven, *The Birth of the Ballets-Russes*, 190. The adoption of primitivism by Russian artists of the day stemmed from the country's nineteenth-century embrace of, as Orlando Figes writes, a "Scythian temperament—barbarian and rude, iconoclastic and extreme, lacking the restraint and moderation of the cultivated European citizen." It was an insistence on choosing to be uncivilized, as the author continues in quoting the Pushkin lines "Now temperance is not appropriate, I want to drink like a savage Scythian." See Orlando Figes, *Natasha's Dance: A Cultural History of Russia* (New York: Henry Holt, 2002), 416. Celebration of the rebelliousness of the Scythians to express derision of the West was nothing new; but using the world of dance as a vehicle, employing a Stone Age ballet built upon Roerich's Stone Age paintings and designs, was audacious.

8. Quoted in Taruskin, *Stravinsky and the Russian Traditions*, vol. 1, 849.

9. Kirstein, *Four Centuries of Ballet*, 206.

10. Quoted in Jann Pasler, "Stravinsky and the Apaches," *Musical Times* 123/1672 (January 1982): 403–7. In a letter of July 1911, written while the composer was back in Ustilug, Stravinsky wrote to Florent Schmitt, "I am only playing French music—yours, Debussy, Ravel. It is good for me—you know—a great consolation in our Russian desert."

11. Walsh, *Stravinsky: A Creative Spring*, 185. In the summer of 1912 Stravinsky, Diaghilev, and Nijinsky had visited Benois in Lugano, where the composer played parts of his new score. The music was full of "amazing splendour and originality," Benois wrote, adding, however, that "the only thing that disconcerted me was that the choreography of *Sacre* had been entrusted to someone so inexperienced as Nijinsky." *Reminiscences*, 348. Benois recalls Diaghilev's excitement about this new "primitive" work, although only a year earlier the impresario had attempted to steer the composer away from the project in favor of a collaboration with Bakst on, of all things, Poe's *The Mask of the Red Death*, eventually given to

Cherepnin, but never produced. See Taruskin, *Stravinsky and the Russian Traditions*, vol. 1, 662 n.5.

12. Eksteins, *Rites of Spring*, 39. Lieven, *The Birth of the Ballets-Russes*, 128.

13. Stravinsky, *An Autobiography*, 31.

14. See Eksteins, *Rites of Spring*, 39–40. The idea of regeneration and rebirth, Eksteins remarks, was very much in the minds of modernists at the turn of the century. Moreover, the youth of the victim was a necessary condition for the sacrifice.

15. Letter of December 15, 1912, from Clarens. This missive appears in many sources. An easily accessible collection of Stravinsky's letters to Roerich and Findeizen may be found in appendix 2 of the Boosey and Hawkes facsimile edition of the sketches for the ballet. See Igor Stravinsky, *The Rite of Spring: Sketches, 1911–1913* (London: Boosey and Hawkes, 1969). For the letter to Findeizen, see appendix 2, 32.

16. In *Natasha's Dance*, Figes questions the matter of prehistoric sacrifice. "Roerich had found some inconclusive evidence of human sacrifice among the Scythians—a fact he publicized in 1898" (288). The scenario adopted pagan rituals to bolster the prospect of human sacrifice, but as Figes continues, this "change was also based on the findings of folklorists such as Alexander Afanasiev, who had linked these vernal cults with sacrificial rituals involving maiden girls." Garafola remarks that only "certain Aztec maize rituals specifically called for the sacrifice of a young girl." See *Diaghilev's Ballets Russes*, 426–27 n.58, for a brief summary of ancient Mexican mythology as compared to Slavic rites.

17. Stephen Walsh suggests that the research Stravinsky undertook while deciding upon the texts used for both of these pieces may have been germinal in his continued thinking about *The Rite*, at least in terms of the scenario, especially given some of the symbolist references that deal with rituals including fertility and sacrifice. Walsh references Lawrence Morton, who suggested that while working on these vocal pieces Stravinsky encountered the poetry of Gorodetsky, which included three stories of "Yarilo." It was to him that a young maiden would be sacrificed, according to Gorodetsky's verse. See Walsh, *The Music of Stravinsky* (London: Routledge, 1988), 34. Visions of sacrifice and propitiation were ubiquitous at the time, and one cannot determine from where, exactly, Stravinsky drew his initial inspiration.

18. Letter to Findeizen of December 15, 1912, in Stravinsky, *The Rite of Spring: Sketches*, appendix 2, 33.

19. Figes, *Natasha's Dance*, 279.

20. Roerich's scenario formed part of his essay "Joy in Art," which appeared in the *European Courier*, a well-respected Russian journal. See Taruskin, *Stravinsky and the Russian Traditions*, vol.1, 861, for a fuller quotation of Roerich's text.

21. The interview appears in several places, including Nijinska's account of it in *Early Memoirs*, 448–49, where she provides a fuller record of Roerich's relationship with her brother. Nijinska claims that the idea of a "Danse sacrale" was Roerich's point of departure. His influence appears to have touched Nijinsky particularly: "Roerich's art inspires me as much as Stravinsky's powerful music. . . . Roerich has talked to me at length about his paintings in this series that he describes as the awakening of the spirit of primeval man. In *Sacre* I want to emulate this spirit of the prehistoric Slavs." What becomes clear is that regardless of which artist hit upon the idea first, both contributed equally to the project.

22. As usual, Diaghilev bristled at being kept in the dark. In his letter to Roerich, Stravinsky comments that Diaghilev has already asked him for a new work. "I said I was writing one which, for the moment, I did not wish to talk about, and this touched off an explosion, as I might have guessed. 'What? You keep secrets from me, I who do my utmost for you all?' " Stravinsky, *The Rite of Spring: Sketches*, appendix 2, 27.

23. Monteux's description appears in several texts, including Minna Lederman, ed., *Stravinsky in the Theatre* (New York: Da Capo Press, 1948), 128–29. For a fuller version of Monteux's account, in which he remembers fearing that "Stravinsky will surely burst, or have a syncope," so impassioned was his piano playing, see Doris Monteux, *It's All in the Music: The Life and Work of Pierre Monteux* (London: William Kimber, 1965), 90–92. See also the interview with Errol Addison in Drummond, *Speaking of Diaghilev*, 202. Addison danced in the

premiere of Massine's 1920 production of *The Rite*. His recollection of many years later chimes with Monteux's description of Stravinsky's piano playing: "Stravinsky used to play the piano for rehearsals, and he broke four pianos in one week."

24. Claude Debussy, *Debussy Letters*, trans. Roger Nichols, ed. François Lesure and Roger Nichols (Cambridge, Mass.: Harvard University Press, 1987), 265. Although Debussy attended rehearsals of *The Rite* and complimented the composer, some accounts record an unflattering reaction. On May 29, 1913, the day of the premiere (exactly one year after Stravinsky had attended the premiere of *L'Après-midi d'un faune*), Debussy, who had attended the performance, wrote to his friend the composer André Caplet, "*Le sacre du printemps* is extraordinarily wild . . . As you might say, it is primitive music with all the modern conveniences!" (Debussy, *Debussy Letters*, 241). Even so, as Richard Buckle contends, "Debussy doubtless preferred Nijinsky's work for *Le Sacre* to his choreography for *L'Après-midi* and *Jeux*, which he detested." Buckle, *Nijinsky* (New York: Simon and Schuster, 1971), 282. The four-hand version is much more than a workaday piano reduction. Moreover, it was used in rehearsals for the premiere— not so uncommon for Stravinsky's ballets. Often the dancers would not hear the orchestral version until a few days before the final rehearsal. Since virtually every page of the sketchbook for the ballet exposes the work's pianistic roots, performances of the four-hand version (of which there are several recordings) are revealing, providing at least some approximation to the bare-bones sound Stravinsky heard as the composition evolved.

25. Benois, *Reminiscences* 347.

26. Stravinsky, *The Rite of Spring: Sketches*, appendix 2, 32.

27. *Le Figaro*, May 17, 1913. Several abbreviated versions of the scenario exist, including two by Roerich.

28. Stravinsky and Craft, *Expositions and Developments*, 147–48.

29. The musical material for the ballet had mostly been sketched by November 1912 (although details continued to be added through the end of March 1913), as Stravinsky triumphantly wrote in red and blue upon the manuscript, noting that he had an "unbearable toothache." For those interested in tracing the compositional process, there is no better source that the nearly one hundred sketch pages beautifully reprinted in the facsimile published by Boosey and Hawkes in 1969, accompanied by Robert Craft's illuminating commentary. See Stravinsky, *The Rite of Spring: Sketches*.

30. Stravinsky, *An Autobiography*, 5. Stravinsky and Craft, *Expositions and Developments*, 47.

31. For a discussion of the chord's significance, see David J. Code, "The Synthesis of Rhythms: Form, Ideology, and the 'Augurs of Spring,'" *Journal of Musicology* 24/1 (Winter 2007): 112–66.

32. Pierre Boulez, *Notes on an Apprenticeship* (New York: Alfred A. Knopf, 1968), 73–75. "What most astonishes the listener," Boulez writes, "is the massiveness of those repeated chords, of those scarcely carried melodic cells; nonetheless, it is in them that there is manifest in the highest degree Stravinsky's inventiveness, difficult to imagine in 1913, and unequaled during the following twenty-five or thirty years."

33. Kirstein, *Dance*, 297.

34. In his commentary to the sketches, Craft suggests that the arpeggiation of this chord, notated higher on the same sketch page than the chord itself, probably came first; but this is questionable. When the composer was interviewed for the 1965 CBS film *Portrait of Stravinsky*, he spoke of working at the keyboard all of the time, and discovering the "Augurs" sonority "as a rather new chord; but what was really new was the accents—and that is the foundation of the whole piece." Stravinsky's sketches often reveal that the first notes notated at the top of a page were not necessarily the first idea notated, and certainly one cannot assume that they were the first thought that occurred to him. Indeed, the fact that the famous chord itself is first notated whole, without any sketches, would argue that this chord came to him as an entity worked out from his improvisation at the keyboard, just as in *Petrouchka*, and that the arpeggiation above it was a more typical fleshing out of a chord, as is often the case in Stravinsky's sketches. Finally, the four measures beginning at m. 9 of the "Augurs of Spring" (the first instance of the ostinato being interrupted) were sketched originally

as two measures only, then at some (unnotated) point the composer added an exact repetition—one more instance of Stravinsky's simply repeating an idea in order to heighten the drama.

35. The Stravinsky archives are full of calendar slips, cocktail napkins, hotel stationery, and notepads upon which Stravinsky would jot down rudimentary ideas—sometimes only a few notes or quickly sketched rhythmic thoughts. The majority of these embryonic ideas are either developed in the piece upon which the composer was currently working or filed away to be used in a later opus.

36. See the discussion in Peter Hill's *Stravinsky: The Rite of Spring* (Cambridge: Cambridge University Press, 2000), 20–21, where it is argued that the "Ritual Action" was indeed the original sacrificial dance.

37. Stravinsky and Craft, *Memories and Commentaries*, 98. While the melody itself has achieved fame on account of its unusual register (once thought unplayable), Boulez argues that it is its rhythmic disposition that sounds the first signal of Stravinsky's unique compositional approach. See Boulez, *Notes on an Apprenticeship*, 80, for an example of that author's dissection of the work's symmetrical and asymmetrical rhythmic structure.

38. See Lawrence Morton, "Footnotes to Stravinsky Studies: 'Le Sacre du printemps,' " *Tempo* 128 (1979): 9–16; and Richard Taruskin, "Russian Folk Melodies in *The Rite of Spring*," *Journal of the American Musicological Society* 33 (1980): 501–43. See also Taruskin, *Stravinsky and the Russian Traditions*, vol. 1, chapter 12, "The Great Fusion," 849–966, for a discussion of the composer's musical sources and of the varied techniques he used (truncations, repetitions, extensions, interpolations, and so on) in transforming those sources rhythmically and otherwise.

39. Given the numerous documents attesting to the work's theatrical and choreographic roots—established in considerable detail long before the first sheet of manuscript paper was penned—the composer's disavowals in the years following the 1913 premiere are disingenuous. In 1920 he claimed that the music had come first: "Be aware that this idea comes from the music and not the music from the idea. I wrote a work that was architectonic, not anecdotal" (an interview with Michel Georges-Michel entitled "Les Deux *Sacre du printemps*," *Comoedia*, December 11, 1920). But the not-so-hidden agenda here was to distance himself from Nijinsky's original choreography in favor of Massine's new production, premiered four days after his remarks were published. An "enlightened Massine," Stravinsky commented, heard *The Rite* as a concert work. "Thus from the first he perceived that, far from being descriptive, the music was an 'objective construction,' " and that *The Rite* "exists as a piece of music, first and last." By the time of his later conversation books with Robert Craft, Stravinsky had dismissed Massine's choreography too, which in retrospect seemed "too gymnastic and Dalcrozean to please me. I realized then [in 1920] that I prefer *Le Sacre* as a concert piece." Stravinsky and Craft, *Expositions and Developments*, 144. Yet when the later *Themes and Conclusions* was published, readers were encouraged to study the aforementioned Boosey and Hawkes facsimile of his sketchbook, since its appendix 3 reprinted his "measure-by-measure description of the original choreography," a document that now "makes possible the recreation of the ballet as it was conceived." And further, "What better excuse could be found than the chance to revive the Nijinsky original, for the first time since 1913? I would come back to see that myself." Igor Stravinsky and Robert Craft, *Themes and Conclusions* (Berkeley: University of California Press, 1982), 218. Jerome Robbins approached Stravinsky in early 1960, asking permission to mount a new production for the Royal Theater in Copenhagen, although nothing came of this proposal. See Joseph, *Stravinsky Inside Out*, 207–8. Craft remarks that when the 1972 Stravinsky Festival of the New York City Ballet was being planned, Robbins "momentarily considered" mounting the ballet, splitting the choreography with Balanchine. According to Craft, "Balanchine believed that *The Rite* should be heard and not seen." Craft, "*The Rite*: Counterpoint and Choreography," *Musical Times* 129/1742 (April 1988): 171. Yet according to Barbara Horgan, Balanchine's close assistant, the choreographer—contrary to his public stance—wished to stage the four-hand version in the late 1960s. Even earlier, Stravinsky's unedited correspondence reveals that a remounting of *The Rite* was planned in the 1950s, with Picasso

and Pavel Tchelitchev as the desired designers. See Charles M. Joseph, *Stravinsky and Balanchine: A Journey of Invention* (New Haven: Yale University Press, 2002), 367 n.10.

40. "Henri Postel du Mas interviews Stravinsky, 1913," *Gil Blas* 25 (June 4, 1913): 1, reprinted in Thomas Kelly, *First Nights* (New Haven: Yale University Press, 2000), 329. Stravinsky's letter to Steinberg of July 3, 1913, is reprinted in Stravinsky and Craft, *Stravinsky in Pictures and Documents*, 102.

41. C. Stanley Wise, "Impressions of Igor Stravinsky," *Musical Quarterly* 2/2 (April 1916): 251.

42. Stravinsky, *An Autobiography*, 48.

43. Stravinsky and Craft, *Memories and Commentaries*, 37.

44. Jean Cocteau, *Le Coq et l'arlequin* (Paris: Éditions de la Sirène, 1918), reprinted in Kelly, *First Nights*, 325, as are many of the reviews at the premiere.

45. Kirstein, *Four Centuries of Ballet*, 198. And as Kirstein further observed, perhaps with an eye toward Nijinsky's approach to *The Rite*, "Returning instinctively to the sacral birth of theater, he anticipated further uncharted development—dance in itself, no longer diverting, but ritualized."

46. Stravinsky's letter to his mother is dated April 19, 1912, and reprinted in Richard Buckle, *Diaghilev* (New York: Atheneum, 1979), 219–20.

47. By 1910 the Dalcrozean system had become immensely popular, to the point of being viewed as a remedy capable of curing almost any rhythmic affliction. Its "arithmetical" techniques were immediately applied to *Jeux*. Debussy was appalled: "I hold Monsieur Dalcroze to be one of the worst enemies of music! You can imagine what havoc his method has caused in the soul of this wild young Nijinsky." See Edward Lockspeiser, *Debussy: His Life and Mind*, 2 vols. (Cambridge: Cambridge University Press, 1978), vol. 2, 171–72. Likewise, the method's imposition of rigidly applied counting upon *The Rite*'s choreography at first stirred only consternation. Rambert offered three classes to the dancers, who, already completely flummoxed by Stravinsky's score and perhaps harboring resentment over Diaghilev's indifference to Fokine's resignation, boycotted the instruction. These classically trained dancers took umbrage with Rambert (a teacher rather than a performer, they protested), threatening to leave the company, though Rambert's patience ultimately eased some of their anxiety. Kirstein insists that the system armed Nijinsky with a "weapon without which he could not have achieved his masterpiece." See Kirstein, *Dance*, 288. But Stravinsky, like Debussy, found the use of such a mechanical technique absurd, in that it gave the dancers only a perfunctory, one-dimensional understanding of his music.

48. Rambert's comment is recorded in Tony Palmer's 1982 film documentary *Once at a Border*. Both Sokolova's and Bourman's recollections are reprinted in Kelly, *First Nights*, 278–79. Sokolova's memories of dancing the Chosen One ("the longest, the most exhausting, and the most difficult solo dance of all ballets") for the Massine version are also recorded in her memoirs, *Dancing for Diaghilev* (1960), and reprinted in Robert Gottlieb, ed., *Reading Dance* (New York: Pantheon Books, 2008), 1060–62: "With my eyes fixed on a red 'Exit' light at the back of the theatre, without allowing them to blink, I lived the role of the Chosen Virgin of the Sun, completely spellbound in the part I was playing. As the huge group moved back to the count of twenty, I knew the moment had arrived, when with one upward beat of the conductor my ordeal was to begin."

49. The telegrams quoted are from the archives of the Paul Sacher Stiftung and reprinted in Craft, *Stravinsky: Selected Correspondence*, vol. 2, 4–5. The pianola was often used by the Ballets Russes in rehearsals.

50. See Stravinsky, *The Rite of Spring: Sketches*, appendix 3, 35–43, for Stravinsky's many directions. No doubt they were originally intended as a guide for Nijinsky. Among numerous specific comments for the "Sacrificial Dance," the composer simply advises, "The rhythm and phrasing of the choreography are much too complex for verbal description."

51. Nijinska, *Early Memoirs*, 449–50.

52. Stravinsky, *An Autobiography*, 41.

53. See Nijinska, *Early Memoirs*, 449–50. Tony Palmer interviewed Rambert not long before she died. Her memories have been preserved in several interviews, both in print and on film. John Drummond's *Speaking of Diaghilev*, for example, places the rehearsal with Stravinsky in

Budapest, where Stravinsky waged an "epic battle" with Nijinsky over tempo (111). Moreover, she recalls that Diaghilev attempted to prepare the company for Stravinsky's newest ballet, especially in light of the troupe's earlier reluctance to accept Nijinsky's choreography to the two Debussy ballets. "He tried to prepare them. It didn't work very well. I think they hated [The Rite] till the last day, to the last rehearsal, to the last performance."

54. Sally Banes, *Dancing Women* (London: Routledge, 1998), 103–4. See Banes's full discussion of *The Rite of Spring* (100–08), where she contends that "the Chosen One dances herself to death, thus metaphorically marrying Yarilo, the sun god, ruler of spring."

55. The composer claimed that Diaghilev encouraged a huge orchestra of around one hundred players, all crammed into the pit. The orchestration of *The Rite* merits a study of its own, but even a quick glance reveals the constant doubling and tripling of winds, four bassoons, two contrabassoons, bass clarinet, and eight horns, to say nothing of the extraordinarily large percussion section.

56. Grigoriev, *The Diaghilev Ballet*, 83–84.

57. Taken from *Montjoie!* May 29, 1913. Stravinsky later remarked that the interview appeared "in the form of a pronouncement on the *Sacre*, at once grandiloquent and naïve, and, to my great astonishment, signed with my name." *An Autobiography*, 49. Still, the composer's eventual repudiation of the story, which in retrospect surely embarrassed him given its programmatic description of the music, was nothing more than one of numerous attempts to eradicate his earlier narratives on *The Rite*, disavowing its existence as a ballet in favor of its independent standing as a symphonic work. It is true that Stravinsky took exception to the translation of his words, but there is no reason to believe that the content of his message was misinterpreted.

58. See Clement Crisp, "Marie Rambert and Nijinsky's *Le Sacre du printemps*," *Dance Research* 19/1 (Summer 2001): 3–10.

59. Levinson's comments first appeared in "Stravinsky and the Dance," *Theater Arts Monthly* 8 (1924): 741–54. Stravinsky's comment was included in the 1966 film *Portrait of Stravinsky*, directed and produced by David Oppenheim for CBS. Surely the composer was right in gauging the audience's expectation. Moreover, there may simply have been too much information for them to process. The score itself was immensely foreign; the dancing no less so. Separately, the techniques introduced in each would have approached a perceptual overload; together, they were overwhelming. "The chief reason for the thorny theatrical path of *The Rite of Spring*," suggested Boris M. Yarustovsky, was "the novelty of its music, its complex world of sound [which] imperiously demanded the concentrated, undivided attention of the listeners for the full transmittal of its thought and the perception of the purely musical essence of the work. The scenic and choreographic images distracted the listeners from the new and unfamiliar sound configurations." Yarustovsky's comment is reprinted in the foreword to the Dover Miniature Score (Mineola, N.Y.: Dover Publications, 1989), viii.

60. Grigoriev, *The Diaghilev Ballet*, 83. There is no shortage of summary accounts of the "riot." There are many for example, in Buckle's *Nijinsky*, Berg's *Le Sacre du printemps*, Hill's *Stravinsky: The Rite of Spring*, and Kelly's *First Nights*.

61. Jean Cocteau, *Le Coq et l'arlequin*, 87–96. Cocteau's complete review of the performance is reprinted in Kelly, *First Nights*, 324–26.

62. In reviewing one of the London performances, Edwin Evans—admittedly an advocate for Stravinsky's work—remarked that "Nijinsky's new principles of choreography have found acceptance in some influential quarters, and rejection in some others, but there is an increasing tendency to treat them with the respect they deserve, as representing a courageous effort to free the ballet from its perennial taint of mere conventional prettiness." Edwin Evans, "Saison Russe," *Outlook*, July 26, 1913: 128.

63. See Taruskin, *Stravinsky and the Russian Traditions*, vol. 2, 1006–33, for a summary of reactions both to the Paris performance and to subsequent performances of the orchestral score in both Moscow and St. Petersburg in 1914.

64. See Vicente García-Márquez, *Massine: A Biography* (New York: Alfred A. Knopf, 1995), 154–63, for a brief account of the ballet's revival. For a more complete reconstruction, see Berg, *Le Sacre du printemps*, 63–87.

65. For a complete listing of the many choreographic settings of *The Rite*, see "Stravinsky and the Global Dancer," a data source complied by Stephanie Jordan at Roehampton University and discussed in chapter 9. For Balanchine's comment on Béjart's version, see Suzanne Levy, "*The Rite of Spring* at Seventy-Five," *Dance Research Journal* 19/2 (Winter 1987–88): 52–54.

66. A blaze of critical reviews greeted Hodson's research, led by Robert Craft's aforementioned article "*The Rite*: Counterpoint and Choreography." For a complete tracking of the reconstruction process, see Hodson, *Nijinsky's Crime against Grace: Reconstruction Score of the Original Choreography for "Le Sacre du printemps"* (Stuyvesant, N.Y.: Pendragon Press, 1996). Hodson details the lengths she and Roerich scholar Kenneth Archer went to authenticate their efforts. Hodson interviewed Rambert and Massine, traveled the globe in search of primary sources, and, most importantly, studied the four-hand piano score that appeared in 1967, which included Stravinsky's aforementioned choreographic notations. After the 1987 revival by the Joffrey Ballet, Craft presented Hodson with "a photocopy of Stravinsky's score, which showed the composer's handwritten markings, but they did not alter the information already available" (Hodson, *Nijinsky's Crime*, xxi). Added to this was information gleaned from Rambert's own annotated piano score, a source of contention addressed by Craft. Hodson reprints the four-hand score together with the notes of Stravinsky and Rambert, as well as several of Valentine Gross-Hugo's sketches, and other relevant photographs or drawings. For a useful review of the 1987 dance conference in New York that addressed the reconstruction (a symposium in which both Craft and Hodson participated), see Levy, "*The Rite of Spring* at Seventy-Five." Twenty-two years after the Joffrey revival, Hodson and Archer's reconstruction of the ballet was released on DVD in 2009, entitled *Stravinsky and the Ballets Russes: "Le Sacre du printemps," "The Firebird."* Both ballets were recorded live at the Maryinsky Theatre in 2008 conducted by Valery Gergiev, *The Firebird* in the staging of Isabelle Fokine and Andris Liepa, and the dancers including Alexandra Iosifidi as the Chosen One. A documentary interview with Millicent Hodson and Kenneth Archer is included as part of the DVD.

67. See Timothy Ferris, "*Voyager's* Music," in Carl Sagan et al., *Murmurs of Earth: The "Voyager" Interstellar Record* (New York: Random House, 1978), 187. Ferris comments that the inclusion of *The Rite's* famous concluding section was meant to represent "a raid by a keen intellect upon a zone of imagination that developed when our ancestors lived in societies resembling those we now elect to call primitive."

68. *Musical Times* 54/846 (August 1913): 535.

CHAPTER 5: A New Approach—A New Collaboration

1. Grigoriev, *The Diaghilev Ballet*, 85.

2. A furious Diaghilev had dismissed Nijinsky after his marriage in 1913 to Romola de Pulszky; but he was reinstated for the American tour as a result of the contractual conditions set by the financier Otto Kahn, whose backing of the tour was required.

3. From the composer's essay "Some Ideas about My Octuor," *The Arts*, January 1924, reprinted in, among other places, Eric Walter White, *Stravinsky: The Composer and His Works* (Berkeley: University of California Press, 1966), 574–77.

4. Many of the works composed during the Swiss years do not conveniently fit into a conventional ballet form. They involve dancing, sometimes singing, and always some extent of dramatic action. Indeed, it is Stravinsky's instinctual need to question existing musical paradigms, to modify traditional forms to fit his creative needs, that stands as one of the hallmarks of his compositional career. These compositions, as well as other hybrid works from later years, are discussed in chapter 8. Even *Pulcinella*, often thought of as a ballet, includes singers, and as Stravinsky himself remarked is not so much a ballet as an *action dansante*. Consequently, it too is addressed in chapter 8.

5. The comment is cited by Yuri Slonimsky in an interview that was later reprinted in Francis Mason, *I Remember Balanchine* (New York: Doubleday, 1991), 74.

6. Valois's comments are reprinted in Drummond, *Speaking of Diaghilev*, 224–25.

7. Sketches for the symphonic conversion are held, together with the autograph manuscript, by the Morgan Library in New York. As in the sketches for *The Rite*, Stravinsky often drafts short blocks of material which he then labels (A, B, C, D, etc.). Typically, each is a rhythmic variation of some basic melodic figuration, and these variations are then inserted at various points in a scene. And as for other works, the composer continues to make alterations to the autograph manuscript, presumed to be the work's final version.

8. Stravinsky's scenario mainly excerpts quotations from Andersen's original story, and was included in the piano reduction published by Éditions Russes de Musique (later, Boosey and Hawkes). The complete scenario appears in White, *Stravinsky: The Composer and His Works*, 230.

9. For the composer's comments, see his *Autobiography*, 80.

10. Simon Volkov, *Balanchine's Tchaikovsky* (New York: Simon and Schuster, 1985), 165–66.

11. An informative documentation of Dame Alicia's recollections is captured in a 1995 video-tape (that is, made seventy years after the premiere) filmed in London, wherein a still nimble Markova recreates several excerpts of *Le Chant* for Iohna Loots, a young South African balle-rina from the Royal Ballet School. This reconstruction is part of a series of indispensable videotapes being compiled by the George Balanchine Foundation, Archive of Lost Choreography. These videos are accessible in several major research library repositories, including the Dance Collection at Lincoln Center, the Harvard Theatre Collection, the John F. Kennedy Center, and the Music Division, Library of Congress.

12. As Nicolas Nabokov suggests, it was not only the composer's "religious convictions" that turned him away from ballet. Rather, ballet imposed "certain theatrical demands," obligating the composer to write "danceable" music, and to some degree at least, submit to the "formal requirements of the choreographic art." The fact is, Stravinsky may well have declined further ballet commissions had the musically attuned Balanchine not arrived on the scene in the mid 1920s. See Nicolas Nabokov, "Stravinsky and the Drama," in Lederman, ed., *Stravinsky in the Theatre*, 109.

13. Denys Sutton, *André Derain* (London: Phaidon Press, 1959), 32.

14. Stravinsky, *An Autobiography*, 135.

15. "The Dance Element in Stravinsky's Music," *Dance Index* 6 (1947), reprinted in Lederman, ed., *Stravinsky in the Theatre*, 81–82.

16. Stravinsky, *An Autobiography*, 135.

17. Soulima's memories are recorded on an audiotape made by Thor E. Wood in 1977, now held by the Dance Collection of the New York Public Library Performing Arts Division.

18. Mark P. O. Morford and Robert J. Lenardon, *Classical Mythology* (White Plains, N.Y.: Longman, 1991), 209.

19. We know little of Balanchine's involvement in these ballets. In *The Triumph of Neptune*, for instance, the dancing was described as "straightforward," "poetical," and "graceful" without a trace of modernism. (Balanchine actually danced in the production as the black character "Snowball," injuring his knee in a rehearsal and thereby hastening the end of his dancing career.) See Edward Ricco, "The Sitwells at the Ballet," *Ballet Review* 6/1 (1977–78): 80–88.

20. Nicolas Nabokov, "Diaghilev and Music," originally published in his *Old Friends and New Music* (Boston: Little, Brown, 1951), and reprinted in Gottlieb, ed., *Reading Dance*, 511.

21. Morford and Lenardon, *Classical Mythology*, 41–42. Balanchine's remarks appear in George Balanchine and Francis Mason, *101 Stories of the Great Ballets* (New York: Doubleday, 1989), 14. A fuller synopsis of the ballet's scenario appears on pp. 11–16.

22. Jonathan Cross reinforces the notion that "Stravinsky had nothing to do with the Washington production." See his "Stravinsky's Theatres," in Cross, ed., *The Cambridge Companion to Stravinsky* (Cambridge: Cambridge University Press, 2003), 301 n.39. But this is misleading. In letter after letter to those responsible for producing the ballet at the Library of Congress, Stravinsky, quite insistently, directs virtually every facet, from the actual staging of the work, to details of costuming.

23. The list of attendees at the premiere reads like a *Who's Who* of the worlds of music and soci-etal privilege: it includes Amy Beach, Edward W. Bok, Aaron Copland, Howard Hanson,

Alfred A. Knopf, H. L. Mencken, Fritz Reiner, Wallingford Riegger, Oscar Sonneck, and Edgar Varèse.

24. The comments of Engel, Bolm, and Coolidge are included in a file marked "Old Correspondence" in the Library of Congress Music Division. Bolm seemed particularly concerned about space for the dancers on the small stage. In a letter to Engel of February 8, 1928, he writes, "My reaction to the scenario of Stravinsky's ballet is not so very stimulating. I think it makes it obvious that your stage is too small for more than three [sic] muses," leaving one to wonder if more were considered at an earlier point in the scenario's evolution.

25. As another example of the confusion, orchestral musicians were imported from Philadelphia for the premiere, rehearsing the work with the dancers in the Washington auditorium for the first time the day before the performance.

26. Stravinsky, An Autobiography, 142.

27. While Oedipus is often viewed as a precursor to the ballet, one should consider the aforementioned Sérénade en la for piano as an even earlier model. Much of the orchestral fabric of the ballet's "Pas d'action," Apollo's second variation, and the "Pas de deux" is traceable to the piano writing of the Sérénade, especially the "Romanza" and "Cadenza Finale," where Stravinsky employs staccato accompaniments in the style of Apollo's frequent pizzicati, and constant harmonic streams of thirds and sixths as a textural device. Moreover, the much discussed "polarity" of the work, oscillating around the pitch "la," with frequent excursions to both f and c, is typical of key relationships evident in Apollo. For a specific discussion of polarity in the ballet's concluding "Apothéose," see Arnold Whittall, "Stravinsky in Context," in Cross, ed., The Cambridge Companion to Stravinsky, 50–56.

28. Maureen Carr remarks, "Thus the official collaboration between Balanchine and Stravinsky apparently did not take place until after the completion of the musical score. But it is always possible that they joined forces on Apollo much earlier." Maureen A. Carr, Multiple Masks: Neoclassicism in Stravinsky's Works on Greek Subjects (Lincoln: University of Nebraska Press, 2002), 100. In fact there is no question that Balanchine was involved from January 2, 1927. His active participation in the ensuing months is verified by the collective memories of the composer, Diaghilev, Vera Soudeikine, Soulima Stravinsky, and of course Balanchine himself.

29. "Stravinsky is a great composer," Diaghilev remarked. "To me, however, his best works are those of the beginning, those which he wrote before Pulcinella; I mean Petrouchka, Sacre, Les Noces. This does not imply that I don't . . . adore Apollon." Nabokov, "Diaghilev and Music," in Gottlieb, ed., Reading Dance, 512.

30. The translation appears in, among other places, White, Stravinsky: The Composer and His Works, 342.

31. Arthur Lourié, "Stravinsky's Apollo," The Gamut, August–September 1928: 20–21. Asaf'yev, A Book about Stravinsky, 275.

32. Danilova's 1986 comments about Apollo are reprinted in Gottlieb, ed., Reading Dance, 1002–5.

33. Nancy Reynolds, No Fixed Points: Dance in the Twentieth Century (New Haven: Yale University Press, 2003), 69.

34. Carr's Multiple Masks reprints several sketches from the Paul Sacher Stiftung in Basel.

35. Igor Stravinsky and Robert Craft, Dialogues (Berkeley: University of California Press, 1982), 33.

36. The choice of the Apollonian myth as a ballet scenario has many precedents. The Viennese dancer and choreographer Franz Hilverding (who was in fact a ballet master in St. Petersburg and Moscow from 1758 to 1764) produced Apollon et Daphné, ou Le Retour d'Apollon au Parnasse in 1763. Jean-Georges Noverre presented Apollon et les muses in London in 1782. Charles-Louis Didelot, who studied with Noverre, choreographed two Apollo ballets: Apollon et Daphné (1802) and Apollon et Persée (1803). Moreover, as Tim Scholl remarks, "The iconography of Russian ballet from the middle of the nineteenth century until the Diaghilev period is rich with depictions (and often conflations) of Apollo and le roi soleil. Apollo is the hero of Dve zvedy, the Petipa court spectacle. He appears in the apotheosis of Sleeping Beauty dressed as Louis XIV." Tim Scholl, From Petipa to Balanchine (London: Routledge, 1994), 150–51.

37. Carr reproduces two important "dotted rhythm" sketches predating the Apollo sketchbook, suggesting that the rhythmic pattern of the ballet "could be thought of as growing out of

Oedipus Rex" (*Multiple Masks*, 105–6). This is undoubtedly true, but one must note that this signature rhythmic figure not only appears in the 1927 opera-oratorio, but is in fact the germinating motive of the earlier Concerto for piano and wind instruments, begun in 1923, the opening twenty-three measures of which could not be more Lully-like in directly anticipating the courtly music of *Apollo*.

38. Francis Poulenc, *Moi et mes amis* (Paris: Éditions La Palatine, 1963), 194–95.

39. Though Terpsichore, the Muse of dance, is obviously the center of Apollo's attention, the importance of Calliope should not be underestimated. Some mythologies held Calliope as the real leader of the nine Muses.

40. While Stravinsky's overlaying of the alexandrine is most perceptible in Calliope's variation, his reliance upon versification as the primary means of organizing his fundamental musical materials, in terms of both pitch and rhythm, is evident throughout the ballet. Particularly significant is the composer's division of the twelve fundamental syllables of the alexandrine into various groupings (for example, two groups of six or three groups of four).

41. Stravinsky prepares for this structurally important return three measures earlier (at Rehearsal 100, m. 17) by beginning a final melodic ascent in the violins and cellos.

42. Suki Schorer recalls that when she first danced *Apollo*, Balanchine suggested she "study the flat profile figures in the early black and red terra-cotta vases" at the Metropolitan Museum. "He mentioned that parts of the finale of the ballet were meant to look two-dimensional." See *Suki Schorer on Balanchine Technique* (New York: Alfred A. Knopf, 1999), 14.

43. Dale Harris, "Balanchine: Working with Stravinsky," *Ballet Review* 10/2 (Summer 1982): 19–24.

44. See Carter's review in *Theatre Arts* 21/5 (May 1937): 411.

CHAPTER 6: America

1. Lincoln Kirstein, *Flesh Is Heir* (1932; reprint, Carbondale: Southern Illinois University Press, 1975), 220–21. Several Ballets Russes offshoots tried to fill the void. Numerous monographs survey the aftermath of the company's dissolution. See, for example, Jack Anderson, *The One and Only: The Ballet Russe de Monte Carlo* (New York: Dance Horizons, 1981); Richard Buckle, *In the Wake of Diaghilev* (New York: Holt, Rinehart and Winston, 1982); and Kathrine Sorley Walker, *De Basil's Ballets Russes* (New York: Atheneum, 1983).

2. The letter is held among the Parmenia Migel Eckstrom papers in the Harvard Theatre Collection. Soulima Stravinsky's comments were trimmed from Palmer's biopic *Aspects of Stravinsky*, although the uncut transcript is held by the Paul Sacher Stiftung.

3. Falla's letter is reprinted in Craft, *Stravinsky: Selected Correspondence*, vol. 2, 171.

4. Christopher Isherwood, *Diaries*, vol. 1, *1939–1960*, ed. Katherine Bucknell (New York: HarperCollins, 1996), 763–64.

5. Stravinsky, *An Autobiography*, 146.

6. Maes, *A History of Russian Music*, 292.

7. Nijinska served as artistic director and choreographer for the Ida Rubinstein Ballet from 1928 through 1931, creating a dozen new works. In 1928 alone, she prepared ballets to the music of Ravel, Schubert and Liszt, Stravinsky, Bach, Borodin, and Rimsky-Korsakov.

8. Ida Lvovna Rubinstein, born in 1885, was known as both a dancer and an actress. She was a member of Diaghilev's troupe for two seasons (1909–11), dancing important roles, some of them quite controversial, such as that of Salome. Her appearance as Cleopatra in the 1909 ballet of the same name (as part of Diaghilev's first Parisian season) immediately won praise from the likes of Jean Cocteau, who spoke of her as "penetratingly beautiful" as she stood before a "spellbound audience." In view of her limitations, however, she was cast as a mime more than a dancer, and soon left the Ballets Russes to challenge Diaghilev directly by using her wealth to establish a rival company. She commissioned important works from Debussy, Honegger, Ravel, and, of course, Stravinsky. For a summary article of her career, see Charles S. Mayer, "Ida Rubinstein: A Twentieth-Century Cleopatra," *Dance Research Journal* 20/2 (Winter 1988): 33–51.

9. Grigoriev, *The Diaghilev Ballet*, 249–50.
10. The letter appears in Serge Lifar, *Serge Diaghilev: His Life, His Work, His Legend: An Intimate Biography* (New York: Da Capo Press, 1976).
11. Stravinsky, *An Autobiography*, 147.
12. Reinhart's letter is reprinted in Craft, *Stravinsky: Selected Correspondence*, vol. 2, 165–66.
13. See Stravinsky and Craft, *Expositions and Developments*, 84–85, for Stravinsky's brief and incomplete remarks on the use of his sources.
14. See Lawrence Morton's still useful "Stravinsky and Tchaikovsky: *Le Baiser de la fée*," in Paul Henry Lang, ed., *Stravinsky: A New Appraisal of His Work* (New York: W. W. Norton, 1963). Morton cites fourteen pieces, either solo piano works or works for voice with piano accompaniment, that Stravinsky explicitly uses. He works through the entire ballet, pointing out how Stravinsky remolds Tchaikovsky's materials rather than simply quoting his models. In *Stravinsky and the Russian Traditions*, vol. 2, 1610–18, Taruskin adds a number of citations and references to Morton's catalogue of Tchaikovskyan models.
15. Stravinsky, *An Autobiography*, 148.
16. Parts of Roland-Manuel's letter to Stravinsky, dated November 30, 1928, appear in Robert Craft's essay "La Poétique musicale," in his *Stravinsky: Glimpses of a Life* (New York: St. Martin's Press, 1992), 83–84. Of the critical assessments made of the ballet, perhaps the most interesting is Boris Asaf'yev's. The author did not seem to know quite what to make of Stravinsky's newest neoclassical work. He praises it as being a step better than the "vapid" *Apollo*, suggesting that with the re-embracing of Tchaikovsky Stravinsky might be able to extricate himself from western-styled neoclassicism, which was, in Asaf'yev's estimate, an unfortunate rejection of his roots. While he found Stravinsky's melodic control "dry and listless," with his rediscovery of Russian models he was returning to the fold, and Asaf'yev professes faith "in the infallibility of Stravinsky's instinct, in his sensitiveness, in his presentiments of historical necessity." Asaf'yev, *A Book about Stravinsky*, 278–81.
17. Comments taken from liner notes for a Deutsche Grammophon Recording (2530–537) released in 1975.
18. Stravinsky had long been an admirer of the seventeenth-century French poet and satirist La Fontaine, whose friends included Boileau, Molière, and Racine. His timeless fables were told with a blend of mirth and sardonicism that always appealed to the composer. La Fontaine's experiments with poetic meter, as well as his affection for Plutarch, Horace, and Ovid, endeared him to Stravinsky immediately. The composer's complete comments are reprinted in White, *Stravinsky: The Composer and His Works*, 578–79.
19. The letter to Balanchine dates from June 30, 1936. It is one of only a handful held at the Sacher Stiftung. Stravinsky rarely corresponded with Balanchine, no doubt because the choreographer was notoriously lax about responding to letters.
20. Stravinsky's communications with his publisher B. Schotts Söhne through Willy Strecker make it possible to track the composing process. In September 1936, for example, Stravinsky advises his publisher to add missing notes and changes in instrumentation to previously sent manuscript pages. In October he sends sixty-one new pages to be printed, and by early November he has forwarded the opening pages of the piano score, in which he notes that the titles of "deals" should be substituted for the earlier titles of "tableaux." The last pages of the piano reduction were airmailed on December 15, whereupon Balanchine had his first look at the score he was to choreograph, no doubt studying it at the piano. Strecker's letters are held by the Sacher Stiftung. Some are reprinted in Craft, *Stravinsky: Selected Correspondence*, vol. 3.
21. The score's quotations are numerous, inviting listeners to track Stravinsky's use of both familiar and unfamiliar tunes reminiscent of Johann Strauss, Ravel, Delibes, and others. Responding to a question posed by Craft in *Dialogues*, the composer remarks, "I had a certain taste for Lecocq at the time of *Mavra* and I wrote a *souvenir* of him into a flute melody in *Jeu de cartes*" (117). He goes on to mention that he owned several autograph scores of Alexandre Charles Lecocq (1832–1918), who was known for his operettas. Indeed, Stravinsky's library included a number of operatic scores, many of them containing passages marked by the composer.

22. The essay appears in several anthologies, including Lederman, ed., *Stravinsky in the Theatre*, 136–40.

23. Stravinsky disliked the costuming and décor. Sketches of costume designs by Irene Sharaff (for *Jeu de cartes*), Alice Halicka (*Le Baiser de la fée*), and Stewart Cheney (*Apollon musagète*) are reproduced in Carol J. Oja, ed., *Stravinsky in Modern Music (1924–1946)* (New York: Da Capo Press, 1982), 158–59.

24. Kirstein's comments appear in his *Thirty Years*, 60.

25. Kirstein, *Four Centuries of Ballet*, 33.

26. The translation is provided by White, *Stravinsky: The Composer and His Works*, 399.

27. See Alfred Frankenstein, "Stravinsky in Beverly Hills," *Modern Music* 19/3 (March–April 1942): 172–81.

28. The exchange appeared in an interview originally published in *Intellectual Digest*, June 1972.

29. Reynolds, *No Fixed Points*, 291.

30. Comments made in an interview with Ingolf Dahl, published in a 1957 issue of *Cinema*.

31. John Martin, "City Center Opens Season of Ballet," *New York Times*, September 11, 1944. The earlier 1942 *Circus Polka* had already raised critics' concern about the seriousness of Stravinsky's works in the early 1940s. Was America to blame for encouraging the composer to accept commissions for such folderol? The *Circus Polka* is briefly discussed in chapter 9.

32. See Stravinsky and Craft, *Dialogues*, 48–50, which includes the composer's detailed comments about the music and the scenario.

33. Morton's comments are included in his essay "Incongruity and Faith," in Edwin Corle, ed., *Igor Stravinsky* (New York: Duell, Sloan and Pierce, 1949), 194–95. Rose was unhappy with the score. After its Philadelphia preview, he suggested to Stravinsky that Robert Russell Bennett "retouch" the orchestration, but Stravinsky refused. Consequently, only a brief portion of the score, with the composer's name unmentioned, was included in the New York premiere. Stravinsky never saw the show.

34. Francis A. Coleman, "A Talk with Igor Stravinsky," *Dance Magazine* 19/4 (April 1945): 30.

35. Walsh, *The Music of Stravinsky*, 184.

36. Comments made in an interview with Vivian Perlis on June 25, 1980, published in Perlis, *Copland: 1900 through 1942* (New York: St. Martin's/Marek, 1984), 357.

37. See Nancy Goldner, ed., *The Stravinsky Festival of the New York City Ballet* (New York: The Eakins Press, 1973), 168.

38. An edited version of the script appears in Stravinsky and Craft, *Stravinsky in Pictures and Documents*, 380–81.

39. Interview with Tobi Tobias, January/February 1979. Noguchi's comments are excerpted from the transcript of an audiotape held by the Dance Collection of the New York Public Library Performing Arts Division.

40. Balanchine's remarks were made to Jonathan Cott during the summer of 1982 and recorded in Cott's *Portrait of Mr. B* (New York: The Viking Press, 1984), 144.

41. Stravinsky and Craft, *Themes and Conclusions*, 52. The original sheets are reproduced in Joseph, *Stravinsky and Balanchine*, 194.

42. Translation from Ovid, *The Metamorphoses*, trans. Horace Gregory (New York: Penguin Books, 1958), 275.

43. This final description appears in Balanchine and Mason, *101 Stories of the Great Ballets*, 290. For a discussion of the literary sources used for the ballet, see Carr, *Multiple Masks*. Carr's study also includes a discussion of Stravinsky's compositional sketches.

44. Stravinsky himself refers to the similarities between *Apollo* and *Orpheus* in Stravinsky and Craft, *Dialogues*, 34.

45. Nabokov, *Old Friends and New Music*, 203–4.

46. Balanchine and Mason, *101 Stories of the Great Ballets*, 287.

47. Tobias interview, Dance Collection, New York Public Library Performing Arts Division.

48. Maria Tallchief, *Maria Tallchief: America's Prima Ballerina* (New York: Henry Holt, 1997), 95–96.

49. "Balanchine and the Classic Revival," *Theatre Arts* 31/12 (December 1947): 39.

50. The letter is reprinted in several sources, including Craft, *Stravinsky: Selected Correspondence*, vol. 1, 271.

CHAPTER 7: A Counterpoint of Minds

1. Robert Craft, "A Centenary View, Plus Ten," in his *Stravinsky: Glimpses of a Life*, 16–17. Craft's recollection of Stravinsky's moment of crisis is recorded in his essay "Influence or Assistance?" also in *Stravinsky: Glimpses of a Life*, 39.
2. For the details of what eventually led to Balanchine's ballet *Opus 34*, based on a Schoenberg score, see Robert Craft, "On Stravinsky and Balanchine," in Christopher Ramsey, ed., *Tributes: Celebrating Fifty Years of New York City Ballet* (New York: William Morrow, 1998), 56. The work is discussed further in chapter 9.
3. Kirstein, *Thirty Years*, 135.
4. Stravinsky and Craft, *Conversations*, 25.
5. Stravinsky began arranging works by Gesualdo, including "Illumina nos," in 1956. His reconstruction of Gesualdo's music was published in 1957. It would become part of his *Tres sacrae cantiones*, completed in 1959. See chapter 9 for Balanchine's 1960 choreographing of another of Stravinsky's arrangements of Gesualdo's music, *Monumentum pro Gesualdo di Venosa ad CD annum*.
6. The Sacher Stiftung holds Kirstein's original letter and scenario. In this "draft" sketch, Kirstein envisioned seven sections in a scenario consisting of "a vast ballroom in space, between the stars. Music of the spheres." There was to be a "reception of the gods" with Apollo and Terpsichore, Cupid, Pegasus, Prometheus, Orpheus and Bacchante, Venus and Mars, and Zeus. All of this was to lead "up to the final dance when the previous pavane, rigaudon, menuet, waltz, tarantella, polka, develops under Jerome Robbins as Mercury, into a big jazz finale."
7. Letter of September 25, 1953, to David Adams of Boosey and Hawkes (Paul Sacher Stiftung). In an interview of January 30, 1954, the New Orleans *Times Picayune*, Stravinsky remarked, "I proposed to George Balanchine . . . that he give me carte blanche to do a new ballet (*Agon*) for them. . . . I told him that he had done so well in adjusting dances to symphonies that I would like to write a special symphony with the dance in mind. It is to be a dancing symphony." John Taras, "Stravinsky on Art and Artists," *Dance Magazine* 55/4 (April 1981): 65.
8. Eliot and Stravinsky first met in December 1956, although they had encountered each other's work long before then. They discussed another possible collaboration in the late 1950s (leading ultimately to *The Flood*), but Eliot eventually withdrew.
9. Robert Craft, *The Moment of Existence* (Nashville: Vanderbilt University Press, 1996), 279.
10. See Eliot's "The Beating of the Drum," *The Nation and the Athenaeum*, October 1923: 11–12.
11. Stravinsky retained a copy of Kirstein's letter (now in the Sacher Stiftung) in his private papers.
12. Balanchine and Mason, *101 Stories of the Great Ballets*, 2.
13. Again, the Sacher Stiftung holds Stravinsky's letters to Kirstein. Edited versions of this and other letters appear in Craft, *Stravinsky: Selected Correspondence*, vol. 1, 287.
14. For a discussion of the composer's attraction to canonic techniques, see Glenn Watkins, "The Canon and Stravinsky's Late Style," in Pasler, ed., *Confronting Stravinsky*, 217–46.
15. Kirstein offers a similar account of the bransle's history, suggesting that the dance was "linked to the satyr-dance of 'Sikinnis.' They were also know as 'Brawls'; thus our word for rough-house." He also categorizes specific bransles, as did Wildeblood. The "Bransle gai" was danced by the "young marrieds," and the Burgundy Bransles were danced by "youths and maidens . . . from side to side in double-time, like the others, only faster." See Kirstein, *Dance*, 159. The whole of chapter 9, "The Ballet Comique and the Ballet de Cour" (148–67), is useful for understanding the courtly backdrop of *Agon*'s first and second "Pas de Trois." The grouping of bransles into a suite (consisting of four, five, or more dances) was common as early as the sixteenth century.
16. Mersenne, *Harmonie universelle, contenant la théorie et la pratique de la musique*. This translation by Roger E. Chapman is taken from Betty Bang Mather, *Dance Rhythms of the French Baroque* (Bloomington: Indiana University Press, 1987), 37.

17. The sketch appears in Stravinsky and Craft, *Stravinsky in Pictures and Documents*, 429. Vera Stravinsky's comments were made in an audiotape interview with Genevieve Oswald recorded on June 14, 1976, now held by the Dance Collection in the New York Public Library Performing Arts Division.

18. Robert Craft contends that Balanchine actually drew the stick figures; but it makes little difference since the two men worked closely together, trading ideas as their working sessions evolved. See Robert Craft, *Down a Path of Wonder* (Norfolk: Naxos Books, 2006), 139.

19. Balanchine and Mason, *101 Stories of the Great Ballets*, 3.

20. See Irene Alm, "Stravinsky, Balanchine, and *Agon*: An Analysis Based on the Collaborative Process," *Journal of Musicology* 7/2 (Spring 1989): 254–69, for a discussion of the document. A beautiful reproduction is included in Ramsey, ed., *Tributes*, 57.

21. Other sketches in the Basel archives detail the evolution of the divisions of the "Pas de deux"—virtually all of them based upon the same set and developmental procedures. For a more complete analysis of the composer's pitch usage in the "Pas de deux," see van den Toorn, *The Music of Igor Stravinsky*, 408–14.

22. For an extended discussion of *Agon*'s temporal divisions, see Jonathan D. Kramer, "Discontinuity and Proportion in the Music of Stravinsky," in Pasler, ed., *Confronting Stravinsky*, 174–95.

23. Stravinsky marks "1st hexachord and 2nd hexachord" in his score and adds other analytic annotations as well; for example, he labels one form "I.O. transposed," indicating that he has taken the original pitches, inverted them, and transposed them to a new pitch level.

24. Duchamp's recollection is recorded in Edwin Denby's celebrated essay "Three Sides of *Agon*," *Evergreen Review* (Winter 1959), reprinted in Gottlieb, ed., *Reading Dance*, 144–50. Kirstein goes on to discuss Renato Poggioli's *Theory of the Avant-Garde* in relation to "Agonism" and "Futurism." See Kirstein, *Four Centuries of Ballet*, 242–43.

25. Reynolds, *No Fixed Points*, 310.

26. Mason, *I Remember Balanchine*, 359.

27. Mason, *I Remember Balanchine*, 395. If the duet caused a stir in the U.S. during those racially strained times, it was criticized even more intensely by the Soviet Press during City Ballet's first tour of Russia in 1962. As Kirstein recalls in his *Thirty Years*, "In the Muscovite press . . . Balanchine's expression of Stravinsky's mutations of Mersenne and de Lauze's Renaissance dances was interpreted as a Negro slave's submission to the tyranny of an ardent white mistress" (171).

28. Banes, *Dancing Women*, 195.

29. Hayden recounted her memories in an interview for the Los Angeles radio station KFAC that was broadcast as a memorial shortly after the choreographer's death.

30. Robert Tracy with Sharon Delano, *Balanchine's Ballerinas: Conversations with the Muses* (New York: Linden Press/Simon and Schuster, 1983), 123–24.

31. Mason, *I Remember Balanchine*, 134.

32. Richard Buckle, *George Balanchine: Ballet Master* (New York: Random House, 1988), 212–13.

33. Bernard Taper, *Balanchine: A Biography* (Berkeley: University of California Press, 1996), 264–71.

34. Paul Horgan, *Encounters with Stravinsky* (New York: Farrar, Straus and Giroux, 1972), 92.

35. The videotape *The Balanchine Celebration*, part 2, filmed in 1993, is part of the "Dance in America" series, Nonesuch 40190–3. The dancers include the following: "First pas de trois," Peter Boal, Zippora Karz, Kathleen Tracey; "Second pas de trois," Albert Evans, Arch Higgens, Wendy Whelan; "Pas de deux," Darcey Bussell and Lindsay Fischer.

36. The dancers' hand gestures define each of the individual beats in this 9/4 measure. Barbara Milberg, one of the original dancers for the "Gailliarde," remembers that Balanchine gave considerable thought to the choreography for this musically pivotal moment. In articulating these nine beats, he positioned the two women in a "freeze frame." He instructed the dancers to employ movements that were "angular, abrupt rather than graceful, and absolutely precise in tempo." See Barbara Milberg Fisher, *The Balanchine Company: A Dancer's Memoir*

(Middletown: Wesleyan University Press, 2006), especially chapter 18, "*Agon*: Point Counterpoint," 156–70.

37. Horgan, *Encounters with Stravinsky*, 93.

CHAPTER 8: Terpsichorean Hybrids

1. Igor Stravinsky, *Poetics of Music in the Form of Six Lessons*, trans. Arthur Knodel and Ingolf Dahl (1947; reprint, Cambridge, Mass.: Harvard University Press, 1970), 76.
2. Asaf'yev, *A Book about Stravinsky*, 105–7.
3. Stravinsky, *An Autobiography*, 102.
4. Craft, *Stravinsky: Glimpses of a Life*, 26.
5. Asaf'yev, *A Book about Stravinsky*, 109.
6. Taruskin, *Stravinsky and the Russian Traditions*, vol. 2, 1294–95. Taruskin provides a complete translation of the original Afanas'yev text, one of his longest narratives.
7. For the composer's recounting of his instrumentation, see his *Autobiography*, 70. See Ansermet's "La Naissance de *L'Histoire du soldat*," in C. F. Ramuz, *Lettres, 1900–1918* (Lausanne: Éditions Clairefontaine, 1956), 36ff., for his description of the instrumental choices that he and Stravinsky considered.
8. Stravinsky, *An Autobiography*, 72–73.
9. Stravinsky recognized Reinhart's financial support by making an arrangement of *L'Histoire* for violin, clarinet, and piano in 1919, comprising five of the eight pieces included in the original concert suite. The same year, Stravinsky dedicated his Three Pieces for clarinet solo to Reinhart—a short trio of studies reflecting the composer's continuing interest in jazz.
10. Stravinsky and Craft, *Expositions and Developments*, 91.
11. Some of the fundamental ideas for *L'Histoire's* dances are traceable to sketches dating from around 1917 for Stravinsky's *Anthony and Cleopatra*, an earlier project with André Gide that was eventually abandoned. See Maureen A. Carr, ed., *Stravinsky's "Histoire du soldat": A Facsimile of the Sketches* (Middleton, Wisc.: A-R Editions, 2005), 11–13.
12. Stravinsky and Craft, *Expositions and Developments*, 92.
13. Taruskin attributes *L'Histoire*'s rhythmic innovativeness to other models with which the composer would have been acquainted. He suggests, for example, that Stravinsky's ensemble is "a stylized village band compounded out of overlapping cadres of Ustilug *klezmorim*, Vaudois *fanfaristes*, and *pasodoble* players from Seville, all led by a Gypsy fiddler." Taruskin, *Stravinsky and the Russian Traditions*, vol. 2, 1301–18.
14. The description of the rehearsal appears in White, *Stravinsky: The Composer and His Works*, 273–74.
15. See Stravinsky and Craft, *Expositions and Developments*, 95. Stravinsky added that the biggest challenge for George Pitoëff was designing the action for "the smallness of the inner stage, which was only as large as two armchairs together."
16. Pitoëff's recollection originally appeared in "Souvenirs intimes," *Le Quartier latin*, Montreal, March 23, 1945, and is quoted in Stravinsky and Craft, *Stravinsky in Pictures and Documents*, 167.
17. The exchanges originally appeared in Claude Tappolet, ed., *Correspondance Ansermet–Stravinsky* (Geneva: Georg, 1990). The letters are reprinted in various sources, including Roger Shattuck, "The Devil's Dance: Stravinsky's Corporeal Imagination," in Pasler, ed., *Confronting Stravinsky*, 82–88.
18. Maureen Carr provides both reviews, the first from *La Suisse* and the second from the *Gazette de Lausanne*. See her *Stravinsky's "Histoire du soldat,"* 7.
19. Asaf'yev, *A Book about Stravinsky*, 184–85. For the notion of dance as Stravinsky's agent of movement, see again Shattuck, "The Devil's Dance," in Pasler, ed., *Confronting Stravinsky*, where the author points to specific sections of *L'Histoire* as evidence of Stravinsky's inherently dance-like music: "The first three measures say everything. A brisk cornet call to launch us on a regular walking pulse that will keep coming back. . . . I hear it as a physical summons to a performance, to start walking, to find some spring and verve in our bodies" (83).

20. By the 1950s, the composition was so familiar that Stravinsky tried to entice various American notables, including Tennessee Williams, Orson Welles, and Marlon Brando, to become associated with the work as translators or as actors. In 1983, *Sesame Street*'s R. O. Blechman created an animated film for PBS's *Great Performances*, in which Max von Sydow dubbed the voice of the Devil. Crossover pop artist Sting recorded the work with Vanessa Redgrave in 1990. Kurt Vonnegut adapted the original libretto in 1993 to tell the tale of Private Eddie Slovik, an executed Second World War deserter. Frank Zappa included a version of the work's familiar opening "March" as part of his album *Make a Jazz Noise*. In 1998, the Chamber Music Society of Lincoln Center recorded Wynton Marsalis's *A Fiddler's Tale*, based upon Stravinsky's composition.

21. Stravinsky and Craft, *Expositions and Developments*, 112–13.

22. Lynn Garafola, "The Making of Ballet Modernism," *Dance Research Journal* 20/2 (Winter 1988): 28. Much has been made of the exact sources Stravinsky used in assembling *Pulcinella*. At least five composers in addition to Pergolesi served as sources. Perhaps even more informative are the scores Diaghilev held in his own music library, scores he had acquired in London and Naples, many of which are heavily annotated in his own hand.

23. García-Márquez, *Massine*, 142.

24. Léonide Massine, *My Life in Ballet*, ed. Phyllis Hartnol and Robert Rubens (London: Macmillan, 1968), 145–46.

25. Massine, *My Life*, 150.

26. One was the fact that Manuel de Falla had turned down the commission. For Diaghilev's intention to commission Falla for *Pulcinella*, see Jaime Pahissa, *Manuel de Falla: His Life and Works* (London: Museum Press, 1954), 111.

27. Stravinsky, *An Autobiography*, 81.

28. Cyril W. Beaumont, *Complete Books of Ballets* (New York: Grosset and Dunlap, 1938), 741. The complete scenario is outlined in detail, accompanied by Beaumont's comments on the production.

29. Stravinsky and Craft, *Conversations*, 105.

30. Buckle, *Diaghilev*, 361.

31. Stravinsky's memory of the meetings appears in his *Autobiography*, 83. For Cocteau's remarks, see White, *Stravinsky: The Composer and His Works*, 287. For a summary of the many different designs Picasso presented—each in turn rejected by Diaghilev—see García-Márquez, *Massine*, 147–8.

32. Both Tommasini and Respighi, orchestrators of other Ballets Russes Italian period-ballets around this time, were likewise kept under Diaghilev's thumb. Lynn Garafola notes that the often intrusive impresario took a particularly active role in shaping the 1919 *Boutique fantasque*. She rightly asks who the real author was here, Rossini, Respighi, or "Diaghilev who assembled the music for the ballet from numerous compositions, pruned bars and passages, changed chords, keys, and tempi, corrected Respighi's additions, and wrote notes to himself like, 'Don't forget all the chords must approximate stylistically the *old* Rossini of *Barber*.' " Garafola, "The Making of Ballet Modernism," 29.

33. Stravinsky, *An Autobiography*, 83.

34. Stravinsky and Craft, *Expositions and Developments*, 112. For a complete listing of the music by other composers that is employed in the ballet, see Taruskin, *Stravinsky and the Russian Traditions*, vol. 2, 1464–65. For a recent, comprehensive discussion of the work, see Maureen A. Carr, ed., *Stravinsky's "Pulcinella": A Facsimile of the Sources and Sketches* (Middleton, Wisc.: A-R Editions, 2010).

35. Whatever the controversy over the rearrangement, the music quickly became immensely popular with violinists and cellists for whom Stravinsky prepared instrumental suites. The 1922 orchestral suite, in which instruments replace the original vocal parts, remains one of the composer's most popular concert works. Additionally, Stravinsky prepared two different versions for violin, the first in 1925 for Paul Kochanski, and the second in 1933 for his touring partner Samuel Dushkin (the often played *Suite italienne*). Dushkin helped Stravinsky to draft idiomatic violin figurations, as he did for a number of his other violin

works. Even more influentially, Gregor Piatigorsky clearly shaped the composer's 1932 cello version (also entitled *Suite italienne*), as manuscripts in the Stravinsky archives reveal.

36. André Rigaud, "M. Igor Stravinsky nous parle de la musique de *Pulcinella*," *Comoedia*, 15 May 1920, reprinted in part in Walsh, *Stravinsky: A Creative Spring*, 312.

37. Constant Lambert, *Music Ho!* (London: Faber and Faber, 1934), 50, 70.

38. André Levinson, "Stravinsky and the Dance," *Theatre Arts Monthly*, 8 November 1924: 741–54; Buckle, *Diaghilev*, 363.

39. Several reviews are reprinted in Walsh, *Stravinsky: A Creative Spring*, 313. The list of *Pulcinella*'s subsequent stagings is extensive, approaching one hundred revivals or new productions.

40. Bronislava Nijinska, "Creation of *Les Noces*," translated by Jean M. Serafetinides and Irina Nijinska, *Dance Magazine* 48 (December 1974): 61. The statement is quoted in Stephanie Jordan, *Stravinsky Dances: Re-visions across a Century* (Alton, Hampshire: Dance, 2007), 344, as part of the author's discussion of Nijinska's choreographic treatment of the score.

41. Stravinsky, *An Autobiography*, 52.

42. A series of twenty-five early sketches found in the Mary Flagler Carey Collection of the Morgan Library are drafted under the "villageoises" title. These source materials exhibit some of the "block" composing seen in *The Rite*, where Stravinsky sketches three or four discrete rhythmic units then arranges them in various patterns, an example being the rotation of AABAA marked in the sketches at what would become Rehearsal 80 of the score.

43. Stravinsky and Craft, *Expositions and Developments*, 118. Around 1915 the impresario became interested in staging another ballet that would explore the power of ritual, an ecclesiastical spectacle entitled *Liturgie*. Diaghilev brought Natalia Goncharova from Moscow to design the work. See Goncharova's recollections in "The Metamorphoses of the Ballet *Les Noces*," *Leonardo* 12/2 (Spring 1979): 137–43.

44. Stravinsky, *An Autobiography*, 104.

45. Lambert, *Music Ho!* 167–68.

46. Stravinsky and Craft, *Expositions and Developments*, 121.

47. Stravinsky and Craft, *Expositions and Developments*, 116.

48. See Margarita Mazo, "Stravinsky's *Les Noces* and Russian Folk Wedding Ritual," *Journal of the American Musicological Society* 43/1 (Spring 1990): 111 n.35. Mazo traces the first operatic setting of a wedding ritual to Sokolovsky and Ablesimov's *The Miller—a Wizard, a Cheat, and a Matchmaker* of 1779.

49. See Craft's preface to Asaf'yev's *A Book about Stravinsky*, xiii. The composer's statements were gleaned from marginalia found in his copy of the author's book.

50. In *Dancing Women*, Sally Banes addresses the submissive role of young married females in the newly formed Soviet Union—a coerced obedience that was deeply ingrained: "Peasant women, who traditionally bore an enormous burden—working the land, caring for the livestock, bearing and raising children, and running the household, all in a situation of crushing poverty, sometimes coupled with physical and sexual abuse—nevertheless did not rush to embrace the newfound emancipation offered to them by the Bolsheviks" (110).

51. Stravinsky and Craft, *Expositions and Developments*, 118.

52. See Garafola, *Diaghilev's Ballets Russes*, 126. Garafola adds that Nijinska's notebooks reveal constructivist drawings of "spatial architecture" including geometric diagrams of "quadrants, arcs, loops, spheres . . . wedges, triangles, squares," all reflecting the linear and angular formations of the music itself.

53. In a letter to Stravinsky of November 25, 1914, Diaghilev begrudgingly admits, "The invention of the movement for *Noces* is clearly Nijinsky's." Boris Kochno indicates that Nijinsky took part in the original conversations about the work, but that after his falling out with Diaghilev Massine was appointed choreographer, although by the time of the production he too had left the company. See Boris Kochno, *Diaghilev and the Ballets Russes* (New York: Harper and Row, 1970), 186–89.

54. Nijinska, "Creation of *Les Noces*," 58. Nijinska's expression "the nature of tragedy" appeared in an article by John Martin in the *New York Times* of May 3, 1936. For a tracing of Nijinska's inspiration to the art of Russia's icon painters and archaic mosaics, see Robert

Johnson, "Ritual and Abstraction in Nijinska's 'Les Noces,'" *Dance Chronicle* 10/2 (1987): 147–69.

55. Nijinska, "Creation of *Les Noces*." For a feminist perspective, see Banes, *Dancing Women*, 121, where it is suggested that as portrayed by Nijinska the bride in the work is no longer mythologized, but rather a real woman, and in particular a victim of repression—"a victim of social tradition, she wields no political power." In *Diaghilev's Ballets Russes*, Garafola perceives the *pointe* work more explicitly as a direct challenge to romantic notions of *pointes* as an expression of femininity: "The ballet spoke of male power and female pain; the stabbing pointes, 'masculine' in their violence, enacted, so to speak, the drama of sexual penetration" (128). One should remember that Nijinska herself had been cast as the original Chosen One in *The Rite*, but withdrew because of her pregnancy.

56. Stravinsky, *An Autobiography*, 106. Stravinsky adds that Diaghilev was opposed to the idea, and thus the composer's vision went unrealized.

57. Kochno recalls three successive designs by Goncharova, the first two in "folkloristic, peasant style, with brilliant colors, and the other worked out in half-tones which were over embellished with gold and silver embroidery." The final version exhibited "costumes after the cut of the regulation work clothes company dancers wore during rehearsals," although modified so that the female tunics were converted "into *sarafans* (an old style of Russian peasant dress)." See Kochno, *Diaghilev and the Ballets Russes*, 189. Goncharova's own—apparently somewhat biased—account of the evolution of the décor appears in her "The Metamorphoses of the Ballet *Les Noces*."

58. Nijinska, "Creation of *Les Noces*," 59–61.

59. Vuillermoz's review appeared in *Excelsior*, June 18, 1923. See Drue Fergison, "Bringing *Les Noces* to the Stage," in Garafola and Baer, eds., *The Ballets Russes and Its World*, 184–87, for excerpts from several early reviews, including one by Raymond Charpentier in *Comoedia*, one by Roland-Manuel in *L'Éclair*, and a particularly lacerating attack by a churlish André Levinson on "the pedantic and stubborn vampire" Nijinska.

60. Newman's review appeared on June 20, 1926. For the full letter of Wells, which Diaghilev inserted in the printed programs of subsequent performances, see White, *Stravinsky: The Composer and His Works*, 260–61.

61. For a comprehensive analysis of Robbins's version, as well as comments on other productions, see Jordan, *Stravinsky Dances*, chapter 5, "*Les Noces*."

62. See Joseph, *Stravinsky Inside Out*, 251, for correspondence between Stravinsky and Robbins as documented in the Paul Sacher Stiftung.

63. For extended comments about the work, see Stravinsky and Craft, *Dialogues*, 36–37. Stravinsky further comments upon the work in Stravinsky and Craft, *Memories and Commentaries*, 145–53, where several letters to and from Gide are reprinted.

64. For a retracing of the work's origins and sketch materials, see Carr, *Multiple Masks*, chapter 4. Gide's letter appears in Craft, *Stravinsky: Selected Correspondence*, vol. 3, 186–87. More than a decade earlier, Rubinstein had hoped to pair Gide and Stravinsky in preparing a new work for her company. The composer took the offer seriously, and began to sketch incidental music for a version of *Anthony and Cleopatra*, although the work was not completed.

65. See Carr, *Multiple Masks*, 192–200, for a discussion of Charles-Albert Cingria's influence on the composer during this period, including the suggestion that Stravinsky was impressed by Cingria's *Pétrarque*—presented to him as a gift in late 1932—as evinced by several marked pages.

66. In advance of the premiere, a performance of the reduced score, with the composer at the keyboard, was given for the Princesse Edmond de Polignac. The work was also previewed at the home of Stravinsky's close friend Nadia Boulanger.

67. Stravinsky and Craft, *Dialogues*, 36–37.

68. See Walsh, *Stravinsky: A Creative Spring*, 536–37. Walsh includes several critical reviews of the premiere.

69. Walter Terry, "The Dancer's Composer," *Saturday Review*, May 29, 1971: 43.

70. Craft, *Stravinsky: Selected Correspondence*, vol. 3, 481.
71. The first interview, with Robert Lewis Shayon, appeared in *Saturday Review* on June 16, 1962. The second was published two weeks later in the June 30 issue.
72. George Balanchine and Bernard Taper, "Television and Ballet," in Robert Lewis Shayon, ed., *The Eighth Art: Twenty-Three Views of Television Today* (New York: Holt, Rinehart and Winston, 1962), 118.
73. See Arthur Todd, "What Went Wrong," *Dance Magazine* 36 (August 1962): 39, 60–61.
74. See Robert Craft, *Present Perspectives* (New York: Alfred A. Knopf, 1984), 240. Craft records that Stravinsky "pasted several pages of my notes to him" into the manuscript of *The Flood*, notes that dealt with "technical questions as well as musical symbolisms."
75. Todd, 40.
76. The unedited version of this important letter is held in the Sacher Stiftung.
77. Balanchine's comments originally appeared in Shayon, ed., *The Eighth Art*, 246.
78. Although the work is serial in construction, featuring hexachordal structures and rotated series often used by Stravinsky by the early 1960s, some early sketches suggest that he originally thought in remarkably diatonic terms. See Lynn Rogers, "A Serial Passage of Diatonic Ancestry in Stravinsky's *The Flood*," *Journal of the Royal Musical Association* 129/2 (2004): 220–30. Stravinsky and Craft, *Themes and Conclusions*, 106.
79. For a view of how *The Flood* comports with modernist musical theater, see W. Anthony Sheppard, *Revealing Masks* (Berkeley: University of California Press, 2001). Sheppard points out the similarities between the textual sources of Stravinsky's work and those of Britten's *Noye's Fludde*, although the musical treatment is quite different.
80. Don Daniels, "Stravinsky III," *Ballet Review* 10/3 (Fall 1982), 46. Daniels's suggestion was partially realized in a bizarre 1985 adaptation of the original 1962 television production. Produced by NOS-TV and the Stiftung Muzt in Amsterdam, the videotape is commercially distributed through NVC Arts International. This Dutch production, which includes a psychedelic, computer-generated light show, employs the original 1962 "soundtrack" of the Columbia Symphony Orchestra and Chorus.

CHAPTER 9: Dancing a Legacy

1. Balanchine's comment was recorded in Arnold Newman and Robert Craft, *Bravo Stravinsky* (Cleveland: World Publishing Company, 1967). For a short but detailed account of the choreographer's thoughts on the composer's sense of dance, see Balanchine's well-worn but still informative "The Dance Element in Stravinsky's Music," which includes the following assertion: "A pause, an interruption, is never empty space. . . . It acts as a carrying agent from the last sound to the next one. Life goes on within each silence" (Lederman, ed., *Stravinsky in the Theatre*, 76). Adorno later modified his criticism of "the static ideal of Stravinsky's music, its immanent timelessness," by admitting that he "arbitrarily applied . . . an external norm." Still, Adorno found little use for the composer's dance music. See his "Stravinsky: A Dialectical Portrait," in *Quasi una fantasia*, trans. Rodney Livingston (London: Verso, 1992), 150.
2. Interview in *The Observer*, July 3, 1921. The "architectural basis of connection" was, however, lost on early critics such as Volynsky, who found *The Firebird* (like *Petrouchka*) marred by a "jerkiness" and an "endless stop and go in the orchestra, which gives no support even to the intricate acrobatic movements raging on stage." Volynsky, *Ballet's Magic Kingdom*, 77.
3. "Stravinsky and His Music," *Manchester Guardian*, February 22, 1934.
4. It should be added that Balanchine realized the need to educate audiences, as best he could, about unfamiliar, complex contemporary music. In *Opus 34*, for instance, he called for the music to be played twice without interruption, thus providing a predictably skeptical audience with the opportunity to rehear the score. The choreography for each of the iterations was quite contrasting. As Edwin Denby wrote of the premiere in *Dance Magazine*, "What makes the ideas in the ballet appear with such expressive power is the way the stage action at every moment seems to fulfill the intense dramatic potency of the music. When the ballet is

over you are convinced that you 'understood' the score, you have felt its grandeur and theater." Denby's review is reprinted in Gottlieb, ed., *Reading Dance*, 202–6.

5. Croce's comments which originally appeared in *Harper's Magazine*, April 1971, are reprinted in Jordan, *Stravinsky Dances*, 165.

6. The other two works were Darius Milhaud's *Creation of the World*, prepared by Todd Bolender, and Francis Poulenc's *Les Biches*, choreographed by Francisco Monicon.

7. For a more detailed analysis of the work from a choreographic perspective, see Jordan, *Stravinsky Dances*, 194ff.

8. Stravinsky and Craft, *Themes and Conclusions*, 34. Whether or not Stravinsky himself really formulated this statement must, alas, be questioned, given the unreliability of the content of his later conversation books.

9. Reynolds, *No Fixed Points*, 312.

10. In the first edition of his *Stravinsky: Chronicle of a Friendship* (Alfred A. Knopf: New York, 1972), Craft notes in a diary entry of February 13, 1968, that Vera Stravinsky is encouraged by her husband's rekindled interest in composing. Craft further notes that on April 17 the composer began writing "an extra instrumental prelude to the *Requiem Canticles* for a performance of the work in memory of Dr. Martin Luther King" (346 n.1). Craft offers a brief description of the compositional ideas that Stravinsky had originally drafted for the work and that would now become the basis of the added music. Evidently, however, the "prelude was abandoned when he saw that it could not be completed in time" for Balanchine's performance. In a subsequent edition of the chronicle, Craft deletes a portion of the diary entry itself, as well as the footnote cited above.

11. Stravinsky's score was rechoreographed by Jerome Robbins for the 1972 Stravinsky Festival. Stravinsky's unpublished papers include a copy of a review of the original Balanchine production that refers to "the company's principal conductor, Robert Irving, implacable as he continued with his task of molding this difficult Stravinsky score." Ill but quarrelsome as ever, the composer underlined the last four words ("this difficult Stravinsky score") and added, "not more than any of my new scores!"

12. In a note to Stravinsky dated May 14, 1968, just two weeks after the performance, Edward Bigelow wrote, "George wanted you to see this film of *Requiem Canticles* which was done during rehearsal on the afternoon of the Second of May, on the day of the performance. You will note that there are two prints. Two cameras were used and the cameramen were instructed to shoot full stage, which you will note they did not do, but decided instead to 'create'—which means the visual pictures George intended, and accomplished, are rather ruined because of our cameramen's unfortunate 'creative decisions.' However, looking at both prints should give a fair idea of what George did." Unpublished note, Paul Sacher Stiftung.

13. Interview with Louis Botto, "Balanchine: Work in Progress," *Intellectual Digest*, June 1972, reprinted in Selma Jeanne Cohen and Katy Matheson, eds., *Dance as a Theatre Art: Source Readings in Dance History from 1851 to the Present* (New York: Harper and Row, 1974), 188.

14. "Balanchine: Work in Progress," 188.

15. Stravinsky's 1942 *Circus Polka*, surely the most bizarre commission Stravinsky ever accepted, was written for a production by Balanchine entitled "The Ballet of the Elephants"—an appropriate description indeed given its four hundred performances by "Fifty Elephants and Fifty Beautiful Girls in an Original Choreographic Tour de Force," as billed by Ringling Brothers and Barnum & Bailey for its Madison Square Garden premiere. Strictly viewed, it should probably be listed among the composer's original ballet scores. And while Stravinsky did invest some time in the project, as several compositional sketches disclose, it was no more than a manufactured score—quickly drafted and sent to Balanchine without any discussion, let alone collaboration. Today the music is often performed in Robbins's charming choreography, intended for younger ballerinas rather than pachyderms. For Robbins's contributions to the Stravinsky Festival, see Deborah Jowitt, *Jerome Robbins: His Life, His Theater, His Dance* (New York: Simon and Schuster, 2004), 402–8. For Stravinsky's *Circus Polka* and Balanchine's original setting of it, see Joseph, *Stravinsky and Balanchine*, 167–70.

16. Toumanova's interview appears in Mason, *I Remember Balanchine*, 104.

17. Taper, *Balanchine: A Biography*, 321.
18. Dance critic Nancy Goldner's comments are reprinted in Jordan, *Stravinsky Dances*, chapter 3, "George Balanchine's Stravinsky: Collaboration as Challenge," 158ff. For more detailed critiques of Balanchine's setting of Stravinsky's music for the 1972 festival, see Nancy Goldner, *Balanchine Variations* (Gainesville: University Press of Florida, 2008), 106–25. Robert Craft, too, expressed reservations about some of the new choreography prepared for several of Stravinsky's scores. See Craft, "Celestial Motions," in *Stravinsky: Glimpses of a Life*, 270–75.
19. For a fuller exploration of such a view, see Robert Garis, *Following Balanchine* (New Haven: Yale University Press, 1995), especially chapter 5, "Balanchine and Stravinsky," 67–89. Vestiges of belief in dance's rightful domination over music persist. There are those, as Denby commented in his wonderful 1949 article "Against Meaning in Ballet" (reprinted in Gottlieb, ed., *Reading Dance*, 378–82), who continue to attend ballet for its entertainment, "a particularly agreeable way of spending an evening in town," and to be thrilled by the "animal grace" of beautiful bodies in motion. Music is only an afterthought, and should avoid overwhelming the fragility of dance, something for which Levinson regularly criticized Stravinsky's crushingly powerful scores. Indeed Lifar once accused Stravinsky's music of being too present, too good. Consequently, the composer's music "enfeebles dancing," he complained. Its "fatal mistake" was the subjugation rather than the enrichment of the dance. See Serge Lifar, *Ballet: Traditional to Modern*, trans. Cyril W. Beaumont (London: Putnam, 1968), 168.
20. Among Balanchine's most notable contributions was his and Jacques d'Amboise's staging of a new version of *The Flood* (now renamed *Noah and the Flood*), conducted by Robert Craft and narrated by John Houseman. Anna Kisselgoff's June 13 *New York Times* review—citing the performance's "penetrating resonance"—was much kinder than those that had lambasted the television premiere twenty years earlier.
21. Still, it must be said that Balanchine, "the architect of classical ballet in America," as the Dance Heritage Coalition cited him, has been the subject of debate in postmodern studies of modernist choreography. This is especially so regarding his position in relation to feminist issues and "invisibilized" African influences on his choreographic approach. See Ramsay Burt, "The Specter of Interdisciplinarity," *Dance Research Journal* 41/1 (Summer 2009): 3–22.
22. Ashton's Stravinskyan choreography remains practically unknown to musicians. Yet his views on dance and music are revealing: "Just as the greatest music has no program . . . the greatest ballets are the same, or at any rate have the merest thread of an idea which can be ignored, and on which the choreographer may weave his imagination for the combination of steps and patterns." How far is this from the Stravinsky–Balanchine approach? See Ashton's 1951 "Notes on Choreography," reprinted in Gottlieb, ed., *Reading Dance*, 2–4.
23. Alastair Macaulay, "Out of the Flames, into the Rites of Spring, in Ballets Russes Tribute," *New York Times*, May 18, 2009.
24. For a discussion of several important *Rite* choreographies, see Berg, *Le Sacre du printemps*, chapter 7, "Movieola," 107–23.
25. Accessible from the Roehampton University website, www.roehampton.ac.uk/stravinsky, this is a database of all Stravinsky's danced works. It was originally compiled in 2002, though it continues to be updated. While the authors' explanation of their working method is both comprehensive and exemplary, to understand fully the extent and utility of this project one should consult Jordan's aforementioned *Stravinsky Dances*, especially the section entitled "Choreographing Stravinsky: Tales from a Chronology" in chapter 2, "From Stravinsky to Choreography" (107–57). Here and elsewhere in this study, Jordan offers analyses of several Stravinskyan works from an informed musico-choreographic viewpoint. The study is especially useful for musicians who may be unacquainted with many of the choreographers listed in the database. For a useful summary of the database, see Jordan, "The Demons in a Database: Interrogating 'Stravinsky the Global Dancer,' " *Dance Research: The Journal of the Society for Dance Research* 22/1 (Summer 2004): 57–83.
26. Jordan, *Stravinsky Dances*, 116.
27. Jordan notes, for example, several rather bizarre productions of masterpieces such as *Petrouchka* wherein the principal character is variously portrayed as "a rock star . . . drug

addict . . . young thief amongst the clothing in a stylish department store." And in a 1998 production of *Petrouchka* by the Gothenburg Ballet, Petrouchka is cast as a "young soldier . . . returning from war in Afghanistan to a *ménage à trois* with a Mafia boss and his moll." Jordan, *Stravinsky Dances*, 132–33.

28. Reynolds, *No Fixed Points*, 528.

WORKS CITED

Adorno, Theodor. "Stravinsky: A Dialectical Portrait." In *Quasi una fantasia*. Translated by Rodney Livingston. London: Verso, 1992.

Alm, Irene. "Stravinsky, Balanchine, and *Agon*: An Analysis Based on the Collaborative Process." *Journal of Musicology* 7/2 (Spring 1989): 254–69.

Anderson, Jack. *The One and Only: The Ballet Russe de Monte Carlo*. New York: Dance Horizons, 1981.

Asaf'yev, Boris. *A Book about Stravinsky*. Translated by Richard French. Ann Arbor: UMI Research Press, 1982.

Balanchine, George, and Francis Mason. *101 Stories of the Great Ballets*. New York: Doubleday, 1989.

Banes, Sally. *Dancing Women*. London: Routledge, 1998.

Beaumont, Cyril W. *Complete Books of Ballets*. New York: Grosset and Dunlap, 1938.

Benois, Alexandre. *Reminiscences of the Russian Ballet*. London: Putnam, 1941.

Berg, Shelly C. *Le Sacre du printemps: Seven Productions from Nijinsky to Martha Graham*. Ann Arbor: UMI Research Press, 1988.

Berger, Arthur. "Problems of Pitch Organization in Stravinsky." *Perspectives of New Music* 2/1 (Autumn/Winter, 1963): 11–42.

Boulez, Pierre. *Notes on an Apprenticeship*. New York: Alfred A. Knopf, 1968.

Bowlt, John E. *The Silver Age: Russian Art of the Early Twentieth Century and the "World of Art" Group*. Newtonville, Mass.: Oriental Research Partners, 1979.

Buckle, Richard. *Diaghilev*. New York: Atheneum, 1979.

———. *George Balanchine: Ballet Master*. New York: Random House, 1988.

———. *In the Wake of Diaghilev*. New York: Holt, Rinehart and Winston, 1982.

———. *Nijinsky*. New York: Simon and Schuster, 1971.

Burt, Ramsay. "The Specter of Interdisciplinarity." *Dance Research Journal* 41/1 (Summer 2009): 3–22.

Calvocoressi, Michel-Dmitri. "A Russian Composer of To-Day: Igor Stravinsky." *Musical Times* 52 (1911): 511–12.

Carr, Maureen A. *Multiple Masks: Neoclassicism in Stravinsky's Works on Greek Subjects*. Lincoln: University of Nebraska Press, 2002.

Carr, Maureen A., ed. *Stravinsky's "Histoire du soldat": A Facsimile of the Sketches*. Middleton, Wisc.: A-R Editions, 2005.

———. *Stravinsky's "Pulcinella": A Facsimile of the Sources and Sketches*. Middleton, Wisc.: A-R Editions, 2010.

Cocteau, Jean. *Le Coq et l'arlequin*. Paris: Éditions de la Sirène, 1918.

Code, David J. "The Synthesis of Rhythms: Form, Ideology, and the 'Augurs of Spring.'" *Journal of Musicology* 24/1 (Winter 2007): 112–66.

Cohen, Selma Jeanne, and Katy Matheson, eds. *Dance as a Theatre Art: Source Readings in Dance History from 1851 to the Present.* New York: Harper and Row, 1974.

Coleman, Francis A. "A Talk with Igor Stravinsky." *Dance Magazine* 19/4 (April 1945): 30–32.

Corle, Edwin, ed. *Igor Stravinsky.* New York: Duell, Sloan and Pearce, 1949.

Cott, Jonathan. *Portrait of Mr. B.* New York: Viking Press, 1984.

Craft, Robert. *Down a Path of Wonder.* Norfolk: Naxos Books, 2006.

———. *An Improbable Life.* Nashville: Vanderbilt University Press, 2002.

———. *The Moment of Existence.* Nashville: Vanderbilt University Press, 1996.

———. *Present Perspectives.* New York: Alfred A. Knopf, 1984.

———. "*The Rite*: Counterpoint and Choreography." *Musical Times* 129/1742 (April 1988): 171–76.

———. *Stravinsky: Chronicle of a Friendship.* Alfred A. Knopf: New York, 1972.

———. *Stravinsky: Glimpses of a Life.* New York: St. Martin's Press, 1992.

———. *Stravinsky: Selected Correspondence.* 3 vols. New York: Alfred A. Knopf, 1982–85.

Crisp, Clement. "Marie Rambert and Nijinsky's *Le Sacre du printemps*." *Dance Research* 19/1 (Summer 2001): 3–10.

Cross, Jonathan, ed. *The Cambridge Companion to Stravinsky.* Cambridge: Cambridge University Press, 2003.

Daniels, Don. "Stravinsky III." *Ballet Review* 10/3 (Fall 1982): 46–47.

Debussy, Claude. *Claude Debussy: Correspondance, 1884–1918.* Edited by François Lesure. Paris: Hermann, 1993.

———. *Debussy Letters.* Translated by Roger Nichols. Edited by François Lesure and Roger Nichols. Cambridge, Mass.: Harvard University Press, 1987.

Drummond, John. *Speaking of Diaghilev.* London: Faber and Faber, 1997.

Eksteins, Modris. *Rites of Spring.* Boston: Houghton Mifflin, 1989.

Eliot, T. S. "The Beating of the Drum." *The Nation and the Athenaeum,* October 1923: 11–12.

Figes, Orlando. *Natasha's Dance: A Cultural History of Russia.* New York: Henry Holt, 2002.

Fisher, Barbara Milberg. *The Balanchine Company: A Dancer's Memoir.* Middletown: Wesleyan University Press, 2006.

Fokine, Michel. *Memoirs of a Ballet Master.* Translated by Vitale Fokine. Boston: Little, Brown, 1961.

Forte, Allen. *The Harmonic Organization of "The Rite of Spring."* New Haven: Yale University Press, 1978.

Frankenstein, Alfred. "Stravinsky in Beverly Hills." *Modern Music* 19/3 (March–April 1942): 172–81.

Garafola, Lynn. *Diaghilev's Ballets Russes.* New York: Oxford University Press, 1989.

———. "The Making of Ballet Modernism." *Dance Research Journal* 20/2 (Winter 1988): 23–32.

Garafola, Lynn, and Nancy Van Norman Baer, eds. *The Ballets Russes and Its World.* New Haven: Yale University Press, 1999.

García-Márquez, Vicente. *Massine: A Biography.* New York: Alfred A. Knopf, 1995.

Garis, Robert. *Following Balanchine.* New Haven: Yale University Press, 1995.

Ghéon, Henri. "Propos divers sur le Ballet Russe." *Nouvelle Revue française* 4 (1910), 199–211.

Goldner, Nancy. *Balanchine Variations.* Gainesville: University Press of Florida, 2008.

Goldner, Nancy, ed. *The Stravinsky Festival of the New York City Ballet.* New York: Eakins Press, 1973.

Goncharova, Natalia. "The Metamorphoses of the Ballet *Les Noces*." *Leonardo* 12/2 (Spring 1979): 137–43.

Gottlieb, Robert, ed. *Reading Dance.* New York: Pantheon Books, 2008.

Grigoriev, Serge. *The Diaghilev Ballet, 1909–1929.* Translated by Vera Bowen. London: Constable, 1953.

Harris, Dale. "Balanchine: Working with Stravinsky." *Ballet Review* 10/2 (Summer 1982): 19–24.

Hill, Peter. *Stravinsky: The Rite of Spring.* Cambridge: Cambridge University Press, 2000.

Hodson, Millicent. *Nijinsky's Crime against Grace: Reconstruction Score of the Original Choreography for "Le Sacre du printemps."* Stuyvesant, N.Y.: Pendragon Press, 1996.

Horgan, Paul. *Encounters with Stravinsky*. New York: Farrar, Straus and Giroux, 1972.

Hosking, Geoffrey. *Russia: People and Empire*. Cambridge, Mass.: Harvard University Press, 1997.

Isherwood, Christopher. *Diaries*. Vol. 1: *1939–1960*. Edited by Katherine Bucknell. New York: HarperCollins, 1996.

Järvinen, Hanna. " 'The Russian Barnum': Russian Opinions on Diaghilev's Ballets Russes, 1909–1914." *Dance Research* 26/1 (Summer 2008): 18–41.

Johnson, Robert. "Ritual and Abstraction in Nijinska's 'Les Noces.' " *Dance Chronicle* 10/2 (1987): 147–69.

Jordan, Stephanie. "The Demons in a Database: Interrogating 'Stravinsky the Global Dancer.' " *Dance Research: The Journal of the Society for Dance Research* 22/1 (Summer 2004): 57–83.

———. *Stravinsky Dances: Re-visions across a Century*. Alton, Hampshire: Dance, 2007.

Joseph, Charles M. *Stravinsky and Balanchine: A Journey of Invention*. New Haven: Yale University Press, 2002.

———. *Stravinsky and the Piano*. Ann Arbor: UMI Research Press, 1983.

———. *Stravinsky Inside Out*. New Haven: Yale University Press, 2001.

Jowitt, Deborah. *Jerome Robbins: His Life, His Theater, His Dance*. New York: Simon and Schuster, 2004.

Karsavina, Tamara. "A Recollection of Stravinsky." *Tempo* 8 (Summer 1948): 7–9.

———. *Theatre Street: The Reminiscences of Tamara Karsavina*. London: Readers Union, 1950.

Kelly, Thomas. *First Nights*. New Haven: Yale University Press, 2000.

Kirstein, Lincoln. *Dance: A Short History of Classic Theatrical Dancing*. Princeton: Dance Horizons, 1987.

———. *Flesh Is Heir*. 1932. Reprint, Carbondale: South Illinois University Press, 1975.

———. *Four Centuries of Ballet*. Mineola, N.Y.: Dover Publications, 1984.

———. *Thirty Years: Lincoln Kirstein's "The New York City Ballet."* New York: Alfred A. Knopf, 1978.

Kochno, Boris. *Diaghilev and the Ballets Russes*. New York: Harper and Row, 1970.

Kresky, Jeffrey. "Urban Legends for Music Theorists." *Music Theory Spectrum* 25/1 (Spring 2003): 121–25.

Lambert, Constant. *Music Ho!* London: Faber and Faber, 1934.

Lang, Paul Henry, ed. *Stravinsky: A New Appraisal of His Work*. New York: W. W. Norton, 1963.

Lauze, François de. *Apologie de la danse, 1623*. Translated and edited by Joan Wildeblood. London: F. Muller, 1952.

Lederman, Minna, ed. *Stravinsky in the Theatre*. New York: Da Capo Press, 1948.

Levinson, André. "Stravinsky and the Dance." *Theater Arts Monthly* 8 (1924): 741–54.

Levy, Suzanne. "*The Rite of Spring* at Seventy-Five." *Dance Research Journal* 19/2 (Winter 1987–88): 52–54.

Lieven, Prince Peter. *The Birth of the Ballets-Russes*. New York: Dover Publications, 1973.

Lifar, Serge. *Ballet: Traditional to Modern*. Translated by Cyril W. Beaumont. London: Putnam, 1968.

———. *Serge Diaghilev: His Life, His Work, His Legend: An Intimate Biography*. New York: Da Capo Press, 1976.

Lockspeiser, Edward. *Debussy: His Life and Mind*. 2 vols. Cambridge: Cambridge University Press, 1978.

Maes, Francis. *A History of Russian Music: From Kamarinskaya to Babi Yar*. Translated by Arnold J. Pomerans and Erica Pomerans. Berkeley: University of California Press, 2002.

Mason, Francis. *I Remember Balanchine*. New York: Doubleday, 1991.

Massine, Léonide. *My Life in Ballet*. Edited by Phyllis Hartnoll and Robert Rubens. London: Macmillan, 1968.

Mather, Betty Bang. *Dance Rhythms of the French Baroque*. Bloomington: Indiana University Press, 1987.

Mayer, Charles S. "Ida Rubinstein: A Twentieth-Century Cleopatra." *Dance Research Journal* 20/2 (Winter 1988): 33–51.

Mazo, Margarita. "Stravinsky's *Les Noces* and Russian Folk Wedding Ritual." *Journal of the American Musicological Society* 43/1 (Spring 1990): 99–142.

Monteux, Doris. *It's All in the Music: The Life and Work of Pierre Monteux*. London: William Kimber, 1965.

Morford, Mark P. O., and Robert J. Lenardon. *Classical Mythology*. White Plains, N.Y.: Longman, 1991.

Morton, Lawrence. "Footnotes to Stravinsky Studies: 'Le Sacre du printemps.' " *Tempo* 128 (1979): 9–16.

Nabokov, Nicolas. *Old Friends and New Music*. Boston: Little, Brown, 1951.

Newman, Arnold, and Robert Craft. *Bravo Stravinsky*. Cleveland: World Publishing Company, 1967.

Nijinska, Bronislava. *Bronislava Nijinska: Early Memoirs*. Translated by Irina Nijinska and Jean Rawlinson. New York: Holt, Rinehart and Winston, 1981.

———. "Creation of *Les Noces*." Translated by Jean M. Serafetinides and Irina Nijinska. *Dance Magazine* 48 (December 1974).

Oja, Carol J., ed. *Stravinsky in Modern Music (1924–1946)*. New York: Da Capo Press, 1982.

Ovid. *The Metamorphoses*. Translated by Horace Gregory. New York: Penguin Books, 1958.

Pahissa, Jaime. *Manuel de Falla: His Life and Works*. London: Museum Press, 1954.

Pasler, Jann. "Stravinsky and the Apaches." *Musical Times* 123/1672 (January 1982): 403–7.

———. ed. *Confronting Stravinsky*. Berkeley: University of California Press, 1986.

Perlis, Vivian. *Copland: 1900 through 1942*. New York: St. Martin's/Marek, 1984.

Poulenc, Francis. *Moi et mes amis*. Paris: Éditions La Palatine, 1963.

Ramsey, Christopher, ed. *Tributes: Celebrating Fifty Years of New York City Ballet*. New York: William Morrow, 1998.

Ramuz, C. F. *Lettres, 1900–1918*. Lausanne: Éditions Clairefontaine, 1956.

Reynolds, Nancy. *No Fixed Points: Dance in the Twentieth Century*. New Haven: Yale University Press, 2003.

Ricco, Edward. "The Sitwells at the Ballet." *Ballet Review* 6/1 (1977–78): 80–88.

Ridenour, Robert C. *Nationalism, Modernism, and Personal Rivalry in Nineteenth-Century Russian Music*. Ann Arbor: UMI Research Press, 1981.

Rogers, Lynn. "A Serial Passage of Diatonic Ancestry in Stravinsky's *The Flood*." *Journal of the Royal Musical Association* 129/2 (2004): 220–30.

Sagan, Carl. *Murmurs of Earth: The Voyager Interstellar Record*. New York: Random House, 1978.

Scheijen, Sjeng, ed. *Working for Diaghilev*. Schoten: BAI, 2004.

Schloezer, Boris de. *Igor Stravinsky*. Paris: Éditions Claude Aveline, 1929.

Scholl, Tim. *From Petipa to Balanchine*. London: Routledge, 1994.

Schorer, Suki. *Suki Schorer on Balanchine Technique*. New York: Alfred A. Knopf, 1999.

Schwarz, Boris. "Stravinsky in Soviet Russian Criticism." *Musical Quarterly* 48/3 (July 1962): 340–61.

Shayon, Robert Lewis, ed. *The Eighth Art: Twenty-Three Views of Television Today*. New York: Holt, Rinehart and Winston, 1962.

Shepard, John. "L'Oiseau de feu: fac-simile du manuscrit Saint-Petersbourg, 1909–1910." *Notes* 44/4 (June 1988): 804–7.

Sheppard, W. Anthony. *Revealing Masks*. Berkeley: University of California Press, 2001.

Squire, W. H. Haddon. "The Mantle of Diaghilev." *Tempo* 5 (Autumn 1947): 29–31.

Steshko, Joni Lynn. "L'Oiseau de feu [1910]." *Notes* 54/5 (June 1998): 997–1002.

Strainchamps, Edmond, and Maria Rika Maniates, eds. *Music and Civilization: Essays in Honor of Paul Henry Lang*. New York: W. W. Norton, 1984.

Stravinsky, Igor. *An Autobiography*. 1936. Reprint, New York: W. W. Norton, 1962.

———. *Petrushka*. Edited by Charles Hamm. Norton Critical Scores. New York: W. W. Norton, 1967.

———. *Poetics of Music in the Form of Six Lessons*. Translated by Arthur Knodel and Ingolf Dahl. 1947. Reprint, Cambridge, Mass.: Harvard University Press, 1970.

———. *The Rite of Spring*. With a foreword by Boris Mikhailovich Yarustovsky. Mineola, N.Y.: Dover Publications, 1989.

———. *The Rite of Spring: Sketches, 1911–1913*. London: Boosey and Hawkes, 1969.

Stravinsky, Igor, and Robert Craft. *Conversations with Igor Stravinsky*. 1959. Reprint, Berkeley: University of California Press, 1980.

———. *Dialogues*. Berkeley: University of California Press, 1982.

———. *Expositions and Developments*. 1962. Reprint, Berkeley: University of California Press, 1981.

———. *Memories and Commentaries*. 1960. Reprint, Berkeley: University of California Press, 1981.

———. *Themes and Conclusions*. Berkeley: University of California Press, 1982.

Stravinsky, Vera, and Robert Craft. *Stravinsky in Pictures and Documents*. New York: Simon and Schuster, 1978.

Street, Donald. "A Forgotten Firebird." *Musical Times* 119/1626 (August 1978): 674–767.

Sutton, Denys. *André Derain*. London: Phaidon Press, 1959.

Tallchief, Maria. *Maria Tallchief: America's Prima Ballerina*. New York: Henry Holt, 1997.

Taper, Bernard. *Balanchine: A Biography*. Berkeley: University of California Press, 1996.

Tappolet, Claude, ed. *Correspondance Ansermet–Stravinsky*. Geneva: Georg, 1990.

Taras, John. "Stravinsky on Art and Artists." *Dance Magazine* 55/4 (April 1981): 65–67.

Taruskin, Richard. "A Myth of the Twentieth Century: *The Rite of Spring*, the Tradition of the New, and 'The Music Itself.' " *Modernism/Modernity* 2/1 (1995): 1–26.

———. "Russian Folk Melodies in *The Rite of Spring*." *Journal of the American Musicological Society* 33 (1980): 501–43.

———. *Stravinsky and the Russian Traditions*. 2 vols. Berkeley: University of California Press, 1996.

Todd, Arthur. "What Went Wrong." *Dance Magazine* 36 (August 1962): 39, 60–61.

Tracy, Robert, with Sharon Delano. *Balanchine's Ballerinas: Conversations with the Muses*. New York: Linden Press/Simon and Schuster, 1983.

Van den Toorn, Pieter C. *The Music of Igor Stravinsky*. New Haven: Yale University Press, 1983.

———. "Will Stravinsky Survive Postmodernism?" *Music Theory Spectrum* 22/1 (Spring 2000): 104–21.

Van den Toorn, Pieter C., and Dmitri Tymoczko. "Stravinsky and the Octatonic: The Sounds of Stravinsky." *Music Theory Spectrum* 25/1 (Spring 2003): 167–202.

Volkov, Simon. *Balanchine's Tchaikovsky*. New York: Simon and Schuster, 1985.

———. *St. Petersburg: A Cultural History*. New York: Free Press Paperbacks, 1995.

Volynsky, Akim. *Ballet's Magic Kingdom: Selected Writings on Dance in Russia, 1911–1925*. Translated and edited by Stanley J. Rabinowitz. New Haven: Yale University Press, 2008.

Wachtel, Andrew, ed. *Petrushka: Sources and Contexts*. Evanston: Northwestern University Press, 1998.

Walker, Kathrine Sorley. *De Basil's Ballets Russes*. New York: Atheneum, 1983.

Walsh, Stephen. *Igor Stravinsky: A Creative Spring: Russia and France, 1882–1934*. New York: Alfred A. Knopf, 1999.

———. *The Music of Stravinsky*. London: Routledge, 1988.

———. *Stravinsky: The Second Exile: France and America, 1934–1971*. New York: Alfred A. Knopf, 2006.

White, Eric Walter. *Stravinsky: A Critical Survey, 1882–1946*. Mineola, N.Y.: Dover Publications, 1997.

———. *Stravinsky: The Composer and His Works*. Berkeley: University of California Press, 1966.

Wiley, Roland John. *Tchaikovsky's Ballets*. New York: Oxford University Press, 1985.

Wise, C. Stanley. "Impressions of Igor Stravinsky." *Musical Quarterly* 2/2 (April 1916): 249–56.

INDEX